3e

Century 21® Jr.

Computer Applications with Keyboarding

Jack P. Hoggatt, Ed. D.
*Assistant Dean and Director of Center for Advising,
Development, and Enrichment*
University of Wisconsin - Eau Claire
Eau Claire, Wisconsin

Jon A. Shank, Ed. D.
Professor of Education, Emeritus
Robert Morris University
Moon Township, Pennsylvania

James R. Smith, Jr., Ed. D.
Assistant Teaching Professor
North Carolina State University
Raleigh, North Carolina

SOUTH-WESTERN
CENGAGE Learning·

Australia • Brazil • Japan • Korea • Mexico • Singapore • Spain • United Kingdom • United States

SOUTH-WESTERN
CENGAGE Learning

Century 21® Jr. Computer Applications with Keyboarding, Third Edition

Jack P. Hoggatt, Jon A. Shank, James R. Smith, Jr.

SVP Global Product Management, Research, School & Professional: Frank Menchaca

General Manager, K-12 School Group: CarolAnn Shindelar

Publishing Director: Eve Lewis

Executive Editor: Dave Lafferty

Development Consulting Editor: Catherine Skintik

Marketing Manager: Andrea Kingman

Sr. Content Project Manager: Martha Conway

Manufacturing Planner: Kevin Kluck

Sr. Media Editor: Mike Jackson

Production Service: Lumina Datamatics Inc.

Copyeditor: Gary Morris

Sr. Art Director: Michelle Kunkler

Internal and Cover Designer: Grannan Graphic Design

Cover Image: Kamruzzaman Ratan/Digital Vision Vectors/Getty Images

Key reach images: © Cengage Learning®, Cengage Learning/Bill Smith Group/Sam Kolich

Design feature images: High technology design background: © iStockphoto.com/Sigal Suhler Moran; Blue technology infographic: © iStockphoto.com/KruIUA

Intellectual Property Analyst: Kyle Cooper

Intellectual Property Project Manager: Michelle McKenna

Photo Research: Lumina Datamatics Inc.

© 2016, 2010 Cengage Learning

ALL RIGHTS RESERVED. No part of this work covered by the copyright herein may be reproduced, transmitted, stored or used in any form or by any means graphic, electronic, or mechanical, including but not limited to photocopying, recording, scanning, digitizing, taping, Web distribution, information networks, or information storage and retrieval systems, except as permitted under Section 107 or 108 of the 1976 United States Copyright Act, without the prior written permission of the publisher.

For product information and technology assistance, contact us at
Cengage Learning Customer & Sales Support, 1-800-354-9706

For permission to use material from this text or product, submit all requests online at **www.cengage.com/permissions**
Further permissions questions can be emailed to
permissionrequest@cengage.com

MicroType 6 with CheckPro illustrations: © Cengage Learning®

Microsoft Office screen captures: © Microsoft Corporation. Microsoft and Windows are registered trademarks of Microsoft Corporation in the U.S. and/or other countries.

Keyboard images, key reach illustrations, tables, and figures (unless otherwise noted): © Cengage Learning®

The names of all products mentioned herein are used for identification purposes only and may be trademarks or registered trademarks of their respective owners. South-Western disclaims any affiliation, association, connection with, sponsorship, or endorsement by such owners.

The Career Clusters icons are being used with permission of the: States' Career Clusters Initiative, 2007, **www.careerclusters.org**

ISBN: 978-1-133-36534-1

Cengage Learning
20 Channel Center Street
Boston, MA 02210
USA

Cengage Learning is a leading provider of customized learning solutions with office locations around the globe, including Singapore, the United Kingdom, Australia, Mexico, Brazil, and Japan. Locate your local office at:
www.cengage.com/global

Cengage Learning products are represented in Canada by Nelson Education, Ltd.

For your course and learning solutions, visit ngl.cengage.com
Visit our company website at www.cengage.com

Printed in the United States of America
Print Number: 01   Print Year: 2014

Century 21 Jr. Computer Applications with Keyboarding, 3e

Provide your middle school and junior high students with the **best in computing education** from the proven business education leader—now stronger than ever! This Third Edition of *Century 21 Jr. Computer Applications with Keyboarding* helps students prepare for a lifetime of keyboarding and computer success with innovative solutions updated to reflect today's business challenges. Trust the leader who has taught more than 90 million people to type—bringing 100 years of publishing experience and a century of innovations together in a complete line of computing solutions.

The Right Approach, with the Right Coverage

- A cleaner look with a new internal design
- Streamlined and more focused chapters of instruction
- Emphasis on **Ribbon Path** (Tab/Group/Command) enables students to quickly navigate the software.

Learning Outcomes mapped to lesson activities.

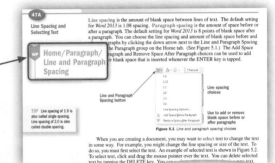

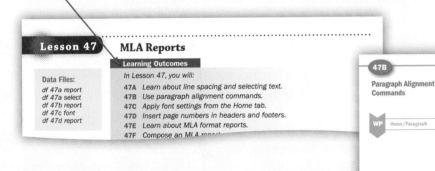

Short generic drills support *Microsoft Office* versions.

CheckPoints help students check completed work along the way.

Trade papers with a classmate. Ask your classmate to proofread your paper and mark errors you may have missed. Make corrections if necessary.

A Proven Approach for Mastering Keyboarding Skills

Triple-control guidelines for timed writings and skillbuilding include three factors—syllabic intensity, average word length, and percentage of high-frequency words—for the most accurate evaluation of students' keying skills.

all letters used

Tested and proven pedagogy provides sound new key learning, skillbuilding, model document illustrations, and triple-controlled timed writings to ensure that assessments are reliable and consistent.

Computer Applications and Beyond!

Core computer application skills are taught and reinforced so that students are prepared for life! Instead of teaching the students the entire application, the critical components are emphasized and mastered.

Word processing skill is enhanced by the model documents provided for letters, tables, reports, and special documents.

Presentations coverage includes creating slides with text, graphics, tables, and charts—and learning the appropriate way to present.

Spreadsheet activities include basic features as well as working with formulas, functions, and charts to help resolve numeric problems for business, education, and personal use.

Database coverage includes creating tables, adding/deleting records and fields, sorting, and creating forms, queries, and reports.

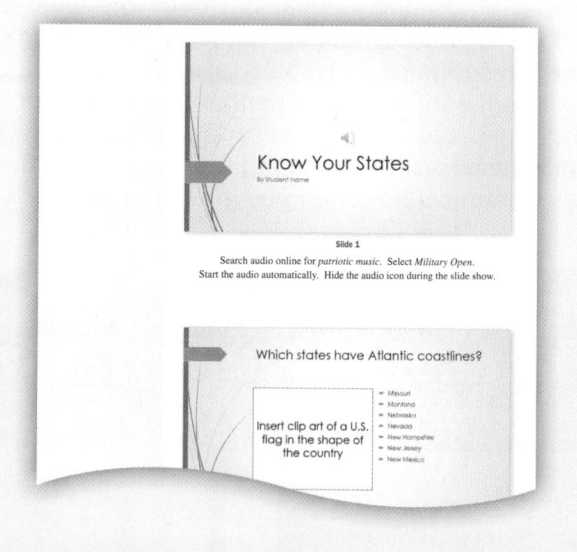

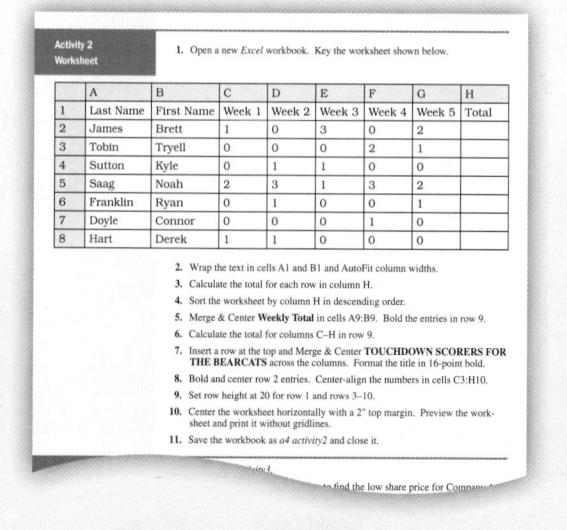

Integrated Learning for Stronger Results

Chapter Review ties learning objectives to concepts taught and applies what is learned.

Across the Curriculum provides curriculum integration with Academic Connections.

Chapter 3 REVIEW
Lessons 11–30

Before You Move On

Answer these questions to review what you have learned in Chapter 3.

1. Describe how you should arrange your work area. LO 11A
2. List five points that describe proper keying position. LO 11B
3. What are the _____ the left hand? What are the home keys for the right hand? LO 11C
4. Tap the ENTER key with your _____ finger. LO 11E
5. Space _____ after a semicolon used as punctuation. LO 13C
6. When keying, keep your wrists low but not _____ the keyboard or desk. LO 11B
7. Keep your _____ on the copy as you key. LO 12A
8. How many times should you space after a period at the end of a sentence? LO 18D
9. To key a capital of the letter *P*, hold down the _____ key. LO 18B
10. To key a capital of the letter *S*, hold down the _____ key. LO 21B
11. The number of standard words keyed in 1' is called _____ (*gwam*). LO 22E
12. To key a series of capital letters, use the _____ key. LO 29B
13. How many times should you space after a question mark at the end of a sentence? LO 29B
14. Word processing software has preset tabs called _____ tabs. LO 30C
15. When you hold down the _____ key, letters to the left of the insertion point will be deleted. LO 30B

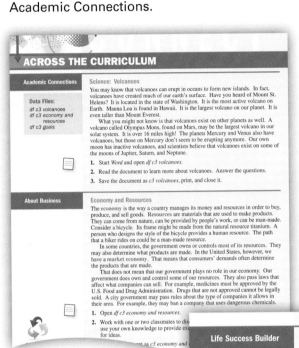

ACROSS THE CURRICULUM

Academic Connections

Data Files:
df c3 volcanoes
df c3 economy and resources
df c3 goals

Science: Volcanoes

You may know that volcanoes can erupt in oceans to form new islands. In fact, volcanoes have created much of our earth's surface. Have you heard of Mount St. Helens? It is located in the state of Washington. It is the most active volcano on Earth. Mauna Loa is found in Hawaii. It is the largest volcano on our planet. It is even taller than Mount Everest.

What you might not know is that volcanoes exist on other planets as well. A volcano called Olympus Mons, found on Mars, may be the largest volcano in our solar system. It is over 16 miles high! The planets Mercury and Venus also have volcanoes, but those on Mercury don't seem to be erupting anymore. Our own moon has inactive volcanoes, and scientists believe that volcanoes exist on some of the moons of Jupiter, Saturn, and Neptune.

1. Start *Word* and open *df c3 volcanoes*.
2. Read the document to learn more about volcanoes. Answer the questions.
3. Save the document as *c3 volcanoes*, print, and close it.

About Business

Economy and Resources

The economy is the way a country manages its money and resources in order to buy, produce, and sell goods. Resources are materials that are used to make products. They can come from nature, can be provided by people's work, or can be man-made. Consider a bicycle. Its frame might be made from the natural resource titanium. A person who designs the style of the bicycle provides a human resource. The path that a biker rides on could be a man-made resource.

In some countries, the government owns or controls most of its resources. They may also determine what products are made. In the United States, however, we have a market economy. That means that consumers' demands often determine the products that are made.

That does not mean that our government plays no role in our economy. Our government does own and control some of our resources. They also pass laws that affect what companies can sell. For example, medicines must be approved by the U.S. Food and Drug Administration. Drugs that are not approved cannot be legally sold. A city government may pass rules about the type of companies it allows in their area. For example, they may ban a company that uses dangerous chemicals.

1. Open *df c3 economy and resources*.
2. Work with one or two classmates to dis... use your own knowledge to provide exa... for ideas.
   ... as *c3 economy and* ...

About Business has activities that cover a number of business topics.

Life Success Builder has activities that involve setting goals and preparing for employment, among other life skills.

The coverage of Career Clusters and the **Career Exploration Portfolio** emphasize critical thinking.

Life Success Builder

Goal Setting

Whether or not you know it, you've probably set goals for yourself in the past. Have you worked hard to earn good grades at school? Have you played hard at practices so that you can improve how you play a sport? Do you practice playing an instrument so that you can master a difficult song? If so, you probably had a goal in mind. Setting goals can motivate you, and achieving goals can make you feel good about yourself.

In this activity, you will analyze goals and set some new goals. As you will learn, goals should be specific, measurable, achievable, realistic, and time specific.

1. Open *df c3 goals*.
2. Read the tips for setting goals and complete the table. Be sure to add ways to improve the goals. Then, set your own goals for the time spans given.
3. Save the document as *c3 goals*, print, and close it.

Career Exploration Portfolio

Activity 2

To complete this activity, you will need the Student Interest Survey that you filled out in Career Exploration Portfolio Activity 1.

1. Look on the last page of your survey and note your top Career Cluster of interest. Find its description on the last two pages of the survey and read it.
2. Go to http://www.careertech.org. Click the **Career Technical Education** button, then click **Career Clusters** in the list at the right. Scroll down on the Career Clusters page and click the link for your top Career Cluster. On the web page for your Career Cluster, click the PDF link following Career Cluster Frame in the information near the top of the page. Read the list of careers in the document and pick one or two in which you are interested. Make a note of the category (called a Pathway) of the career(s) you choose. You will need to know the Pathway in a future activity.
3. Use the Internet to find out specific duties of the career(s) that you chose. You may look for other information that interests you as well.
4. Use *Word* to write a summary of what you learned. Save the document as *c3 career 1 details*, print, and close it.

Online Resources:

ngl.cengage.com/c21jr3e

The addition of **21ˢᵗ Century Skills** and **Digital Citizenship** add interesting and relevant topics for classroom discussion.

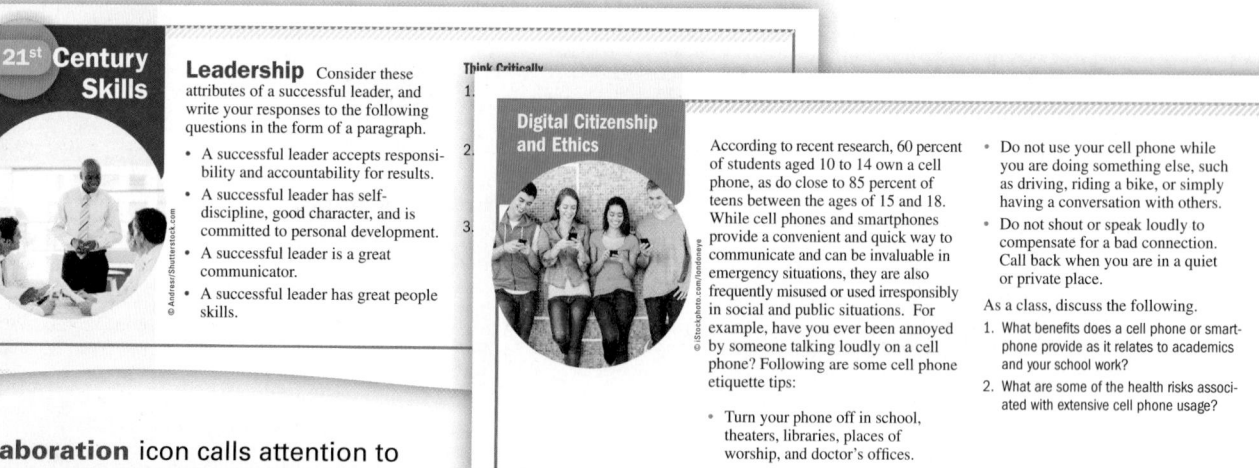

Collaboration icon calls attention to places where students work together.

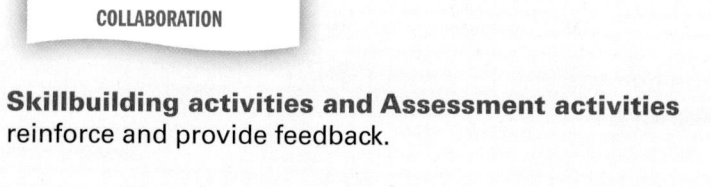

Skillbuilding activities and Assessment activities reinforce and provide feedback.

Capstone projects provide real-world projects that integrate all skills.

Digital Solutions Take You Beyond the Book!

For supporting software that is motivating, teaches new keys, checks documents for speed and accuracy, and is built for student success, *MicroType™ 6* and *MicroType 6 with CheckPro™* are your ideal solutions.

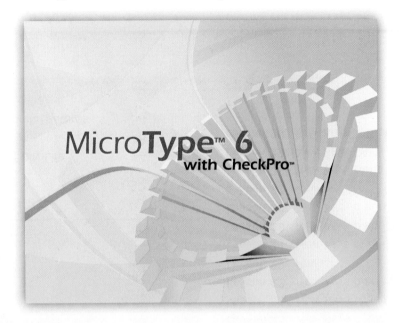

MicroType 6 includes touch-typing instruction for alphabetic and numeric keyboarding and the numeric keypad.

MicroType 6 with CheckPro checks keystrokes and formatting in *Microsoft Word* and *Excel*, providing the most comprehensive teaching and learning tool.

If you need only new-key learning and skillbuilding, then *MicroType 6* is your solution. With either solution, textbook marginal references will indicate the appropriate points for incorporating the software. Skillbuilding lessons can be used throughout the course to continue to build those essential productivity skills.

An **Interactive eBook** provides students with an interactive, online-only version of the printed textbook to be used at school or at home with indexing, highlighting, and quick navigation.

Visit Us Online!

For more information on this innovative textbook—as well as a wealth of teaching and learning resources—visit ngl.cengage.com/c21jr3e today!

- ▶ Tests
- ▶ Data Files
- ▶ Flashcards
- ▶ Lesson Plans
- ▶ *PowerPoint* Presentations
- ▶ Solution Files
- ▶ Web Links
- ▶ And much more!

Cengage Learning Testing Powered by Cognero is a flexible, online system that allows you to author, edit, and manage test bank content from multiple Cengage Learning solutions; create multiple test versions in an instant; deliver tests from your learning management system, your classroom, or wherever you want!

Contents

Unit 3 Word Processing, Desktop Publishing, and Document Formatting

Unit 4 Computer Applications

FEATURES

Unique Chapter Features	Selected Pages
ABOVE and BEYOND	64, 193, 335
checkpoint	8, 58, 81, 129, 175, 210, 243, 266, 313, 364, 392
Instant Message	2, 50, 88, 134, 183, 254, 320, 390
MicroType	81, 91, 101, 111, 122, 129, 138, 150, 156
TECHNIQUE TIP Reach out with little finger SPACING TIP Tap the ENTER key twice to insert a DS between 2-line TIP In Windows 8.1, there is no reason to shut down your computer completely—	12, 53, 81, 89, 128, 139, 159, 172, 198, 204, 226, 238, 259, 264, 281, 292, 306, 316, 338, 354, 382, 387, 416
COLLABORATION	36, 46, 86, 134, 175, 206, 254, 266, 303, 313, 364, 392
WP File/Save As	22, 172, 177, 184, 211, 214, 219, 237, 242, 250, 253, 264, 267, 271, 276
PP View/Presentation Views	315, 317, 321, 328, 333
SS Page Layout/Sheet Options	355, 356, 361, 366, 370, 375
DB Create/Tables/Table Design	390, 395, 401, 407

Chapter 1 — Computer Hardware/Software and Information Management

Lessons 1–6

Imagine a world without computers. Cars would quit running, phones would stop ringing, people could not buy anything with credit or debit cards, airplanes would be grounded, and lights would turn off. Sort of hard to imagine, isn't it?

Computers are powerful tools. They help us work, learn, and play. If you need to communicate, look something up, or get something done, chances are a computer can help. Computers do many other things, such as:

- Diagnose illness to help heal the sick.

- Guide telescopes that explore distant galaxies.

- Control the lighting, air conditioning, and security systems in buildings.

- Analyze traffic patterns to reduce traffic jams and congestion.

- Make calls, store phone numbers, and send text messages.

- Share music and video, play games, and run programs.

- Animate movies such as *The Hobbit*, *Monsters University*, and *Frozen*.

© Denys Prykhodov/Shutterstock.com

Figure 1.1 *Smartphones are powerful online computers.*

From
Janet Marshall

One more improvement for the workbook: Can you add a chart to the Sheet 2 worksheet? See my suggestions, attached.

JM   5/21

Let's create a chart that compares the total sales of each sales agent. You can select the agent's name in column D and the total sales for each agent in column E and then create a column chart.

Insert an appropriate chart title, and then apply a chart style of your choice.

Mr. Newhouse would like a hard copy of this information, so please position the chart so that you can print both the data and the chart on one sheet.

Computer Hardware and Software

Learning Outcomes

In Lesson 1, you will:

1A Discover various types of hardware.
1B Identify three types of software.
1C Learn the five steps of information processing.

1A

Hardware

Figure 1.2 *Microprocessors are the brains inside a computer.*

Instant Message

Microprocessors are digital. This means that they calculate with two digits—0 and 1. Stringing billions of digits together in just the right order, such as 01011101, will make a microprocessor jump into action and do what you want it to do.

Computer **hardware** includes all the parts of a computer that you can touch with your hands. Hardware can be found either inside of or connected to computers. For example, inside your computer you may find a **hard drive** that stores data. Computers also have **microprocessors**, as shown in Figure 1.2, inside them. A microprocessor is a small circuit board that controls all the work a computer does. The microprocessor is the brain of the computer, which makes it the most important part. A microprocessor is also called a **processor** or a **CPU**, which stands for **central processing unit**. Hardware can also be connected to a computer. Examples of this type of hardware include a keyboard, mouse, or monitor.

Microprocessors are found in computers of all shapes and sizes. They are located in laptops, MP3 players, phones, cameras, remote controls, and cars. They control streetlights and fire alarms, and they dispense money at ATMs.

Computers of all types are called digital communication tools, or **DigiTools**. Figure 1.3 shows several different DigiTools.

Desktop PC

Laptop PC

Tablet PC

Smart phones and handhelds

Wearable tech

Figure 1.3 *DigiTools come in a variety of sizes and shapes.*

Project 13

**From
Janet Marshall**

Attached (*df heber house photos*) are the photos to complete the slide show.

Please see the instructions I've supplied for completing the presentation.

JM   5/20

The photos of the Heber house are now available and have been stored in the df heber house photos file. Please copy and paste pictures to their correct slides, and then resize and reposition the pictures so they are about the same height and at the same location on each slide. Apply a picture style of your choice to all three pictures. Don't forget to delete any placeholders you don't use.

Let's change the bulleted list on slide 7 to a SmartArt list—you can choose which one, and then modify colors as you like.

At the right side of slide 7, please add a Double Wave shape and insert the text And Much More! Make sure the shape is appropriately sized and apply a shape style of your choice.

Apply transitions of your choice to some or all slides for added visual interest.

Project 14

**From
Janet Marshall**

Mr. Newhouse thought you did a great job with the *Sales Commission* worksheet. He would like you to add a worksheet to the workbook with the information shown on the attached, grouping the sales for each agent.

JM   5/21

Address of Homes Sold	City	State	Sales Agent	Sales Price
872 Oak Terrace	White Bear Lake	MN	Chen	$289,900
Agent Total			Chen	$289,900
705 Shenandoah Lane N.	Minneapolis	MN	McIntyre	$265,000
535 Birch Lake Avenue	White Bear Lake	MN	McIntyre	$230,000
1729 Hawthorne Drive	Hopkins	MN	McIntyre	$285,000
338 Betty Crocker Drive	St. Louis Park	MN	McIntyre	$148,900
Agent Total			McIntyre	$928,900

Include an "Agent Total" for each agent as shown above and below and a "Total Company Sales" at the bottom as shown below.

875 St. Albans Street	Roseville	MN	Stone	$165,900
873 St. Croix Heights	Hudson	WI	Stone	$225,000
Agent Total			Stone	$390,900
Total Company Sales				$2,639,100

Personal Computers

As you study this book, you will probably use a **personal computer**, or **PC**. A PC is designed for an individual user. It may be a multimedia desktop PC, a laptop PC, or a tablet PC. You also may use a handheld computer.

A personal computer may have many parts. Examine the parts of the typical desktop PC in Figure 1.4. Do you have all of these parts in your computer system?

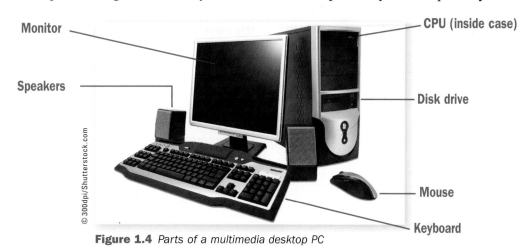

Monitor

CPU (inside case)

Speakers

Disk drive

Mouse

Keyboard

© 300dpi/Shutterstock.com

Figure 1.4 *Parts of a multimedia desktop PC*

Peripherals

A computer cannot do everything by itself! It needs help to perform various tasks. Other devices that work with a computer are called **peripherals**. (See Figure 1.5.) Printers, digital tablets, scanners, and headsets are examples of peripherals.

Handwriting tablet

Hilary Morgan / Alamy

Scanner

© Mile Atanasov/Shutter stock.com

Speech recognition headset

© ZIGROUP-CREATIONS/ Shutterstock.com

Printer

© Alexandr Makarov/ Shutterstock.com

Figure 1.5 *Computer peripherals*

Instant Message

DigiTools, which include computers and peripherals, are also called devices, electronic devices, and, consumer electronics.

Project 11

From
Janet Marshall

Please format the attached as a letter for my signature. Address the letter to:

Mr. and Mrs. Parker Anderson
1320 Lorl Lane #3
Ogden, UT 84404-4396

JM   5/19

Dear Mr. and Mrs. Taylor:

Judith Johnson, personnel manager of Owen & Caden Production Company, informed me that you have accepted a position with them and will be moving to Minnesota the first part of July. I know you will enjoy living in this area.

A copy of the "Mover's Guide" published by our real estate company is enclosed. It is designed to give helpful hints on making the move as painless as possible. We hope you will find it useful as you organize for the move to Minnesota.

If we can be of assistance to you in locating a place to rent or a home to purchase, please telephone our office (612-555-0101).

Sincerely,

Project 12

From
Janet Marshall

Create a database and then create a new table to store the information taken from the *Sales Commission* work-sheet. Use the column headings for the data-base fields. Save the table as *Agent Sales Commissions.*

JM   5/20

Address of Homes Sold	City	State	Sales Agent	Sales Price	Sales Agent Commission
872 Oak Terrace	White Bear Lake	MN	Chen	$289,900.00	$7,247.50
705 Shenandoah Lane N.	Minneapolis	MN	McIntyre	$265,000.00	$6,625.00
535 Birch Lake Avenue	White Bear Lake	MN	McIntyre	$230,000.00	$5,750.00
1729 Hawthorne Drive	Hopkins	MN	McIntyre	$285,000.00	$7,125.00
338 Betty Crocker Drive	St. Louis Park	MN	McIntyre	$148,900.00	$3,722.50
108 Franklin Terrace	Minneapolis	MN	O'Dell	$395,900.00	$9,897.50
719 Comstock Lane	Minneapolis	MN	Perez	$299,000.00	$7,475.00
88 North William Street	Stillwater	MN	Perez	$179,000.00	$4,475.00
1218 Jessamine Avenue	St. Paul	MN	Perez	$155,500.00	$3,887.50
875 St. Albans Street	Roseville	MN	Stone	$165,900.00	$4,147.50
873 St. Croix Heights	Hudson	WI	Stone	$225,000.00	$5,625.00

After you complete the database, please create a query that shows the sales agent, the sales price, and sales agent commission. Use McIntyre as the criteria for the sales agent field. Save as McIntyre Sales Commission.

1. Discuss with your class or team the many different DigiTools. Answer these questions:

   - What is the first thing you remember doing with a computer?

   - Which digital communication tools do you use most and why?

   - What peripheral tools have you used? Have you ever used a scanner, a speech or recording headset or microphone, an artist drawing or writing tablet, or a digital camera? If so, what work or activity did you do with these tools?

   - Have you seen anyone use a smartphone (such as an iPhone, an Android, or a BlackBerry), digital video recorder, desktop PC, laptop PC, handheld computer, tablet PC, or global positioning system (GPS)?

   - Have you ever used a DigiTool such as an iPod or MP3 player, a digital video recorder, a cell phone, or a game console just for entertainment reasons?

   - If you have a cell phone, what games can you play on your phone? Can you download music, ringtones, and web pages on your phone? Does your phone have fingertip (multi-touch) control (like the iPhone) or a keypad for text messaging? What do you like most about your phone? What do you dislike about your phone? What would you improve if you could?

2. Study the typical computer system shown in Figure 1.4. Discuss these questions:

   - Is it nearly the same as the computer system you will be using?

   - In what ways might it be different?

   - Do you have a computer at home? If so, what is it like?

1B

Software

Figure 1.6 *Video games are examples of software.*

Source: Microsoft

Computers need instructions to work properly. These instructions are called **software**. Software gives instructions to a computer's microprocessor. It tells the computer hardware what to do.

Do you make calls or send text messages? Do you visit websites? Do you download music or take pictures? If the answer is yes, then you are already using software. For example, if you play a video game like the one shown in Figure 1.6, the game you play is the software program. (The game console is hardware.) Word processing, spreadsheet, and drawing programs are also examples of software.

There are three types of software:

- **Operating systems (OSs)** control how computers communicate with the hardware and how they interact with you, the user.

- **Applications** allow you to complete a specific task. Applications let you create a report, browse the Internet, edit a multimedia video, or calculate a math problem. Applications are generally installed on a local computer.

- **Online apps** also let you complete specific tasks such as editing photos, playing games, and viewing multimedia. Online apps run over the Internet inside a web browser. (See Figure 1.7.)

Newhouse Realty

From
Janet Marshall

I've attached a copy of the Parade of Homes schedule I sent to Justin O'Dell for June 5. Please use the *df newhouse memo* template and create his schedule for June 6. Use a different color for the table to distinguish it from the June 5 schedule. Use the *Clients* table in the database for the phone numbers.

Send a copy of the memo to Blake Newhouse and me.

JM   **5/19**

Memo

To:	Justin O'Dell
From:	Janet Marshall
cc:	Blake Newhouse
Date:	May 19, 20--
Re:	Schedule for June 5

Justin, the table below shows your schedule for showings on June 5. Please let me know if you have any questions.

Client	Phone	Time
Mr. and Mrs. Warren Sabbatini	651-555-0179	10 a.m.
Miss Candace Wilcox	651-555-0115	
Dr. and Mrs. Michael Vaughn	608-555-0144	1 p.m.
Mr. Timothy Giani	651-555-0120	
Ms. Alison Koosman	651-555-0147	4 p.m.
Mr. and Mrs. Felipe Garcia	612-555-0164	
Mr. and Mrs. Chase McNally	715-555-0122	7 p.m.
Mr. Scott Sackett	612-555-0184	

Schedule for Justin O'Dell
June 6

Mrs. Jayne Boyer	10 a.m.
Mr. Brandon Vanderbilt	
Dr. Javier Tallmadge	1 p.m.
Dr. and Mrs. Evan Ross	
Ms. Tasha Lang	4 p.m.
Mr. Loren Rizzo	
Ms. Stacy Rice	7 p.m.
Mr. Theodore Farrell	

Instant Message Online apps work much like the applications on your PC. Online apps can create documents, publish web pages, send email, and post your personal calendar online.

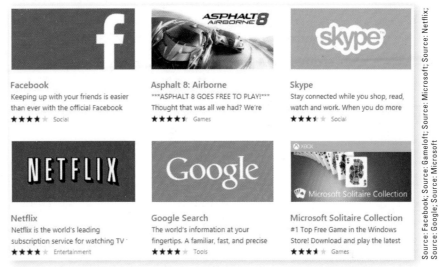

Source: Facebook; Source: Gameloft; Source: Microsoft; Source: Netflix; Source: Google; Source: Microsoft

Facebook
Keeping up with your friends is easier than ever with the official Facebook
★★★★☆ Social

Asphalt 8: Airborne
ASPHALT 8 GOES FREE TO PLAY!
Thought that was all we had? We're
★★★★½ Games

Skype
Stay connected while you shop, read, watch and work. When you do more
★★★½☆ Social

Netflix
Netflix is the world's leading subscription service for watching TV
★★★★☆ Entertainment

Google Search
The world's information at your fingertips. A familiar, fast, and precise
★★★★☆ Tools

Microsoft Solitaire Collection
#1 Top Free Game in the Windows Store! Download and play the latest
★★★½☆ Games

Figure 1.7 *Online apps for free or purchase run through a web browser.*

Can you suggest to a friend the name of an application or online app he or she can use to solve specific problems? There are so many to choose from. You can often guess the use of a program from its name. A few commonly used applications and online apps are listed below. Match the program name with its use.

a. *Spider Solitaire*   ___ 1. Word processing

b. *Intuit QuickBooks*   ___ 2. Web page creation software

c. *Blogger*   ___ 3. Popular game

d. *Microsoft Word*   ___ 4. Drawing program

e. *Internet Explorer*   ___ 5. Internet/web browser

f. *iTunes*   ___ 6. Accounting program

g. *Google Sites*   ___ 7. Image-editing software

h. *Paint*   ___ 8. Music downloading software

i. *Photoshop*   ___ 9. Online opinion, news, and information sharing software

1C

Information Processing

We interact with computers using a five-step process. This process is called **information processing** and is illustrated in Figure 1.8. Information processing puts words, pictures, and numbers (called **data**) into forms we can use and understand.

From
Janet Marshall

Please see the instructions I've attached for this project.

JM   5/19

Create a PowerPoint presentation featuring one of the homes built by Newhouse for our private showing during the Parade of Homes. I've outlined the text and layout for each slide below.

The photographer took pictures of the home yesterday. Once the pictures are available, you can include those as well. Use your judgment and creativity for putting the presentation together. The content for the slides is provided below.

Slide 1: Title Slide

The Heber House
20-- Parade of Homes

Slide 2: Picture with Caption

Picture: To come
Caption: **Stylish Contemporary**

Slide 3: Title and Content

About the Home . . .

- Two-story
- 4,025 Sq. Feet
- 3 Bedrooms
- 2½ Baths
- Professionally Decorated

Include a *For Sale* sign from online pictures.

Slide 4: Two Content

The Great Room

- Two-Story Ceiling
- Large Wall of Windows
- Elegant Fireplace

Picture of great room to come for second content placeholder.

Slide 5: Two Content

Spacious Kitchen

- Island
- Corner Pantry
- Gas Double Ovens
- Gas Cooktop

Picture of kitchen to come.

Slide 6: Two Content

Master Bedroom Suite

- Walk-In Closet
- European Glass Shower
- Double Sinks
- Garden Tub
- Cathedral Ceiling

Picture of master bedroom to come.

Slide 7: Two Content

Additional Rooms and Spaces

- Two Bedrooms
- Play Area for Kids
- Family Room with Wet Bar and Fireplace
- Home Office
- Balcony Reading Room
- First-Floor Laundry

Slide 8: Title and Content

Title: **Property Information**

Content: Table with the following information.

Column 1	Column 2
Architecture	Contemporary
Basement type	Full, poured
Heating	Gas forced air
Lot size	75 × 145
Semiannual taxes	$4,609
Sewer, water	Public
Schools	Woodland Park Elementary
	Brooklyn Junior High School
	Champlin Park Senior High

Slide 9: Title Slide

June 7 – 21
20-- Parade of Homes

Insert an online picture of a sketch of a home.

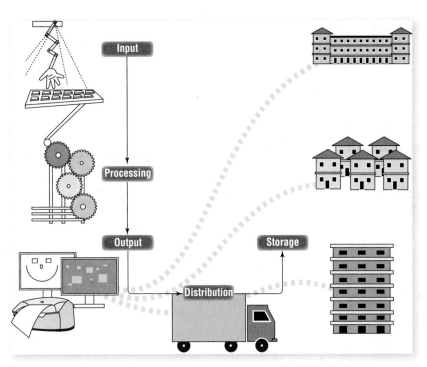

Figure 1.8 *The five steps of information processing*

- **Input** lets you put data into a computer. You can use your fingers on a touch screen, an electronic pen on a drawing tablet, a keyboard, a speech headset, a scanner, a camera, and other tools to input data.

- **Processing** lets you change or manipulate data using software. You may add numbers, sort a list of names, and alter the colors on a picture.

- **Output** is the way you get data from a computer. You can read a text message, print a report, and view your photos on a monitor.

- **Distribution** involves sharing information with the people who want it. For example, you may post a blog, build a website, and use a phone to send a picture to a friend.

- **Storage** lets you save data for later use. You can store on your local hard drive, save on a small flash drive, and save on the Internet.

When you transfer photos from a digital camera to your computer, you may do all five of the information processing steps. Match the tasks listed below with the five information processing steps.

a. Input   ___ 1. View your photo on the screen

b. Processing   ___ 2. Transfer your picture from a camera to a computer

c. Output   ___ 3. Save a copy of the photo in an online photo gallery

d. Distribution   ___ 4. Attach the photo to an email or text message and send it to a friend

e. Storage   ___ 5. Use software to enhance or improve the photo

**From
Janet Marshall**

Three more clients accepted invitations to the showing. Send the attached letter, *df acceptance letter*. You will need to replace the information in red with the appropriate information. The letters go to:

Ms. Stacy Rice
Mr. and Mrs. Travis
    McDowell
Mr. Theodore Farrell

Their addresses are in the *Clients* table of our database.

Justin O'Dell will show Ms. Rice and Mr. Farrell the homes on Saturday, June 6, at 7 p.m. Maria Perez will show Mr. and Mrs. McDowell the homes on Friday, June 5, at 1 p.m.

JM   **5/16**

Newhouse Realty

315 Parkview Terrace
Minneapolis, MN 55416-3430

May 16, 20--

Mr. and Mrs. Jackson Higgins
825 W. Oak Street
Stillwater, MN 55082-4122

Dear Mr. and Mrs. Higgins:

We are pleased to have you take part in our private showing of the homes that will be in this year's Parade of Homes. The eight homes you will see combine quality construction, professional decorating, and exclusive landscaping to make this year's show the best ever.

I have made arrangements with (AGENT'S NAME) to show you the homes. Please meet (HIM/HER) at our office at (TIME) on (FRIDAY/SATURDAY), June (5/6). It will take approximately two hours to visit the homes.

I am looking forward to hearing your comments about the homes after the showing. If you have any questions prior to the showing, please telephone me.

Sincerely,

Janet Marshall
Office Manager

xx

c (NAME OF AGENT)

Operating System Basics

In Lesson 2, you will:

2A   *Learn about operating systems.*
2B   *Study the **Windows** Start screen and Charm bar.*
2C   *Sharpen your mouse skills.*
2D   *Turn off your computer.*

2A

Operating Systems

An operating system (OS) is the most important software on any computer. It controls the hardware. The OS also makes it possible to run other types of software. Think of your operating system as a control center. An OS will guide you through tasks such as:

- Entering your login name and password.
- Helping you find the applications and files.
- Choosing among available printers.
- Reminding you to save before you turn off your computer.

Login Names and Passwords

As a police officer checks a driver's license when making a traffic stop, an OS checks for your login and password when you start a computer.

- A **login name** identifies you to a computer.
- A **password** is a series of letters and/or numbers and symbols that you key to gain access.

 Instant Message Passwords protect your data, files, pictures, email, websites, and other information from misuse by others.

Your login name and password may be assigned by your school. However, you may be able to create your own password. If you do, choose it carefully. Your password is your main security device. Follow these password rules:

- Keep your password secure. Never share it with others.
- Respect others. Do not ask them for their passwords.
- Do not sneak to find someone else's password, even as a prank.
- Think of a password you will remember.
- Do not create a password that someone else can easily guess.

9. 872 Oak Terrace | White Bear Lake | MN | Chen | $289,900

10. 1218 Jessamine Avenue | St. Paul | MN | Perez | $155,500

11. 108 Franklin Terrace | Minneapolis | MN | O'Dell | $395,900

Mr. Newhouse would like some additional information on the worksheet. Add a totals row for the Sales Price, Company Commission, and Sales Agent Commission. Beneath the Totals row of the Sales Agent Commission column, display and label the Lowest (MIN), Highest (MAX), and Average (AVERAGE) sales agent commission as shown below.

875 St. Albans Street	Roseville	MN	Stone	$165,900.00	$9,954.00	$4,147.50
873 St. Croix Heights	Hudson	WI	Stone	$225,000.00	$13,500.00	$5,625.00
	Totals			Total	Total	Total
	Lowest					MIN
	Highest					MAX
	Average					AVERAGE

Project 7

From
Janet Marshall

Please create a copy of our client database and name it *newhouse project 7*. Then make the corrections to the database and create the report described on the attached.

JM   5/15

1. The spelling for Malarie McNally should be Mallory McNally.

2. Felipe Garcia got married; his wife's name is Jessica. Also change the title for this record to Mr. and Mrs.

3. Tyler Bunnell's address is 670 Myrtle Street rather than 671.

4. Tarin Chan's phone number should be 612-555-0188.

Create a report using all of the fields except Title. Group the report by State and then by City. Sort by Last Name in ascending order. Use Stepped Layout and Landscape orientation. Use Clients Report for the title.

The strongest passwords contain letters, symbols, and numbers. They are not words found in the dictionary. A password such as *secr375et* is an example of a strong password. A poor example is an obvious word such as *password* or a string of numbers such as *1234*.

If your computer is on a network or runs an older version of *Windows*, your login steps may be different. Follow your instructor's directions to log in.

1. Turn on your computer and click the icon that displays your name. If no icon with your name appears, ask your instructor how to log in.

2. Think of a password or ask your instructor for your assigned password.

3. Create or change your password as instructed. In Figure 1.9, Max is creating his password. He must key his password in the first and second boxes. *Windows* requires that you key a password twice to make sure it has been keyed correctly.

Figure 1.9 *Create a password.*

Your password creation screen may look a little different. However, password creation steps are similar on most systems.

4. Key a hint to help you remember your password. Other users may be able to see your hint, so be sure to make it one that only you will understand.

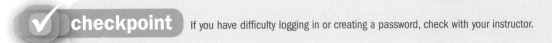

checkpoint If you have difficulty logging in or creating a password, check with your instructor.

2B

Windows Start Screen and Charm Bar

After you log in, you will see the *Windows* **Start screen**. The Start screen, shown in Figure 1.10, is a collection of tiles, each representing an application. Your Start screen may look different from the one shown in the figure.

The Start screen is a **graphical user interface (GUI)**. A **user interface (UI)** allows users, like you, to interact with the computer.

The Start screen is your home base. You can open applications or "apps," check your mail or calendar, or go to the Desktop. You can add apps to your Start screen so that you just need to click a tile to start that app.

Project 5

From
Janet Marshall

Design a flyer for the Parade of Homes. Be sure to include all the information shown on the attached sheet. The seven builders are listed with some of the other documents I've given you to key. Make sure to list them in alphabetical order. Include an online picture of a home at the bottom of the flyer.

JM   **5/14**

20-- Parade of Homes

June 7 – 21

Monday – Friday 5 p.m. to 9 p.m.

Saturday & Sunday 10 a.m. to 6 p.m.

Featuring homes built by

[List the seven homebuilders in alphabetical order]

Sponsored by Newhouse Realty Company

Project 6

From
Janet Marshall

Create a worksheet titled **Sales Commissions Since May 1**. The company commission is 6% of the sales price; the agent's commission is 2.5%. Try to get the information to fit on one page. I've attached the information for the 11 homes that have sold along with the columns I would like on the worksheet.

After entering the information, sort by sales agent.

JM   5/15

Columns on worksheet:

A. Address of Homes Sold

B. City

C. State

D. Sales Agent

E. Sales Price

F. Company Commission (0.06)

G. Sales Agent Commission (0.025)

Homes sold:

1. 705 Shenandoah Lane N. | Minneapolis | MN | McIntyre | $265,000
2. 719 Comstock Lane | Minneapolis | MN | Perez | $299,000
3. 875 St. Albans Street | Roseville | MN | Stone | $165,900
4. 535 Birch Lake Avenue | White Bear Lake | MN | McIntyre | $230,000
5. 1729 Hawthorne Drive | Hopkins | MN | McIntyre | $285,000
6. 88 North William Street | Stillwater | MN | Perez | $179,000
7. 338 Betty Crocker Drive | St. Louis Park | MN | McIntyre | $148,900
8. 873 St. Croix Heights | Hudson | WI | Stone | $225,000

Tiles can be static or dynamic. Live or dynamic tiles let you preview information about the associated application. For example, if you have a news app, you can see the latest news headlines in the tile without opening the application. Static tiles serve as a gateway to applications such as *Office* programs, the Internet, games, pictures, or videos you have stored on your computer.

Static tiles

Dynamic tiles

Figure 1.10 *The Windows 8.1 Start screen*

Figure 1.11
Charm bar

The **Charm bar** is a universal tool that can be accessed from anywhere no matter what you are doing or what application you are running. To access the Charm bar, move the mouse pointer or swipe from the upper- or lower-right corner of your screen. The Charm bar will appear on the right. See Figure 1.11.

There are five charms on the Charm bar. They are *Search*, *Share*, *Start*, *Devices*, and *Settings*. Let's take a brief look at each of these elements.

The **Search** charm allows you to search for a particular keyword. The Search charm's behavior changes depending on the application that is currently active. For example, if you are in the news app, it will let you search for a particular story.

The **Share** charm allows you to share information from an app with family, friends, and classmates. The default sharing method is email, but you can install *Twitter*, *Facebook*, or other social media platforms.

The **Start** charm takes you to the Start screen.

The **Devices** charm allows you to work with devices attached to your computer, such as printers and additional monitors. When you are viewing content of a Start screen app, such as Maps, for example, you can select a printer to print the map or control how the screen displays on multiple monitors.

The **Settings** charm allows you access to settings for the network, volume, screen brightness, notifications, power, and language. You also find the option to customize your Start screen.

Project 3

From
Janet Marshall

Justin McIntyre would like us to invite Mr. and Mrs. Jacob Nivins to the home showing. I've attached a hard copy of the letter template we are using since my computer isn't letting me access the electronic file.

After you rekey the letter, save it because our sales agents may have others they want invited. The address information is in our client db.

JM   5/13

May 1, 20--

(Title) (First Name) (Last Name)
(Address)
(City), (State) (ZIP)

Dear (Courtesy Title) (Last Name)

The 20-- Parade of Homes will be held June 7 – 21. This year we are planning something new. A limited number of our previous home buyers from Newhouse Realty are being invited to participate in a private showing prior to the public opening of the Parade of Homes.

The private showing will give Newhouse Realty agents the time needed to point out the many fine features of the quality homes being shown this year and to answer any questions you may have. With so many people taking part in the Parade of Homes, it is difficult to give our preferred customers the attention they deserve during the days the homes are shown to the public.

If you are interested in this free showing, sign and return the enclosed card. We look forward to showing you the outstanding homes built for this year's home show.

Sincerely,

Janet M. Marshall
Office Manager

Project 4

From
Janet Marshall

Key the listing of homes that will be in this year's Parade of Homes. Use **Parade of Homes** for the main heading and **June 7 – 21, 20--**, as the secondary heading. Center column headings. After you key the table, sort the builders in ascending alphabetical order.

JM   5/14

Address	Builder	Price
360 Brookdale Lane	Greenway Construction	$375,000
608 Candlewood Court	Newhouse Realty	$579,000
625 Candlewood Court	Newhouse Realty	$429,000
900 Hawthorne Avenue	Gill & Sons Construction	$639,000
3809 Glacier Place	Kasota Contractors	$329,000
608 Hillswick Trail	Anderson Builders	$475,000
712 Kirkwood Circle	Lancaster & Sons	$599,000
376 Brookdale Lane	Knox Home Builders	$409,000

The mouse is a hovering and pointing device. It is a navigation tool that controls a pointer on your screen, which is used to control your OS. Just as a helicopter can hover above a city, a mouse can hover over any part of your *Windows* desktop. After you move your mouse into position, you can click one of its buttons to activate commands on your computer. A typical mouse is shown in Figure 1.12.

Mouse wheel

Left mouse button

Right mouse button

© Tatiana Popova/Shutterstock.com

Figure 1.12 *Parts of a typical mouse*

Many people use a digital pen in addition to a mouse. Laptop computers usually have a track pad that you can use instead of a mouse. On some computers, you can use your fingers as a pointing device. A variety of pointing devices are shown in Figure 1.13.

Instant Message

If you are using a digital pen, hover ¼ inch above the surface and move the pointer around the screen as you would with a mouse. If you have a multi-touch screen, use your fingers like a mouse pointer.

© Anna Jurkovska/Shutterstock.com

Track pad

© microstocker/Shutterstock.com

Ergonomic mouse

© Paulo Resende/Shutterstock.com

Digital pen

PictureNet/Corbis

Fingertip multi-touch screen

© Aga_Rafi/Shutterstock.com

Roller ball

Figure 1.13 *Other pointing devices*

**From
Janet Marshall**

Prepare a table from the information shown on the attached. Use **Featured Homes** for the main heading and **Week of June 14 – 21** for the secondary heading. Use *df home photo1*, *df home photo2*, *df home photo3*, *df home photo4*, and *df home photo5* for the inserts.

JM   5/13

Insert *df home photo1*	$998,900 678 Centennial Place Minneapolis, MN 55404 5 Beds 4,780 Sq. Ft. 3 Full Baths 1 Half Bath
Insert *df home photo2*	$989,500 8400 Cottagewood Terrace NE Minneapolis, MN 55432 5 Beds 4,600 Sq. Ft. 3 Full Baths 2 Half Baths
Insert *df home photo3*	$650,000 6300 Stauder Circle Edina, MN 55436 4 Beds 3,970 Sq. Ft. 2 Full Baths 2 Half Baths
Insert *df home photo4*	$499,900 10308 52nd Avenue N Plymouth, MN 55446 4 Beds 3,300 Sq. Ft. 2 Full Baths 1 Half Bath
Insert *df home photo5*	$425,000 3513 Sheridan Avenue S Minneapolis, MN 55410 3 Beds 3,150 Sq. Ft. 2 Full Baths 1 Half Bath

Place your mouse on a mouse pad or hard surface. Slide your mouse (or a pen or your fingers, depending on your computer) to move the pointer around your desktop. If you are using a track pad on a laptop, touch the track pad and slide your finger in any direction to move the pointer on your screen.

As you move the mouse or other pointing device, watch the pointer move on the screen. It will move in the direction that you move your pointing device. The pointer often takes the shape of an arrow. At other times, the pointer looks like a hand. When using different applications, your pointer can change appearance to other shapes too. You can move your pointer to any spot on the desktop.

If your mouse cannot be moved any further, lift it off the surface on which you are sliding it. Move it a few inches and place the mouse back on the surface and continue. After positioning the pointer over the icon or object you wish to use, you can:

- Left-click to select something.

- Double-click to open an application, a file, or an image.

- Click and drag objects around the screen.

- Right-click to open pop-up menus.

ABOVE and BEYOND

Mouse Safety

If you use your mouse improperly, you can injure yourself. Follow these safety tips.

- Place your mouse in a comfortable position.
- Position your mouse close to elbow level and not too far away.
- Do not grip your mouse tightly. Keep your hand relaxed.
- Use relaxed movements starting from the shoulder.
- Do not bend your wrist up, down, or to the side.
- Keep your elbow bent comfortably. Do not extend your arm out straight. Instead, move your mouse pad closer to you.
- Do not press hard on the mouse button. Use a light touch.
- Do not hold onto the mouse if you are not using it.
- Take a break every few minutes. Place your hand to your side and stretch it or shake it gently.

1. Make sure the Start screen is showing on your screen.

2. Move your mouse pointer or swipe around the Start screen. Notice the speed and direction required to achieve a particular movement on the Start screen.

3. Notice the tiles on your Start screen. Some tiles are static such as the desktop or apps like Skype. Some tiles are dynamic like the Weather tile that constantly updates, indicating the current weather conditions.

4. Display the Charm bar.

5. Tap or click the **Search** charm. Key **Mail** in the search box and tap ENTER. The Mail application opens.

6. Display the Charm bar again and tap or click the **Devices** charm. Review the devices available when the Mail application is open.

7. Display the Charm bar again and tap or click the **Start** charm to return to your Start screen.

8. Tap or click your Internet browser. Notice that your browser opens immediately.

9. Explore other tiles on your Start screen to see the information and apps available when you start your computer.

**From
Janet Marshall**

Mr. Newhouse pre-
pared these emails
on the train on the
way to work today.
The first one goes to
our five agents. The
second one goes to
Rebecca St. John.
Please get their email
addresses from the
company database
(*df newhouse realty*).

Remember to copy
Mr. Newhouse and
Bcc me.

JM   5/12

The response from former home buyers who are interested in the private showing of this year's Parade of Homes has been excellent. Meeting with past customers to determine if we can be of further assistance to them with their housing requirements is a real opportunity for us. All of the individuals invited have been in their present homes for over five years and may be ready to consider the purchase of a new home.

Janet will be coordinating schedules for the two days of the private showing. We should have your schedule ready within the next two or three days. A meeting will be held on May 20 at 8:30 a.m. to discuss specific details for the Parade of Homes.

Rebecca, last month when we were discussing some of the details for the Parade of Homes private showing, you indicated that you would be willing to handle the arrangements for refreshments. I would like to take you up on that offer if it still stands.

Please stop by my office sometime this week so that we can discuss a few of the specifics.

Exiting a computer the proper way will help you avoid losing important information. Exiting is sometimes called "shutting down," "logging out," or "logging off." When *Windows* shuts down, it completes tasks such as:

- Closing any open applications.

- Saving unsaved data.

- Closing open connections to networks or the Internet.

- Saving current settings.

When your computer is on, your OS, applications, and data are stored in **memory** chips inside the computer. One type of memory is called **RAM**, or **Random Access Memory**. Another type of memory is called **flash memory**. When the computer is turned off, the memory in RAM is erased or cleared. Any unsaved data will be lost.

After you have practiced with the mouse, follow these steps to turn off your computer.

TIP In *Windows 8.1*, there is no reason to shut down your computer completely—put it in sleep mode instead. This uses little power, and your computer starts up faster. Your work is automatically saved, and the computer (laptop or tablet) is turned off if the battery is too low. Sleep is the default shutdown mode.

1. Close any application you have open—you may be prompted to save your work.

2. Display the Charm bar and click the **Settings** charm.

3. Tap or click **Power;** then tap or click **Shut down.** See Figure 1.14.

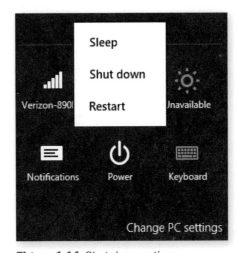

Figure 1.14 *Shut down options*

4. After the computer has shut down, turn off the power switch on the monitor and any peripheral devices you have been using.

5. Review the other options available from the shutdown list that are explained in Table 1.1

Client Information

A table with client information has been included in the *df newhouse realty* database. The *Clients* table includes client names, addresses, and phone numbers.

Newhouse Letter Format

Letters are to be keyed in block format with mixed punctuation. Use 12-point Arial. Include your reference initials on all letters.

When something is enclosed with a letter, key **Enclosure** at the left margin one line beneath reference initials.

Copy notations are keyed at the left margin one line beneath reference initials (or one line beneath the enclosure notation, if an enclosure is included). Leave one space after the c before keying the name of the person receiving the copy. (This is different from what you previously learned. Many companies have their own variation of what you learned in the textbook. Of course, you will always adhere to their guidelines.)

Newhouse Realty

315 Parkview Terrace
Minneapolis, MN 55416-3430

May 16, 20--

Mr. and Mrs. Jackson Higgins
825 W. Oak Street
Stillwater, MN 55082-4122

Dear Mr. and Mrs. Higgins:

We are pleased to have you take part in our private showing of the homes that will be in this year's Parade of Homes. The eight homes you will see combine quality construction, professional decorating, and exclusive landscaping to make this year's show the best ever.

I have made arrangements with Maria Perez to show you the homes. Please meet her at our office at 10 a.m. on Friday, June 5. It will take approximately two hours to visit the homes.

I am looking forward to hearing your comments about the homes after the showing. If you have any questions prior to the showing, please telephone me.

Sincerely,

Janet Marshall
Office Manager

jm

c Maria Perez

Table 1.1 *Shut down menu options*

Sleep	Puts your computer to "sleep" but keeps enough power in memory to keep your work available exactly where you left it. Recommended for short breaks.
Shut down	Turns off the computer system completely.
Restart	Shuts down completely and then restarts. Often used to clear a computer's memory and to refresh the system.

21st Century Skills

© Andrest/Shutterstock.com

Leadership Consider these attributes of a successful leader, and write your responses to the following questions in the form of a paragraph.

- A successful leader accepts responsibility and accountability for results.
- A successful leader has self-discipline, good character, and is committed to personal development.
- A successful leader is a great communicator.
- A successful leader has great people skills.

Think Critically

1. What attributes of a successful leader apply to ethical and appropriate computer use?

2. Describe ways in which you have demonstrated leadership abilities when using the computer, the Internet, or a mobile device such as a cell phone.

3. Write your responses in paragraph form and give the page to your instructor.

Lesson 3

Windows OS Basics

Learning Outcomes

In Lesson 3, you will:

3A   *Open applications.*
3B   *Learn the parts of a **Windows** application.*
3C   *Resize, minimize, maximize, and restore windows.*
3D   *Learn more about pointers.*

3A

Open Applications

Your computer gives you several different ways of starting applications, depending on the operating system and version.

- The application you want may appear on the Start screen as a tile. Click the tile to start the application.

Ms. Marshall will attach general processing instructions to each task you are given. If a date is not provided on the document, use the date included with the instructions. If the instructions given with the document are not sufficiently detailed, use your decision-making skills to process the document. Use the textbook as a reference when needed.

Documents should be attractively formatted. You are expected to produce error-free documents; proofread and correct your work carefully before presenting it for approval. Print each project when completed unless otherwise directed by your instructor.

As with a real job, you will be expected to work independently and learn on your own how to do some things that you haven't previously been taught using resources that are available to you. You will also be expected to use your decision-making skills to arrange documents attractively whenever specific instructions are not provided. Since Newhouse Realty has based its word processing manual on the *Century 21* textbook, you can refer to this text in making formatting decisions. In addition, you can use the Help feature of your software to review a feature you may have forgotten or to learn new features you may need.

Data Files:

df newhouse realty
df home photo1
df home photo2
df home photo3
df home photo4
df home photo5
df acceptance letter
df newhouse memo
df heber house photos

Filenames

In order to quickly assess information, Newhouse Realty has established a file-naming system that is used by company employees. It is very simple. All files you create should be named with *newhouse*, followed by the project number (*newhouse project 1*, *newhouse project 2*, etc.).

Data Files

Some of the projects you will be working on have already been started or require information from previously created documents. You will need to access the company data files to complete these projects.

Company Email

Company email addresses are available in the *Company Email Addresses* table of the *df newhouse realty* database.

When an email is sent to more than one individual, put email addresses in alphabetical order by last name.

Emails for Mr. Newhouse

Mr. Newhouse often creates email messages in longhand. When Janet Marshall keys the messages for him, she uses the following subject line: *Message from Blake Newhouse*. You should use the same subject line for messages you key for him.

Mr. Newhouse would like a copy of all emails sent on his behalf. Bcc Ms. Marshall on all correspondence.

- From the Start screen, display the Charm bar. Tap or click the Search charm. Key the name of the application you wish to open in the **search box**. In Figure 1.15, we are searching for *PowerPoint*. As you start to key the word, application programs that contain the word will appear on the list of results. Click the app to begin work.

- Click the Desktop tile to display the *Windows* **desktop**. An application's icon may appear on the desktop or be pinned to the taskbar.

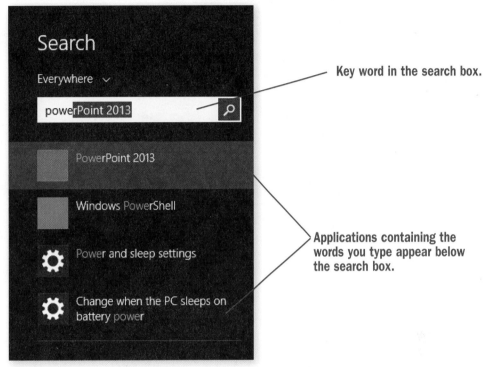

Figure 1.15 *Search for apps.*

Key word in the search box.

Applications containing the words you type appear below the search box.

3B

Parts of a Windows Application

The *Windows* OS opens each application in a separate frame called a **window**. That is how the *Windows* OS got its name. Many windows look similar to each other even though they may contain different applications. In Figure 1.16, look at the parts in an application called *PowerPoint*. Like many applications, it has a **ribbon** where all the commands are displayed.

PROJECT

Newhouse Realty: An Integrated Project

Dr. Jack P. Hoggatt

Work Assignment

Newhouse Realty hires students to work during seasonal peak periods. You have been hired as an office assistant to help Janet Marshall, office manager, prepare documents for the annual *Parade of Homes*, which is sponsored by Newhouse Realty. The owner of Newhouse Realty, Blake Newhouse, has several projects that he needs completed as well.

The *Parade of Homes* is a showing open to the general public of newly constructed homes that feature the latest innovations in the housing industry. This year, Newhouse Realty agents (Steve Chen, Justin McIntyre, Justin O'Dell, Maria Perez, and Cynthia Stone) will be inviting former clients to attend a private showing prior to the *Parade of Homes*.

The position will provide you with the opportunity to utilize many of the computer application skills you have learned. You will use:

- *Word* to process letters, tables, and a flyer
- *Outlook* to process emails
- *Access* to create and update databases
- *Excel* to construct a worksheet to calculate commissions
- *PowerPoint* to design a slide presentation for the open house

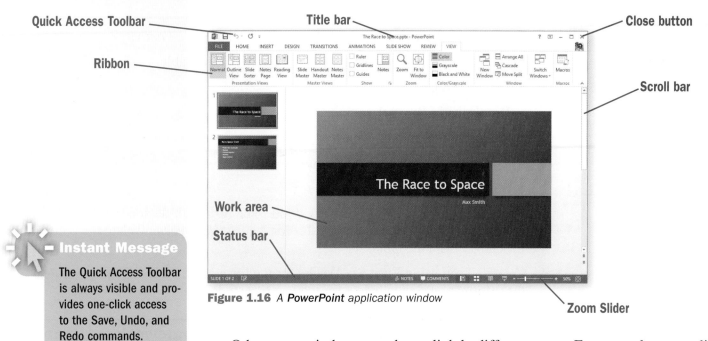

Quick Access Toolbar

Ribbon

Title bar

Close button

Scroll bar

Work area

Status bar

Figure 1.16 *A PowerPoint application window*

Zoom Slider

Instant Message

The Quick Access Toolbar is always visible and provides one-click access to the Save, Undo, and Redo commands.

Other open windows may have slightly different parts. For example, an application used to edit photos has a menu bar and buttons for issuing commands as well as window control buttons. (See them in Figure 1.17.)

Menu bar

Close button

Buttons

Figure 1.17 *A photo-editing application window*

1. Start *Windows*, if necessary. Move the pointer to the upper-right corner of the Start screen to display the Charm bar.

2. Click the **Search** charm.

3. Key **PowerPoint** in the search box.

Data File:

df a4 activity7

1. Open the database *df a4 activity7*; save the database as *a4 activity7*.

2. Make the changes shown below to the *First Six Weeks* table.

   • Jimanez should be spelled Jimenez

   • Brooks had a 98 on the exam

   • Van Horn had an 8 on Quiz 1

   • Thompson had a 64 on the exam

   • Suzuki had a 6 on Quiz 3

3. The scores on Quiz 3 were not very good. The instructor decided not to use those grades in calculating the grades for the first six weeks. Delete the column for Quiz 3 from the table.

4. Create a form using **First Six Weeks** for the form name. Use the form to enter the information shown below for the last two students.

Student Name	Homework 1	Quiz 1	Homework 2	Quiz 2	Homework 3	Exam
Young, C	10	6	9	6	10	67
Zelmer, W	5	10	7	10	8	88

5. Use Query Design to create a query showing students with exam scores of 90 or above. Include the student name and the exam score. Sort the exam scores in Descending order. Print the query. Save the query as **Exam Scores of 90 or Above**.

6. Use the Report Wizard to create a report with the following fields and specifications:

   • Student Name

   • Homework 1

   • Homework 2

   • Homework 3

   Grouping: none

   Sort: none

   Layout: Tabular

   Orientation: Portrait

   Title of report: **Homework**

7. View the report in Print Preview, print the report, and then close the report.

8. Close the database.

4. Click **PowerPoint** in the list of results.

5. When the *PowerPoint* window opens, click **Blank Presentation**. In the new presentation, look for the parts shown in Figure 1.16.

6. Click on the *Click to add title* placeholder and key your name.

7. Click the minus (–) sign on the Zoom Slider. Then click the plus (+) sign. Notice what happens to your name.

8. Close *PowerPoint* by clicking the **Close** button as shown in Figure 1.16. (Do not save.)

3C

Resize, Minimize, Maximize, and Restore Windows

Application windows can be different sizes and placed in different areas on the desktop. If a window does not cover the entire desktop, you can move it or resize it.

To move a window, click the title bar and drag the window. To resize a window, place the pointer on the top, bottom, or side edge of the window to display a double-sided arrow. This arrow will let you know when resizing can take place. Then drag in the direction you want to resize. To change the height and width of a window at the same time, hover the pointer over a corner. The pointer will change shape to a double-sided arrow as shown in Figure 1.18. Click and drag the arrow in any direction until the application is the size you want it to be.

Drag the title bar to move a window.

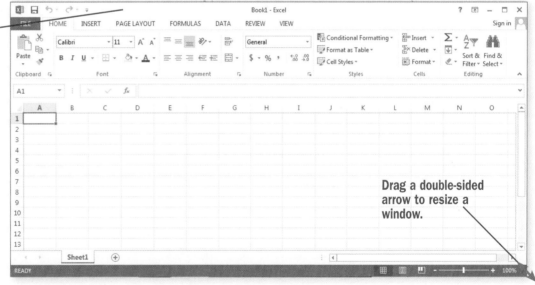

Drag a double-sided arrow to resize a window.

Figure 1.18 *Resize and move a window.*

You can "hide" an application window by clicking its **Minimize** button. (See Figure 1.19.) This sends the window to the **taskbar**. This is called *minimizing* the window. When you minimize a window, its program does not close. It simply moves from the screen. To display the window again, click that program's icon on the taskbar.

1. Create a new database using *a4 activity6* for the filename.

2. Create and save a table using **First Six Weeks** for the table name; use the information below for the field names.

   - Default ID field
   - Student Name
   - Homework 1
   - Quiz 1
   - Homework 2
   - Quiz 2
   - Homework 3
   - Quiz 3
   - Exam

3. Enter the records given below in the table.

Student Name	Homework 1	Quiz 1	Homework 2	Quiz 2	Homework 3	Quiz 3	Exam
Abbott, J	10	9	10	8	10	8	98
Anderson, J	9	8	8	7	9	6	76
Brooks, H	10	8	10	9	9	8	88
Chen, S	9	8	10	9	8	6	56
Cook, I	8	8	9	9	10	6	95
Denver, G	8	7	9	7	10	6	83
Etheridge, M	8	7	9	8	8	7	50
Fernandez, M	5	8	7	9	8	8	77

4. Adjust each column width to fit the longest item in the column.

5. Sort the records in descending order by Exam.

6. Print the table and then close it.

7. Close the database.

The Maximize and
Restore Down buttons
trade places depending
on the size of the window.
When a window is full size,
the Restore Down button
displays so you can reduce
the size of the window.
When the window is not full
size, the Maximize button
displays so you can make
the window full size.

To make the window fill the entire screen, click the **Maximize** button. To restore a window to its previous size, click the **Restore Down** button. Practice with these buttons in the next activity.

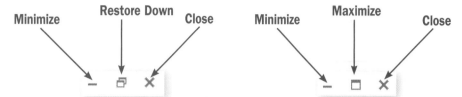

Figure 1.19 *Minimize, Maximize, Restore Down, and Close buttons*

1. Start *Excel*.

2. If the program window does not cover the entire desktop, click or tap the **Maximize** button. The window will change to full size.

3. Click or tap the **Restore Down** button. The window is now smaller than full-screen size.

4. Hover the mouse pointer over the lower-right corner of the *Excel* window. When the pointer changes to a double-sided arrow, click and drag down and to the right to make the window bigger. (See Figure 1.18 on page 16.)

5. Click or tap the **Minimize** button shown in Figure 1.19. The window will disappear from the screen.

6. Restore *Excel* by clicking its icon on the taskbar.

7. Hover the mouse pointer over the lower-right corner of the window. Use the double-sided arrow to make the window smaller.

8. Click and drag the *Excel* title bar to move the window to the upper-right corner of the screen. Then move it to the lower-left corner of the screen.

9. Close *Excel*.

3D

Learn More about Pointers

In Lesson 2, you learned that the pointer sometimes changes shape. The shape lets you know what you can do at a particular place on the desktop. Study Table 1.2 to learn about the most common pointer shapes. You will discover a few new ones when you complete the next activity using the *Paint* application.

Table 1.2 *Mouse and pen pointer shapes*

	Select or **Arrow.** Tells you where the mouse is located as you move it across the screen.
I	**Text Select** or **Insertion Point.** Moves the insertion point (flashing line) to the exact spot where you need to key words or numbers. Also helps you select text.

(Continued)

6. Merge & Center cells H1 and H2.

7. Key **YTD % Change** in the merged cell and wrap the text.

8. In cell H3, calculate the YTD % Change by entering this formula: **=(G3−B3)/B3**. Copy the formula to cells H4:H10.

9. Format numbers in columns B–G and I–K in Currency with two decimal places.

10. Format numbers in column H as Percentage with two decimal places.

11. Merge cells A1 and A2.

12. In cell A11, key **Average**.

13. In cell B11, calculate the average share price in column B. Copy the formula to cells C11:G11

14. Bold entries in row 11.

15. Apply 12-point bold format in rows 1 and 2.

16. Use center align in cells A3:A11.

17. Use center align in rows 1 and 2.

18. Set column widths to 10.

19. Insert a row at the top of the worksheet and center **YEAR-TO-DATE STOCK PORTFOLIO ANALYSIS** as a title across columns A–K using a bold, 16-point font.

20. Change orientation to Landscape, center the worksheet horizontally and vertically on the page, and select to print gridlines.

21. Preview and print the worksheet.

22. Save the workbook as *a4 activity3* and close it.

Activity 4
Column Chart

Data File:
df a4 activity4

1. Open the workbook *df a4 activity4*.

2. Insert a 2-D column chart using the default layout and chart elements. Use the worksheet title for the chart title and add data labels to the chart.

3. Print the chart and the worksheet together.

4. Save the workbook as *a4 activity4* and close it.

Activity 5
Change Chart Type and Style

Data File:
df a4 activity5

1. Open the workbook *df a4 activity5*.

2. Change the pie chart to a doughnut chart. Change the chart style to Style 3.

3. Print the chart only.

4. Save the workbook as *a4 activity5* and close it.

Table 1.2 (*Continued*)

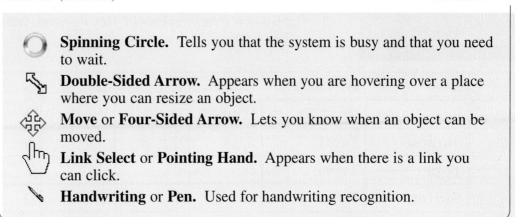

Spinning Circle. Tells you that the system is busy and that you need to wait.

Double-Sided Arrow. Appears when you are hovering over a place where you can resize an object.

Move or **Four-Sided Arrow.** Lets you know when an object can be moved.

Link Select or **Pointing Hand.** Appears when there is a link you can click.

Handwriting or **Pen.** Used for handwriting recognition.

1. Start the *Paint* program and click or tap the **Maximize** button if necessary.

2. Point to different icons on the ribbon. Hesitate for a few seconds over each icon. The name and a brief description of each will appear. For example, Figure 1.20 shows the pointer hovering over the Pencil tool so that its name and description appear.

Step 2

Figure 1.20 *Read the on-screen tip for each tool.*

3. Click or tap the **Fill with color** tool. It looks like a bucket spilling paint. Move the pointer down to a blank part of the window. Notice how the pointer changes appearance to look like a bucket.

4. Next, click or tap the **Magnifier** tool; it looks like a magnifying glass. Move back to the work area and see how your pointer changes to display the tool with which you are working.

5. Click or tap the **Pencil** on the toolbar. (See Figure 1.20.) Move the pointer to the work area. Click and hold the mouse button and drag the pencil pointer to write your first name. You can release the mouse button to add spaces between letters.

6. Choose a different color from the Colors tool palette and write your last name.

7. Click the **Eraser** on the Home tab. Drag it to erase one letter of your name.

8. Use *Paint* to practice drawing. Try many of the tools and colors on the tabs and tool palettes. Experiment!

9. Click or tap the *Paint* window's **Close** button. (Do not save.)

1. Open a new *Excel* workbook. Key the worksheet shown below.

	A	B	C	D	E	F	G	H
1	Last Name	First Name	Week 1	Week 2	Week 3	Week 4	Week 5	Total
2	James	Brett	1	0	3	0	2	
3	Tobin	Tryell	0	0	0	2	1	
4	Sutton	Kyle	0	1	1	0	0	
5	Saag	Noah	2	3	1	3	2	
6	Franklin	Ryan	0	1	0	0	1	
7	Doyle	Connor	0	0	0	1	0	
8	Hart	Derek	1	1	0	0	0	

2. Wrap the text in cells A1 and B1 and AutoFit column widths.

3. Calculate the total for each row in column H.

4. Sort the worksheet by column H in descending order.

5. Merge & Center **Weekly Total** in cells A9:B9. Bold the entries in row 9.

6. Calculate the total for columns C–H in row 9.

7. Insert a row at the top and Merge & Center **TOUCHDOWN SCORERS FOR THE BEARCATS** across the columns. Format the title in 16-point bold.

8. Bold and center row 2 entries. Center-align the numbers in cells C3:H10.

9. Set row height at 20 for row 1 and rows 3–10.

10. Center the worksheet horizontally with a 2" top margin. Preview the worksheet and print it without gridlines.

11. Save the workbook as *a4 activity2* and close it.

1. Open *df a4 activity3*.

2. In cell H3, use the MIN function to find the low share price for Company A. Copy the formula to cells H4:H10.

3. In cell I3, use the MAX function to identify the high share price for Company A. Copy this to cells I4:I10.

4. In cell J3, enter a formula to subtract cell H3 from cell I3. Copy this formula to cells J4:J10.

5. Insert a column between columns G and H.

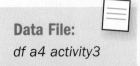

Data File:
df a4 activity3

Microsoft Word and Ribbon Basics

Data File:

df 4d microsoft
and google

Learning Outcomes

In Lesson 4, you will:

4A   *Explore the **Word** ribbon.*
4B   *Key and edit text in **Word**.*
4C   *Save a document.*
4D   *Open an existing file and save with a new name.*
4E   *Preview and print a document in **Word**.*
4F   *Use numbered lists and discuss acceptable use policies.*

4A

Explore the Word Ribbon

Microsoft Word is a word processing application. You will need to use *Word* in many of the chapters to come. This lesson will teach you a few basics, just enough to complete your work successfully. In Unit 3, you will learn to use the features of *Word* in greater detail.

A key feature of *Word* is the ribbon. The ribbon displays most of *Word*'s commands along the top of the screen. (See Figure 1.21.)

Figure 1.21 *Commands on the Home tab*

When you open a document in *Word*, the commands on the Home tab display by default. To view more commands, click or tap the tabs at the top of the ribbon. Commands are organized into *groups*. The Home tab has five groups: Clipboard, Font, Paragraph, Styles, and Editing.

You can display additional commands and options using other features of the ribbon:

- Click a *dialog box launcher* arrow, at the lower-right corner of a group, to display a **dialog box** that contains additional commands relating to that group.

Assessment 4   Worksheets and Database

Warmup Practice

Key each line twice. If time permits, key the lines again.

Alphabet

1 Gus Javon quickly baked extra pizza for the women.

Figures/Symbol

2 Janet paid Jon $1,347.75; John paid Ken $2,690.85.

Speed

3 Kamela may work with the city auditor on the form.

gwam 1' | 1 | 2 | 3 | 4 | 5 | 6 | 7 | 8 | 9 | 10 |

Activity 1
Assess Straight-Copy Skill

Key one or two 2' or 3' timed writings on all paragraphs combined. Print, proofread, circle errors, and determine *gwam*.

A   all letters used

	gwam	2'	3'

Liz, who is nearing the end of her third year of   5   3
high school, is a quality young person. She is an   10   7
above-average student who always makes high grades.   15   10
Liz is taking challenging English, math, and computer 21   14
application courses and an advanced science class for   26   17
which she can earn college credit. She has played   31   21
soccer and softball for three years and was one of   36   24
the top soccer players in the county last year. She   42   28
holds offices in several student organizations and is 47   31
a member of the honor society at her high school.   52   35

Liz, like many other young adults, is trying to   5   38
make career plans. She is very good with computers,   10   41
math, and science and enjoys these classes. She   15   45
thinks she would like to be a physics teacher. She   20   48
has, however, received signals from many friends and   26   52
family members that she should not aspire to a career 31   55
in science, especially physics, because it is a field 36   59
dominated by men. She does not want such discouraging 42   62
comments to shake her desire.   45   64

A teacher who supports her career goal suggested   5   68
she research roles for women in science. An Internet 10   71
search quickly led her to associations that help women 16   75
in science network with each other. Also, many of   21   78
these groups provide opportunities for girls to be   26   82
mentored by women in their field of interest. Liz is 31   85
encouraged by her research. She plans to enroll in   37   89
the next mentoring program of the chapter of women   42   92
scientists in her city.   44   94

gwam 2' | 1 | 2 | 3 | 4 | 5 |
     3' | 1 | 2 | 3 |

- Click a More button for a *gallery* such as the Styles gallery to display the entire gallery.
- Click a down arrow on a command button to see additional commands for that button.

1. Start *Windows*. Click the **Search** charm from your Charm bar. Key **Word** in the search box and tap ENTER.
2. Click **Blank document** to open a new document. If it is not already selected, click the **Home** tab.
3. Click the **Insert** tab to display the tab shown in Figure 1.22. Note the ten groups in which the commands are organized.

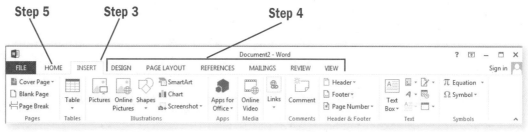

Figure 1.22 *Insert tab commands*

Do you understand the organization of the commands within each group in each tab? For example, look at each command within the Paragraph group on the Home tab. Why is each placed in that group? Understanding the organization will help you find commands when you need them.

4. Display the hundreds of commands available by clicking each of the remaining tabs: **Design**, **Page Layout**, **References**, **Mailings**, **Review**, and **View**. You can also click the **File** tab. Unlike the other tabs, the File tab shows its commands in a vertical menu.
5. Return to the Home tab and view the groups on this important tab. Find the following commands or features in each group. If you are not sure what some commands do, hover your pointer over them for a brief description.
    - **Clipboard:** Find the Cut and Copy commands. They are light gray, indicating they are not currently active.
    - **Font:** Find the Font Color button and click the small downward-pointing arrow on the button to display the Font Color palette. Click anywhere on the screen to close the palette.
    - **Paragraph:** Click the Paragraph group's dialog box launcher to open the Paragraph dialog box. Click the **Cancel** button in the dialog box to close it.
    - **Styles:** Click the **More** button at the lower-right corner of the Styles gallery to see all the styles in the gallery.
    - **Editing:** Locate the Find and Replace commands, and then click the down arrow on the Find button to see additional commands.
6. Close *Word* by clicking the **Close** button. (Do not save.)

COLLABORATION

1. Open *df c12 college database instructions*. Print and close the file.

2. Follow the instructions given on your printout to research at least ten schools that offer degrees related to a career you are interested in. Then work with a group of classmates to design and create a database and create a table, form, queries, filters, and reports.

Career Exploration Portfolio

Online Resources:

ngl.cengage.com/c21jr3e

Activity 11

To complete this activity, you must first complete Career Exploration Portfolio Activities 1–10.

1. Review your Student Interest Survey. Reread all of the summary paragraphs that you wrote as you completed Career Exploration Portfolio Activities 2–10.

2. Think about all of the information that you learned through the Career Exploration Portfolio activities. Use this information to pick the one career you are most interested in. Remember that this may or may not be the same career that is listed as your first choice on your Student Interest Survey.

3. Use *Word* to write a summary of the career that you chose. Be sure to explain the reasons you like this career better than the other two. Describe the pros and cons, including information about the duties of the jobs, skills needed, and education needed.

4. Save your document as *c12 top career choice*, print, and close it.

To key text, tap each key on the keyboard or other input device that you are using. If you press a wrong key, you can use the BACKSPACE key to delete your mistakes. As you key text, remember to:

- Tap the Space Bar once to space between words.
- Tap the Space Bar once after a comma (,).
- Tap the Space Bar twice after a period (.), a question mark (?), an exclamation mark (!), and a colon (:).
- Hold down the SHIFT key to create a capital letter.
- Tap ENTER only at the end of a paragraph.

TIP Do not tap ENTER when you reach the end of a line! When a line is full, the next word will automatically jump to the next line. This is called wordwrap.

1. Start *Word*, create a new document, and click the **Home** tab if necessary.

2. Key the following text in the document.

   Space Exploration [Enter]

   <your name> [Enter]

   The Russians were the first to send someone into space. The Russians called their astronauts by the name cosmonauts. The first cosmonaut left Earth on April 12, 1961.

Instant Message

Notice that when you move the pointer around the work area of a *Word* document, it changes in appearance to the pointer called an *I-beam*. This pointer tells you that you can click to insert text.

3. Move the mouse pointer so that it is positioned to the left of the first word in your document (right before *Space Exploration*). Click once to place the insertion point (blinking line) before this line.

4. Key the first change (the text marked in green) as shown below.

   The History of Space Exploration

5. Position the insertion point at the end of your name and tap ENTER. Key the changes shown below that are marked in green.

   The Russians [Enter]

   The Russian and the American space programs were in competition. The Russians were the first to send someone into space. The Russians called their astronauts by the name cosmonauts. The first cosmonaut, Yuri Gagarin, left Earth on April 12, 1961. [Enter]

   The Americans [Enter]

   The Americans were eager to catch up. The United States sent their first astronaut, Alan Shepard, into space on May 5, 1961. [Enter]

TIP You may also move the insertion point by tapping the up, down, left, and right arrow keys.

ACROSS THE CURRICULUM

Academic Connections

Data Files:
df c12 books database instructions
df c12 books
df c12 outsourcing instructions
df c12 college database instructions

Language Arts: Book Database

How do you think libraries keep track of all the books that they own and lend? Without computers, this would be a huge task! Most libraries have a specific system that they use to track their books; one part of these systems usually involves a database. In this activity, you will work with a database that a team of teachers uses to track books that they have purchased for use in their classrooms. You will edit, sort, and query the database.

1. Start *Word* and open *df c12 books database instructions*. Print and close the file without saving it.

2. Read the instructions on your printout to start *Access* and open *df c12 books*.

3. Make changes to the database as instructed. Then save database objects and close the database.

About Business

Outsourcing

Companies must react quickly to changes in customers' wants and needs in order to be successful. Outsourcing is a practice that helps companies do this. **Outsourcing** means that a company hires another company or person to do work. This is done rather than having the work performed by other company employees.

Outsourcing work lets a company focus on its main business. Other jobs that are not related to the primary business of the company may be handled by outside firms. For example, a company that makes bikes may want to focus on jobs that relate directly to producing bikes. Other jobs, such as providing building security, preparing payroll, and providing technical support for the company's computers, may be outsourced.

1. Open *df c12 outsourcing instructions*. Print and close the file.

2. Follow the instructions given on your printout to research some companies in your area that can be hired to do outsourced work. Then design and create a database that holds the information that you find.

Life Success Builder

College Choices

What factors will help you decide where to go to college? A lot of students think about where a college is located and how much it costs. One big factor to consider is what majors, or areas of study, a college offers. If you want to be a dentist, you probably wouldn't attend a school that specializes in theater.

In this activity, you'll have the chance to research some schools that offer degrees in a field you are interested in. Then you'll work with a team of classmates to design and create a database of schools.

Save a Document

WP   File/Save As

As soon as you create a new file, you should save it. A file that has been saved can be opened again so you can edit the text. Use the Save As command on the File tab to begin the process of saving a file. You will then have to navigate to the location on your computer or other storage area where you want to store the file.

1. Click the **File** tab on the ribbon. Then click **Save As** as shown in Figure 1.23.

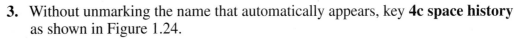

Figure 1.23 *Choose the Save As command on the File tab.*

2. Click **Computer** and then click **Browse**. The **Save As** dialog box opens.

3. Without unmarking the name that automatically appears, key **4c space history** as shown in Figure 1.24.

TIP *Word* automatically gives your document a name. To change it, you can key over it (if it is highlighted). If you accidentally unmark the name, click to place the insertion point right after it and tap BACKSPACE until it is deleted.

TIP The following characters cannot be used in file or folder names: \ / : * ? " < > |.

Figure 1.24 *Naming a file in the Save As dialog box*

4. Follow your teacher's instructions to find and open the folder where you will store the file.

5. Click or tap **Save**.

6. Close the document and exit *Word*.

TECHNIQUE TIP
Quickly tap the Space Bar after the last letter in each word. Immediately begin keying the next word.

1 The sign is on the mantel by the antique ornament.
2 Pamela kept the food for the fish by the fishbowl.
3 I paid the man by the dock for the bushel of corn.
4 The box with a shamrock and an iris is by the car.
5 To the right of the big lake is the dismal shanty.

gwam 30" | 2 | 4 | 6 | 8 | 10 | 12 | 14 | 16 | 18 | 20 |

Speed Building

1. Key three 1' timed writings on each paragraph, striving to key more on each timing; determine *gwam*.

2. Key a 2' or 3' timed writing on all paragraphs combined, striving to maintain your highest 1' *gwam*.

A all letters used

	gwam 2' 3'
"I left my heart in San Francisco." This	4 3
expression becomes much easier to understand after	9 6
an individual has visited the city near the bay.	14 9
San Francisco is one of the most interesting areas	19 13
to visit throughout the entire world. The history	25 16
of this lovely city is unique. Even though people	30 20
inhabited the area prior to the gold rush, it was	35 23
the prospect of getting rich that brought about	39 26
the fast growth of the city.	42 28
It is difficult to write about just one thing	5 31
that this exquisite city is known for. Spectacular	10 34
views, cable cars, the Golden Gate Bridge, and	15 37
Fisherman's Wharf are only a few of the many things	20 40
that are associated with this amazing city. The	25 43
city is also known for the diversity of its people.	30 46
In fact, there are three separate cities within the	35 50
city, Chinatown being the best known.	39 53

gwam 2' | 1 | 2 | 3 | 4 | 5 |
3' | 1 | 2 | 3 |

Open an Existing File and Save with New Name

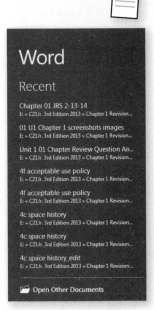

Figure 1.25 *Open Other Documents command in* **Word** *start window*

TIP Triple-click {*Your Name*} to quickly highlight the entire line.

WP   File/Save As/Save

Throughout this book, you will need to open data files and save them with new names. A data file contains information you will use to complete an activity. With a data file, part of the work has already been done for you.

Data filenames start with *df* for *data file*, then list the "activity number" followed by a "descriptive name." For example, *df 4d microsoft and google*. When you save a file you have completed, you will be given the filename to use.

1. Start *Word*.

2. In the *Word* opening screen, click **Open Other Documents** in the lower-left corner of the screen (Figure 1.25).

3. Following your instructor's directions, choose the network or local folder where your instructor has placed the data files.

4. Click the data file named **df 4d microsoft and google** as shown in Figure 1.26.

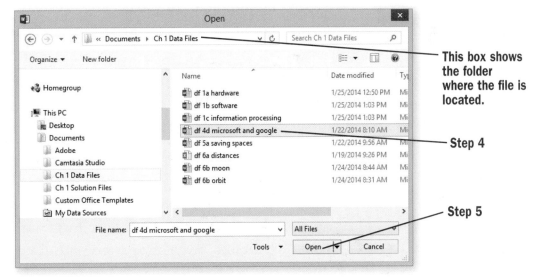

Figure 1.26 *Select and open a data file.*

5. Click **Open**. The document will appear on the screen.

6. Read the document. You may need to use the scroll bar to scroll to the bottom.

7. Drag your insertion point over the words *{Your Name}* to highlight them, and then release the mouse button. Key your name. It will replace the highlighted text.

8. Replace *{Class Name}* and *{Today's Date}* with the appropriate information.

9. Scroll to the bottom of the document and click the insertion point in the blank space for the first similarity. Key the first similarity.

10. Key the rest of your answers in the appropriate spaces.

11. Click the **File** tab and click **Save As**.

KEYBOARDING SKILLBUILDING

Warmup Practice

Key each line twice. If time permits, key the lines again.

Alphabet

1 Jack Gable explained most of his very low quizzes.

Figure/Symbol

2 He used check #208 and #259 to pay invoice #31647.

Speed

3 The eight busy men did the problems for the girls.

gwam 1' | 1 | 2 | 3 | 4 | 5 | 6 | 7 | 8 | 9 | 10 |

Improve Keying Technique

Key each line twice, striving to maintain a continuous pace.

TECHNIQUE TIP
Do not rest your palms on the keyboard or desk as you key.

Space Bar

1 it is be no box zap six ace save nice make ill joy
2 up in to and tax yes help gone face down quit were

SHIFT keys

3 Rio de Janeiro; Port of Spain; Mount Saint Helens;
4 Jan and Seth left on Monday to go to Mt. Rushmore.

Adjacent keys

5 union open oil cash here wet where brass part bids
6 Wes Marti was the last guy to weigh before dinner.

Long direct reaches

7 my ice any run sum nut gum hut many curb vice nice
8 Bob Cox broke my record to receive a bronze medal.

Word response

9 girl down coal held paid land rush odor iris hands
10 Pamela may wish to make a bid for their auto maps.

gwam 1' | 1 | 2 | 3 | 4 | 5 | 6 | 7 | 8 | 9 | 10 |

12. Find the folder where your instructor has told you to save your files.

13. Key **4d applications and apps** in the File name box and click **Save**.

14. Close the document and exit *Word*.

Preview and Print a Document in Word

WP   File/Print/Print

Sometimes you will need a printed copy of your work. Print by clicking the File tab followed by the Print command. This command opens the Print screen shown in Figure 1.27. On this screen, you can choose your printer, select the number of copies to print, and choose other options. You can also preview your document to check for any last-minute errors or formatting issues before you print.

1. Start *Word* if it is not already open.

2. Open the *4c space history* file you created earlier.

3. Click the **File** tab on the ribbon.

4. Click **Print**. The screen to the right of the Print command changes as shown in Figure 1.27.

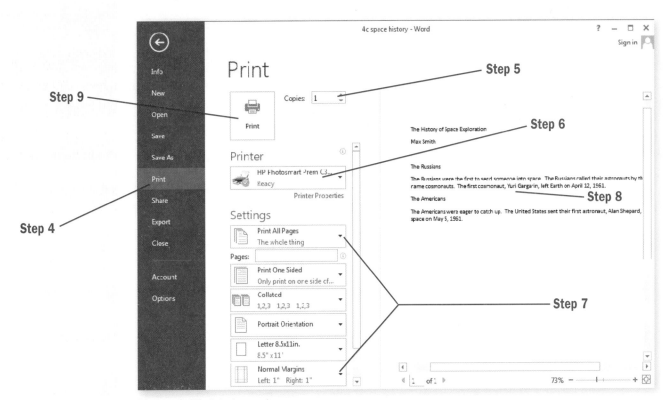

Figure 1.27 *Printing options*

5. Make sure the number of copies is set to **1**. If it is not, use the arrow keys to change it. You can also highlight the number in the box and key the number you want.

6. Choose the printer assigned by your instructor.

c. The complete title for Beethoven's composition is **Symphony No. 5 in C minor, Op. 67**. Update the field.

d. Correct the dates for Franz Haydn. They should be **1732–1809**.

3. Print and then close the table. Close *Access* or continue with the next activity.

Design and Create a Database

You and two of your classmates have been asked by your principal to design a database that will allow the school to:

- Locate a student at any time during the school day.

- Send information to the home address of a student's parent(s) or legal guardian.

- Contact a student's parent(s) or guardian during the school day for an emergency.

COLLABORATION

1. Work with two classmates to plan the fields that will be needed in a database table to store this information. Read steps 2 through 5 to see how the data will be used.

2. Working alone, create a new database file. Name the file *c12 school records*. Create a table for the database using the fields you planned with your classmates. Remember to use an appropriate data type and enter a description for each field. Set a field for the primary key. Save the table using an appropriate name.

3. Enter data in the table for five students. Make up names, addresses, and other data so you do not share real personal information.

4. Create a query that is based on your database table. Include fields that result in a table showing the student's first name, the student's last name, and the number where a student's parent(s) or guardian may be contacted during the day. Save the query using an appropriate name.

5. Create a report based on your query. Include all of the fields in the report. Sort the data in the report by the student's last name. Save the report using an appropriate name. Print the report.

6. Close the *c12 school records* database. Close *Access*.

7. Review the other options in the list.

8. Look at the picture of your document to the right. If you catch a last-minute mistake, click another tab on the ribbon and make changes to the document. Save the changes and then go back to step 4.

9. Click the **Print** button near the upper-left corner of the screen.

10. Close the document and exit *Word*.

4F

Numbered Lists and Acceptable Use Policies

When you are using a computer, you need to follow certain rules as well. Chances are your school has rules you should follow. These rules are called acceptable-use policies, or AUPs. In the next exercise, you will key an AUP using a numbered list.

Numbered lists can be used to track steps of instruction, lists of items, and more. When you key a list where each item is preceded by 1, 2, 3, 4, and so on, you are creating a numbered list. When creating a numbered list:

- Key the number 1.
- Key a period.
- Tap the Space Bar once.
- Key text for the line and then tap ENTER.

If *Word*'s automatic numbering feature has been turned on, the remaining numbers in your list should be automatically added each time you tap ENTER. If automatic numbering has been turned off, just type the numbers.

1. Start *Word* if it is not already open. In a new, blank document, key the following AUP:

Acceptable-Use Policy [Enter]

<your Name> [Enter]

Seven Rules [Enter]

1. Never share your password. [Enter]
2. Never use your computer to lie or offend others. [Enter]
3. Do not forward suspicious email or other messages. [Enter]
4. Do not steal digital data from others. [Enter]
5. Do not download graphics, music, videos, or other data from the Internet without permission. [Enter]
6. Do not bring food or drink into the lab. [Enter]
7. Organize and clean your workstation area every day. [Enter]

2. When you tap ENTER after the last line, a number 8 will appear if automatic numbering is on. Simply tap BACKSPACE to delete it.

Instant Message

Compare the rules in this activity to the ones you must follow at your school.

TIP Save your document often to avoid losing your work. Once you have saved a file with a name, you can use the Save button on the Quick Access Toolbar or the File tab.

Before You Move On

Answer these questions to review what you have learned in Chapter 12.

1. A database is a collection of information that is stored in database objects. Name four database objects that you used in this chapter. LO 78A

2. A database _____ contains all of the information about one person or item. LO 78B

3. A database _____ holds one piece of information from a database record. LO 78B

4. The _____ determines the kind of data a field can hold. LO 78B

5. Data can be entered into a database table in Datasheet view or using a database _____. LO 79B

6. The data type used for letters or numbers that do not require calculations is _____. LO 78B

7. You create a form automatically based on a table that has 12 fields in each record. Which of those fields will be included in the form? LO 79B

8. When you create a form using the Form Wizard, which fields can you include in the form? LO 79C

9. Explain the difference between Landscape and Portrait orientation. LO 79C

10. To add a field to an existing table, open the table in _____ view. LO 80A

11. What is the purpose of a query? LO 81A

12. What is the purpose of a filter? LO 81B

13. What software feature can be used to arrange the data in a column in a database table in ascending order? LO 81C

14. What is a database report? How does it differ from a database table? LO 82A

15. A field chosen to identify each record in an *Access* database table is called the _____. *Access* will not allow duplicate data to be entered in this field. LO 78A

Applying What You Have Learned

Edit Records in a Database

1. Start *Access*. Open *df c12 composers* and use Save As to rename the database *c12 composers*.

2. Open the *Composers (1600–1799)* table. Make the following changes.

    a. Enter **Joseph** for Franz Haydn's middle name.

    b. Enter **Amadeus** for Wolfgang Mozart's middle name.

Data File:

df c12 composers

3. Save the file as *4f acceptable use policy*.

4. Change the color of the first rule to blue.

   a. First, highlight the line with your pointer. (If automatic numbering is turned on, the number and the period following it will not be highlighted.)

   b. Next, click the **Home** tab and, in the Font group, click the **Font Color** button's down arrow. See Figure 1.28.

   c. In the palette that displays, choose any blue color, such as Blue in the Standard Colors.

5. Change the color of the other rules in your document using colors from the Font Color palette. Make each rule a different color.

6. Select the title *Acceptable-Use Policy* and click the **Bold** button in the Font group on the Home tab.

7. Select your name and click the **Italic** button in the Font group on the Home tab.

8. Select the heading *Seven Rules* and click the **Underline** button's down arrow to display the palette of underline styles. Click the **Double underline** style.

9. Click the **Save** button on the Quick Access Toolbar (shown in Figure 1.28) to quickly save the file.

10. Print and close the file. Exit *Word* and shut down the computer unless your instructor tells you otherwise.

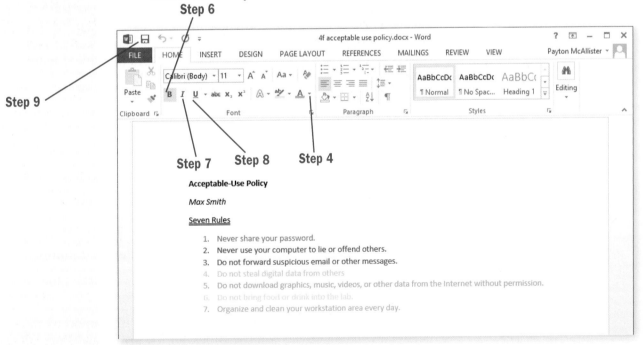

Figure 1.28 *Apply colors and Font group formats.*

9. The report will be saved and will open in Print Preview. Compare your report with the top portion of the report shown in Figure 12.30.

Figure 12.30 *Lincoln Junior High Students report*

10. Print the report and then close it.

82B

Create a Query and a Report

For this activity, you will create a report showing the first name, last name, class, and instructor for all students taking a class from Mr. Johnson during first period. Before creating the report, you will need to create a query to get the data for the report.

1. In the *82 lincoln* database, create a query in Design view. Base the query on the *Student Schedules* table. Include these fields in the query: First Name, Last Name, Class Period 1, Instructor 1. In the Instructor 1 column on the Criteria row, key **Johnson**. The query design grid should look like Figure 12.31.

Field:	First Name	Last Name	Class Period 1	Instructor 1
Table:	Student Schedules	Student Schedules	Student Schedules	Student Schedules
Sort:				
Show:	✔	✔	✔	✔
Criteria:				"Johnson"
or:				

Figure 12.31 *Query design grid*

2. Run the query. Look over the query results. You should see six records. Save and close the query results table using the name **Period 1 Johnson**.

✔ **checkpoint**

Compare your printed report with the one shown in Figure 12.27 on page 411.

3. Create a report using the Report Wizard. Base the report on the *Period 1 Johnson* query. Include all of the fields in the report.

4. Group the report by the Class Period 1 field. Sort the report by the Last Name field in ascending order. Choose **Block** for the layout and **Portrait** for the orientation.

5. Key **Johnson's Period 1 Class** as the report title.

6. Print the report. Then close the database and exit *Access*.

Exploring and Organizing Your Digital Space

Data File:

df 5a saving
    spaces

Learning Outcomes

In Lesson 5, you will:

5A Learn about storage spaces.

5B Navigate files and folders in **Windows**.

5C Create folders.

5D Rename and delete folders.

5E Copy and move folders.

5F Follow a path to a folder or file.

5A

Storage Spaces

You will want to save your important information, called *data*. Digital data is stored in files. You can create and save text, pictures, video, and sound files. You can store (or save) your files in a variety of storage places:

- On your PC
- On peripherals connected to your PC
- On local networks
- On the Internet

<u>On your PC</u>: A hard drive is the most common storage device inside a computer. **Compact disc (CD)** drives also are built into most PCs. There are several types of CD drives. CD-RW (ReWritable) drives let you save your data only one time.

<u>On peripherals connected to your PC</u>: **USB flash drives** and memory cards are common storage devices (see Figure 1.29). They can be used with many DigiTools: PCs, handheld computers, cameras, and cell phones. They are small enough that you can take them with you wherever you go.

Instant Message

Portable storage tools go by many names: USB flash drives, pen drives, jump drives, thumb drives, key drives, and memory sticks.

© Bomshtein/Shutterstock.com

© ExaMedia Photography/Shutterstock.com

© Galushko Sergey/Shutter stock.com

Figure 1.29 *USB flash drives, memory cards, and CDs are common storage devices.*

<u>On local networks</u>: You may be asked to save on your school's local network. This is often called a **LAN**, or **local area network**. To use a LAN, you need an account. Since many people can save to the same network, security is an issue. To keep networks safe, LAN accounts require login names and passwords. After you connect to your network, you can save your files in your own assigned folders. Local networks are managed by experts called **system administrators**.

TIP If you move the wrong field to the Selected Fields column, highlight the field name and click the left arrow to move the field back to the Available Fields column.

4. Click the **First Name** field in the list under Available Fields. Click the right arrow (>) button to move the field to the Selected Fields box. Do the same for the other fields to be included in the report: Last Name and Grade. Your screen should look like Figure 12.28. Click **Next**.

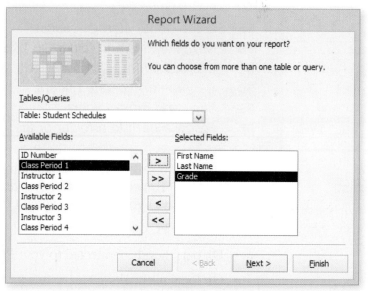

Figure 12.28 *Report Wizard opening screen*

5. The next prompt asks if you want to add any grouping levels. Select **Grade** and click the right arrow button to move the field name to the next column. Click **Next** to continue.

6. The next prompt asks for the sort order you want for detail records. Click the down arrow in the first box and select **Last Name** (Figure 12.29). You would like the report in **Ascending** order. Click **Next** to continue.

Figure 12.29 *Report Wizard sort order screen*

7. The next screen allows you to select a report layout. Select **Stepped** for the layout and **Portrait** for the orientation. Click **Next** to continue.

8. On the last screen, key **Lincoln Junior High Students** for the report title. Select **Preview the report**. Click **Finish**.

<u>On the Internet</u>: The Internet is the biggest network of all. You can save your information on the Internet instead of on your personal computer or on your school's LAN. This is called "saving to the **cloud**."

There are several advantages to saving files online. When you save on the Internet, you do not need to carry around a laptop, USB flash drive, CD, or memory card. You can access your files from any computer connected to the Web. Also, if your hard drive crashes, you do not need to worry. Your files will still be safe online. Many Internet-based companies let you save online for free or for a small fee. Google, Yahoo!, and Apple will let you save to their cloud storage. *Microsoft Office 2013* allows you to save to the **OneDrive** using the Save As command on the File tab, as shown in Figure 1.30. Using a login name and a password, you can open an account for these services. You can store word processing, spreadsheet, presentation, picture, video, email, and many other types of files.

Instant Message

Use your web browser to learn about saving files online. For Google's Docs & Spreadsheets service, key docs.google.com in your web browser. For Microsoft's OneDrive, key onedrive.live.com.

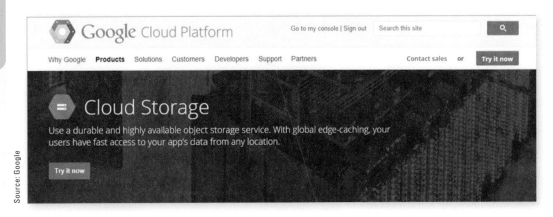

Source: Google

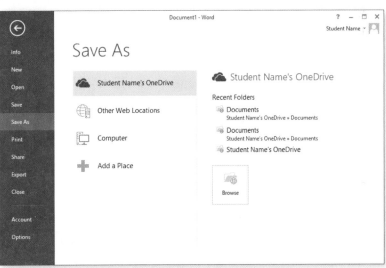

Figure 1.30 *Google and Microsoft let you save files on the Internet.*

Working with Database Reports

Data File:

df 82 lincoln

Learning Outcomes

In Lesson 82, you will:

82A Create a report.

82B Create a query and report.

82A

Create a Report

A **report** is a database object used to display data. Reports can be formatted to show data in a format that is easy to read. The top part of a report is shown in Figure 12.27. Reports can contain data from tables or queries. You can create an AutoReport from an open table or query. You can use the Report Wizard to create a report or mailing labels. In this lesson, you will create a report using the Report Wizard.

Johnson's Period 1 Class

Class Period 1	Last Name	First Name	Instructor 1
U.S. History	Chu	Chou	Johnson
	Foster	Erika	Johnson
	Garner	Shelby	Johnson
	Hansen	Brittany	Johnson
	Hennessy	Mathew	Johnson
	Martinez	Ricardo	Johnson

Figure 12.27 *Database report*

The Report Wizard

The Report Wizard allows you to create a report by making a series of choices. You can choose the:

- Table or query on which the report is based.

- Fields to include in the report.

- Way fields will be grouped in the report.

- Way records will be sorted in the report.

- Layout of the report.

If you do not like the results of your choices, you can delete the report and create a new one using different choices. You also can make changes to a report in Layout or Design view.

1. Open *df 82 lincoln*. Save the database as *82 lincoln*.

2. You will create a report to show data from the *Student Schedules* table. On the Create tab in the Reports group, click **Report Wizard**.

3. Select the *Student Schedules* table under Tables/Queries.

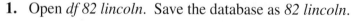

1. Start *Word* and open the document *df 5a saving spaces*.

2. Print the document and then close it.

3. Using information supplied by your instructor, complete the table. Keep this document as a reference guide to places you can store your files.

5B

Navigate Files and Folders in Windows

Files are used to store digital information. Files can be stored inside **folders**. Think of a folder as a box in which you can put all of your files. Inside the box, you can put smaller boxes. System administrators often call these **subfolders**.

Good file organization begins with giving your files and folders names that are logical, relevant, and easy to understand. You can use *File Explorer* (formerly *Windows Explorer*) to see how files and folders are organized on your computer. See Figure 1.31. This feature may be somewhat different on your computer, depending on your *Windows* version and setup.

Ribbon tabs

File Explorer ribbon

Navigation Pane

Document window

Preview pane

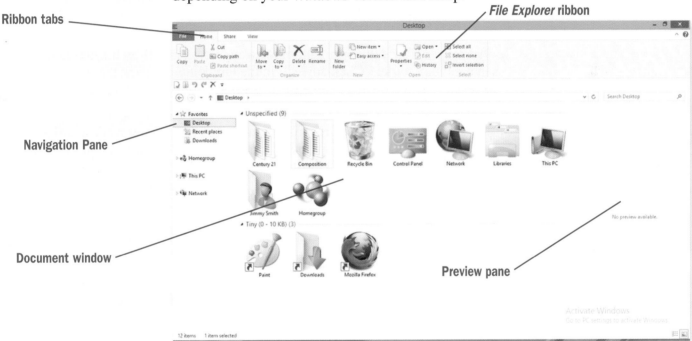

Figure 1.31 *File Explorer* window

As in *Word*, *File Explorer* uses a ribbon to organize common tasks, such as copying and moving, creating new folders, and changing the view. *File Explorer* has three tabs—Home, Share, and View. The Home tab contains commands such as Copy, Paste, Move to, Delete, and Rename. The Share tab lets you email files or folders and even burn them to a disc. The View tab lets you preview a file and set how *Windows* sorts your icons.

1. Start *Windows* if necessary and display the Charm bar. Tap or click the **Search** charm.

2. Key **File Explorer** in the search box and tap ENTER. *File Explorer* opens and displays the resources on your PC.

Sort Records

The Sort feature allows you to arrange the information in a table or query in a certain order. The information can be sorted in ascending order (0 to 100 or A to Z) or descending order (100 to 0 or Z to A).

In this activity, you will use the Sort feature to arrange records in the *Student Schedules* table in various ways.

1. Click any cell in the Last Name field. Click the **Ascending** button in the Sort & Filter group on the Home tab. The buttons used to sort data are shown in Figure 12.26. The Last Name field should be alphabetized starting with *Barneson*.

Figure 12.26 *Sort buttons*

2. Now you will use the Sort feature to arrange the records by the Grade field in ascending order. Click any cell in the Grade field. Click the **Ascending** button. The data will be shown with all seventh-graders first and then all eighth-graders.

3. Now you will arrange the records by the Grade field in descending order. Click any cell in the Grade field if necessary. Click the **Descending** button. The data will be shown with all eighth-graders first.

4. Close the *Student Schedules* table. Choose **No** if asked if you want to save design changes to the table. Close the database.

Query, Filter, and Sort Records

In this activity, you will create a query in a database that contains information for a newspaper delivery route.

1. Open *df 81 newspaper* and use Save As to rename the database as *81 newspaper* in the folder where you save your work for this class.

2. Create a query in Query Design view. Base the query on the *Customer Information* table. Include the First Name, Last Name, and Address fields in the query.

3. Run the query. Select (highlight) *only* the word **Hyacinth** in the Address field in the first record in the results table. Click the **Selection** button on the Home tab. Click **Contains "Hyacinth"**. Only records that have the word *Hyacinth* in the street address should be displayed.

checkpoint

Does your query results table have 11 records? The address of the first record should be 13400 Hyacinth Court, and the address of the last record should be 13452 Hyacinth Court.

4. Click a cell in the Address field. Click the **Ascending** sort button to arrange the customers by their street address in ascending order.

5. Print the query results table that has been filtered and sorted. Use Portrait orientation.

6. Close the query results table without saving changes. Close *Access*.

3. Click a folder in the Navigation Pane such as the Documents folder. The Home tab displays. Notice the various functions you can perform in the Home tab.

4. Tap or click the **Share** and **View** tabs to see the functions you can perform in each.

5. In the Navigation Pane, click **Desktop**. Notice the contents of the desktop are now displayed. Click other places in the Navigation Pane to see what changes.

6. Tap or click **This PC** in the Navigation Pane. Tap or click the triangle to the left of *This PC*. Notice the folders that appear.

7. Click one of the folders. The contents of the folder are displayed.

8. Some of the folders displayed may have triangles beside them. Tap or click one of the triangles to display subfolders.

9. Within a subfolder, click one of the files inside. Click the **View** tab and then click **Preview pane** to see a preview of the contents of the file.

10. Close *File Explorer* by clicking the **File** tab and clicking **Close**.

5C

Create Folders

You need to give each new folder a name. The name should tell you the type of information in the folder. This way you can find files more easily. For example, you can place a file called *All about Moon Rocks* in the Moon Rocks folder. (You would not place it in a folder called Maps to Mars.)

Let's take a closer look at the Home tab of *File Explorer* in Figure 1.32. From the Home tab, you can create, rename, delete, and move folders.

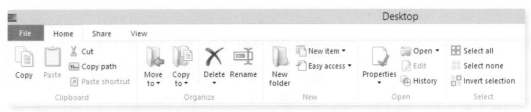

Figure 1.32 *File Explorer* Home tab

 Instant Message For the following activities, your instructor may direct you to create your folders in a different place. Substitute with the directions that your instructor gives you.

TIP You also may right-click the middle of the Documents window, click **New**, and then click **Folder** from the pop-up menu.

1. Open *File Explorer*. Tap or click **This PC**.

2. Select the Documents folder.

3. Click **New folder** on the Home tab.

4. Where you see New folder, key **Computers**. (See Figure 1.33.)

Figure 1.33 *Name a folder.*

1. Open the *Student Schedules* table.

2. Click in a cell in the Class Period 1 column that contains the entry *U.S. History*. On the Home tab in the Sort & Filter group, click the **Selection** button. Select **Equals "U.S. History"**. (See Figure 12.24.) Only records with *U.S. History* in the Class Period 1 field will display.

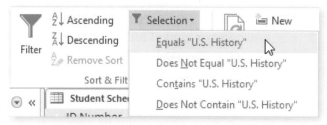

Figure 12.24 *Selection button*

3. Click a cell in the Instructor 1 column that contains *Johnson*. Click the **Selection** button again. Select **Equals "Johnson"**. Only records for seventh-graders with *U.S. History* in the first class period who have *Johnson* for an instructor will display.

4. Leave *Access* open. Start *Word*. Open *df 81 memo* from your data files. Save the file as *81 memo* in the location where you store files for this class.

5. Make *Access* the active window. In the *Student Schedules* filtered table, select the following columns: ID Number, Last Name, First Name, Grade, Class Period 1, and Instructor 1. (Point to the first column head and drag across to select the columns.) Click the **Copy** button in the Clipboard group on the Home tab.

6. Make *Word* the active window. Click the blank line below the paragraph of the memo. Click the **Paste** button in the Clipboard group on the Home tab. The table will appear in your memo. Center the table horizontally.

7. Change **Student Name** to your name in the memo heading. Add the current date in the heading. Save the memo again, using the same name. Print and close the memo. Close *Word*.

8. Make *Access* the active window if necessary. The Toggle Filter button can be used to remove the filter or to apply the filter. Click the **Toggle Filter** button in the Sort & Filter group to remove the filter. (See Figure 12.25.)

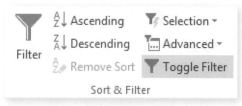

Figure 12.25 *Toggle Filter button*

9. All records should now be displayed in the table. Click **Toggle Filter** again to apply the filter. The six records for the seventh-graders with *U.S. History* in the first class period taught by *Johnson* will again be displayed. Click **Toggle Filter** to remove the filter. Leave the *Student Schedules* table open.

 **checkpoint**

Do you have nine new folders? One folder should be named Computers. The others should have the names shown in step 6.

5. Tap ENTER or click outside the folder to have the computer accept the folder name you keyed in step 4.

6. Create eight new folders in your Documents folder. Use the following names for the folders:

Space	*Stars*
Moon Rocks	*Perfect Planets*
Maps to Mars	*Comets*
Saturn	*Asteroids*

5D

Rename and Delete Folders

Sometimes you decide a different name would be better for a folder. Some folders are no longer needed and should be deleted. You can use the Rename and Delete commands on the *File Explorer* Home tab to accomplish these tasks.

1. Reopen *File Explorer* if necessary and select the **Documents** folder.

2. Click the **Perfect Planets** folder to select it.

3. Click **Rename** on the Home tab.

4. Key the new name **Planets** and tap ENTER to confirm the new name.

5. Rename the *Moon Rocks* folder to the new name **Moon**.

6. Click the **Comets** folder to select it.

7. Click **Delete** on the Home tab.

8. Choose **Yes** to confirm that you want to send the folder to the Recycle Bin. (See Figure 1.34.)

TIP You can also rename a folder by right-clicking the folder and choosing **Rename** from the pop-up menu. Key the new name. You can also delete folders using the right-click method.

Figure 1.34 *Confirm delete.*

9. Delete the folders Maps to Mars and Asteroids. Click **Yes** to confirm that you want to send each folder to the Recycle Bin.

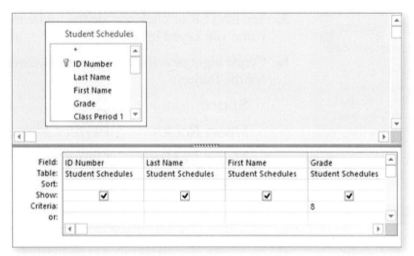

Figure 12.22 *Query design grid*

8. On the Query Tools Design tab in the Results group, click the **Run** button (Figure 12.23). The query results will display in a table.

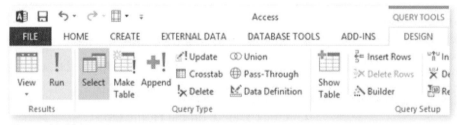

Figure 12.23 *Run button*

9. Click the **Close** button on the query results tab and click **Yes** to save the query. For the query name, key **Grade 8 Students**. Click **OK**.

10. Read the following CheckPoint. Close the query window. Continue with the next activity.

 **checkpoint** Did the query results table show 13 records? All records should be for students in grade 8.

81B

Filter by Selection

Another way to find information is by using a filter. A **filter** hides records in a table that do not match your criteria. For example, suppose you want to find all of the records for students who are taking English in second period. You can apply a filter that will hide all other records. Filtered records are not deleted, just hidden. They will be displayed again when the filter is removed.

Ms. Tonia Cross, the principal at Lincoln Junior High, has requested some information that you can obtain from the database. She wants to know which seventh-grade students have U.S. History during first period with Mr. Johnson. In this activity, you will use the Filter by Selection feature to provide the information the principal wants.

Copy and Move Folders

A folder that is inside another folder is called a *subfolder*. Subfolders hold information related to the topic of a main folder. In Figure 1.35, the Space folder shows four subfolders: Moon, Planets, Saturn, and Stars. To create a subfolder, copy or move a folder into another folder.

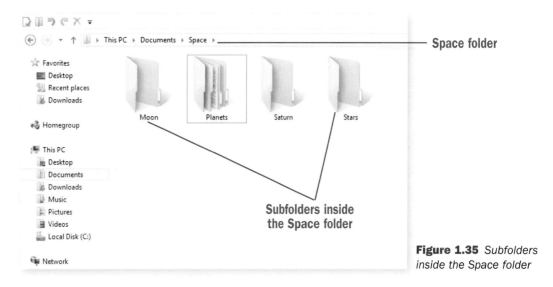

Figure 1.35 *Subfolders inside the Space folder*

TIP Another way to move a folder is to use the Move to command on the Home tab.

1. Select the folder to move.
2. Click the **Move to** button.
3. Click **Choose location** at the bottom of the drop-down menu.
4. In the Move Items dialog box, navigate to the folder you want to move into.
5. Click **Move** to complete the move.

Move a Folder by Dragging

You can move folders into other folders by selecting and dragging them.

1. Reopen your Documents folder using *File Explorer* if necessary.

2. Click the **Moon** folder and drag it on top of the Space folder as shown in Figure 1.36.

3. Practice by dragging the **Stars** folder into the *Space* folder in the same way.

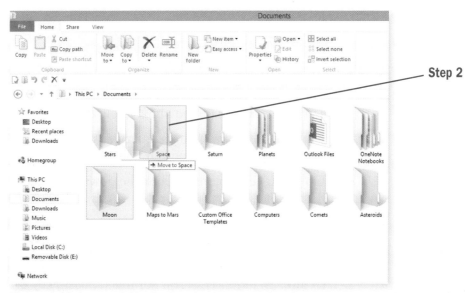

Figure 1.36 *Move a folder by dragging it to a new location.*

a certain field, or data that is not in a field. For example, the database for Lincoln Junior High has records for students in grades 7 and 8. You can create a query that will display only records for students in grade 8. A query allows you to include all of the fields included in a table or only selected ones. When you create the query to show only records for eighth-grade students, for example, you may want only their first name, last name, and grade included.

In this activity, you will create a query to show the Last Name, First Name, and Grade fields for records for eighth-grade students.

1. Open *df 81 lincoln*. Save the database as *81 lincoln* in the folder where you are storing files for this lesson.

DB Create/Queries/
Query Design

2. In the *81 lincoln* database file, follow the path at the left and click **Query Design**. The query design grid will open as shown in Figure 12.21. The Show Table dialog box will be open.

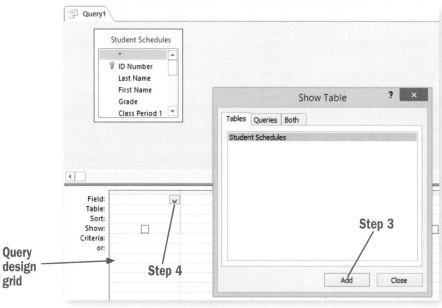

Figure 12.21 *Show Table dialog box and query design grid*

3. The table *Student Schedules* will be selected in the Show Table dialog box. Click **Add**. The *Student Schedules* fields list box will appear in the query window. Click **Close** on the Show Table dialog box.

4. Click the down arrow in the query design grid in the first column by *Field*. The list of field names will appear. Select **ID Number**.

5. Tab to the next column. Click the down arrow in the second column and select **Last Name**.

6. Tab to the next column. Click the down arrow in the third column and select **First Name**.

7. Tab to the next column. Click the down arrow in the fourth column and select **Grade**. In the Criteria row for this column, key **8**. Your design grid should look like the one in Figure 12.22.

Copy or Move a Folder Using Ribbon Commands

You can use the Copy or Cut and Paste commands to copy or move a folder.

1. Click the **Planets** folder.

2. Click the **Copy** button on the Home tab. (See Figure 1.37.)

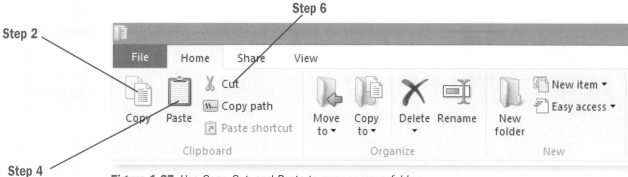

Step 6

Step 2

Step 4

Figure 1.37 *Use Copy, Cut, and Paste to copy or move folders.*

3. Double-click the **Space** folder to open it.

4. Finally, click **Paste** on the Home tab and the folder is pasted into the Space folder.

5. Click the **Saturn** folder.

6. Click the **Cut** button on the Home tab.

7. Open the Space folder and then click **Paste** to move the Saturn folder into the Space folder.

8. Double-click the **Computers** folder to open it.

9. Create 12 new subfolders inside the Computers folder. Create folders for Chapter 1, Chapter 2, Chapter 3, and so on, to Chapter 12. Your teacher may instruct you to use these folders to store files you work with in this course.

10. Close *File Explorer.*

checkpoint

Do you have four subfolders (Moon, Planets, Saturn, and Stars) in your Space folder?

5F

Follow a Path to a Folder or File

As you work with applications, you will find that you sometimes must follow a precise path through your folders to the files you need. The **path** for a file is shown in the address box at the top of the document window in *File Explorer.* You can also see the path at the top of dialog boxes such as Save As or Open.

A path statement can be written in a type of shorthand from folder to folder until you get to your file. For example:

Documents\Space\Planets\Saturn*5f all about saturn*

Instant Message The marks (\ ) between folder names are called *backslashes.*

Digital Citizenship and Ethics

Corbis RF/Glow Images

File-sharing technology lets you search for and copy files from someone else's computer. (This is called "peer-to-peer" or P2P technology.) File sharing is most often used to trade MP3s, but movies, games, and software programs can also be shared. BitTorrent, uTorrent, Kazaa, FrostWire, and Shareaza are popular file-sharing programs. They give you direct access to other computers without having to go through a central server.

File-sharing programs are a convenient way to share public domain files (material that isn't owned by anybody). But file sharing can quickly turn into

piracy. **Piracy** is sharing or downloading copyrighted material without paying for it. It is another form of stealing, and it is illegal. Burning copies of CDs or DVDs and even swapping MP3 files with your friends are forms of piracy.

As a class, discuss the following.

1. "Borrowing" someone's copy of the latest computer game and installing it on your own PC is piracy. Why do you think this is considered stealing?

2. How could illegal file sharing cause harm or damage to the holders of copyrighted materials?

Lesson 81

Working with Database Queries, Filters, and Sorts

Learning Outcomes

Data Files:

df 81 lincoln
df 81 memo
df 81 newspaper

In Lesson 81, you will:

81A *Create a query in Design view.*
81B *Filter data by selection.*
81C *Sort records.*
81D *Query, filter, and sort records.*

81A

Create a Query in Design View

Data is stored in a database so that it can be used later. The data can be used to answer questions. The question may be as simple as "What is John Smith's telephone number?" or as complex as "What is the net operating profit for our company for the fourth quarter?"

Generally, databases contain large amounts of data. Queries and filters are used to display only certain records from the database. For example, you may want to know how many seventh-grade students are enrolled in Algebra I this semester. A query would allow you to extract from the database all the students who are enrolled in Algebra I this semester who are seventh graders. In this lesson, you will learn to use queries and filters to find (mine) data to answer questions.

Database Queries

A **query** is a database object that displays certain data that you describe. You describe the data by entering criteria. The criteria might be the field name, data in

1. Open *File Explorer*.

2. Follow this path to locate the Planets folder that you copied earlier to the Space folder: **Documents\Planets**.

3. Right-click on the **Planets** folder in the Navigation Pane and then click **Delete** on the shortcut menu.

4. Click **Yes** to confirm the deletion.

5. Close *File Explorer*.

Lesson 6

Working with Application Files

Learning Outcomes

Data Files:

df 6a distances
df 6b moon
df 6b orbit

In Lesson 6, you will:

6A Learn about the **Excel** application window.
6B Work in multiple applications and files.
6C Manage files.

6A

Excel Application Window

As you have learned, *Microsoft Office* applications have many features in common. All of them have a ribbon with tabs containing commands for working with the application. All of them have the same resizing and closing commands, as well as a Quick Access Toolbar, a status bar, and zoom controls.

Excel's application window has tools and features that let you work with numbers and formulas. The main portion of the *Excel* window is organized into columns, rows, and cells. These parts are marked in Figure 1.38. In the cells, you can key words or numbers. You also can key formulas to do math calculations.

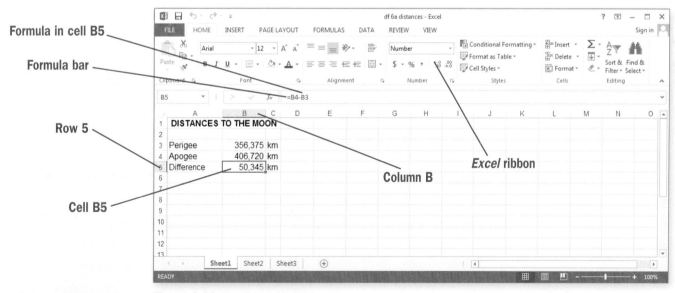

Figure 1.38 *The Excel window*

8. Miss Hintze, who teaches math, was recently married. Her new last name is Hintze-Braun. You will use the Replace feature to update the table with her new name. Click **Replace** from the Find group of the Home tab. The Find and Replace dialog box will appear as shown in Figure 12.20.

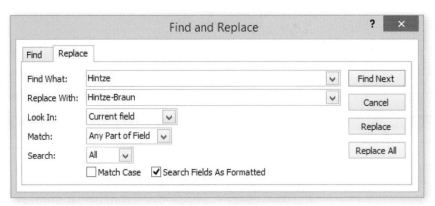

Figure 12.20 *Replace tab in the Find and Replace dialog box*

9. In the Find What box, key **Hintze**. In the Replace With box, key **Hintze-Braun**. In the Look In box, select **Current document**. The computer will search the entire table rather than just the field that is currently selected.

10. Click **Replace All**. A dialog box will appear telling you that you will not be able to undo this operation. Click **Yes** to continue. Click **Cancel** to close the Find and Replace box.

11. Using the Replace feature, edit all records in the table to change **Education** to **Ed** (no period in the abbreviations). Click the **Match** down arrow and select **Any Part of Field**.

12. Widen or shorten the columns in the table as needed to display the complete field title and the complete information in the field. Close the table. Save layout changes.

80C

Modify a Database Table

The principal of Lincoln Junior High would like the *Student Schedules* table in the *80 lincoln* database modified to include a field for the grade level of the students. The field should be placed after the First Name field. Use **Grade** for the field name. Use **Number** as the data type and **Grade Level of Student** for the description.

After you add the field to the table, enter the grade level for all students. Ferrero, Chang, Bjorkman, Guillermo, Thomson, J. Hefner, LaRoche, Hansen, Sisson, Castillo, Crandall, McMillian, and Painter are all in grade 8; the rest of the students are in grade 7. Close the table and exit *Access*.

1. Start *Windows*, if necessary, and display the Charm bar. Key **Excel** in the search box and tap ENTER.

2. In the *Excel* start screen, click **Open Other Workbooks**.

3. Follow the path to the folder that contains the data files for this class as directed by your instructor. Select the *df 6a distances* file. Click **Open**.

4. Navigate to the Moon folder you created in the last lesson by following this path: **Documents\Space\Moon**.

5. Key **6a distances** for the filename and click **Save**.

6. Close the document and exit *Excel*.

6B

Work in Multiple Applications and Files

The *Windows* OS allows you to have several documents open at the same time. This can help you find information in one file while reading questions in another file. You can display both files on the screen at the same time.

Remember that you can work only in the active program. Tap or click inside an application window to make it active. You also can click the program name on the taskbar to make it active. A program is active when the text in the title bar is black rather than gray.

Use a *Word* Document to Find Information

Switch between active and inactive documents to find information and to answer questions.

TIP If necessary, zoom to about 80% so that you can see all of the data on the page.

1. Start *Word*. Open the document *df 6b moon* and save it as *6b moon project* in the Chapter 1 folder you created in the last lesson (Documents\Computers\Chapter 1). Key your name, class name, and instructor name beneath the title.

2. Open *df 6b orbit* and save it as *6b orbit* in the Moon folder (Documents\Space\Moon).

3. Click **View** and then click **View Side by Side** in the Window group. You can now see both documents on the screen at the same time.

4. Click back and forth several times between the two documents. Watch how the color of the text in the title bar changes to show the active window.

5. Read the *6b orbit* file and find the answers to the first five questions in the *6b moon project* file.

6. In the *6b orbit* file, select the text that answers the first question. Click **Copy** in the Home tab's Clipboard group. (See Figure 1.39.)

Step 7

Step 6

Figure 1.39 *The Home tab's Clipboard group*

In a small table, you can locate records easily by scrolling through the rows. However, many databases are large, and scrolling to find a certain record to edit is not so easy. You can use the Find feature to locate a record quickly. You can use the Replace feature to change several occurrences of data in a table. You can make edits to records in Datasheet view or using a form.

In this activity, you will edit records in the database you used earlier in this lesson.

1. Open the *80 lincoln* database you worked with in 80A Activity 1.

2. Open the *Student Schedules* table. You need to edit the record for the student with ID 48263. Click the first record that appears in the ID Number field.

3. On the Home tab, click **Find** in the Find group. In the Find What box, key **48263**. (See Figure 12.19.) Click **Find Next**. The record for the student with this ID, Rico Martinez, will be displayed in *Student Schedules*.

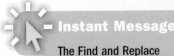

Instant Message

The Find and Replace features can be used in either the Datasheet or Form view.

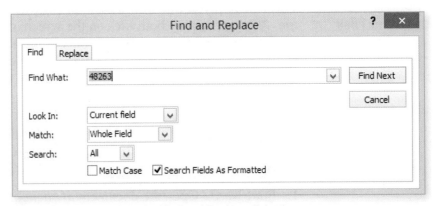

Figure 12.19 *Find tab in the Find and Replace dialog box*

4. Click **Cancel** to close the Find box. Use the mouse or the TAB key to move to the First Name field. Change the name from Rico to **Ricardo**.

5. Use Find to move to the record for Felipe Santos, ID Number 25781. Felipe has changed Biology instructors. He has switched from Baker to **Boyer**. The class still meets during the fourth class period. Update his record.

6. Brittany Hansen, ID Number 35981, has **U.S. History** during the first class period and **English** during the second class period. Her English teacher is **Fenn**. Her history teacher is **Johnson**. Update her record.

7. Mary Castello moved last week. You need to delete her record from the table. Since you do not know Mary's ID Number, use the Find feature to locate her last name. Once you find Mary's record, click any field of the record. From the Records group of the Home tab, click the down arrow on the Delete button. Click **Delete Record**. Note that the next record is now displayed. Choose **Yes** when asked if you are sure you want to delete the record.

7. Click in the *6b moon project* file to make it the active window. Click the blank line under the first question where you want the answer to appear. Click the **Home** tab and click **Paste** to paste your answer into the file.

8. Repeat the copy-and-paste process to paste answers to the second, third, fourth, and fifth questions in the *6b moon project* file.

9. Close the *6b orbit* file. Save the *6b moon project* file and leave it open for the next activity if you have time to continue working. If not, close the file.

COLLABORATION

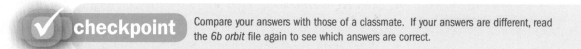

✓ **checkpoint**   Compare your answers with those of a classmate. If your answers are different, read the *6b orbit* file again to see which answers are correct.

Use an *Excel* Spreadsheet to Find Information

1. Start *Word* if it is not already open. Open the *6b moon project* file. Resize the window so that it occupies half the screen.

2. Start *Excel*. Open the *6a distances* file that you saved earlier (path: Documents\Space\Moon). The *6a distances* file shows the answer to the final question in the *6b moon project* file.

3. Resize the *Excel* window so that it occupies the other half of the screen.

4. Select cell **B5** containing the answer (50,345 km) in the *Excel* file. Click the **Home** tab and click **Copy** in the Clipboard group.

5. Make the *6b moon project* file the active window. Click the blank line under the question where you want the answer to appear. Click the **Home** tab and choose **Paste**. This will paste your answer into the file.

6. Make the *Excel* file the active window. Close the *6a distances* file and exit *Excel*.

7. Maximize the *6b moon project* window. Save your changes, close the file, and exit *Word*.

6C

Manage Files

Sometimes keeping your files organized will require you to rename, move, or copy files. As you learned in Lesson 5, *File Explorer* lets you delete, rename, move, and copy folders. You can use the same buttons on the Home tab of *File Explorer* to manage files. (See Figure 1.40.)

Figure 1.40 *File Explorer* Home tab

Activity 2

In this activity, you will add and delete fields in an existing database.

Instant Message

Enter the composer's name in a search engine or an online encyclopedia to find data about him.

COLLABORATION

checkpoint

Exchange tables with a classmate and check each other's work. Make corrections to your table if necessary.

1. Open *df 80 composers* and use Save As to create *80 composers* in the folder in which you save your work for this class.

2. Open the *Composers (1600–1799)* table in Design view.

3. Insert a new field after the Life field. Key **Birthplace** for the field name. Select **Short Text** for the data type. For the description, key **Composer's Birthplace**.

4. Switch to Datasheet view and save the changes to the table. Print the table in Landscape orientation. Close the database.

5. Work with another student to find the country where each composer was born. For example, Bach was born in Germany. Access the Internet and find the birth country for three of the remaining composers. Your classmate should find data for the other three composers. Share your data with each other.

6. Open *80 composers*. Open the *Composers (1600–1799)* table. Update the table with the birthplaces you found in your research.

The table has data in the Teachers field for only one record. You have decided that this data is not needed.

7. Switch to Design view. Right-click the row that has Teachers for the field name. Choose **Delete Rows** from the pop-up menu.

8. You will be asked whether you want to permanently delete the selected field(s) and all of the data in the field(s). Click **Yes**. The field will be deleted.

9. Switch to Datasheet view and click **Yes** to save the table. Print the table in Landscape orientation. Close the database.

Congratulations! You now know how to update records as well as add and delete fields in an existing database table.

80B

Edit Records

Reasons for Editing Records

Information changes over time. Errors are sometimes made in entering data. As a result of these errors and changes, the data in a database may need to be corrected or updated. Edits (changes and corrections) may be needed for a variety of reasons. For example, if a person moves to a new house, his or her address data would need to be updated. A student may change classes. An incorrect address may be entered. All of those situations require that edits be made to the database.

Methods for Editing Records

Editing database records is similar to editing word processing documents. You begin by moving to the location where the change is to be made. You can use the DELETE or BACKSPACE keys to delete data. You also can delete entire records.

Delete Files

1. Start *File Explorer*. Follow the path to find your *Excel* file *6a distances*.
2. Select the **6a distances** file.
3. Click the **Delete** button on the Home tab of *File Explorer*.
4. Click **Yes** when asked whether you want to send the file to the Recycle Bin.

Rename a File

1. Follow the path to find your *Word* file *6b orbit*.
2. Select the **6b orbit** file.
3. Click the **Rename** button on the Home tab of *File Explorer*.
4. Key the new name **6c moon data** and tap ENTER.

Copy a File

1. Follow the path to find your *Word* file *6c moon data*.
2. Select the **6c moon data** file.
3. Click the **Copy** button on the Home tab of *File Explorer*.
4. Then, open the Chapter 1 subfolder (path: **Documents\Computers\Chapter 1**) and click **Paste**.

Move a File

1. Follow the path once again to find the original copy of your *Word* file *6c moon data*.
2. Click **Rename** and key **6c earth to the moon** for the new filename.
3. Click the renamed *6c earth to the moon* file and then click **Cut** on the Home tab of *File Explorer*.
4. Then open the Moon subfolder (path: **Documents\Space\Moon**) and click **Paste**.
5. Close *File Explorer* and turn off your computer.

TIP If you insert the row in the wrong place, click the **Undo** button.

6. Repeat the procedure to insert a row for the name of the instructor for each class period. For the last class (Period 6), enter the data in the blank row under *Class Period 6*. (See Figure 12.18.)

Field Name	Data Type	Description (Optional)
ID Number	Short Text	Student's ID number
Last Name	Short Text	Student's last name
First Name	Short Text	Student's first name
Class Period 1	Short Text	Name of period 1 class
Instructor 1	Short Text	Name of Instructor for Class Period 1
Class Period 2	Short Text	Name of period 2 class
Instructor 2	Short Text	Name of Instructor for Class Period 2
Class Period 3	Short Text	Name of period 3 class
Instructor 3	Short Text	Name of Instructor for Class Period 3
Class Period 4	Short Text	Name of period 4 class
Instructor 4	Short Text	Name of Instructor for Class Period 4
Class Period 5	Short Text	Name of period 5 class
Instructor 5	Short Text	Name of Instructor for Class Period 5
Class Period 6	Short Text	Name of period 6 class
Instructor 6	Short Text	Name of Instructor for Class Period 6

Figure 12.18 *Table with fields added*

7. Switch to Datasheet view. Click **Yes** to the prompt *Do you want to save the table now?* to save the changes to the table design.

8. Create a form automatically (**Create/Forms/Form**). Once the form is created, close it. Click **Yes** to the prompt *Do you want to save the changes to the design of the form?* Key **Student Schedules** (**Form 3**) for the name of the form. Click **OK**.

9. Open *Student Schedules* (*Form 3*) and enter the names of the instructors for each class for the students shown below. Use the TAB or ENTER key to move from field to field.

	Chu	Santos	Hansen	Martinez	Castello
Instructor 1	Johnson	Fenn	Ramos	Johnson	Baker
Instructor 2	Fenn	Hintze	Johnson	Hintze	Strauss
Instructor 3	Hamilton	Hamilton	Hamilton	Vasquez	McDowell
Instructor 4	Boyer	Baker	Wallace	D'Angelo	Vasquez
Instructor 5	Hintze	Burdette	Strauss	Ramos	Fenn
Instructor 6	Burdette	McDowell	Boyer	Baker	Wallace

10. Close the form. Close the *80 lincoln* database.

Digital Citizenship and Ethics

COLLABORATION

According to recent research, 60 percent of students aged 10 to 14 own a cell phone, as do close to 85 percent of teens between the ages of 15 and 18. While cell phones and smartphones provide a convenient and quick way to communicate and can be invaluable in emergency situations, they are also frequently misused or used irresponsibly in social and public situations. For example, have you ever been annoyed by someone talking loudly on a cell phone? Following are some cell phone etiquette tips:

- Turn your phone off in school, theaters, libraries, places of worship, and doctor's offices.

- Do not use your cell phone while you are doing something else, such as driving, riding a bike, or simply having a conversation with others.

- Do not shout or speak loudly to compensate for a bad connection. Call back when you are in a quiet or private place.

As a class, discuss the following.

1. What benefits does a cell phone or smartphone provide as it relates to academics and your school work?

2. What are some of the health risks associated with extensive cell phone usage?

Adding Fields, Deleting Fields, and Editing Records

Learning Outcomes

In Lesson 80, you will:

80A *Add and delete table fields.*

80B *Edit database records.*

80C *Modify a database table.*

Data Files:

df 80 lincoln
df 80 composers

80A

Add and Delete Table Fields

After creating a database table, you might want to add or delete fields. For example, in the *Student Schedules* table, including the name of the instructor for each class period would be helpful. If Lincoln High School changed to a five-period day, Period 6 would need to be deleted from the table.

To add fields to a table, you begin by opening the table in Design view. You insert a new row in the table where you want the field to appear. Then you enter a field name, data type, and description. After you save the table, you are ready to enter data in the new field for the existing records or for new records.

To delete fields from a table, you begin by opening the table in Design view. Then you select and delete the field. You will learn to add and delete fields in the activities that follow.

Access has a Save As command like the one you have used in other *Office* applications to save files using a new name. This feature is useful when you want to make changes to a database and still keep a copy of the original database.

DB File/Save As/Access Database (default)

Activity 1

In this activity, you will add fields to a database table.

1. Open the *df 80 lincoln* database.

DB Home/Views/Design View

2. Use the Save As command to save the database as *80 lincoln* in the folder in which you save your work for this class.

3. In the *80 lincoln* database, open the *Student Schedules* table in Design view.

4. Right-click anywhere in the row with the field name Class Period 2. Choose **Insert Rows** from the pop-up menu. (See Figure 12.17.)

5. A new row will be inserted above the selected row. In the new row, key **Instructor 1** for the field name. Choose **Short Text** for the data type. For the description, key **Name of Instructor for Class Period 1**.

TIP Virus protection software can disable some database content. If the message "Security Warning Some active content in the database has been disabled" is displayed when you open a database, click the **Enable Content** button. Depending on your virus protection software, you might have to enable content every time you open a database.

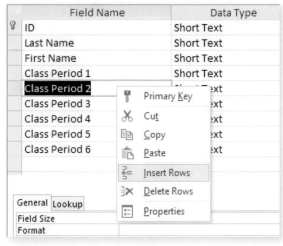

Figure 12.17 *Insert a new row.*

Before You Move On

Answer these questions to review what you have learned in Chapter 1.

1. The physical parts of a computer that you can touch are called
   _____. LO 1A

2. Explain the difference between an operating system, an application, and an
   online app. LO 1B

3. The five steps of information processing are _____, processing,
   _____, distribution, and _____. LO 1C

4. The _____ is the most important software on a computer. LO 2A

5. A(n) _____ is a series of letters, numbers, and symbols that you
   key to gain access to a computer. LO 2A

6. List three things you can do to avoid injury when using a mouse. LO 2C

7. _____ closes any open applications and turns off the
   computer. LO 2D

8. *Microsoft PowerPoint*'s commands are displayed on its _____.
   LO 3B

9. Explain the difference between the Minimize, Maximize, and Restore Down
   buttons. LO 3C

10. To print a document, choose _____ from the _____
    tab. LO 4E

11. What are four of the seven rules for acceptable computer use? LO 4F

12. List three common devices or places used to store computer files. LO 5A

13. Folders stored inside other folders are called _____. LO 5B

14. Explain how you would cut, copy, delete, and move files and folders.
    LO 5D, 5E, 6C

15. Which characters cannot be used in file or folder names? LO 4C

16. The series of folders and subfolders that lead you to the location of a file is
    called the _____. LO 5F

17. The main portion of the *Microsoft Excel* window is organized into
    _____, _____, and _____. LO 6A

18. The View _____ command allows you to view two documents
    next to each other. LO 6B

19. _____ and _____ allow you to remove a file or
    folder from one place and move it to another. LO 5E, 6C

TIP Before opening Print Preview, double-click the right border line of each column heading to adjust the width of the columns.

9. Close the form and open the *Student Schedules* table. Notice that the records you added using the form are now included in the table. Notice that the records have again been arranged by ID Number.

10. Open Print Preview. In the Page Layout group, change the Orientation to **Landscape**. Refer to 78D, if needed.

11. While in Print Preview, determine whether the *Student Schedules* table will print on one page. If it doesn't fit on one page, what suggestions would you have for making it fit on one page?

12. Complete the CheckPoint, and then close the database.

 **checkpoint** Check each record for spelling and keying errors. Make the necessary corrections, adjust the width of any fields if necessary, and close the table. Save any layout changes if necessary.

21st Century Skills

Joachim E. Röttgers/imageBROKER/Alamy

Use and Manage Information

As discussed in this chapter, databases are an effective tool for organizing and managing large amounts of information. Educational institutions use databases to organize information on students, teachers and staff, and class offerings. Governments use databases to manage information on personnel, taxes, and public programs and facilities. Businesses use databases to store information about customers, employees, sales, inventories, and more.

But how is all this information obtained? Most of it is provided voluntarily. For example, individuals provide information when they file a tax return, apply for a credit card, enroll at a school or college, apply for a driver's license, fill out a job application, or answer a survey.

Think Critically

1. Most organizations obtain and use database information for legitimate business reasons. Provide examples of how a business might use customer purchasing information to increase sales.

2. What dangers or risks are involved with supplying information about yourself that will be stored in an electronic database?

3. If you created a database of friends, family, and other contacts, what type of information would you store on each person? Is there any information you think would be inappropriate to share with others?

Create Subfolders

Your Computers folder has subfolders to hold your work for this class. You need to create subfolders for other subjects and classes you are taking. That way all of your assignments will have a home.

1. Start *File Explorer* and open your primary saving space or folder.

2. Create a folder called **Subjects**.

3. Open your new Subjects folder. Inside, create a new subfolder for all of the classes you have in school. For example, create Math, Science, Language Arts, and History folders. Now you have a place to save all of the assignments for all of your other classes!

4. Move your Computers folder into the Subjects folder along with all of the other subject folders you just created.

5. Close *File Explorer*.

Rename and Move Files

Filenames should be relatively short and very descriptive. This means that a file-name should give you an idea of what is in the file. One of the files you created in Chapter 1 needs to be renamed and moved into the Subjects\Computers\Chapter 1 folder.

1. Start *File Explorer* and locate and open the folder in which you saved the files you created in Chapter 1.

2. In the right pane, select the file **4d applications and apps**. Rename the file as *c1 compare apps*.

3. Move the renamed *c1 compare apps* file into your Subjects\Computers\ Chapter 1 folder.

4. Close *File Explorer*.

TIP The > button moves only the highlighted field over to the Selected Fields window.

3. Notice that your *Student Schedules* table is identified in the Tables/Queries box and its fields are listed in Available Fields. Because you have only one table, the name of that table (*Student Schedules*) appears in the Tables/Queries box. If you had several tables, you could select the table from which you wanted to prepare the form. (To select a table, click the down arrow and choose the desired table.)

4. Click the double-arrow (>>) button to select all of the fields and include them in the form. Click **Next**.

5. The next Wizard screen lets you select the form layout. Select **Tabular** and then click **Next**.

6. Finally, you will be prompted to give the form a title. Key **Student Schedules (Form 2)**. Select the option **Open the form to view or enter information**. (See Figure 12.16.) Click **Finish**.

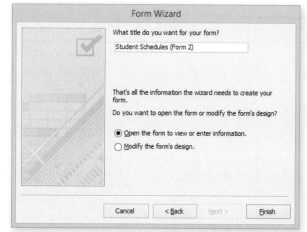

Figure 12.16 *Enter a title for the form in the Form Wizard.*

7. The form appears on your screen in Form view displaying the nine records that you entered earlier.

8. Move to a new blank record at the bottom of the form. Enter data for the three records shown below.

ID Number	52798	63156	23927
Last Name	Schuricht	Talbot	Davenport
First Name	Jessica	Dane	Mitchell
Period 1	Algebra	Keyboarding Apps	Biology
Period 2	U.S. History	U.S. History	U.S. History
Period 3	Physical Ed	English	English
Period 4	Chorus	Algebra	Algebra
Period 5	English	Chorus	Chorus
Period 6	Biology	Biology	Keyboarding Apps

ACROSS THE CURRICULUM

Academic Connections

Data Files:

df c1 ancient greece
df c1 sparta and
    athens
df c1 business
df c1 leadership
    skills
df c1 budget

Social Studies: Sparta and Athens

Ancient Greece was made up of several separate city-states. Two of the most powerful were Sparta and Athens. While these two city-states were alike in many ways, some of their basic beliefs were very different.

1. Start *Word* and open the data file named *df c1 ancient greece*. Print and close the document.

2. Follow the directions given on your printout to create a paragraph that compares and contrasts Athens and Sparta.

About Business

Supply and Demand

Supply and demand are the main forces in a market economy. **Supply** is the amount of a product or service that producers (companies) offer for sale. The relationship between a product's price and the amount produced is called the *law of supply*. Other factors being the same, when a product's price falls, companies will produce less of it. When a product's price rises, companies will produce more.

Demand is the amount of a product or service that consumers are willing and able to buy. The relationship between a product's price and the demand for a product is called the *law of demand*. Consumers will buy more of a product when the price goes down. They will buy less when the price goes up.

Consumers want to buy products at low prices. Producers want to sell products at high prices. Consumers and producers must compromise to reach an agreement on a product's price. The price at which consumers are willing to buy and producers are willing to sell is called the **market price**.

COLLABORATION

1. Working with one or two classmates, open *df c1 business*. Save the file as *c1 business* in the Subjects\Computers\Chapter 1 folder of one of your group members.

2. Replace the text in the top-left corner with your group members' names, class, and date. Read and discuss each question with your group. After each question, key your answer in bold text. Save, print, and close the file.

3. Have one person in your group use *Windows* to copy the *c1 business* file and paste it in his or her Social Studies folder that was created in the previous activity. Then rename the file in the Social Studies folder to *c1 supply and demand*. Each person in your group should repeat this step so that you each have a *c1 supply and demand* file in your Social Studies folder.

4. Each group member should then delete the *c1 business* file from the Chapter 1 folder.

TIP When you tap TAB in the last field of a record, a new blank record is created.

ID Number	11583	25781	22854
Last Name	Chu	Santos	Hefner
First Name	Chou	Felipe	Amanda
Period 1	U.S. History	English	Algebra
Period 2	English	Algebra	U.S. History
Period 3	Keyboarding Apps	Keyboarding Apps	Physical Ed
Period 4	Biology	Biology	Biology
Period 5	Algebra	Art	English
Period 6	Art	World History	Chorus

5. When you finish entering the data, close the form by clicking its **Close** button.

6. Open the *Student Schedules* table. (If it is already open, you must close and reopen it in order to see the records that were just added.)

7. Notice that the new records are in the table. The records were automatically arranged in ascending order by ID Number. Read the following CheckPoint and then close the table.

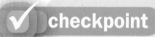 **checkpoint** You should now have nine records in the *Student Schedules* table.

79C

Create a Form Using a Wizard

Using the Form command is a quick way to create a form. Forms can also be created using the Form Wizard. The Form Wizard will ask a series of questions and create the form based on the answers. The Form Wizard gives you more choices about how the form will look and what fields you will include.

1. Open the database *79 lincoln* that you created in 79A if necessary.

2. Click the **Create** tab on the ribbon. In the Forms group, click **Form Wizard**. The Form Wizard will open as shown in Figure 12.15.

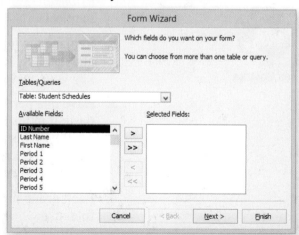

Figure 12.15 *Form Wizard*

Leadership Skills

Do you have what it takes to be a good leader? Many people define a leader as a person who guides, directs, and encourages others to achieve. What makes a good leader? Good leaders:

- Are trustworthy, honest, and dependable; they do what they say they will do.
- Listen to the opinions of others.
- Inspire, motivate, and build the skills of those around them.
- Are good communicators; they keep everyone informed and give clear instructions.
- Adapt to new situations.

1. Open *df c1 leadership skills*.

2. Follow the instructions to rate yourself on each skill listed. Key your rating number for each skill in the box in front of the skill.

3. Calculate your total to determine your level of leadership today.

4. Think about the areas where you rated yourself the lowest. How can you develop your leadership skills for the future? Key your ideas in the area provided at the bottom of the document.

5. Save the file as *c1 leadership skills* in your Social Studies folder, print, and close it.

Math and Personal Finance: Budgets

A **budget** is an itemized spending plan. Budgets help you determine the amount of money you need for a certain period of time. You can make a budget for any amount of time, such as a week, a month, or a year.

Planning a budget requires you to make choices. Some items you want to buy may cost more than you have in your budget. You need to figure out what is most important to have and save for items that you can buy later.

1. Using *File Explorer*, create a new folder in your Chapter 1 folder named Business.

2. Open *df c1 budget* and save it as *c1 budget* in the Chapter 1\Business folder. Print and close the document and exit *Word*.

3. Follow the directions in the file to create a budget and practice math skills.

Online Resources:

ngl.cengage.com/c21jr3e

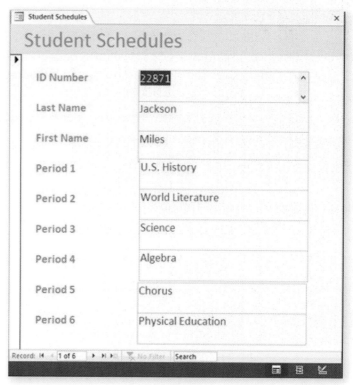

Figure 12.14 *Student Schedules* form

2. The arrows at the bottom of the screen can be used to move from record to record. Click each of the arrows in turn. As you click each arrow, notice the record that is displayed before and after clicking the arrow.

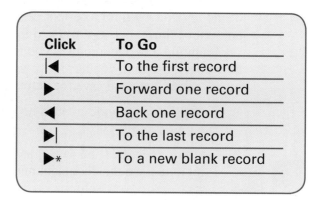

Click	To Go
I◄	To the first record
►	Forward one record
◄	Back one record
►I	To the last record
►*	To a new blank record

3. Click the tab for the *Student Schedules* table. Click the table's **Close** button. Click the form's **Close** button. Click **Yes** to save changes to the design of the *Student Schedules* form. Save the form as **Student Schedules (Form 1)**.

4. Open *Student Schedules (Form 1)*. Go to a new blank record (*). Enter the data for three students as shown below.

Chapter 2   Connecting to the World's Information

Lessons 7–10

Computers have totally changed the way we work, live, and think. Computers have integrated themselves into all aspects of our lives and society. *Instagram*, *Twitter*, and *Facebook* have changed how we connect and communicate with each other. Logging onto a computer or "smart" device instantly connects us to the world. While most of these advancements have been positive, they have also presented challenges to personal privacy and to the ethical use of technology.

In this chapter, you will think about how technology affects people's daily lives. The Internet has affected society greatly in recent years. You will learn to search for and find information on the Internet. You also will learn about ways of using the Internet as a good digital citizen.

© Bloom Design/Shutterstock.com

© pistolseven/Shutterstock.com

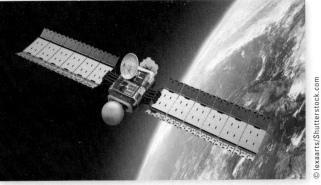
© lexaarts/Shutterstock.com

3. Click the **ID Number** field name row. Click the **Primary Key** button on the Table Tools Design tab to set this field as the primary key.

4. Use the *Switch to Datasheet View* path at the left to display Datasheet view. Save the table as **Student Schedules**.

5. Three student records are shown below. Enter the records into the *Student Schedules* table. After you enter the data, adjust the column widths to fit the longest entry in each column.

ID Number	35981	48263	52596
Last Name	Hansen	Martinez	Castello
First Name	Brittany	Rico	Mary
Period 1	English	U.S. History	Biology
Period 2	U.S. History	Algebra	Chorus
Period 3	Keyboarding Apps	Physical Ed	World History
Period 4	Algebra	Chorus	Physical Ed
Period 5	Chorus	World Literature	English
Period 6	Biology	Biology	Algebra

6. Enter the schedules for Jan Blake (ID Number: 73381), Miles Jackson (ID Number: 22871), and Rebecca Mead (ID Number: 88201). Refer to 78C for their schedules.

7. Leave the table open to complete 79B.

79B

Create a Form

You have already learned how to enter data into the database table using Datasheet view. Data can also be entered using a database form. A form is an object used to enter or display data. The Form command automatically creates a form based on an open table and includes all of the fields from the table.

A new form you create using the Form command displays in Layout view. This view can be used to adjust the appearance of the form. To enter records using a form, you must use Form view.

You are now ready to create a form from the *Student Schedules* table in the *79 lincoln* database.

DB Create/Forms/Form

1. With the *Student Schedules* table open, follow the path at the left and click **Form**. A form with all of the fields in the *Student Schedules* table will automatically be created. The new form displays in Layout view. Miles Jackson's record is shown in Figure 12.14.

Computers and Daily Life

Learning Outcomes

In Lesson 7, you will:

7A *Study the history of computers.*
7B *Describe how computers improve productivity.*
7C *Consider how computers are part of everyday life.*

7A

History of Computers

The first electronic computers were introduced in the mid-1900s. These computers were very big, as you can see in Figure 2.1. Some computers were housed in large rooms and weighed hundreds of pounds.

Bettmann/CORBIS

Figure 2.1 *Early computers were large and heavy.*

Early computers could perform only basic operations. For example, they could add, subtract, divide, and multiply. They could do these tasks many times faster than a person could. However, they were painfully slow compared with today's computers.

Advances in computers came slowly at first. Once computers had a way to store information, the demand for them grew. People started building smaller computers. In 1977, the Apple personal computer was introduced. Since that time, computers have steadily changed and improved. Some important milestones in the history of computing are shown in Table 2.1.

Table 2.1 *Computing history milestones*

1946	The first large-scale electronic computer, called ENIAC, was created.
1951	UNIVAC, one of the first commercial computers, was bought by the U.S. Census Bureau.
1963	The computer mouse was developed by Douglas Engelbart.

(Continued)

Creating a Database Form

Learning Outcomes

In Lesson 79, you will:

79A *Create a database, create a table, and enter records.*

79B *Create a database form.*

79C *Create a form using a wizard.*

79A

Plan and Create a Database

Instant Message

To review creating a database, see 78A. To review creating a table, see 78B.

DB *Create Table in Design View*
Create/Tables/Table Design

When you design a database, it is important to make it easy to use the data. You need to consider whether you can have all the data in one table or if you need several tables.

The database you created in Lesson 78 is not designed for storing and using large amounts of data. If there are 600 students at Lincoln Junior High, it would be very cumbersome, and users would become very frustrated trying to find a specific student's table out of the 600 tables created to accommodate each student's information individually. Schedules would have to be viewed one at a time. Searching or sorting the data would be difficult.

A database with one table that includes all students would be more useful. It would allow users to search and sort the data much more efficiently. In the next activity, you will create a database with one table to store schedule data for students at Lincoln Junior High.

1. Start *Access* and create a new database. Use *79 lincoln* for the filename. Close the default Table1 table.

2. Use the **Create Table in Design View** path at the left to create a table. Enter the field names, data types, and descriptions shown below.

Field Name	Data Type	Description
ID Number	Short Text	Student's ID Number
Last Name	Short Text	Student's Last Name
First Name	Short Text	Student's First Name
Period 1	Short Text	Class Period 1
Period 2	Short Text	Class Period 2
Period 3	Short Text	Class Period 3
Period 4	Short Text	Class Period 4
Period 5	Short Text	Class Period 5
Period 6	Short Text	Class Period 6

Table 2.1 (*Continued*)

1965	Minicomputers were introduced. These were the first computers to use integrated circuits.
1969	Small computers helped astronauts land on the moon.
1977, 1981	Apple PCs and IBM PCs were introduced. Personal computers became practical for business and personal use.
1983	Notebook computers were introduced.
1984	Apple introduced the Macintosh computer and the graphical interface using pictures, or icons, instead of text commands.
1991	The World Wide Web was developed. Internet use began to increase rapidly.
1993	PDAs were introduced, which were the first small, handheld computers. They gave inspiration to today's smart cell phones.
2001	Tablet PCs were introduced. Handwriting and speech continue to become more popular as input methods.
2007	Apple released the iPhone, which is both a handheld computer and a phone with wireless Internet capabilities. As an input tool on the iPhone, fingertips replace the mouse.
2008	Google released Google Chrome as a new and unique web browser.
2009	Google's Gmail was released and the Bing search engine was released by Microsoft.
2010	Apple unveiled the iPad, changing the way consumers view media and jumpstarting the tablet computer market. The online photo and video sharing service *Instagram* was introduced as the newest form of social media.
2011	IBM's Watson supercomputer won *Jeopardy* in February and on October 5th Steve Jobs, Apple Computer co-founder, died.
2012	Microsoft released *Windows 8*, which featured a much faster startup, integrated web apps, and improved support for digital media.
2013	Connected TVs and tablets moved into the mainstream as media providers such as Netflix and Snagfilm rival broadcast and cable companies. Also, identity theft, data breaches, privacy issues, and national security topped headlines throughout the year.
2014	Seven new web domain names are released including .guru, .clothing, and .bike.

From the 1970s, computer makers have been in intense competition. Each seeks to create faster, smaller, easier to use, and less expensive computers. The results have been a huge success. The power of computers has more than doubled every two years for the past 35 to 40 years. That is a lot!

5. Enter Rebecca Mead's schedule into the table from the information shown below.

ID	Class Period	Class	Teacher
1	Period 1	Keyboarding Apps	Mr. Dexter
2	Period 2	Civics	Ms. Blakely
3	Period 3	Biology	Mr. Weston
4	Period 4	Algebra	Mr. Carver
5	Period 5	World Literature	Mr. Dexter
6	Period 6	Physical Education	Ms. Gomez

6. Close the table.

78D

Preview and Print a Table

When in Print Preview, you can use the features in the Page Size and the Page Layout groups to change the paper size, orientation, and margins, as shown in Figure 12.13. If the document is currently set for Portrait orientation and you want Landscape orientation, simply click the Landscape button. Margins can be changed by using the Margins button for preset margins or Page Setup to specify custom margins.

TIP Changes made in Print Preview are not saved. They must be made every time you print.

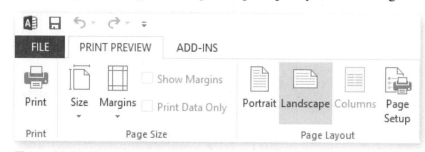

Figure 12.13 *Change page layout.*

 **DB** File/Print/Print Preview

1. Open the table for Miles Jackson.

2. Follow the path at the left to see how the table looks using Print Preview.

3. Click the table a couple of times to switch between a full-page and a close-up view of the table. Notice that the table name (*Miles Jackson*) and the current date appear at the top of the page. *Page 1* appears at the bottom of the page.

4. Change the orientation to Landscape.

5. Change the top margin to 2".

6. Print the table by clicking **Print** on the Print Preview tab.

7. Click **Close Print Preview**.

8. Close the table and then click the **Close** button to exit *Access*.

Close Print Preview

✓ checkpoint Check your printed table. Have you completed all instructions? Are names spelled correctly? Great job! You now know how to create a database table and enter records.

Today's fast, tiny, and powerful computers are finding their way into the most unlikely places. Often without knowing it, we use dozens of computers every day (Figure 2.2). They have become more important in our lives with every passing year. As a result, they now influence the way we work, live, and play.

HDTV

iPhone

Wii

Figure 2.2 *Computers are part of many common devices.*

7B

How Computers Improve Productivity

COLLABORATION

People worked and lived for thousands of years without computers. So why have we become so dependent on them now? The simple answer is that computers help us get more done. They increase our productivity. **Productivity** is a measure of how much work can be done in a certain amount of time.

1. Work in a group or team. Pick one member as a scribe to take notes. Brainstorm as many answers as you can to these three questions:
   a. How do computers make people more productive? List and explain your ideas.
   b. Can computers make people less productive? List and explain your answers.
   c. Can you get along without a computer, a cell phone, or other digital tools? List and explain your answers.

2. Present and discuss your answers with the class or with another team and compare your ideas. What answers and ideas did your group identify that other groups did not? What answers and ideas did other teams come up with that your group may have missed?

7C

How Computers Are Part of Everyday Life

Imagine if all computers suddenly disappeared. As you go through your day today, think about how things would be different without computers.

School

Think about your school. Most likely the heating, cooling, emergency, and communication systems all use computers. Obviously, the computer labs would disappear. Most clocks would stop, and the lights would not turn on. Fire alarms might not work properly. In addition, your teacher could not enter your grades without the help of a computer. How many of your assignments require the use of a computer?

Activity 2

You now know how to create a table and enter data. Practice what you have learned by creating a table for Miles Jackson's schedule like the one you created for Jan Blake.

Use Table Design to create the table. Use Datasheet view to enter the information displayed below. Review 78B as needed for creating the table design. The design will be the same as the one created for Jan Blake.

ID	Class Period	Class	Teacher
1	Period 1	U.S. History	Mr. Chan
2	Period 2	World Literature	Ms. Jepson
3	Period 3	Science	Mr. Sanchez
4	Period 4	Algebra	Ms. Schultz
5	Period 5	Chorus	Mr. Fields
6	Period 6	Physical Education	Mr. Gerig

Activity 3

When the design of a new table is to be the same as a table previously created, you can copy the existing table rather than repeating all the steps to create the design of the table. Create a table for Rebecca Mead's schedule and enter the information displayed below by completing these steps.

1. Click on Jan Blake's table in the Navigation Pane and copy (CTRL + C) and paste (CTRL + V).

2. In the Paste Table As dialog box (Figure 12.12), select **Structure Only**; otherwise, all the data in Jan Blake's table will be copied in the new table.

3. Select the table name *Copy Of Jan Blake* and key **Rebecca Mead**. Click **OK**.

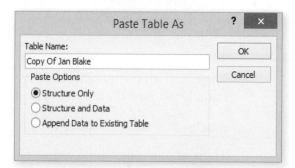

Figure 12.12 *Copy and name a table.*

4. The new table for Rebecca Mead appears in the Navigation Pane beneath the tables that have already been created. Double-click on the table to open it.

Transportation

Think about transportation. Without computers, most modern cars would stop working. Many of the safety, pollution control, and starter systems on cars use computers. Cars with onboard computers can now parallel park and anticipate movements of vehicles surrounding them to avoid accidents. Traffic lights and warning systems use computers. The Amber Alert system warns motorists to be on the lookout for missing children. Many lives have been saved as a result of computer alert systems.

Home

Think about your home. Most appliances, clocks, and other electronic devices would stop working. Your digital phone would not exist. Your televisions, radios, DVD players, and computer games would quit working, too! There would be no more Internet, email, or instant messaging. Your home security alarm would fail to work (Figure 2.3).

Figure 2.3 *Security alarms do not work without computers.*

Money and the Mall

Think about your money and shopping trips to the mall. Money transactions are routed and recorded by computers. All ATMs require computers to help distribute cash. Credit card systems would cease to work. You would not be able to buy anything at the mall or superstore because the registers would quit working. Besides that, the mall's elevators and escalators would stop working. There would be no lighting, no air conditioning, and no security systems.

The Space Program

Think about the space program. Without computers, spaceships would never get off the ground. Satellites would quit working. The International Space Station would crash to Earth. We might not discover new opportunities in our expanding universe.

You know how computers are used in many areas of people's everyday lives. You will explore some other areas where computers are important in this activity.

1. Work in a team with three or four classmates. Ask one team member to take notes and ask another to lead the discussion.

COLLABORATION

3. Enter the remaining classes shown in the following table.

ID	Class Period	Class	Teacher
1	Period 1	U.S. History	Mr. Chan
2	Period 2	Algebra	Ms. Boston
3	Period 3	Chorus	Mr. Fields
4	Period 4	English	Ms. Ramirez
5	Period 5	Keyboarding Apps	Mr. Dexter
6	Period 6	Physical Education	Ms. Gomez

4. Look at record 5 that contains *Keyboarding Apps*. The column is not wide enough to show all of the information. You can adjust column widths to fit the data.

5. Place the pointer on the column border (vertical line) to the right of the word *Class* (the column head). The pointer will appear as a double-headed arrow with a vertical line. (See Figure 12.11.) Double-click the column border. The column width will adjust to fit the longest item in the column.

TIP The data is automatically saved when a table is closed.

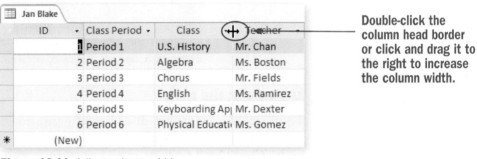

Double-click the column head border or click and drag it to the right to increase the column width.

Figure 12.11 *Adjust column width.*

COLLABORATION

6. Close the table. You will be asked whether you want to save changes to the layout of the table. Click **Yes**.

7. Complete the CheckPoint below.

 **checkpoint** Switch seats with one of your classmates. Open your classmate's *Jan Blake* table to see if it is set up correctly. Make sure all classes are included. Check for keying and spelling errors.

2. Brainstorm how computers are used in each of the categories listed below. Make a list of as many ideas as you can.

- Science
- Medicine
- Business and industry
- Arts and entertainment
- Protecting the environment

3. Discuss your list with the class or with another group of students in your class.

Lesson 8

Internet Basics

Learning Outcomes

In Lesson 8, you will:

8A   *Learn about networks and the Internet.*
8B   *Learn about connecting to the Internet.*
8C   *Explore the parts of a web browser window.*
8D   *Access and navigate web pages.*

8A

Networks and the Internet

Networks

When one computer links to another computer, a **network** is created. A small network may have only a few computers. A large network can include thousands of computers. A network with computers located within a short distance (such as within the same school) is called a *local area network (LAN)*.

When many LANs link to one another, a web of networks is created (Figure 2.4). The **Internet** is a web of computer networks that spans the Earth. Files on the Internet are stored on powerful computers called **servers**.

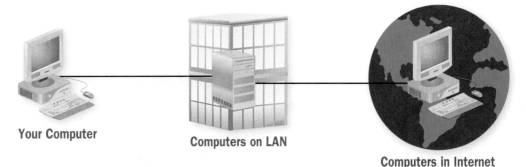

Your Computer   **Computers on LAN**   **Computers in Internet**

Figure 2.4 *Using your computer, you can find information on a LAN or on the Internet.*

TIP You can also click the **Primary Key** button to set the primary key for a table.

Figure 12.9 *Save the table design.*

4. A prompt will appear asking whether you want to create a primary key. Click **Yes**. *Access* will create a field named ID to be the primary key. *Access* will prevent any duplicate values from being entered in the primary key field.

You are now ready to add records to the table.

78C

Add Records to a Table

As you work in an *Access* database, you will use a number of different views. You create a table in Design view, for example, but you must switch to Datasheet view to enter records in the table. You use the View command in the Views group on the Home or a Design tab to switch between different *Access* views.

Activity 1

You have now created a database file (*78 schedule*) and a database table (*Jan Blake*). In this activity, you will add records to the table.

1. Open the *Jan Blake* table in Datasheet view if necessary by double-clicking the object in the Navigation Pane.

TIP Move from column to column by tapping TAB, by clicking a cell, or by using the arrow keys.

2. Click to place the insertion point beneath *Class Period* and key **Period 1**. Tap TAB once to move the insertion point to the Class field. Key **U.S. History**, which is Jan Blake's first class. Tap TAB to move the insertion point to the Teacher field. Key **Mr. Chan**, the name of Jan Blake's history teacher. (See Figure 12.10.)

Figure 12.10 *Jan Blake* database table

Note: The ID field in the table was created automatically when you chose to create a primary key. The field type is AutoNumber. This means that you do not enter data in this field. *Access* will automatically assign a number in this field to each record you create.

The Internet

The Internet created new ways for people to communicate. People use the Internet to research topics, exchange messages, buy and sell products, and promote organizations and ideas.

Electronic mail, commonly called email, is a popular use of the Internet. **Email** is the electronic transfer of messages. It allows users to exchange information quickly and easily. Blogs and instant messaging also are popular uses of the Internet. A **blog** allows users to post messages for others to read. Blogs are usually organized around a particular topic, such as music or sports, or around people's lives. There are blogs for millions of different topics and people. **Instant messaging** allows users who are online to key text messages. The messages are displayed almost instantly for the person you are chatting with.

An important part of the Internet is the World Wide Web. It is often called simply *the Web*. The **World Wide Web** is a system of computers that can handle documents formatted in a special language. This language is called *HTML (Hypertext Markup Language)*. HTML documents, called *web pages*, can display text as well as graphics. They allow users to move from one document to another using hyperlinks. A group of related web pages is called a *website*.

Websites are created for many reasons. One reason is to sell products. The selling and buying of products on the Internet is called **e-commerce**. Billions of dollars' worth of products are sold each year through e-commerce. Clothes, cars, groceries, medicine, movie tickets, books, and music are just a few of the items that customers can buy online. See Figure 2.5.

Source: Amazon.com

Figure 2.5 *People can search for and buy products of all kinds online.*

Websites are also used by people, companies, governments, and other groups to provide information. For example, you can access a website provided by the White House. On this site, you can find articles about current news events related to the U.S. president. You also will find information about our government, the latest news and updates, and you can blog on current events. See Figure 2.6.

Primary Key

When you create an *Access* table, you can select one field in the table to be the primary key. A **primary key** is a field chosen to identify each record in a table. *Access* will not allow duplicate data to be entered in the primary key field. The value in the primary key must be unique for every record.

For example, in a table containing data for students at a school, each student would have a student ID number. Each student's ID number would be different from all other ID numbers. The field that holds the student's ID number can be set as the primary key. This would prevent a user from accidentally entering the same ID number for two different students.

You can choose a field to set as the primary key. You also can let *Access* create a primary key field for you.

The *78 schedule* database that you created will store data about class schedules in a simple table. The table will have four fields: ID, Class Period, Class, and Teacher. The data type for the ID field will be AutoNumber, and the other fields will use the default Short Text data type.

1. In the *78 schedule* database, click the **Create** tab. In the Tables group, click **Table Design** (Figure 12.7).

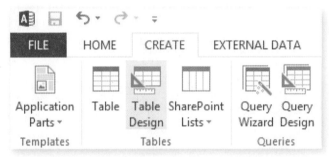

Figure 12.7 *Create a new table using Table Design.*

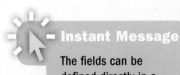

2. The new table opens in Design view with the insertion point blinking under *Field Name*. Key **Class Period**. Tap TAB to move to the Data Type field; then tap TAB to accept the default data type and move to the Description field. Key the information shown in Figure 12.8. Use TAB to move from field to field or use the mouse to click where you want to key.

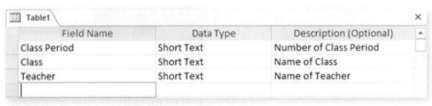

Figure 12.8 *Table in Design view*

3. Click the table's **Close** button. Click **Yes** to save changes to the table design. Key **Jan Blake** for the Table Name and click **OK** (Figure 12.9).

Figure 2.6 *Information about our government can be found on the White House website.*

Connecting to the Internet

To access the Internet from a home computer, you may need to set up an account with an Internet service provider. An **Internet service provider (ISP)** is a company that provides customer connections to the Internet. AT&T, Verizon, CenturyLink, and Comcast are examples of popular ISPs. Many schools provide ISP service through their LANs.

In the past, most computers were connected to their networks by wires. This has limited us as to how and where we connect to the Internet. Wireless Internet connections now allow freedom of movement. Computers can be linked to the Internet without wires through a device called an *access point*. The area around an access point is called a *hot spot*. With the proper equipment, you can connect to the Internet when you are in a hot spot. Hot spots can be created in schools, restaurants, airports, hotels, and even some public parks.

> **Instant Message** Wireless connections are often called **Wi-Fi**. Sometimes they are called **802.11** connections. Another short-range wireless connection is called **Bluetooth**.

Parts of a Web Browser Window

A **web browser** is a program that lets you find and view web pages. *Internet Explorer*, *Chrome*, *Safari*, and *Firefox* are popular web browsers. Look at the *Internet Explorer* window shown in Figure 2.7. You will see a title bar, tabs, scroll bars, and control buttons like those you have learned about in other *Windows* programs. A *Chrome* browser window is shown in Figure 2.5. Notice the similarities between *Chrome* and *Internet Explorer*.

Create and Save a Table

Tables

Once you create a database file, you can create tables to store data. A **table** is a database object used for organizing and storing data. A table is made up of records and fields. A **record** is a row of information (data) in a table (Figure 12.5). A **field** is a column of information (data) in a table (Figure 12.6).

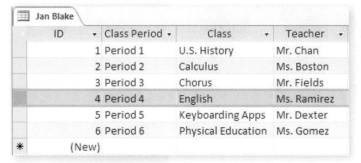

Figure 12.5 *Record (row)*

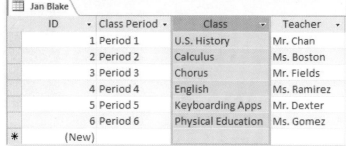

Figure 12.6 *Field (column)*

Table Design

Before creating a table, you should take time to plan the design of the table. Planning the design will save you the time and frustration of having to modify it later. You should consider the types of data (names, amounts, descriptions) that will be stored in the table. You also should consider how the data will be used. For example, sorting data by state will be easy if you include a State field in the table, rather than store state data along with other information in an Address field.

Data Types

Choosing the data type for each field is an important step in designing a table. The **data type** determines the kind of data a field can hold. You can use several types of data, some of which are shown in Table 12.1.

Table 12.1 *Data types*

Data Type	Description
Short Text	For letters or numbers that do not require calculations
Number	For numbers to be used in calculations
Date/Time	For dates and times
Currency	For dollar values
AutoNumber	Numbers assigned in order by *Access*
Yes/No	For data that can only be Yes or No

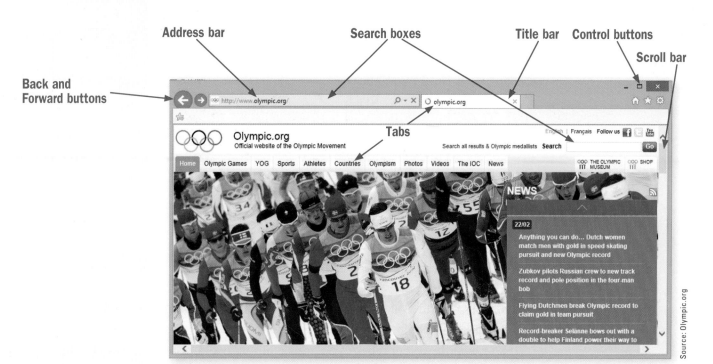

Figure 2.7 *The Internet Explorer browser window*

Source: Olympic.org

8D

Access and Navigate Web Pages

Web Addresses

In Chapter 1, you learned to follow a path to locate a file on your computer. In a similar way, you must locate web pages you want to view. A **uniform resource locator (URL)** is an address for a website. You can key a URL into the address bar of a web browser. After you key a URL and give the appropriate command, the browser will look for the address and display the site's web page.

URLs contain **domain names**. For example, the domain name *nasa.gov* is part of the address for the National Aeronautics and Space Administration website. The *.gov* at the end of the URL stands for *government*. Domain names can give you some insight into the purpose of the sites you visit. Table 2.2 shows a few examples:

Table 2.2 *Example domain names*

.edu	Educational	.gov	Governmental
.mil	Military	.net	Network providers
.org	Organizational	.us	Country code for the United States
.biz	Business	.mx	Country code for Mexico
.com	Commercial	.ca	Country code for Canada
.pro	Professional	.jp	Country code for Japan
.info	Informational	.cn	Country code for China

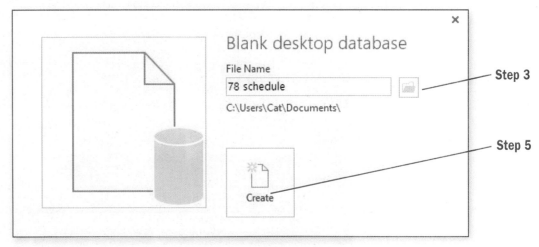

Figure 12.3 *Name the new database.*

3. Click on the folder icon next to the filename and navigate to the location where you are saving files for this chapter.

4. Open the folder where you are saving the work you do in this chapter and click **OK** to save *78 schedule*.

5. Click **Create** to create the blank database.

6. *Access* opens the new database with a sample Table1 displayed, as shown in Figure 12.4. Click the table's **Close** button to close the sample table.

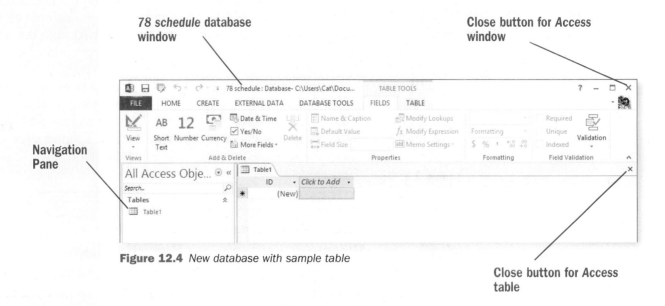

Figure 12.4 *New database with sample table*

In this activity, you will use a URL to find the NASA welcome page. Instructions given are for *Internet Explorer*. If you have a different browser, the directions will be similar.

1. Follow your teacher's instructions to log on to the Internet.

2. Start *Internet Explorer* (or another browser). Click the address bar. The current address should be highlighted. If it is not, click and drag over the address to select it. In the address bar, key **www.nasa.gov** as shown in Figure 2.8.

Figure 2.8 *Internet Explorer address bar.*

Instant Message

In a URL, **http://** is short for Hypertext Transfer Protocol. HTTP is the means by which information is shared over the Web.

3. Tap ENTER. The characters *http://* will be automatically added to the beginning of the address. A welcome page similar to the one shown in Figure 2.9 should appear.

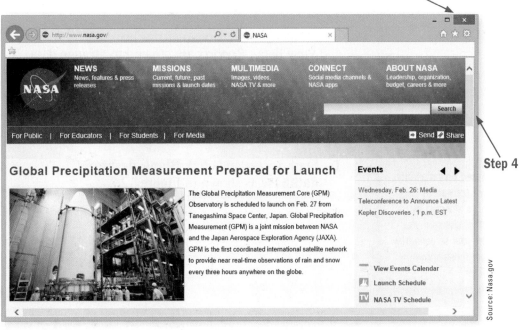

Figure 2.9 *The NASA welcome page.*

Instant Message

The first page you visit on a website is called a *welcome page*. Welcome pages change often. Your page may look different from the one in Figure 2.9.

4. Use the scroll bar to move down the NASA welcome page.

5. To visit another website, key **www.nasm.si.edu** in the address bar and tap ENTER. The Smithsonian National Air and Space Museum welcome page should display.

6. Using the scroll bars, examine the welcome page. Click the **Close** button on the browser window to close *Internet Explorer*.

Creating a Database

In Lesson 78, you will:

78A *Create a database.*
78B *Create and save a table.*
78C *Add records to a table.*
78D *Preview and print a table.*

78A

Create a Database

In this chapter, you will use *Microsoft Access* to create electronic databases. The first step in creating a database is to save a new database file. Within the database file, you can create database **objects**. Common objects are tables, queries, forms, and reports, as shown in Figure 12.1. *Tables* are created to store data. *Queries* are created to find data to answer questions. *Forms* are created to enter and view data. *Reports* are created to arrange data in a way that is easy for others to understand.

In this lesson, you will create a database and design a table to store data for a student's school schedule. Creating a database using *Access* is similar to creating a document using *Word*.

1. Start *Access* and click **Blank desktop database** as shown in Figure 12.2.

TIP Based on installation options or software preferences selected by you or other users on your computer, your screens may differ from those shown in this chapter.

Figure 12.1 *Objects list in* **Access**

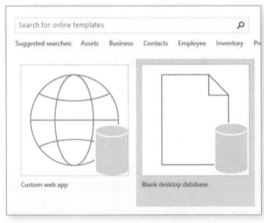

Figure 12.2 *Initial screen in* **Access**

2. Click in the box under File Name and key *78 schedule* for the filename as shown in Figure 12.3.

TIP When the pointer passes over a hyperlink, it becomes a hand with a pointing finger.

TIP You do not have to key www to access a web page. You can save time by just keying the domain name.

Hyperlinks

Many web pages have hyperlinks. A **hyperlink** can be text, a button, or a graphic. When you click a hyperlink, you are taken to a new location. Not all of the pictures or words on a web page are hyperlinks. How can you find hyperlinks on a web page? Simply move the pointer (usually an arrow) around the page with your mouse, finger, or digital pen. When the pointer changes to a hand with a pointing finger, you have found a hyperlink.

When you click a hyperlink, the browser moves to a new location. If you want to return to the previous page, click the **Back button** in the browser window. To return to the page you just left, click the **Forward button**. To return to your home page or starting point, click or tap the **Home button**.

1. Log on to the Internet. Start *Internet Explorer* or another browser. In the address bar, key **msn.com**.

2. Move the mouse pointer around the welcome page. Watch the pointer become a pointing finger when it passes over a hyperlink.

3. Click a hyperlink such as **Entertainment**. Quickly scan the new page. Click the **Back** button. (See Figure 2.10.) This will take you back to the previous page.

Figure 2.10 *Internet Explorer's buttons.*

4. Click the **Forward** button. This will take you to the page you just left.

5. Click the **Home** button. This will take you to your starting home page.

6. Click the **Close** button on the browser window to close *Internet Explorer*.

Lessons 78–82

Data are facts and figures. Your name is an example of data. The price of a car is an example of data. People have more data to deal with today than ever before. For data to be valuable, it must be easy to find and understand.

A database is an organized collection of information such as facts and figures. A phone book is an example of a database. The data in a phone book are arranged by last name in alphabetical order. This makes the data easy to find and use.

A database can be in printed form or electronic form. Your school has a database with information about you and your classmates. The database includes your guardian's contact information in case of an emergency, your class schedule so you can be contacted should the need arise, your attendance record for reporting purposes, and a record of your academic performance. In this chapter, you will learn how to create an electronic database and store data. You also will learn how to find and arrange the data in a useful way.

© Nejron Photo/Shutterstock.com

Lesson 9

Browser and Search Features

Learning Outcomes

In Lesson 9, you will:

9A   *Use the History and Favorites features of the browser.*
9B   *Use the Search feature on a website.*
9C   *Employ techniques to search the entire Web.*
9D   *Improve search techniques.*
9E   *Use power search techniques to find information.*

9A

Browser History and Favorites

Browser programs such as *Internet Explorer*, *Chrome*, *Safari*, and *Firefox* have features that can help you find and revisit websites. The **History** feature shows you a list of links for sites you have visited recently. Some browsers let you change the display of sites in the History list to show sites visited by date, by order, or by frequency. You may also be able to use the browser's address bar to view links to sites you have recently visited.

The **Favorites** feature allows you to create a list of links for sites you visit often. (Some browsers call these links Bookmarks rather than Favorites.) You can use the links to move quickly to a site. You can organize them into folders to make it easier to locate the link you want.

Activity 1

1. Log on to the Internet and start *Internet Explorer* or your default browser.

2. Locate and display your History list. (In *Internet Explorer*, click the **Favorites** icon and then click the **History** tab. See Figure 2.11.)

3. On the History list, click the link for the NASA site (www.nasa.gov) that you visited earlier.

4. Display the History list again. If you are using *Internet Explorer*, click the down arrow to the right of *View By Date*, and select **View By Order Visited Today**.

5. Click the **Smithsonian's National Air and Space Museum** link.

6. Click the **Show Address bar Autocomplete** down arrow on the address bar to see a list of sites you have recently viewed. (See Figure 2.12.)

TIP The History list can display all of the pages you have visited. If you are using a different computer, the NASA site might not be on the History list. In that case, key the URL in the address bar.

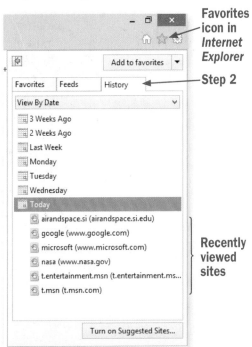

Favorites icon in *Internet Explorer*

Step 2

Recently viewed sites

Figure 2.11 *History list in Internet Explorer.*

Personal Finance Skills

You may be dreaming about it—the day you finish school and move out on your own. Of course, with every dream comes reality. Your perfect place will cost money, and you will have other bills that must be paid as well.

In this activity, you will develop a monthly budget. You must determine your income and expenses such as rent, car payments, gas, utilities, and more.

1. Open the document *df c11 monthly budget* and save it as *c11 monthly budget*.

2. Follow the directions to calculate a monthly income for a job of your choice. Then research to find typical expenses of a working adult. Last, continue to follow directions to enter the data into a new worksheet and balance a personal budget.

Activity 10

To complete this activity, you will need the Student Interest Survey that you filled out in Career Exploration Portfolio Activity 1. Completing Career Exploration Activities 2–9 would also be helpful but is not mandatory.

1. Review your Student Interest Survey. Note your *third* Career Cluster of interest. Reread its description.

2. Go to http://www.careertech.org. Click the **Career Technical Education** button, and then click **Career Clusters**. Click the name of your third Career Cluster choice near the bottom of the page.

3. Scroll through the categories available within that Career Cluster. Click the Plan of Study **Excel** link under the category you are most interested in to download the file to your system. (Choose the same category, or Pathway, that you used in Activities 4 and 7 if you completed them.)

4. Locate and open the downloaded *Excel* workbook. Read the list of classes you should take in high school to get ready for this career. Then read the list of classes that you should take after high school.

5. Search the Internet to find one or more colleges or technical schools that offer degrees in this career.

6. Use *Word* to write a summary of what you learned in this activity. Save the document as *c11 career 3 skills*, print, and close it.

Online Resources:

ngl.cengage.com/c21jr3e

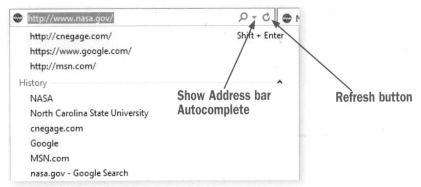

Figure 2.12 *Recently viewed pages in **Internet Explorer**.*

TIP If a page does not load properly or needs to be updated, click the **Refresh** button.

TIP You can also key a word or phrase in the address bar and click the Search button to search for a website.

7. You also can open a previously viewed page by keying the first part of the URL. Start keying **msn** in the address bar. The full URL will appear in the recently viewed list as shown in Figure 2.13.

Figure 2.13 *Previously accessed website in **Internet Explorer**.*

8. Click the link for **msn.com**. Your browser will move to this site. Leave your browser open for the next activity.

Activity 2

1. The MSN.com website contains the latest headlines from around the world, weather, sports, and other information that you can use every day. To make visiting the site easy, you will add it to your Favorites list. Click the **Favorites** icon (it may look like a star) to display the Favorites menu or a bookmark dialog box.

2. Click the **Add to favorites** button, shown in Figure 2.14.

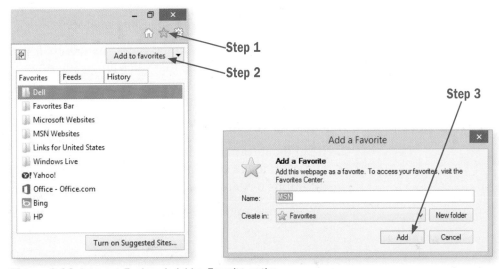

Figure 2.14 ***Internet Explorer's** Add a Favorite option.*

ACROSS THE CURRICULUM

Academic Connections

Data Files:

df c11 fundraiser instructions

df c11 fundraiser

df c11 economic factors

df c11 monthly budget

Math: Calculate Results of a Fund-raiser

You may not realize it, but math is used in everyday life. *Excel* can help perform calculations quickly and easily. In this activity, you'll have the chance to use both formulas and functions to find results and analyze data.

1. Start *Word* and open the document *df c11 fundraiser instructions*.

2. Follow the instructions to calculate totals, percents, and averages. You will also practice formatting and sorting data.

About Business

Economic Indicators

"Unemployment rates are down." "The stock market was up today with moderate trading." Why do news reporters, politicians, and people on the street talk so much about the economy? People talk about the economy because it affects their everyday lives.

The measurements that people use to describe how well the economy is doing are called **economic indicators**. Some examples are:

- Sales of new homes
- New claims for unemployment benefits
- Trends in the stock market
- Personal income
- How much people are spending at stores

Watching the changes in the economy can help you plan. For example, if you work at a store and you see that sales are going down, your boss might ask you to work fewer hours. This will affect your pay, so it probably wouldn't be a good time to buy a new car or another big purchase.

1. Open the document *df c11 economic factors*. Save it as *c11 economic factors*.

2. Read the information in the file and follow the directions to create a worksheet and chart about unemployment rates. Analyze your data to answer the questions in step 7 of *c11 economic factors*.

3. The Add a Favorite dialog box will appear with the site name. (See Figure 2.14.) Click **Add**.

4. Click the **Home** button to go to your home page. Then click the **Favorites** button. (Use Bookmarks in *Firefox* or *Chrome*.) Click the **Favorites** tab if necessary.

5. Locate the link on your Favorites list for the MSN.com site. Click the link to go to this site.

6. Use any method to display the NASA site you visited earlier and then add the NASA site to your Favorites list.

9B

Search for Information on a Website

You can use a search feature to find information. Services such as Google and Yahoo! search the entire Web. Other search tools search a single site, such as NASA or the Library of Congress.

To search either the Web or a single site, key a word (called a keyword) into a search text box and tap ENTER or click the Search or Go command. An example of the search box from the NASA site is shown in Figure 2.15.

| satellites | Search |

Figure 2.15 *The NASA website search feature.*

Each time you search for something on the Web, you are conducting a query. A query is a problem you want the search tool to resolve. Search tools use mathematical logic to satisfy a query based on the keyword(s) you enter.

Answers to a query are called results. When the search is complete, a list of results (also called *hits*) appears. Scroll through the results and choose the one that seems to have the information you need.

Sample search results for the NASA search are shown in Figure 2.16. To access an item from the list, click the link. If you want to go back to the list to try another link, use the Back button. Some search engines list the results in pages. To see more results, click the page number or Next.

Activity 1

1. Log on to the Internet and start your browser. Use the Favorites link to go to the NASA website at http://www.nasa.gov.

2. Look for a search box similar to the one shown in Figure 2.15.

3. Key the term **satellites** in the search box. Click the **Search** button to begin the search, as shown in Figure 2.15.

Improve Keying Technique

1. Key lines 1-5 twice.
2. Take three 30" timed writings on line 5. If you complete the line, key it again.

Balanced-hand words of 2-5 letters

1 or me go am do if so box did end due for many city
2 of the six and but may pay man own for pan doe map
3 make them such paid sign work both down name forms
4 sip pen wish both pans lame keys gowns right eight
5 Pam and the busy man may fix the eight city signs.

gwam 30" | 2 | 4 | 6 | 8 | 10 | 12 | 14 | 16 | 18 | 20 |

Speed Building

1. Key three 1' timed writings on each paragraph, striving to key more on each timing; determine *gwam*.
2. Key a 2' or 3' timed writing on both paragraphs combined, striving to maintain your highest 1' *gwam*.

A all letters used

gwam 2' 3'

The first part of the constitution deals with   5   3
the structure and powers of the legislative, the   10   6
executive, and the judicial branches of the government. 15 10
The legislative branch is there to make the law, while 21 14
the executive branch is there to carry out the law. 26 17
A person must be a citizen to be elected to positions 31 21
in either of these two areas of the government. The 37 24
judicial branch is there to interpret the laws when   42 28
questions or concerns come up about them. Positions 47 31
in the judicial branch are appointed. To be appointed 53 35
to this area of government, an individual must also 58 39
be a citizen.   59 39

Division of power is a critical concept to our   5 43
system of governing. The powers of the government   10 46
are divided among the three branches. Doing so   15 49
provides for a structure with checks and balances of 20 52
each of the divisions of the government. None of the 25 56
branches has enough influence to dominate the other two. 31 60
Each branch of the governing body has some authority 36 63
over what the other branches are able to do.   41 66

gwam 2' | 1 | 2 | 3 | 4 | 5 |
3' | 1 | 2 | 3 |

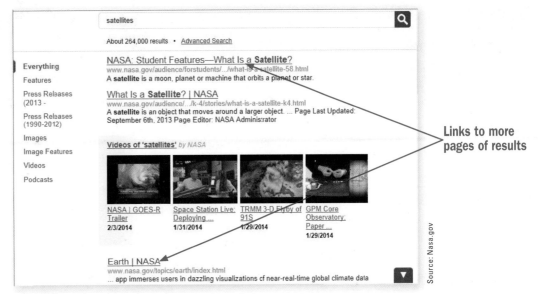

satellites

About 264,000 results • Advanced Search

Everything

Features

Press Releases
(2013 -

Press Releases
(1990-2012)

Images

Image Features

Videos

Podcasts

NASA: Student Features—What Is a **Satellite**?
www.nasa.gov/audience/forstudents/.../what-is-a-satellite-58.html
A **satellite** is a moon, planet or machine that orbits a planet or star.

What Is a **Satellite**? | NASA
www.nasa.gov/audience/.../k-4/stories/what-is-a-satellite-k4.html
A **satellite** is an object that moves around a larger object. ... Page Last Updated:
September 6th, 2013 Page Editor: NASA Administrator

Videos of 'satellites' *by NASA*

NASA | GOES-R
Trailer
2/3/2014

Space Station Live:
Deploying ...
1/31/2014

TRMM 3-D Flyby of
91S
1/29/2014

GPM Core
Observatory:
Paper ...
1/29/2014

**Links to more
pages of results**

Earth | NASA
www.nasa.gov/topics/earth/index.html
... app immerses users in dazzling visualizations of near-real-time global climate data

Source: Nasa.gov

Figure 2.16 *Search results on the NASA website.*

4. Scroll through the results to find an item that interests you. Click the link and read the first paragraph of the article. Use the Back button to return to the main list and read parts of one or two other articles.

5. Open *Word* and start a new, blank document. Summarize in a paragraph what you read in the three articles. Save the document as *9b nasa* and close it.

Activity 2

1. If necessary, log on to the Internet and start your browser. In the address bar, key **nps.gov**. This is the URL for the U.S. National Park Service website.

2. On the welcome screen, look for a search box. Key the name of a U.S. national park in the search box. For example, you could key **Yosemite** or **Yellowstone**. Click **Search** or the button provided to start the search.

3. Scroll through the hits to find an item that interests you. Click the link and read the first paragraph of the article. Use the Back button if desired and read one or two more articles.

4. Open a new, blank *Word* document. Write a short statement summarizing what you read in each of your three articles from this exercise. Save the document as *9b nps* and close it.

Activity 3

1. If necessary, log on to the Internet and start *Internet Explorer*. Use the History feature to go to the U.S. National Park Service website (http://www.nps.gov).

2. Add this site to your Favorites list.

3. In the site's search box, key **Yellowstone**. Click **Search** or the button provided to start the search.

KEYBOARDING SKILLBUILDING

Warmup Practice

Key each line twice. If time permits, key the lines again.

Alphabetic

1 Jack Vezquil and six women had fun at a big party.

Figure

2 Flight 9804 sat at Gate 367 for 125 minutes or so.

Speed

3 The busy girls may wish to visit the town chapels.

gwam 1' | 1 | 2 | 3 | 4 | 5 | 6 | 7 | 8 | 9 | 10 |

Tabulation Practice

Set tabs at 2.5" and 4.5". Key the text at right. Key three 1' timings. For each timing, try to increase the amount of text you key.

TECHNIQUE TIP
Reach out with your little finger and tap the ENTER key quickly. Return your finger to the home key.

Arkansas	Kentucky	Louisiana
Little Rock	Frankfort	Baton Rouge
Delaware	Massachusetts	Michigan
Dover	Boston	Lansing
Idaho	Missouri	Montana
Boise	Jefferson City	Helena
Kansas	New Hampshire	New Jersey
Topeka	Concord	Trenton

Improve Keying Technique

Key each line twice, striving to maintain a continuous pace.

TECHNIQUE TIP
Think, say, and key the words as words, not letter by letter.

3rd row

1 it up tie yet toy put wet you true quiet were ripe

2 us we or pop top toe pew rope your pout ripe equip

Home row

3 lad ask add had gas sad ash lash half sash haggles

4 has gaff asks fall glass hall lads adds gash lakes

Bottom row

5 can zinc numb van oxen climb bronze buzz cave back

6 man exact bunk noun event vacancy convene minimize

gwam 1' | 1 | 2 | 3 | 4 | 5 | 6 | 7 | 8 | 9 | 10 |

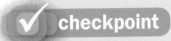

4. Open a new, blank *Word* document.

5. Read the items in the search results as needed and answer the following questions in your document:

   • In what state(s) is the park located?

   • What is the size of the park?

   • When was the park established as a park?

   • What are some of the main attractions of the park?

6. Save the document as *9b questions* and close it.

checkpoint

Compare your answers with those of a classmate. If the first two answers differ, check the website again for accurate information.

9C

Search the Entire Web

TIP To learn more about search engines, visit a site such as Search Engine Showdown (http://www .searchengineshowdown .com). The site provides detailed comparisons of various search engines.

It is one thing to search a site such as NASA with thousands of pages of information. It is quite another to search the entire Internet containing billions of possible results. Articles and reports can be found on almost any topic from millions of sites. Finding the exact information you need can be a challenge.

Web-based search engines can help you meet this challenge. A search engine is a program that performs keyword searches to pinpoint the Internet content you need.

To use a search engine, log on to the Internet and open your browser. Key the URL of any search engine in the address bar. The addresses of some common search tools are listed here:

• Google   google.com

• Yahoo!   yahoo.com

• Ask   ask.com

Narrow a Search

You will often need to narrow your search results by adding keywords to your search phrase, as you learn in the next activity.

1. If necessary, start your browser and key **google.com** (or pick another search tool) in the address bar; then tap ENTER.

2. Key the words **hiking trails** in the search window shown in Figure 2.17 and tap ENTER.

Figure 2.17 *Google search engine*

Complete a Worksheet

1. Open the workbook *df c11 statistics*.

2. Wrap the text in row 1 so the long headings will appear on two lines. Adjust the width of any column to format the headings correctly. Use Bottom Align.

3. In cell N1, key **Batting Average**. Wrap the text if it does not wrap automatically. In column N, rows 2 through 17, calculate each player's batting average by dividing Hits by At Bats. Use three decimal places.

4. In cell A18, key **Totals** and center it in cells A18:C18. In row 18, columns D through M, calculate the totals for each column. In cell N18, compute the team batting average.

5. In cell A19, key **Least** and center it in cells A19:C19. In cell A20, key **Most** and center it in cells A20:C20. In cell A21, key **Average** and center it in A21:C21.

6. In row 19, record the lowest value for rows 2 through 17 in each column in columns D through M.

7. In row 20, record the highest value for rows 2 through 17 in columns D through M.

8. In row 21, record the average value for rows 2 through 17 in columns D through M. Express the averages in D21:M21 as whole numbers.

9. Insert one row at the top of the worksheet. In row 1, key **CRENSHAW CROWS BASEBALL STATISTICS**. Center the title across columns A through N.

10. Format the worksheet to make it easy to read by changing font sizes and effects, alignment, column widths, row heights, etc. Change the orientation to Landscape, center the worksheet horizontally and vertically, and print it on one page.

11. Save the workbook as *c11 statistics* and close it.

3. Open a new, blank *Word* document. Save the document as *9c search*. Record the number of results you received. As illustrated in Figure 2.18, the results probably number in the millions.

Instant Message

You will see *sponsored links* at the right side (or sometimes at the top) of your results. These links are advertisements sponsored by companies that want to sell products. Unless you plan on buying something, do not click sponsored links or you'll see an advertisement.

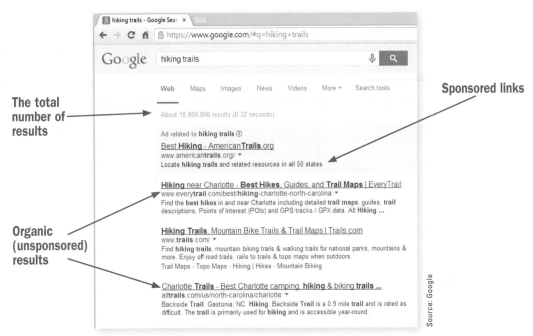

The total number of results

Sponsored links

Organic (unsponsored) results

Figure 2.18 *A few keywords can produce millions of results.*

4. Scroll down and review the organic, or unsponsored, results that have been returned. Notice that they can encompass any hiking and/or hiking trail–related topics. For example:

- Mountain bike trails
- Hiking trails nearby
- Day hiking trails
- Trails for all-terrain vehicles
- Dog-friendly trails

Since these results are so broad, we will narrow the search geographically.

5. Key the search words **hiking trails north carolina** and tap ENTER.

6. In your *9c search* document, record how many results you received when you limited the search by geographical location.

These results are still a little broader than you may need. So we will narrow the search further to include only information on trails you can hike in North Carolina parks.

7. Key **hiking trails north carolina parks** as shown in Figure 2.19 and tap ENTER.

Figure 2.19 *Narrow your search.*

	A	B	C	D	E	F
13	Homziak	95	98	98	97	98
14	Macy	80	75	83	90	95
15	Mahli	95	96	100	97	100
16	Rice	95	92	100	93	95
17	Robins	68	92	92	93	93
18	Tarzia	77	94	90	80	95
19	Vazza	71	88	96	85	93
20	Wayne	84	96	96	98	95
21	Wehner	67	72	85	92	88
22	Zehnder	86	94	94	80	100
23	Zigerell	80	96	94	90	95

5. In column G, use AutoSum to calculate the total points for all test scores for each student.

6. In column H, enter a formula to calculate an average point score for each student. Format the cells for one decimal place.

7. In cell B24, enter a formula to find the average test score for Test 1. Copy the formula to cells C24:F24. Format the cells for one decimal place.

8. In cell B25, enter a formula to find the highest test score for Test 1. Copy the formula to cells C25:F25.

9. In cell B26, enter a formula to find the lowest test score for Test 1. Copy the formula to cells C26:F26.

10. Apply a bottom border to cells A2:H2 and to cells B23:H23. Apply bold to cells A24:A26. Set the column width for all columns to 9.

11. Delete the row that contains data for Homziak.

12. Sort the data in rows 3 through 22 by the Average column in descending order and then by the Student column in ascending order.

13. Select cells **B2:F2**, hold down CTRL, and select cells **B23:F23**. Create a column chart from this data. For the chart title, key **AVERAGE TEST GRADES**. Place the chart below the data on the worksheet so it appears to be centered below the worksheet.

14. Center the data horizontally and vertically on the page. Preview the data and scale it to fit on one page, if necessary, so the worksheet and the chart are printed on the same page.

15. Save the workbook as *c11 grades* and close it.

8. In your *9c search* document, record how many results you received. Compare the total number of results with each succeeding search.

9. Close your browser. Save the *Word* document and close it.

Analyze Search Results

Search results may contain dozens, thousands, hundreds of thousands, or even millions of entries. The main lists of results are often called **organic results**. (See Figure 2.18.) These results occur naturally based on the search criteria and the detailed mathematics applied by Google or another search engine. They are *not* influenced by advertising dollars.

Depending on the search tool, you may see a heading for **sponsored links**. (See Figure 2.18.) These links often appear shaded in color, flanking the results on the side and/or near the top. Advertisers have paid to list these sites. They may not be the most relevant to your search if you are looking for academic information. However, if you are looking to buy something, they may be exactly what you want.

21st Century Skills

Access and Evaluate Information

The Internet and World Wide Web have given computer users quick and easy access to information on virtually any topic. But how do you know that the information is accurate, timely, and written by a reliable and knowledgeable source? Following are some tips:

- Verify any information by checking another source.

- Identify the author or organization that publishes or sponsors the site and identify the date the content was created or last updated.

- On the home page, look for a statement or purpose for the site.

- Examine the language of the site. Does it provide facts, opinions, or both? A reliable site should present information in a balanced and objective manner and should be free of spelling and grammatical errors.

Think Critically

Open a new word processing document and compose your answers to the questions below.

1. Why is it important to evaluate information you read on the Web?

2. Do you think the Internet is as reliable a source of information for computer help as the documentation that comes with your computer or software?

3. Describe ways in which you evaluate information you obtain in various formats, including the Internet, television, print publications, and in person.

4. Save as directed by your teacher.

© LIUSHENGFILM/Shutterstock.Com

Before You Move On

Answer **True** or **False** to each question to review what you have learned in Chapter 11.

1. Each workbook can contain only one worksheet. LO 72A

2. A worksheet has rows that run vertically and columns that run horizontally. LO 72A

3. Letters are used to identify worksheet columns. LO 72A

4. Cells can be merged in a word processing table but not in a worksheet. LO 73E

5. By default, numbers are automatically right-aligned when they are entered. LO 72D

6. A worksheet can be printed with or without gridlines. LO 72E

7. The contents of one cell cannot be copied to more than one other cell. LO 74C

8. More than one row or column can be inserted or deleted at the same time. LO 76A

9. A function is a predefined formula. LO 74C

10. The contents of a cell can be cleared, but the format cannot be cleared. LO 75C

11. Words in a worksheet can be sorted only in ascending order. LO 76B

12. An *Excel* worksheet can be prepared in a *Word* document. LO 76D

13. Charts that have a title should not have a legend. LO 77A

14. Bar charts present information in vertical columns. LO 77A

15. Chart titles and legends are included in the default chart elements. LO 77A

Applying What You Have Learned

Data Files:

df c11 grades
df c11 statistics

Create Worksheet and Chart

1. Open the workbook *df c11 grades*.

2. Insert a row above row 1. In cell A1, key **HEALTH TEST GRADES** for the worksheet title. Apply bold and a 14-point size to the title. Center the title across columns A through H.

3. Apply bold and center alignment to the column heads in row 2.

4. Insert rows so you can key the following data beginning with row 13. Key the data as shown.

TIP Results are sorted by order of relevance. This means that the websites or documents most likely to contain the information you want are listed first. But if you do not get the information you want, you may need to improve your keyword choices and try again.

As you surf the Internet looking for information, remember some of these important Google tips.

- Search engines such as Google find the **stem** of a word (for example, *hike*) and include related words with different endings or tenses in the search (for example, *hiking*, *hiker*, and *hiked*).

- Do not worry about capitalization. *North Carolina* is the same as *north carolina.*

- If you use multiple words such as *hiking trail parks*, you will receive a list of results that correlates with all three words. But the correlation may be random. For example, you may be taken to a Web article that contains information about *locations you can mountain bike, parks that allow use of all-terrain vehicles.* This may not be at all what you are seeking.

- You can turn individual words into phrases by using quotation marks; for example, *"appalachian trail."* This is called **phrase searching**. The quotation marks force a search for the exact sequence of words enclosed within the marks.

- Google throws out small or insignificant words such as *and*, *I*, *it*, *the*, and *or* and single digits such as *1* and *7*. This helps speed up the search, so do not bother entering them.

- If a normally insignificant word is absolutely essential to the success of a search, put a + directly in front of it preceded by a space; for example, *+1.*

In the next activity, you will use phrase searching to locate a specific Utah ski resort high in the Wasatch Mountains east of Salt Lake City (SLC), Utah. Imagine that you can recall only the vaguest details but do remember that it is in *Big Cottonwood Canyon.*

© Patrik Mezirka/Shutterstock.com

Figure 2.20 *Finding what you are looking for is easy online.*

1. Start your browser if necessary and key the address **google.com**.

2. Key the words **big cottonwood canyon** within quotation marks following your other search words:

ski snowboard utah "big cottonwood canyon"

TIP Use the exact name, **Solitude Mountain Resort**, to narrow your search further. Did you find http://www.skisolitude.com?

3. Open a new, blank *Word* document. Record how many results came from your query. Did Google return results and links that mention the Solitude Mountain Resort? If so, record a few samples in your notes.

Instant Message The *I'm Feeling Lucky* option on Google will take you directly to Google's most relevant website result for your query.

3. Chart the data using a chart style you choose. Include all default chart elements; however, you may include additional ones.

4. Save the workbook as *77d report*, print the chart and data on the same worksheet, and close the workbook.

 **checkpoint** Compare your chart with that of a few classmates and discuss if all present the data in an accurate, attractive, and easy-to-read format.

21st Century Skills

Productivity and Accountability

Spreadsheets are a powerful tool for calculating, managing, and analyzing numerical data. Businesses use spreadsheets to record market research, measure performance, and create financial documents. Another valuable use of spreadsheets is creating charts and graphs to help illustrate complex numerical information and identify trends.

Assume you are the production manager for a manufacturing company. You want to analyze the productivity of workers on first shift (6 a.m.–2 p.m.), second shift (2 p.m.–10 p.m.), and third shift (10 p.m.–6 a.m.). To do this, you have collected the following information on the number of units produced per shift.

	Shift 1	Shift 2	Shift 3
Monday	145	120	109
Tuesday	147	119	112
Wednesday	144	123	112
Thursday	147	125	111
Friday	140	124	110

1. Open a new workbook and enter the data shown above.

2. Create a column chart to illustrate the number of units produced per shift. Save the workbook as directed by your teacher.

3. Evaluate the chart. What might account for the lower outputs for shifts 2 and 3?

4. Click the down arrow by the web address for Solitude Mountain Resort. Choose the **Similar** link. See Figure 2.21. Notice that pages with a high correlation to the page you just selected are revealed. Use this technique when you want to dig deeper into a topic.

Down arrow

Solitude Mountain Resort & Ski Vacation | Utah Ski Resorts
www.skisolitude.com/ ▾ Solitude Mountain Resort ▾
Check out the latest in s ⎡ Cached ⎤ ⎤oard equipment from DPS, Elan, Soul Poles,
Surface Skis and many ⎣ ⎦ for a meet and greet with several U.S. ...
Season Passes - Lodgir ⎣ Similar ◄ ⎦ent - Summer
                                       └Step 4

Figure 2.21 *Locate similar results.*

5. In your document, copy the top three URLs for the results you found similar to the Solitude Mountain Resort.

6. Save the document as *9d search* and close it.

9E

Power Search Techniques

Searches are much easier, more powerful, and more fun than they were in the past. In this next activity, you will try some powerful search techniques. You will:

- Search for the types of books you like to read.

- Query for a definition by entering the **define** operator.

- Search for a street map by entering an address along with the city and state.

- Query a stock quote by entering the appropriate ticker symbol.

- Conduct queries to find the weather in a city or at an airport.

- Search for great places to eat in Utah.

- Use the negative operator (–) to exclude things you do not want in your search.

- Pose queries in the form of natural questions.

Todd Gipstein/National Geographic Creative

Figure 2.22 *Try new keyword combinations to improve your search results.*

Chart Styles button that can be used to change the overall appearance of your chart, including the color of bars, columns, lines, pie slices, etc. The bottom button, Chart Filters, can be used to choose the data points and names to display on the chart.

In this activity, you will change layout and styles of two charts.

1. Open *77a sales* and click the chart to select it. Click the **Chart Elements** button.

2. To display data labels in the chart, check the **Data Labels** box. Notice that values for each column have been inserted above that column.

3. To display axis titles in the chart, check the **Axis Titles** box. Notice that Axis Title boxes have been inserted to the left of the vertical axis and below the horizontal axis. Click the vertical axis box, key **Sales**, and then click outside the box. *Sales* will display as the axis title. Click the horizontal axis box, key **Salesperson**, and then click outside the box to display *Salesperson* as the axis title.

TIP If you cannot see the axis title box clearly, resize the chart by selecting a corner sizing handle and dragging it outward until the axis title box is clearly visible.

4. To change the chart style, click the **Chart Styles** button (the middle button) and scroll through the options. Select **Style 8** from the options.

5. Save the workbook as *77c sales* and close it.

6. Open *77a school*.

7. Display the chart with axis titles and data labels, and without gridlines.

8. Key **Grade** as the vertical axis title and **Students** for the horizontal axis title.

9. Choose a chart style that you prefer.

10. Save the workbook as *77c school*, print the chart and the data on the same worksheet, and close the workbook.

77D

Worksheet and Chart

1. Open a new workbook.

2. Key the following in the worksheet, formatting the data so it is attractive and easy to read.

MONTHLY SALES				
Month	George Aiken	Pedro Aramez	Carla Homas	Kris Nedra
July	$ 66	$ 82	$ 75	$ 78
August	$ 64	$ 77	$ 68	$ 68
September	$ 69	$ 66	$ 70	$ 80
October	$ 58	$ 74	$ 72	$ 69
November	$ 63	$ 76	$ 69	$ 74
December	$ 64	$ 68	$ 67	$ 76

1. Start a new, blank *Word* document and save it as *9e search*; then start your browser if necessary. Go to **google.com.**

2. Search for the following books:

   books about skiing

   books on snowboarding

3. Conduct a search for the types of books you like to read. List the top three results in your *9e search* document.

4. Find a map for a location near Solitude Mountain Resort by keying the following:

   12000 e big cottonwood canyon rd ut

   or

   12000 e big cottonwood canyon rd 84121

5. Click the map to expand it. Use the zoom control to move out from the location until you see the entire state of Utah.

6. Use your street address and ZIP Code to find a map that zooms in on your street in your community.

7. Conduct a query to find the current stock price for Google, Apple, and Microsoft. Use the following ticker symbols:

   goog

   aapl

   msft

   Record the price of all three stocks in the *9e search* document.

8. Find the weather in Salt Lake City, which is about 30 miles from Solitude Mountain Resort. Key the following:

   weather slc

   or

   weather slc airport

   Record the current conditions in the *9e search* document.

9. Find a list of great restaurants in Utah, but exclude Italian food. Key the following: **utah restaurants –Italian**.

   Record the three top results in the *9e search* document.

10. Find a list of restaurants in your area, but exclude fast-food restaurants. How complete a list did you obtain? Key the number in the *9e search* document.

11. Use a natural question to find answers to the following queries:

    What is the population of Utah?

    Who is the governor of Utah?

    Record the answers to those questions in the *9e search* document.

Change Chart Type

The chart you initially select to display your data can be changed to other chart types to help you decide which type best displays your data. In addition to column, bar, and pie charts, you can select line, area, and doughnut charts.

In this activity, you will change a column chart to a line chart (see Figure 11.26), a bar chart to an area chart (see Figure 11.27), and a pie chart to a doughnut chart (see Figure 11.28).

Figure 11.26 *Line chart*

Figure 11.27 *Area chart*

Figure 11.28 *Doughnut chart*

SS Insert/Charts/Insert Line Chart

1. Open *77a sales* and click the chart to activate it.
2. Follow the path at the left and select the **Line with Markers** chart type to change the column chart to a line chart.
3. Save the workbook as *77b sales* and close it.
4. Open *77a school* and click the chart to activate it.

SS Insert/Charts/Insert Area Chart

5. Follow the path at the left and select the **Area** chart type to change the bar chart to an area chart.
6. Save the workbook as *77b school* and close it.
7. Open *77a expenses* and click the chart to activate it.

SS Insert/Charts/Insert Pie or Doughnut Chart

8. Follow the path at the left and select the **Doughnut** chart type to change the pie chart to a doughnut chart.
9. Save the workbook as *77b expenses* and close it.

Change Chart Layout and Styles

Once you have created a chart, you can change the chart layout to display chart parts such as axis titles, data labels, gridlines, etc., that are not displayed in the default layout. Also, you can choose not to display chart parts such as the chart title and legend that are displayed in the default chart layout.

The three buttons shown in Figure 11.29 appear at the right of a selected chart. The Chart Elements button (the plus sign icon) shows the list of major chart elements you can display or not display in your chart. Those with a checkmark display, and those not checked will not display. You can change what is displayed by adding or removing checks. The middle button is the

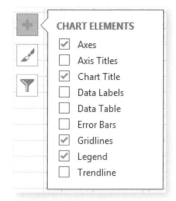

Figure 11.29 *Chart Elements, Chart Styles, and Chart Filters buttons*

12. Define and record three words you do not know the meaning of. Use the define operator followed by the word. For example:

define: snowboarding

define: skiing

13. Save your answers and notes in the *9e search* document and close it.

Wikipedia

One of the most exciting resources on the Web is called Wikipedia. Visit Wikipedia by keying wikipedia.org into your browser. See Figure 2.23.

Wikipedia is an online encyclopedia. It can be edited by nearly anyone in the world. It allows people with different backgrounds and knowledge to collaborate and research together. This can be a great thing, having the collective wisdom of thousands. Then again, some of those contributors may be wrong about the facts. So it is up to the Wikipedia community to patrol the pages for accuracy.

Wikipedia has become so popular that you often find that a Wikipedia article will be the first, second, or third result in a search query. Search queries are chosen by how relevant they are and by how many people link to those sites. Clearly, if Wikipedia comes up in the top ten results, hundreds of millions of people are choosing Wikipedia as a key source of information.

However, never limit yourself to just one resource. Always check what you learn on Wikipedia with other resources. Always double-check the accuracy of the information presented on any website. Do not limit yourself to just one source.

Figure 2.23 *Visit Wikipedia for answers.*

Source: Wikipedia.org

1. Start your browser if necessary and go to **wikipedia.org**.

2. If necessary, choose the language you want to search (probably English).

3. Use Wikipedia's search capabilities to learn more about space exploration. Key the following search query: **space exploration**.

4. Reopen your *Word* document called *9b nasa*. At the end of the page, list five key milestones or key events in space exploration history.

5. Save the document as *9b nasa wikipedia* and close it.

In this activity, you will prepare a column, bar, and pie chart using the default chart style and default chart elements. Default chart elements include a **chart title** that identifies the chart contents and a **legend** that identifies the chart's data categories. The charts you will create are shown in Figures 11.23, 11.24, and 11.25.

Figure 11.23 *Column chart*

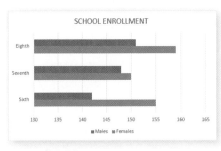

Figure 11.24 *Bar chart*

Figure 11.25 *Pie chart*

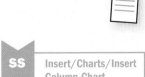

1. Open the workbook *df 77a sales*.

2. Begin a column chart by selecting cells **A2:C5** as the range of cells to be charted.

3. Follow the path at the left to display column chart types. Click **Clustered Column** in the 2-D Column section.

4. Click the **Chart Title** text box and key **SALES REPORT** as the chart title. Click outside the text box to enter the text. Notice that the chart has a legend as well as the chart contents.

5. To print just the chart, select the chart and then print it as you would print other worksheets. To print both the chart and the data on the worksheet, select the chart, move it to the left below the data, click outside the chart area, and then print. In this activity, print just the chart.

6. Save the workbook as *77a sales* and close it.

7. Open *df 77a school*.

8. Begin a bar chart by selecting cells **A2:C5** as the range of cells to be charted.

9. Follow the path at the left to display bar chart types. Click **Clustered Bar** in the 2-D Bar section.

10. Key **SCHOOL ENROLLMENT** as the chart title.

11. Print the chart and the data on one worksheet (refer to step 5 above, if needed).

12. Save the workbook as *77a school* and close it.

13. Open the workbook *df 77a expenses*.

14. Begin a pie chart by selecting cells **A2:B7** as the range of cells to be charted.

15. Follow the path at the left to display pie chart types. Click **3-D Pie** in the 3-D Pie section.

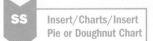

16. Key **MONTHLY EXPENSES** as the chart title.

17. Print the chart on the page without the data.

18. Save the workbook as *77a expenses* and close it.

The SS path labels at left:

Insert/Charts/Insert Column Chart

Insert/Charts/Insert Bar Chart

Insert/Charts/Insert Pie or Doughnut Chart

Basics of Good Digital Citizenship

Data File:

df 10a opportunity

Learning Outcomes

In Lesson 10, you will:

10A *Learn about ethics and netiquette rules.*

10B *Learn about computer crime.*

10C *Learn about safety issues related to using the Internet.*

10D *Learn about copyright issues.*

10A

Ethics and Netiquette

Computer users must be concerned with ethics related to information and networks. **Ethics** are moral standards or values. They describe how people should behave. **Netiquette** is a term often used to describe rules for proper online behavior.

To communicate successfully, you follow certain rules of ethical behavior. For example, you would not answer your cell phone and start shouting at someone. That would be considered rude. You also should follow rules of polite behavior when communicating online. The word *netiquette* is formed from the words *etiquette* (the requirements for proper social behavior) and *net* (from the word *Internet*).

Some netiquette rules relate to email and instant messages. For example, do not key or text in ALL CAPS. That is like shouting your message and is considered rude. Here are some other netiquette rules that you should know.

- Do not give out phone numbers or other personal information unless you are sure the site is safe.

- Never give out personal information about other people without their permission.

- Do not forward messages from other people without their permission.

- Send information only to those who need it. Busy people do not want to spend time reading messages that do not relate to them.

- Do not send large attachments without the receiver's permission.

- Do not send spam. **Spam** includes any unsolicited or unwanted message.

- Be courteous to others in all online messages and on web pages. Do not use offensive or biased language.

- Respect the privacy of others. Do not read email or other material that is meant for someone else.

- Assume that messages (email, instant messages, phone conversations, blog postings, and *Facebook* postings) are not secure. Do not include private information.

- Be ethical. Do not copy material from the Web and use it as your own without paying for it and listing it as a source.

- Do not use another person's computer or cell phone without his or her permission.

- Do not use the Internet for anything that is illegal.

5. In cell A6, key **Totals**. In cells B6:G6, find the sum of the children from age 0 to 17.

6. Center-align all cell contents; use one decimal place for numbers in cells B3:G6; bold the entries in rows 1, 2, and 6.

7. When the worksheet is completed, use the bottom sizing handle to hide all rows below row 6. (Only rows 1 through 6 should be visible, as shown in Figure 11.22.)

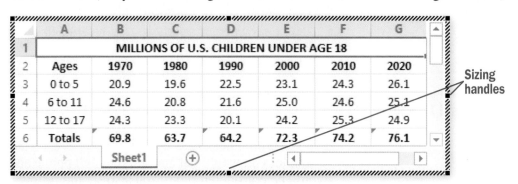

Figure 11.22 *Resize the worksheet to hide unused rows.*

8. Click outside the worksheet to view the worksheet object in the document. If necessary, insert/delete space above and below the worksheet to balance the white space around the worksheet. *Note:* If you need to return to the *Excel* worksheet to make changes, double-click the worksheet object—*Excel* will reopen.

9. Save the document as *76d memo*. Print the memo. Close *Word*.

Lesson 77

Worksheets with Charts

Learning Outcomes

In Lesson 77, you will:

Data Files:

df 77a sales
df 77a school
df 77a expenses

77A Create column, bar, and pie charts.
77B Change chart type.
77C Change chart layouts and styles.
77D Create a worksheet and chart.

77A

Column, Bar, and Pie Charts

Charts are important because they show information graphically. This allows the audience to better understand the data. You can create many different kinds of charts with spreadsheet software, including column, bar, and pie charts. **Column charts** and **bar charts** compare values across categories of data. **Pie charts** show what percentage each value is of a total value. If you need help deciding which chart type to use, you can use *Excel*'s Recommended Charts feature.

COLLABORATION

1. Start *Word.* Open the document *df 10a opportunity.* Read the email message contained in this document.

2. Work with one or two classmates to evaluate the email message. Does the message follow netiquette rules (listed in the previous section)? On a separate sheet of paper, make a list of any rules this message violates.

3. Can your team identify any potential problems with the offer being made in this message? If so, list them.

4. Compare your team's responses to other teams in your class. Discuss any differences in team responses.

Computer Crime

Individuals and businesses alike can be victims of computer-related crime. People and companies must be careful to protect their private data. They also must protect the data gathered from others. For example, companies may have medical records or credit card numbers of customers. Those records are often stored on computers. This makes the records vulnerable to computer crime.

Computer Viruses and Hackers

One type of illegal activity related to computing is spreading computer viruses. A **computer virus** is a destructive program. A virus can be loaded onto a computer and run without the computer owner's knowledge. Viruses are dangerous. They can destroy data quickly. They also can cause a computer or network to stop working properly. Some viruses can travel across networks and get past security systems. Antivirus programs can find and remove viruses before they do harm. To protect their data, users should back up (make a copy of) important data and keep it in a safe place.

Another computer crime is called **hacking**. Hacking is accessing computers or networks without permission. People who do this are called **hackers**. Hacking is both unethical and illegal. Penalties for hacking can be up to 20 years in prison!

Hackers may be able to access and misuse information that belongs to others. For example, a hacker might steal a customer's credit card number to buy products over the Internet. This is an example of computer fraud.

Identity Theft

Sometimes a criminal may steal more than a credit card number. He or she may steal a person's identity. The criminal will find as much personal information about a victim as possible. For example, bank account numbers, social security numbers, job information, family information, and spending records may be hacked. Personal information also may come from a stolen purse or wallet.

Once a criminal has this type of information, he or she can pretend to be the person who owns that information. This is called **identity theft**. Money may be moved out of the victim's bank account. A new credit card account, using the victim's name, may be opened. Vacations, cars, and other expensive items may be charged to the victim's credit card. When the credit card bills are not paid, the overdue account is reported on the victim's credit report. The victim may be turned down for loans or may not be hired for jobs because of the bad credit report.

Modify a Worksheet

1. Open the workbook *df 76c dinner*. Save the workbook as *76c dinner by ticket*.

2. Select **A2:F2** and use the Wrap Text feature to display the column headings on two lines.

3. Use the AutoFit Column Width feature to adjust the column widths.

4. Click cell **C3**. Sort the data below the column heads by ticket number from smallest to largest.

5. Center the worksheet horizontally and vertically on the page.

6. Access the Print Preview screen (Print on the File tab). Notice that the preview displays page 1 of a two-page worksheet. You can print it on one page by changing the scaling option. Click the No Scaling down arrow in the Settings list. Choose the **Fit Sheet on One Page** option. *Excel* scales down the size of the columns and rows so the worksheet appears on one page.

7. Save the workbook again, but do not close it.

8. Save the *76c dinner by ticket* workbook as *76c dinner by name*.

9. Sort the data below the column heads in ascending order by last name and then by first name. Check to see that the sorted list has the names in alphabetical order.

COLLABORATION

10. Save the workbook again. Print the worksheet with gridlines. Complete the CheckPoint below and then close the workbook.

✓ **checkpoint** Compare your printed worksheet with that of a classmate. Make corrections if necessary.

Create a Worksheet in a Word Processing Document

WP Insert/Tables/Table/ Excel Spreadsheet

In this activity, you will create an *Excel* worksheet in a *Word* document.

1. Start *Word*. Open the document *df 76d memo*.

2. Position the insertion point at the end of the first paragraph and tap ENTER to insert a line. Position the insertion point at the center of the line (Home/Paragraph/Center).

3. Follow the path at the left to insert an *Excel* worksheet in the word processing document.

4. When the *Excel* ribbon and worksheet appear, key the information shown below.

MILLIONS OF U.S. CHILDREN UNDER AGE 18						
Ages	1970	1980	1990	2000	2010	2020
0 to 5	20.9	19.6	22.5	23.1	24.3	26.1
6 to 11	24.6	20.8	21.6	25.0	24.6	25.1
12 to 17	24.3	23.3	20.1	24.2	25.3	24.9

Millions of Americans have been victims of identity theft. Individuals and businesses have lost billions of dollars to this type of crime. The U.S. Federal Trade Commission (FTC) provides resources for victims of identity theft. (See Figure 2.24.) The FTC also provides tips for reducing this crime. To reduce the chances of being a victim of identity theft, you can:

- Request and review a copy of your credit report every year.

- Use strong passwords on credit card, bank, and phone accounts.

- Avoid giving out personal information on the phone, through the mail, or over the Internet unless the site is reputable.

- Shred charge receipts, credit records, checks, and bank statements before throwing them away.

- Keep your social security card and number in a safe place.

- Protect access to home computers and guard against computer viruses.

Figure 2.24 *The U.S. Federal Trade Commission provides resources for identity theft victims.*

Source: Consumer.ftc.gov

Scams

Some criminals run scams on the Internet. A **scam** is a scheme used to take money under false pretenses. For example, someone may want to sell you stolen music or will take your money without sending you the product you bought. To avoid being the victim of a scam, buy only from reputable companies. Do not give out personal information or credit card numbers unless you are certain the company is honest and the website is safe.

5. Verify that the names are sorted in alphabetical order. Verify that the first names also are in alphabetical order when the last names are the same.

6. Set the top margin to 2". Select the option to center the data horizontally on the page. Print the worksheet. Save the workbook, using the same name. Close the workbook.

7. Open the workbook *df 76b art* again. To quickly sort the list by the Period column so the reader can easily see a list of students for each class, select cell **C3**. Follow the *Smallest to Largest* path at the left and select **Sort Smallest to Largest**. Check the sorted data. The information should be sorted by period. The first six names should be the same as those shown in Figure 11.20. Save the workbook as *76c art by period* and close it.

SS   *Smallest to Largest*
Home/Editing/Sort & Filter

	A	B	C
1	ART CLASS ENROLLMENT		
2	Last Name	First Name	Period
3	Graff	Vincent	2
4	Graff	Robert	2
5	Hall	Doris	2
6	Julian	Betty	2
7	Nevin	Stan	2
8	Nevin	Bill	2

Figure 11.20 *Sort by period.*

8. Open the workbook *df 76b art* again. This time you will sort the list by period from smallest to largest and then alphabetically by first and last name within each period.

9. Click cell **A3**. Access and select **Custom Sort**. In the first-level Sort by box, choose **Period**. Click **Add Level** and select **Last Name** in the Then by box. Click **Add Level** and select **First Name** in the second Then by box. Click **OK**.

10. Verify that your list is sorted by period with period 2 listed first and then alphabetically by last name and then first name within each period. The first seven names in your list should be the same as those shown in Figure 11.21.

	A	B	C
1	ART CLASS ENROLLMENT		
2	Last Name	First Name	Period
3	Allen	James	2
4	Biddle	Claire	2
5	Biddle	Mary Ann	2
6	Davis	David	2
7	Davison	Jay	2
8	Graff	Robert	2
9	Graff	Vincent	2

Figure 11.21 *Sort by period and name.*

11. Save the workbook as *76b art by both* and close it.

In this activity, you will access a website that has information about computer crimes. You will follow hyperlinks to find an article about one crime case and print the article.

1. If necessary, log on to the Internet and start *Internet Explorer* or another browser. In the address bar, key **cybercrime.gov**. This site is hosted by the U.S. Department of Justice. (If you are using a different browser, follow the appropriate steps to complete this activity.)

2. Click hyperlinks related to computer crime and computer crime cases. Read about one computer crime case. Ask your instructor or a classmate for help if you cannot find an article.

3. Right-click and then click **Print preview** from the shortcut menu to see how the document will appear when printed. Note the page numbers that include the article you chose. Close Print Preview.

4. Right-click and then click **Print** from the shortcut menu. Select your printer if needed. Choose to print 1 copy of only the pages on which your article appears. Click **Print**.

5. Read the case again from your printed copy. Use a marker or pen to highlight the main points of the article. Be prepared to share these points with the class.

10C

Internet Safety

Using the Internet is a great way to communicate and interact with other people. As in the real world, many people you meet will be honest and kind. They will have no intention of harming you or cheating you. However, as in the real world, some people in the virtual world try to cheat or harm others. For this reason, computer users must be concerned about safety.

Personal Safety

As a computer user, you should be concerned about your personal safety. When you meet someone on the Internet, you have only this person's word about who he or she is. You probably cannot see the person. The person may say that his or her age is 14 when it is really 40. The person may claim to be a woman when he is really a man. The person may pretend to be interested in the things that interest you to gain your trust. The person's real motive may be to deceive you or harm you.

To protect yourself, never give out your full name, personal address, phone number, school address, or other private information to individuals you do not know personally. Never send your picture to someone you do not know personally. Never agree to meet in person someone you have met on the Internet unless you have a parent or guardian present.

The person you meet might really be your age and share your interest in a hobby or sport. In that case, Mom or Dad can wait at the next table while you and your new friend talk and enjoy pizza. Your new friend probably brought Mom or Dad along, too. If the person you meet turns out to be different than you expected, you will be glad you have Mom or Dad nearby.

5. Key the following information in the rows:

| Row 4 | James | 211 | 11 | 83 |
| Row 5 | Long | 197 | 7 | 71 |

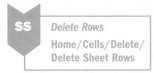

SS *Delete Columns*
Home/Cells/Delete/
Delete Sheet Columns

6. To delete column B, click a cell in column B and then use the ***Delete Columns*** path at the left to select **Delete Sheet Columns**. Column B (Cars) will be deleted and all columns to its right will move to the left. Click the **Undo** button to restore the column.

SS *Delete Rows*
Home/Cells/Delete/
Delete Sheet Rows

7. To delete row 6 (Nedro), point to the row heading, click to select the row, and then use the ***Delete Rows*** path at the left. Row 7 becomes row 6. Click the **Undo** button to restore the row.

8. Save the workbook as *76a vehicles* and close it.

76B

Sort Worksheet Data

As you learned in Lesson 58 of Chapter 7, sorting means arranging or grouping items in a particular order. You can sort data in a worksheet the same way you sort data in a table. Use *ascending* order to arrange text from A to Z or numbers from lowest to highest. Use *descending* order to arrange text from Z to A or numbers from highest to lowest.

You may want to rename and save a workbook before doing a sort. This lets you keep a copy of the information in its original order.

1. Open the workbook *df 76b art*. Save the workbook as *76b art by name*.

2. To sort the data by names in columns A and B in ascending order, click cell **A3**.

SS Home/Editing/Sort &
Filter

3. Follow the path at the left and select **Custom Sort** from the Sort & Filter drop-down list. The Sort dialog box opens.

4. Select **Last Name** in the Sort by box list if necessary. Click the **Add Level** button in the upper-left corner. Click the arrow at the right of the Then by box and choose **First Name**. Verify that the Sort On text boxes display Values and that the Order text boxes display A to Z. The My data has headers checkbox in the upper-right corner of the dialog box should be selected. Your Sort dialog box should match the selections shown in Figure 11.19. Click **OK**.

Figure 11.19 *Sort dialog box*

Safety of Data

Computer users should be concerned about the safety of their private data. Many people buy products from websites. Doctors have patients fill out medical history forms online. Bank customers make transactions online. All of those situations require entering personal information. How can you make sure your data will be safe when you use these kinds of websites?

Reputable companies take measures to ensure that the data will be safe. Internet browsers have built-in features that can help protect your personal information and identity. Settings in your browser help identify unsafe sites and let you set the security levels for trusted sites. A secure site address begins with https://, and a lock icon appears next to the site name in the address bar. See Figure 2.25.

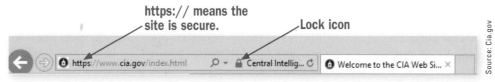

Figure 2.25 *Address bar of a secure website.*

A **digital certificate** verifies the identity of a person or indicates the security of a website. These certificates are issued by trusted companies such as VeriSign. Clicking the lock icon reveals security information about the website (see Figure 2.26). The address bar is color-coded to let you know that your transactions are over a secure connection. For example, red means the certificate is out of date. Green is the most secure. Yellow means the certification authority cannot be verified and there might be a problem.

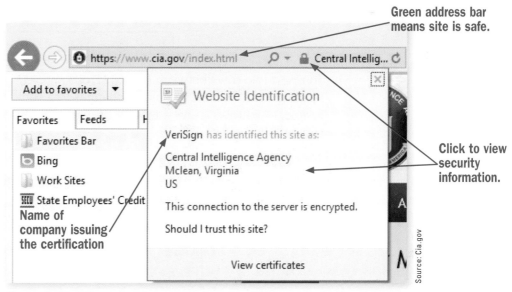

Figure 2.26 *Information about a website's certification.*

Once a company has your private data, it should take measures to keep it safe. Companies can use special hardware and software called **firewalls** to help prevent unauthorized users from getting to your data.

Lesson 76

Enhancing Worksheet Skills

Learning Outcomes

In Lesson 76, you will:

76A *Insert and delete rows and columns.*
76B *Sort worksheet data.*
76C *Modify a worksheet.*
76D *Create a worksheet in a word processing document.*

Data Files:

df 76a vehicles
df 76b art
df 76c dinner
df 76d memo

76A

Insert and Delete Rows and Columns

When you create or edit worksheets, you may find that you need to delete a row or column of data. You also may find that you need to insert a row or column of data. One or more rows or columns can be inserted at a time. Columns may be added at the left edge or within a worksheet. Rows may be added at the top edge or within a worksheet.

1. Open the workbook *df 76a vehicles*.

2. To insert a column between columns B and C, click a cell in column C. Follow the **Insert Columns** path at the left to insert a new column C. Key the following data in the appropriate cells:

Cell C2	Trailers
Cell C3	13
Cell C4	17
Cell C5	21

SS *Insert Columns*
Home/Cells/Insert/
Insert Sheet Columns

3. To insert two rows between rows 3 (Holt) and 4 (Nedro), point to the row 4 heading area. When the pointer changes to a right arrow, click and drag down to select two rows (rows 4 and 5). Release the mouse button. Selected rows are shown in Figure 11.18.

	A	B	C	D
1		**VEHICLE RECORDS**		
2	Name	Cars	Trailers	Vans
3	Holt	225	13	115
4	Nedro	243	17	97
5	Peters	212	21	87
6				

Figure 11.18 *Selected rows*

SS *Insert Rows*
Home/Cells/Insert/
Insert Sheet Rows

4. Use the **Insert Rows** path at the left to insert two new rows. (*Excel* inserts the number of rows that are selected when you click the Insert feature.)

You should be aware of what a company plans to do with your data. Many companies post a privacy policy on their websites. A **privacy policy** is a document that tells how personal data will be used. A link such as *Privacy Statement* or *Privacy Policy* is often shown at the bottom of a site's welcome page. The first part of a typical privacy statement is shown in Figure 2.27. Before entering your data, read the site's privacy policy to see if you approve of how your data will be used.

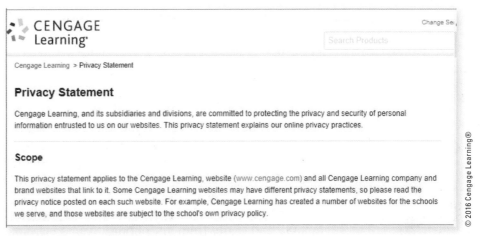

Figure 2.27 *Privacy statement for a website.*

1. If necessary, log on to the Internet and start *Internet Explorer* or another browser. In the address bar, key one of the following URLs or a URL given to you by your teacher.

   google.com

   yahoo.com

   ask.com

2. In the search box, key **online safety**. Click a button such as **Go** or **Search** to begin the search.

3. Scroll down the list of hits. Choose a hit that you think will have an article or tips for online safety. Look at several sites until you find one with good advice about online safety for teens.

4. Add the best site you found to your Favorites list. For this site, list the following information:

   • URL for the website.

   • Website name.

   • Organization that sponsors or posts the site. (*Note*: You may need to follow links such as *About Us* to find the company or organization that sponsors the site.)

   • The type of information you found (article, guidelines or rules, videos, and so on).

5. Share information about the site with your class or a group of classmates as directed by your teacher.

14. In cell F3, enter a formula to calculate the percent the March Savings amount is of the Budget Savings amount. Format cell F3 for Percent Style with no decimal places. Copy the formula to cells F4:F14.

15. AutoFit the column widths and set the top margin to 2". Select the option to center the data horizontally on the page. Print the worksheet with no gridlines.

16. Save the workbook as *75d budget*, print it, and close it.

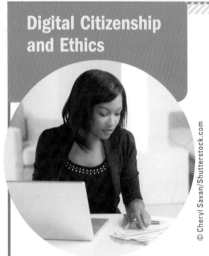

Digital Citizenship and Ethics

Through the Internet, people are now able to conduct many of their banking and financial transactions without ever having to leave their homes. Using electronic fund transfers (EFTs), you can move money from one account to another, make deposits, and pay bills quickly and easily from your home computer. EFTs require that you have electronic access to your bank account and have the authority to conduct transactions. Most people find EFTs to be convenient and effective, but there are some concerns:

- Errors can occur even in an automated system. You should check your account statements diligently.

- Funds are usually released quicker from your accounts than when using a paper system, so you must be sure there is enough money in the account to cover the transaction.

- When paying bills, there is often a two- to four-day processing period, so you must initiate the payment early enough to avoid a late payment and a late fee.

As a class, discuss the following:

1. Provide examples of how you already use EFTs or could use them to manage your personal finances.

2. What security risks should you consider when using EFTs?

© Cheryl Savan/Shutterstock.com

People or companies that create works that are new, useful, and potentially profitable may be granted a copyright for those works. A **copyright** is a form of protection granted by the U.S. government. Copyright laws and rules tell how copyrighted works can be legally used. Works such as books, articles, music, plays, movie scripts, and artwork can be copyrighted. Copyrighted material may carry the © symbol. However, you should assume that material is copyrighted even if you do not see the symbol.

As a general rule, you may not use copyrighted material legally unless you have the owner's permission. However, you may be able to use a small portion of a copyrighted work for educational purposes. The rules that relate to this type of use are called the **fair use doctrine**.

Fair use doctrine does not allow plagiarism. The term **plagiarism** refers to using material created by another person and claiming it as your own. For example, suppose you find a report on the Internet that fits the assignment you were given. You print the report and turn it in with your name as the writer. This is plagiarism. Plagiarism in schoolwork may result in suspension or another serious punishment.

Copyright rules also affect what you can do with some works after you purchase them. For example, movies and music are often sold with certain terms and conditions. These terms may limit how you can use the movie or music. You may be able to make one or two copies of a song for backup purposes or to use on an MP3 player. However, you may not be allowed to make copies of the song to give to friends. In the next activity, you will explore some terms of use for music purchased online.

1. If necessary, log on to the Internet and start *Internet Explorer* or another browser. In the address bar, key one of the following URLs or a URL given to you by your teacher.

   google.com
   yahoo.com
   ask.com

2. In the search box, key **music download**. Click a button such as **Go** or **Search** to begin the search.

3. Choose links in the results list to find a site that sells music online. For example, Amazon.com sells music and books online that you can download. Access the site.

4. If the site has many departments, you may need to choose a link such as *Music*. You may need to choose another link such as *Download Music*. Follow links as needed to reach a page where you can buy and download songs.

5. Follow a link such as *Terms of Sale* or *Usage and License Rules* to learn how you may use the music you purchase from this site. These links are often located at the bottom of the web page. If you have difficulty finding this information, ask your instructor or a classmate.

6. Make a list of the main points given in the terms of use. What copies are you allowed to make? What copying is specifically not allowed? Be prepared to discuss your findings with the class.

1. Open the workbook *df 75c schedule*.

2. Select cell **F2**. Tap the DELETE key. This clears (deletes) the cell contents only; the cell format remains. In cell F2, key **Friday** and tap ENTER. Notice that the text appears in bold because the format was not deleted.

3. Select cell **B5**. Press the CTRL key and click cell **B7**. Both cells should be selected. Still pressing the CTRL key, click cell **D5**. All of these cells should be selected (highlighted). Release the CTRL key.

COLLABORATION

4. Click the **Clear** button in the Editing group on the Home tab. Choose **Clear Formats** as shown in Figure 11.17. The data will remain, but the bold format will be removed from these cells.

5. Select cells **A10:F11**. Click the **Clear** button and choose **Clear All** to clear the contents and formats in these cells.

✓ checkpoint

Compare your printed copy with that of a classmate to see if the contents and formats have been deleted or cleared correctly.

6. Select the remaining names that have bold or italic format. Clear the cell formats.

7. Center the worksheet horizontally and vertically and print it with gridlines.

8. Save the workbook as *75c schedule* and close it.

75D

Modify a Worksheet

1. Open the workbook *df 75d budget*.

2. Change cell A1 to **BUDGET AND MONTHLY EXPENSES**. Apply 14-point bold formatting. Center the title over columns A through F.

3. Apply center alignment and bold to the column heads in row 2.

4. Use Cut and Paste to move the data in cells A18:B18 to cells A3:B3.

5. Clear the contents of cells A16:E17.

6. Change the value in cell E15 to **95**.

7. Copy cell B3 to cells C3:E3. Copy cell B4 to cells C4:E4.

8. Clear the contents in cells A10:B10.

9. Move cells A15:E15 to A10:E10.

10. Apply a bottom border to cells B14:E14.

11. Enter formulas in cells B15:E15 to calculate the sum of the numbers in columns B, C, D, and E.

12. Select cells **B3:E15** and apply the Accounting number format with no decimal places.

13. Go to cell F2 and key **March %**. Apply bold and center alignment if it is not applied automatically.

Peter Dazeley/The Image Bank/Getty Images

COLLABORATION

A **cyber predator** is someone who uses the Internet to hunt for victims whom they take advantage of in many ways—sexually, emotionally, psychologically, or financially. Cyber predators know how to manipulate kids. They create trust and friendship where none should exist.

Cyber predators are the dark side of social networking and other forms of online communication. They frequently log on to chat groups or game sites and pose as other kids. They try to gradually gain your trust and encourage you to talk about your problems. Even if you don't chat with strangers, personal information you post on sites such as *Facebook* can make you a target.

As a class, discuss the following.

1. Give examples of how to identify a cyber predator.

2. How can you avoid being the victim of a cyber predator?

3. What should you do if you receive a message that is suggestive, obscene, aggressive, or threatening?

4. You also can change a column width by using the AutoFit Column Width feature. Click the column C heading to select the column. Click the **Format** button on the Home tab. Select **AutoFit Column Width** in the Cell Size section. (See Figure 11.16.) The width will become wide enough to accommodate the longest item in the column.

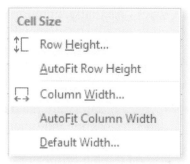

Figure 11.16 *AutoFit Column Width feature*

5. Another way to change the column width using the mouse is to move your pointer to the right border of the column heading area. When the pointer changes to a two-sided arrow, drag the right column border so it is slightly wider than the longest item in the column. Release the mouse button, and the column width will change. Use this procedure to change the width of column D.

6. Select the row 1 content. Increase the font size from 11 to 14. Notice that the row height increases automatically to fit the larger font size.

7. Select cell **C2**. Key **Requested** before *Position*. Wrap the text in cell C2.

8. To make rows 3 through 8 taller, select the row headings for rows 3 through 8. Click **Format** on the Home tab and then click **Row Height** to open the Row Height dialog box. Key **20** in the Row Height dialog box. Click **OK**.

9. Save the workbook as *75b players* and close it.

75C

Clear and Delete Cell Contents and/or Formats

When you select one or more cells to edit the cell contents, only the text or numbers are changed. If the cell has been formatted, any new text you key will have the same format. As shown in Figure 11.17, you can use the Clear button to clear the contents of a cell (Clear Contents), the format of a cell (Clear Formats), or both (Clear All).

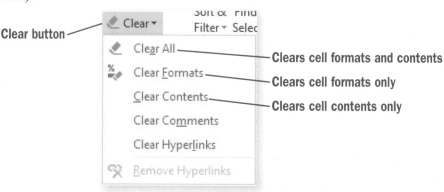

Figure 11.17 *Clear options*

Before You Move On

Answer these questions to review what you have learned in Chapter 2.

1. Describe early computers in terms of how big they were and what they could do. LO 7A

2. In what year were notebook computers introduced? LO 7A

3. A measure of how much work can be done in a certain amount of time is called _____. LO 7B

4. List three ways that computers are used in everyday life. LO 7C

5. When one computer links to another computer, a(n) _____ is created. LO 8A

6. What is the Internet? LO 8A

7. What is e-commerce? LO 8A

8. What is an Internet service provider? Give two examples of ISPs. LO 8B

9. A program that lets you find and view web pages is called a(n) _____. LO 8C

10. To go to a certain website, what do you key in the browser's address bar? LO 8D

11. What happens when a user clicks a hyperlink on a web page? LO 8D

12. Explain what the History feature and the Favorites feature of a browser allow you to do. LO 9A

13. Items in a search results list are called _____. LO 9B

14. A website that allows you to enter search criteria and find related websites is called a(n) _____. LO 9C

15. Define the terms *ethics* and *netiquette*. LO 10A

16. Give examples of three different types of computer-related crime. LO 10B

17. What can you do to protect your personal safety online? LO 10C

18. What color code lets you know that your transactions are over a secure connection? LO 10C

19. What can you do to protect the safety of your personal data online? LO 10C

20. What is a copyright? LO 10D

1. Open the workbook *df 75a lockers.*
2. Select cell **C4**. Click the Formula bar. Tap the BACKSPACE or DELETE key to delete **8**. Key **7**. Tap ENTER.
3. Select cell **A6** and replace *Jane* with **Dora**.
4. Select cell **B8**. Click the Formula bar. Delete the digit **2** in the locker number. Key a **4** in its place so the number is 86640.
5. Print the worksheet with gridlines, a 2" top margin, and centered horizontally.
6. Save the workbook as *75a lockers* and close it.

75B

Change Column Width and Row Height

You can use several methods to change the column width and row height in a worksheet. You can specify a column width or row height. You can change the column width and row height by using the mouse. You can use the AutoFit Column Width or AutoFit Row Height features. By default, row height changes automatically to fit the largest font used in a row.

SS Home/Cells/Format

1. Open the workbook *df 75b players.*
2. To set the width of column A to 10 characters, select any cell in column A. Follow the path at the left and click **Column Width** in the Cell Size section of the Format drop-down menu. Key **10** in the Column Width dialog box as shown in Figure 11.14. Click **OK**.

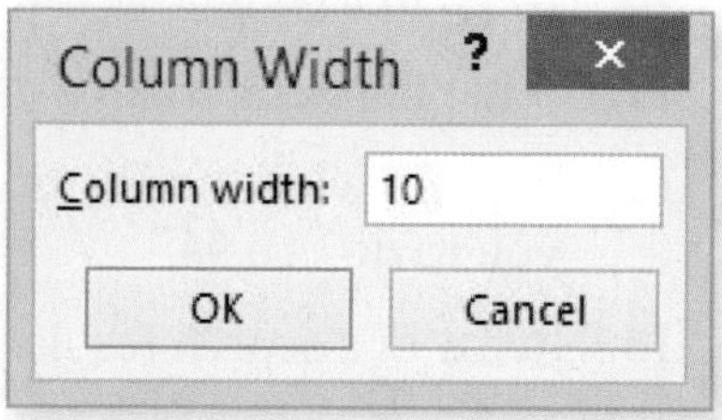

Figure 11.14 *Column Width dialog box*

3. To resize column B using your mouse, move your pointer to the right border of the column B heading area. The pointer will change to a two-sided arrow as shown in Figure 11.15. Double-click the left mouse button. The column width will adjust to display the longest item in the column.

TIP You can set a specified width or use AutoFit Column Width for several columns at one time. Select the column headings of the columns to be changed. Apply the desired width change by using the Column Width dialog box or by double-clicking one of the selected column heading borders.

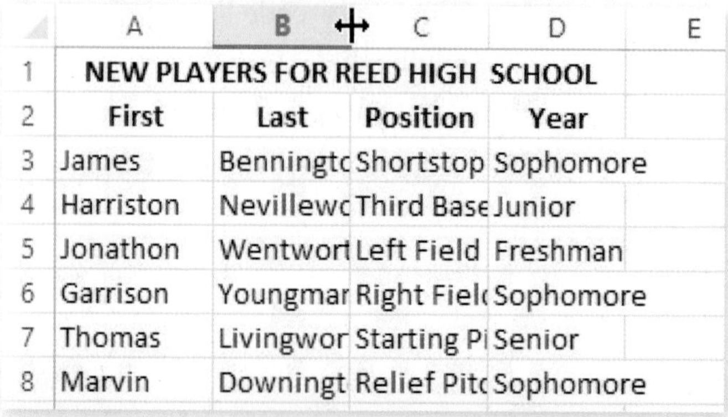

	A	B	C	D	E
1	NEW PLAYERS FOR REED HIGH SCHOOL				
2	First	Last	Position	Year	
3	James	Benningtc	Shortstop	Sophomore	
4	Harriston	Nevillewc	Third Base	Junior	
5	Jonathon	Wentwort	Left Field	Freshman	
6	Garrison	Youngmar	Right Fiel	Sophomore	
7	Thomas	Livingwor	Starting Pi	Senior	
8	Marvin	Downingt	Relief Pitc	Sophomore	

Figure 11.15 *AutoFit column width using mouse*

Research Spyware

Have you ever heard the term *spyware*? In this activity, you will research this term on the Internet. You will use a search engine to find an online dictionary. You also will find articles related to spyware. Your goal is to find online resources to help you answer the following questions:

- What is spyware? What does it do?

- How can you protect your computer system so that spyware is not loaded onto it?

1. Log on to the Internet and start *Internet Explorer* or your default browser. In the address bar, key one of the following URLs or a URL given to you by your teacher.

   google.com

   yahoo.com

   msn.com

2. In the search box, key **computer dictionary**. Choose one of the sites from the results list. On the dictionary site, search using the term *spyware*. Read the information provided.

3. Go back to the search results list. Access another online dictionary and find a definition for *spyware*. Read the information provided.

4. Go back to the search engine you used in step 1. Key **spyware** in the search box. Click a button such as **Go** or **Search** to begin the search. Another search term you may want to use is *spyware blocker*.

5. Choose links in the results list to find articles about spyware. Read two or three articles.

6. In your own words, write an answer for each question given at the beginning of this exercise. Save your work in a document named *c2 spyware*. Be prepared to discuss your answers with the class.

Formulas and Functions

1. Open the workbook *df 74d stats*.

2. Enter a formula in cell F3 to calculate the individual batting averages (Hits/At Bats) using three decimal places. Copy and paste this formula to cells F4:F10.

3. In cell B11, use the AutoSum function to calculate the total for cells B3:B10. Copy and paste this formula to cells C11:E11.

4. In cell F12, enter a formula using the MIN function to display the lowest average. Adjust the format for three decimal places if necessary.

5. In cell F13, enter a formula using the MAX function to display the highest average. Adjust the format for three decimal places if necessary.

6. Change the top margin to 2" and center the worksheet horizontally. Print the worksheet without gridlines.

7. Save the workbook as *74d stats* and close it.

Lesson 75

Editing Worksheets

Learning Outcomes

Data Files:

df 75a lockers
df 75b players
df 75c schedule
df 75d budget

In Lesson 75, you will:

75A Edit cell contents.

75B Change column widths and row heights.

75C Clear and delete cell contents and formats.

75D Modify a worksheet.

75A

Edit Cell Contents

You can edit (change) text or numbers you have keyed in a cell. To edit data, select the cell that contains the data. (See Figure 11.13.) Click the Formula bar. Use the DELETE or BACKSPACE keys to delete old data. Key the new data. Tap ENTER or click the Enter icon on the Formula bar. You also can select the data you want to change in the cell and key the new text or numbers to replace it.

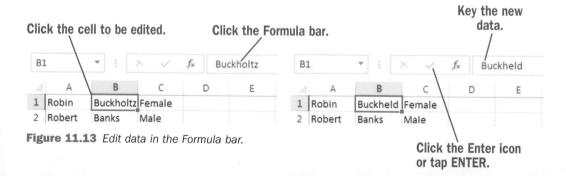

Figure 11.13 *Edit data in the Formula bar.*

ACROSS THE CURRICULUM

Academic Connections

Data Files:

df c2 maps
df c2 global markets

Science: Solar Energy

The rays of the sun that reach Earth create solar energy. This energy can be transformed, or changed, into other forms of energy that we can use. For instance, solar energy can be used to heat water and buildings. It can also be turned into electricity to run machines or light homes. One of the greatest benefits of using solar energy is that it does not pollute the air or land.

1. Open your web browser and use a search engine to find information about solar energy. Find basic facts about how it works. Also research areas and conditions where solar energy works best. Take notes on or print the best information that you find.

2. Find at least two examples of solar energy in use today. Add the websites where you find this information to your Favorites list.

3. Review your notes. Also look at your websites again by accessing them from your Favorites list. Then write an email that summarizes what you learned. Make sure you follow netiquette rules, and send the email to your teacher.

Social Studies: Read a Map

Have you ever visited a new city and had trouble finding your way to the places you wanted to visit? Did you have a map that helped you to locate the buildings you wanted to see and learn information you needed to know?

In this activity, you will go to a website that provides maps for areas all over the world. Using the site, you will find a map of Greensboro, North Carolina.

1. Start *Word*. Open the document *df c2 maps* and save it as *c2 maps*.

2. Follow the directions in the data file and key answers to the questions. Resave and close the document when you are finished.

About Business

The Global Marketplace

Market is a word used to describe a company's customers. The geographical area in which a company sells its products is called a **marketplace**. Some companies sell from only one store in one location. Others sell products in many cities or states. Still others sell products around the world. When a company sells its products around the world, they operate in a **global marketplace**.

Selling products to other countries can be hard. Companies must be able to ship their products across the world instead of just across the United States. They must also learn the cultures of the countries to which they sell. Handling payments in foreign currencies also takes more work.

1. Open *df c2 global markets* and save it as *c2 global markets*.

SS   Formulas/Function
Library/AutoSum
or
Home/Editing/
AutoSum

If the range selected by *Excel* is not correct, key the correct range or use the mouse to select the correct range. Click the Enter icon to calculate the answer. The Auto-Sum button can be accessed by following one of the paths given at the left.

1. Open a new workbook and key the following data. Center the title across columns A through G. Apply 12-point bold to the title. Apply center alignment and bold to the column heads in row 2.

	A	B	C	D	E	F	G
1	COMPUTER CLASS QUIZ SCORES						
2	Name	Quiz 1	Quiz 2	Quiz 3	Quiz 4	Quiz 5	Quiz 6
3	Joe	90	90	90	100	90	90
4	Mary	89	90	90	79	90	90
5	Paul	100	100	100	100	100	100
6	Carl	100	80	90	100	90	90
7	Sue	90	100	100	100	100	80
8	Twila	90	90	90	80	80	80

2. Go to cell H2 and key **Total**. Apply bold and center alignment if necessary.

3. Go to cell H3, click the **AutoSum** down arrow, and select **Sum**. Verify the range of cells in the formula is correct. If not, edit the cell range. Tap ENTER or click the Enter icon to calculate the answer, which should be 550.

4. You can copy and paste formulas to one or more other cells by using the Copy and Paste commands. The formula will adjust to contain cell addresses for the new cells. To copy the formula in cell H3 to H4:H8, select cell **H3** and click **Copy** (note that the selected cell is indicated by a dashed cell border). Select cells **H4:H8**. Click the **Paste** button. Tap ESC on the keyboard to remove the dashed border of the cell that was copied.

5. Go to cell I2 and key **Average**. Apply bold and center alignment if necessary.

6. Go to cell I3 and use the AVERAGE function to find the average of the numbers in cells B3:G3. The correct answer is 91.66667.

7. Copy and paste the formula in I3 to cells I4:I8.

8. Go to cell A9 and key **MIN**. Select cell **B9** and use the MIN function to find the smallest number in cells B3:B8. The correct answer is 89. Copy and paste the formula in cell B9 to C9:G9.

9. In cell A10, key **MAX**. In cell B10, use the MAX function to find the highest score in cells B3:B8. The correct answer is 100.

10. Copy and paste the formula in cell B10 to cells C10:G10.

11. Select cells **A8:G8** and apply a bottom border.

12. Center the worksheet title over cells A1:I1.

13. Change the top margin to 2". Select the option to center the table horizontally on the page. Print the worksheet without gridlines.

14. Save the workbook as *74c quiz*. Complete the CheckPoint.

COLLABORATION

✓ **checkpoint**   Ask a classmate to check your worksheet. Make corrections and print the worksheet again if errors are found. Then close the workbook.

2. Follow the steps in the data file to research a product and the company that sells it. Answer each question in the document.

3. Follow the last couple of steps to convert U.S. dollars to other currencies. Compare your answers to those of your classmates. Save, print, and close the document.

Life Success Builder

Public Speaking

Spiders, heights, the dark, and public speaking. What do these four things have in common? They describe the worst fears of many people! Sometimes the best way to get over a fear is to just do it. With a few basic tips, you can learn how to become a better, more comfortable public speaker, which can help you succeed in school and in life.

COLLABORATION

1. Working with a partner, create a new, blank *Word* document. Save it as *c2 public speaking*.

2. Open your web browser. Search for tips on how to improve your public speaking skills, bookmarking your favorite sites. Key the ten tips that you and your partner find most helpful into your *Word* document. Make sure that you describe the tips using your own words.

3. Next, find at least three organizations that offer classes on public speaking. Key a few details about each organization or class into your *Word* document.

4. Add a heading above each of your lists. Save, print, and close your document.

Career Exploration Portfolio

Activity 1

Many different career opportunities are available to you once you graduate from high school. The career exploration activities at the end of each of the following chapters will help you learn more about careers in which you may have an interest. Begin your exploration by completing the following steps.

Online Resources:

ngl.cengage.com/c21jr3e

1. Open your browser and go to http://www.careertech.org.

2. Click the **Career Technical Education** button, and then click **Career Clusters Resources** in the list at the right. Scroll down on the Career Clusters Resources page and click the **Student Interest Survey** link.

3. Click the link for either the English or Spanish survey. The survey will automatically download to your computer.

4. Locate the survey in your downloaded files and open it in your PDF reader. Print the survey and close it.

5. Follow the instructions at the top of the printout to complete the survey. Be sure to list your top three career clusters at the bottom of the last page.

3. The T-shirts cost $3.00 each. In cell D4, key **=3*25** and tap ENTER. The answer (75) should appear in the cell.

4. In cell E3, calculate the total receipts from games, food, and T-shirts by keying **=B3+C3+D3** as the formula. The answer (763.25) should appear in the cell.

5. In cell E4, enter a formula to find the total expenses for games, food, and T-shirts. (*Hint:* The answer should be 276.33.)

6. Profit is the amount of money from receipts that is left after expenses are paid. To find the profit for games, key **=B3-B4** in cell B5. The answer should be 239.50.

7. In cell C5, enter a formula to find the profit for food. In cell D5, enter a formula to find the profit for T-shirts. In cell E5, enter a formula to find the total profit. (*Hint:* The total profit should be 486.92.)

8. Click in cell F2 and key **T-Shirts %**. If needed, apply bold and center alignment.

9. You want to record the percent of the total profit that came from T-shirt sales in cell F5 by keying **=50/E5** as the formula. The answer (0.102686) should appear in the cell.

10. Format cells B3:E5 using Accounting Number Format with 2 decimals, and format cell F5 in Percent Style with no decimals.

SS   Home/Font/Borders

11. Select cells **B4:E4**. Follow the path at the left to the Borders feature. Click the down arrow on the Borders button and select **Bottom Border**.

12. Change the top margin to 2". Center the table horizontally. Print the worksheet without the gridlines showing.

13. Save the workbook as *74b festival* and close it.

74C

Functions

Spreadsheet software has built-in functions. A **function** is a predefined formula that can be used to perform calculations. For example, the SUM function is used to add numbers. Other commonly used functions include the following.

- The AVERAGE function finds the average of the numbers in a range of cells.

- The COUNT function counts how many entries there are in a range of cells.

- The MIN function finds the smallest number in a range of cells.

- The MAX function finds the largest number in a range of cells.

Instead of keying the function's name (Sum, Average, Min, or Max) and the cell range in the Formula bar, you can click the cell in which you want the answer to appear, click the AutoSum button (see Figure 11.12), and select the desired option from the menu. *Excel* will automatically select the cell range next to the active cell and identify the range selected with a moving border.

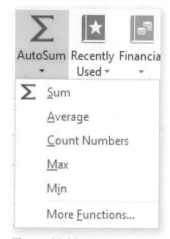

Figure 11.12 *AutoSum options*

UNIT 2

Keyboarding

Chapter 3   Letter Keys

Lessons 11–30

We live in the *Information Age* (also called the *Computer Age*). Computers are used to gather, create, and share information for personal, educational, and business uses. Information that once took days or even weeks to create and distribute can now be created and shared very quickly. Using various types of software programs, the computer can be used to create spreadsheets, databases, presentation visuals, emails, and other business documents such as reports, letters, and tables. Once created, these documents can be sent to another person almost anywhere in the world in a matter of seconds.

The higher the level of keyboarding skill, the faster the computer can be used to complete the software application. The keyboard is used not only to input information into the computer but also to extract information as well. The more skilled a user is at the keyboard, the faster he or she can gather, create, and share information.

© Andrey_Popov/Shutterstock.com

9. Format cells in A12:D12 using Long Date format.

10. Format cells in A13:D13 using Date, Type: March 14, 2012.

11. Save the workbook as *74a numbers2* and close it.

Formulas are equations that perform calculations on values in a worksheet. You can key formulas to add, subtract, multiply, and divide numbers. To enter a formula to solve math problems, select the cell in which the answer is to appear. Key an equal (=) sign to indicate that the following text and numbers will be a formula. Enter the formula and tap ENTER or click the Enter icon on the Formula bar. The formula will appear in the Formula bar, and the answer will appear in the cell as shown in Figure 11.10.

Figure 11.10 *Formulas appear in the Formula bar.*

Formulas are solved in this order:

1. Calculations inside parentheses are done before those outside parentheses.

2. Multiplication and division are done in the order they occur.

3. Addition and subtraction are done in the order they occur.

In this activity, you will use formulas to calculate dollar amounts and percentages related to games, food, and T-shirt sales at a school festival.

1. Open the workbook *df 74b festival*.

2. At the festival, 25 T-shirts were sold at $5.00 each. To calculate the Receipts for the T-shirts, key **=5*25** in cell D3. As you key the formula, it will appear in both the cell and the Formula bar. Tap ENTER or click the Enter icon on the Formula bar. The answer (125) should appear in the cell (see Figure 11.11).

TIP When entering formulas, you can click on the cell address to enter it rather than keying it.

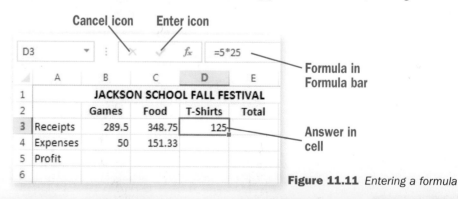

Figure 11.11 *Entering a formula*

Home Keys (asdf jkl;)

Learning Outcomes

In Lesson 11, you will:

- *Learn control of home keys (**asdf jkl;**).*
- *Learn control of the Space Bar and ENTER key.*

11A

Work-Area Arrangement

Arrange your work area as shown in Figure 3.1.

- Keyboard directly in front of chair
- Front edge of keyboard even with edge of desk
- Monitor placed for easy viewing
- Book at right of monitor

© Cengage Learning®

Figure 3.1 *Work-area arrangement*

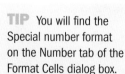

Lesson 74 — Using Formulas and Functions

Learning Outcomes

In Lesson 74, you will:

74A *Format numbers.*
74B *Use formulas.*
74C *Use functions.*
74D *Create a worksheet with functions and formulas.*

Data Files:

df 74a numbers1
df 74a numbers2
df 74b festival
df 74d stats

74A

Format Numbers

SS Home/Number

When numbers are keyed into a worksheet, the software formats them as General, the default format. As you learned in the previous lesson, you can use features in the Number group to change the format to a more appropriate format. In this activity, you will use the formats you have learned as well as others that are available.

You can select predefined number formats from the Number Format list (see Figure 11.9). If the predefined format doesn't provide the desired format, click the Number Format dialog box launcher at the lower right of the Number group to open the Format Cells dialog box with the Number tab displayed. You can select the desired number format in the Category list, and then select additional formatting choices from any options that are shown to the right of the Category list. You can also access this dialog box by selecting More Number Formats at the bottom of the Number Format list (see Figure 11.9).

Figure 11.9 *Number Format list*

Worksheet 1

1. Open the workbook *df 74a numbers1* and format the numbers as directed.

2. Save the workbook as *74a numbers1* and close it.

Worksheet 2

1. Open the workbook *df 74a numbers2*.

2. Format cells in A1:A7 using Number format, three decimal places, and comma separators.

3. Format cells in B1:B7 using Currency format and two decimal places.

4. Format cells in C1:C7 using Accounting format with no decimal places.

5. Format cells in D1:D7 using Percentage format with two decimal places.

6. Format cells in A9:D9 using Special, Type: Phone Number.

7. Format cells in A10:D10 using Special, Type: Social Security Number.

8. Format cells in A11:D11 using Short Date format.

TIP You will find the Special number format on the Number tab of the Format Cells dialog box.

KEYING TIP The way
you sit when you use the
keyboard is important. You
can key more accurately
when you sit correctly.

The features of correct keying position are shown in Figure 3.2 and listed below.

- Fingers curved and upright over home keys
- Wrists low, but not touching keyboard
- Forearms parallel to slant of keyboard
- Body erect
- Feet on floor for balance
- Eyes on copy

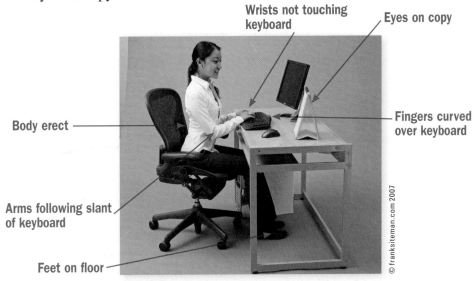

Figure 3.2 *Keying position at the computer*

The keys on which you place your fingers to begin keying are called the **home keys**. The home keys are **a s d f** for the left hand and **j k l ;** for the right hand.

1. Find the home keys on the keyboard illustration shown below in Figure 3.3.
2. Locate and place your fingers on the home keys on your keyboard.
3. Keep your fingers well curved and upright (not slanting).
4. Remove your fingers from the keyboard. Place them in home-key position again. Curve and hold your fingers lightly on the keys.

Figure 3.3 *Home-key position*

Create a Worksheet

1. Open a new workbook and key the worksheet data below. Wrap the text in the cell range A2:E2.

2. Format the worksheet title in 14-point bold and center it across the columns.

3. Format the column headings in 12-point bold and center them vertically and horizontally.

4. Format the numbers using Accounting number format with no decimals.

5. Center the worksheet horizontally and vertically on the page in Portrait orientation and change the setting to print gridlines.

6. Preview the worksheet, make any necessary changes, and then print it.

7. Save the workbook as *73f worksheet* and close it.

SIX MONTH SALES				
Month	Gregg Abels	Luiz Callia	Maria Forde	Sandra Sharpe
January	55.67	66.23	73.59	69.02
February	24.57	76.54	35.69	64.32
March	69.30	30.96	57.92	79.08
April	47.83	62.12	43.90	54.02
May	50.42	50.92	45.00	53.21
June	54.30	60.98	57.81	60.23

When you key, tap each key lightly with the tip of the finger. Keep your fingers curved as shown in Figure 3.4. The Space Bar is used to place a space between words. Tap the Space Bar with the right thumb. Use a quick down-and-in motion (toward the palm). Avoid pauses before or after spacing.

Curve fingers and tap the keys.

Tap the Space Bar with a quick down-and-in-motion.

Figure 3.4 *Keying and spacing technique*

1. Place your fingers in home-key position.

2. Key the line below. Tap the Space Bar once at the point of each arrow.

3. Review proper position at the keyboard (11B). Key the line again.

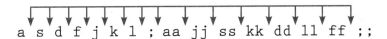

a s d f j k l ; aa jj ss kk dd ll ff ;;

ENTER key reach

The **ENTER** key is used to return the insertion point to the left margin and to move it down one line. The **margin** is the blank space between the edge of the paper and the print. Tap the ENTER key once to **single-space (SS)**. This moves the insertion point down one line. Tap the ENTER key twice to **double-space (DS)**. This moves the insertion point down two lines. Study the illustration at the left.

1. Place your fingers on the home-row keys.

2. Reach the little finger of the right hand to the ENTER key.

3. Tap the key.

4. Return the finger quickly to home-key position.

5. Practice tapping the ENTER key several times.

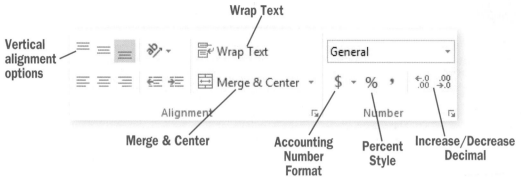

Figure 11.8 *Alignment and Number groups*

1. Open the workbook *df 73e format*.

2. Position your pointer over each of the features in the Alignment and Number groups, and read the description of each feature that is displayed.

3. Key the following data in the cell range A9:C12. After keying the second number, tap ENTER to complete the formulas in column D.

Rhonda	74	68
Sandy	64	68
Tom	54	58
Vera	61	70

4. Select the cell range **A2:D2** and use **Wrap Text**, **Middle Align**, and **Center** in the Alignment group and **Bold** in the Font group to format the column headings.

5. Select the cell range **B3:C12**. Click the **Accounting Number Format** button and then click the **Decrease Decimal** button twice so no decimals are displayed.

6. Select the cell range **D3:D12**. Click the **Percent Style** button, and then use the **Increase Decimal** feature to display one decimal place.

7. Key **COOKIE SALES REPORT** in cell A1. Select the cell range **A1:D1**. Click **Merge & Center**, then **Bold**, and then increase the font size to **14**.

8. Center the worksheet horizontally and vertically on the page and preview it.

9. Save the workbook as *73e format* and close it.

Home Keys and Space Bar

SPACING TIP Tap the ENTER key twice to insert a DS between 2-line groups.

Keep fingers curved and upright.

Key each line once single-spaced. Double-space between 2-line groups. Do not key the line numbers.

```
1 a aa s ss d dd f ff j jj k kk l ll ; ;; asdf jkl;
2 a aa s ss d dd f ff j jj k kk l ll ; ;; asdf jkl;
```
Tap the ENTER key twice to double-space (DS)

```
3 f ff d dd s ss a aa ; ;; l ll k kk j jj fdsa ;lkj
4 f ff d dd s ss a aa ; ;; l ll k kk j jj fdsa ;lkj
```
DS

```
5 sj sj ld ld a; a; jf jf lj da k; fs ksj dla ;f ja
6 sj sj ld ld a; a; jf jf lj da k; fs ksj dla ;f ja
```
DS

11G

ENTER Key

TECHNIQUE TIP
Reach out with little finger and tap the ENTER key. Quickly return your finger to home key.

Key each line once single-spaced. Double-space between 2-line groups.

```
1 ;; dd aa jj
2 ;; dd aa jj

3 ll ss kk ff dd j
4 ll ss kk ff dd j

5 sa sa jd jd lk lk f;f
6 sa sa jd jd lk lk f;f

7 da da jk jk s; s; fl fl kk
8 da da jk jk s; s; fl fl kk
```

MicroType

Use *MicroType* Lesson 1 for additional practice.

 **checkpoint** Does your **J** finger remain in place as you tap the ENTER key? If not, make an effort to improve your reach technique.

Select a Range of Cells

A range of cells may be selected to perform an operation (move, cut, copy, clear, format, print, etc.) on more than one cell at a time. A *range* is identified by the cell in the upper-left corner and the cell in the lower-right corner, usually separated by a colon. For example, B4:C10 is the range of cells from cell B4 through C10.

To select a range of cells, highlight the cell in the upper-left corner of the range. Hold down the left mouse button, and drag to the cell at the lower-right corner of the range. Once the range has been selected, release the mouse button and perform the desired operation(s) to format cell content in much the same way as text is formatted in a word processing document. To deselect a range of cells, click a cell outside the range.

1. Open the workbook *df 73d range*. Use features from the Font group to make the following changes:

    a. Select the range of cells A1:D1 and apply bold.

    b. Select the range of cells A2:D5 and change the font color to red.

    c. Select the range of cells A6:D7 and change the font style to italic.

    d. Select the range of cells A8:D9 and use a yellow fill.

2. Save the workbook as *73d range* and close it.

73E

Format Worksheets and Cell Content

SS   Home/Alignment or Number

Worksheets that you create for your own use can be very informal. You may enter data quickly and think little about the format. However, worksheets that will be attached to reports or letters or shared with others should be formatted carefully. The worksheet should present data in a format that is easy to read. Follow these general guidelines for worksheet appearance:

A **worksheet title** describes the content of a worksheet. Unless otherwise directed, key the title in all capital letters. Apply bold and center-align the title across the columns that have data.

A **column heading** appears at the top of a column and describes the data in the column. Unless directed otherwise, key column heads in bold, capital and lower-case letters, and use center alignment.

Key data in cells using the default font unless otherwise directed. Data in cells can be aligned left, aligned right, or centered. Usually, numbers are aligned right and words are aligned left or centered.

Center worksheet data horizontally on the page. Center worksheet data vertically on a page or set a 2" top margin.

You can use features on various tabs (Home, Page Layout, etc.) to format worksheets as you have done with word processing documents. Some of the Alignment and Number group features that will be used in this activity are shown in Figure 11.8. In Lesson 74, you will learn more features in the Number group.

Review

Learning Outcomes

In Lesson 12, you will:

- *Review control of home keys (**asdf jkl;**).*
- *Review control of the Space Bar and ENTER key.*

12A

Work-Area Arrangement and Keying Position

Arrange your work area as shown in Figure 3.5.

- Keyboard directly in front of chair
- Front edge of keyboard even with edge of desk
- Monitor placed for easy viewing
- Book at right of monitor

Figure 3.5 *Work-area arrangement*

Figure 3.6 *Keying position*

Review Figure 3.6 for keying position.

- Fingers curved and upright over home keys
- Wrists low, but not touching keyboard
- Forearms parallel to slant of keyboard
- Body erect
- Feet on floor for balance
- Eyes on copy

12B

Home-Key Position

1. Find the home keys on the chart: **a s d f** for the left hand and **j k l ;** for the right hand.

2. Locate and place your fingers on the home keys on your keyboard with your fingers well curved and upright (not slanting).

3. Remove your fingers from the keyboard; then place them in home-key position again, curving and holding them lightly on the keys.

Margins and Page Orientation

SS *Margins*
Page Layout/Page Setup/Margins

SS *Page Orientation*
Page Layout/Page Setup/Orientation

The Margins feature can be used to change the amount of white space between the top, bottom, left, and right edges of the worksheet. The default setting is typically 0.7" for the left and right margins and 0.75" for the top and bottom margins. Other frequently used margins can be selected, or custom margins can be set. See Figure 11.6 for the Margins tab in the Page Setup dialog box that displays when Custom Margins is selected. The path at the left can be used to change margins.

As in *Word*, the default page orientation for *Excel* is Portrait, which prints vertically on 8½" × 11" paper. Landscape orientation can be selected and will print vertically on 11" × 8½" paper. The path at the left is used to set page orientation. See Figure 11.7.

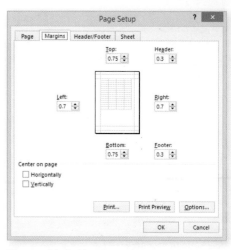

Figure 11.6 *Margins tab*

1. Open the workbook *df 73a worksheet*.

2. Change page orientation to Landscape.

3. Change the margins to 2" by selecting **Custom Margins** from the Margins menu to open the Page Setup dialog box with the Margins tab active. Key **2"** in the top, bottom, left, and right margin boxes.

4. Preview the worksheet and then print it without making additional changes.

5. Save the workbook as *73b worksheet*, but do not close it.

Figure 11.7 *Page orientation*

Center Worksheets

SS Page Layout/Page Setup/Margins/ Custom Margins

Worksheets, like tables in *Word*, can be centered horizontally and/or vertically to make them more attractive when printed.

1. If needed, open *73b worksheet*.

2. Change margins to Normal and page orientation to Portrait.

3. Follow the path at the left to access the Page Setup dialog box and then check **Horizontally** and **Vertically** under Center on page (see Figure 11.6).

4. Preview the worksheet. *Note:* You can click the Print Preview box at the bottom of the Page Setup dialog box to go directly to the same print preview that is displayed when you select Print on the File tab.

5. Save the workbook as *73c worksheet* and close it.

Home Keys and Space Bar

Keying technique

Spacing technique

SPACING TIP Tap the ENTER key twice to insert a DS between 2-line groups.

When you key, remember to tap each key lightly with the tip of the finger. Tap the Space Bar with the right thumb. Use a quick down-and-in motion (toward the palm). Avoid pauses before or after spacing.

Key each line once single-spaced. Double-space between 2-line groups. Do not key the line numbers.

```
1  a s d f dd aa ff ss j k l ; ll jj ;; kk fd as j;kl
2  a s d f dd aa ff ss j k l ; ll jj ;; kk fd as j;kl
```
Tap the ENTER key twice to double-space (DS)

```
3  ll aa jj dd ;; ss kk ff jj aa ll ;; ss dd kk ff ll
4  ll aa jj dd ;; ss kk ff jj aa ll ;; ss dd kk ff ll
                                                    DS

5  ka ls ;f jd ak sl f; dj lf jd ka ;s fl dj ak s; js
6  ka ls ;f jd ak sl f; df lf jd ka ;s fl dj ak s; js
                                                    DS

7  sjs kak f;f ldl jsj aka ;f; dld sjs a;a fsf kdk ll
8  sjs kak f;f ldl jsj aka ;f; dld sjs a;a fsf kdk ll
                                                    DS
```

ENTER Key

ENTER *Right little finger*

Use the correct reach for the ENTER key. Reach the little finger of the right hand to the ENTER key. Tap the key. Return the finger quickly to home-key position.

Key each line once single-spaced. Double-space between 2-line groups.

```
1  s ss l ll;
2  s ss l ll;

3  f ff j jj d dd;
4  f ff j jj d dd;

5  k kk a aa l ll s ss;
6  k kk a aa l ll s ss;

7  j jj f ff d dd ; ;; a aa;
8  j jj f ff d dd ; ;; a aa;

9  s ss l ll a aa k kk s ss f ff;
10 s ss l ll a aa k kk s ss f ff;
```

Lesson 73 | Format and Print Worksheets

Learning Outcomes

In Lesson 73, you will:

73A *Preview and print a worksheet.*
73B *Set margins and page orientation.*
73C *Center worksheets horizontally and vertically.*
73D *Select a range of cells.*
73E *Format worksheets and cell content.*
73F *Create a worksheet.*

Data Files:

df 73a worksheet
df 73d range
df 73e format

73A

Preview and Print a Worksheet

SS *Print Preview*
File/Print

SS *Print*
File/Print/Print

Worksheets can be previewed so you can see how the worksheet will look when printed. As shown in Figure 11.5, you can display a page of a worksheet by using the Print Preview feature that displays when the Print screen is accessed via the Print Preview path at the left. If you want to enlarge the worksheet, click the Zoom to Page icon at the lower-right corner. If you want to display the margins, click the Show Margins icon at the lower-right corner. After previewing the worksheet, you can return to it to make additional changes, or, if no changes are needed, you can print it using the Print path at the left.

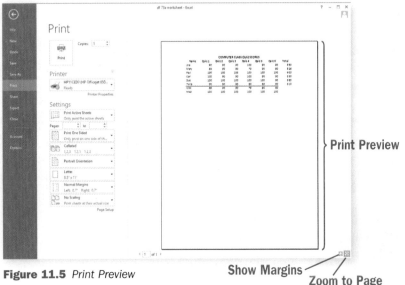

Print Preview

Show Margins
Zoom to Page

Figure 11.5 *Print Preview*

1. Open the workbook *df 73a worksheet*.

2. Follow the ***Print Preview*** path to preview it.

3. Return to the worksheet and change cell B7 to **70**.

4. Follow the ***Print*** path to print the worksheet.

5. Save the workbook as *73a worksheet* and close it.

Key each line once single-spaced. Double-space between 2-line groups. Do not key the red lines between groups of words.

```
1 as; as;|ask ask|ad; ad;|add add|all all|fall fall;
2 as; as;|ask ask|ad; ad;|add add|all all|fall fall;

3 a sad lass; a sad lass;|all fall ads all fall ads;
4 a sad lass; a sad lass;|all fall ads all fall ads;

5 add a; add a;|ask a lad ask a lad|a salad a salad;
6 add a; add a;|ask a lad ask a lad|a salad a salad;
```

SPACING TIP

¶ Click the **Show/ Hide ¶** button in the Paragraph group on the Home tab to display formatting marks for spaces and paragraphs.

12F

End-of-Class Routine

MicroType

Use *MicroType* Lesson 2 for additional practice.

At the end of each class period, complete the following steps.

1. Exit the software.

2. Turn off equipment if directed to do so.

3. Store materials as instructor directs.

4. Clean up your work area and push in your chair before you leave.

Digital Citizenship and Ethics

© Monkey Business Images/Shutterstock.com

Bullying is unacceptable! Bullying comes in many forms, from teasing and name-calling to pushing and hitting to excluding others from a group. Now, technology has provided new ways for people to bully each other. Cyberbullying—or using online communications technology to harass or upset someone—has become increasingly common as more and more people use cell phones and the Internet.

Cell phones and email can be used to send hateful calls or messages or to share humiliating images. Threatening messages can be sent via chat rooms, message boards, and social networking sites. Name-calling and abusive remarks are thrown at players on gaming sites. What can you do about cyberbullying? As a class, discuss the following.

1. What are three things you can do so that you do not become a victim of cyberbullying?

2. If you've been the victim of cyberbullying, what course of action should you take?

1. Open a new workbook.

2. Go to cell A4 and begin keying the data shown below in cells A4:C10. Notice that the text in column A is left-aligned. The numbers in columns B and C are right-aligned.

	A	B	C
1			
2			
3			
4	Ann	13579	7
5	Barb	24680	7
6	Connie	14703	8
7	Dora	25814	8
8	Eve	97532	7
9	Flora	86420	7
10	Grace	63074	8

3. Save the workbook as *72d data* but do not close it.

72E

View and Print Gridlines and Row and Column Headings

SS Page Layout/Sheet Options

Gridlines (cell borders) and headings (row numbers and column letters) may or may not be viewed on the monitor or printed on a worksheet. The default settings are to display (view) the headings on the monitor but not print them. Therefore, if you want to print the gridlines or headings, you will need to check the appropriate Print checkbox shown in Figure 11.4. If you do not want to view the gridlines or headings on the monitor, you will need to deselect the appropriate View checkbox shown in Figure 11.4.

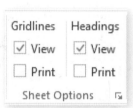

Figure 11.4 *Gridlines and headings*

1. If needed, open *72d data*.

2. Follow the path at the left to access the Sheet Options group. Set the sheet options to view and print the gridlines, but do not view or print the headings.

3. Save the workbook as *72e data* and close it.

Lesson 13

New Keys h and e

Data File:

df 13d check sheet

Learning Outcomes

In Lesson 13, you will:
- *Learn reach technique for **h** and **e**.*
- *Combine **h** and **e** smoothly with home keys.*

13A

Warmup

Key each line twice single-spaced. Double-space between 2-line groups.

All keystrokes learned

```
1  aa jj ss ;; ff kk dd ll jj aa ;; ss kk ff ll dd aa

2  ask; ask; sad; sad; lad; lad; all; all; fall; fall

3  a lad asks; ask a sad lass; all fall ads; a salad;
```

Tap ENTER twice to double-space (DS) between lesson parts.

13B

Plan for Learning New Keys

All of the remaining keys that you learn will require your fingers to reach from the home keys to tap other keys. Follow the plan given below to learn the reach for each new key.

Standard Plan for Learning New Keys

1. Find the new key on the keyboard chart provided.
2. Look at your keyboard and find the new key on it.
3. Study the picture at the left of the practice lines for the new key. Note which finger is used for the key.
4. Curve your fingers and place them in home-key position (over **asdf jkl;**).
5. Watch your finger as you reach to the new key and back to home position a few times. Keep your finger curved.
6. Key the set of drill lines according to the directions provided, keeping your eyes on the copy as you key.

2. Use the mouse to make cell A12 active. Use the mouse to make cell B24 active. You may need to use the scroll bars to display the area you want.

3. Use the arrow keys to make cell D11 active. Use the arrow keys to make cell F30 active. Use the arrow keys to make cell P30 active.

4. Use PAGE DOWN and arrow keys to make J100 active. Use PAGE UP and arrow keys to make L40 active.

5. Tap the F5 key (found in the row of function keys at the top of the keyboard) to open the Go To dialog box. Key **H100** in the Reference box. Click **OK**. H100 should be the active cell.

6. Tap CTRL + HOME to make cell A1 active. Tap the TAB key once to make cell B1 active. Tap the ENTER key to make cell A2 active.

7. Close the workbook without saving it.

TIP Using the F5 key is often the quickest way to move to a cell that is far from your current location.

72D

Enter and Align Labels and Values

Data keyed into a cell is automatically assigned a label or value status. When only numbers are keyed into a cell, the value status is assigned and the data is right-aligned (see Figure 11.3). When letters and/or symbols (with or without numbers) are keyed into a cell, the label status is assigned and the data is left-aligned.

To record the data entered, tap TAB or ENTER. You also can click the Enter icon on the Formula bar to record the data. The Enter icon is shown in Figure 11.3. If you want to change the alignment that was automatically assigned to labels and values, use the desired alignment option in the Alignment group on the Home tab.

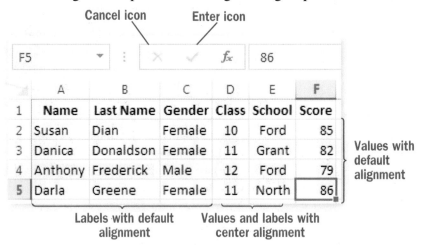

Figure 11.3 *Label and value alignment*

If you make a mistake when entering data, use the DELETE or BACKSPACE key to remove text or numbers. If you find an error after you have left a cell, select the cell that has the error. Key the correct data and tap TAB or ENTER. The new data you key will replace the error.

You might begin keying data and then want to stop, perhaps because you realize you are in the wrong cell. To cancel data entry, tap the ESC key before tapping TAB or ENTER. You also can click the Cancel icon on the Formula bar to cancel data entry. The Cancel icon also is shown in Figure 11.3.

13C

New Keys h and e

h Right index finger

e Left middle finger

Use the *Standard Plan for Learning New Keys* (page 85) for each key that you learn. Review the plan now. Relate each step of the plan to the illustrations and copy shown below. Then key each line twice. Do not key the line numbers, the vertical lines separating word groups, or the labels.

Learn h

```
1 h j h j|hj hj|j h j h|jh jh|had had|has has|shall;
2 jh jh|ash ash|hash hash|shad shad|half half|flash;
3 lash lash|dash dash|half half|hash hash|hall hall;
```

Learn e

```
4 e d e d|ed ed|d e d e|de de|feel feel|deeds deeds;
5 less less|feed feed|deal deal|fake fake|seal seal;
6 sale sale|keel keel|sell sell|desk desk|jade jade;
```

Combine h and e

```
7 she she|held held|shed shed|head head|shelf shelf;
8 he he|heal heal|shell shell|shade shade|jade jade;
9 heed heed|heel heel|flesh flesh|leash leash|he he;
```

Tap ENTER twice to double-space (DS) between lesson parts.

13D

Technique Check

Techniques are very important. In the early stages of learning to key, it is helpful to have others observe your techniques and tell you how you are doing. Sometimes your teacher will provide the feedback. Other times you will receive feedback from one of your classmates.

1. Open *df 13d check sheet*. Print the document. Close the file.

2. Work with a classmate. Ask your classmate to key lines 7–9 (above) as you watch for proper techniques. Mark notes on your check sheet. Share your comments with your classmate.

3. Ask your classmate to rate your techniques as you key lines 7–9. Discuss your ratings with your classmate.

COLLABORATION

 **checkpoint** Check your classmate's technique.

Active cell: Highlighted with a thick border, it stores information that is entered while the cell is active.

Columns: Identified by *letters* that run horizontally.

Rows: Identified by *numbers* that run vertically.

Worksheet tab: Identifies the worksheet in the workbook.

Scroll bars: Used to move the display horizontally or vertically within a worksheet.

1. Start *Word.* Open the document *df 72a worksheet.* Complete the activity as directed, referring to Figure 11.1 as needed.

2. Save the document as *72a worksheet* and close *Word.*

72B

Open and Close Excel and Open and Save a Workbook

Excel spreadsheet software is opened and closed in the same manner that you opened and closed *Word* and *PowerPoint* software in preceding chapters. Likewise, new and existing workbooks are opened, saved, and closed the same as word processing documents and presentation slide shows.

1. Start *Excel.* Click **Blank workbook**. A new workbook opens with cell A1 (the cell address) active in the Sheet1 worksheet. Key your first name in cell A1.

2. Save the workbook as *72b first* and close it.

3. Open the workbook *df 72b last* and key your last name in cell A1. Save the worksheet as *72b last* and close it. Close *Excel.*

72C

Move Around in a Worksheet

When you enter information in a worksheet, it is placed in the active cell. The active cell is the current location of the insertion point. Thus, the active cell changes when you move the insertion point from cell to cell. You can identify the active cell by looking at its border. The active cell is the cell with the thick border around it. (See Figure 11.1.)

To activate (select) a cell with the mouse, move the pointer to the desired cell and click the mouse. You also can use the arrow keys and the TAB and ENTER keys to activate a different cell.

To move from one cell to another quickly, you can use keyboard shortcuts. For example, to move to the first cell in a row and make it the active cell, tap HOME. To move to cell A1, press CTRL + HOME. To move the active cell up one page, tap PAGE UP.

In this activity, you will practice moving around a worksheet using the mouse and the keyboard.

1. Open a new workbook. Click cell **C4** to select it. Cell C4 is now the active cell. Note that the active cell address appears in the Name box as shown in Figure 11.2.

Figure 11.2 *The active cell is shown in the Name box.*

13E
Key Mastery

Key each line twice.

```
1 ask ask|seek seek|half half|leaf leaf|halls halls;

2 ask dad; he has jell; she has jade; he sells leeks

3 he led; she has; a jak ad; a jade eel; a sled fell

4 she asked a lass; she led all fall; she has a lead

5 he led; she had; she fell; a jade ad; a desk shelf
```

MicroType

Use *MicroType* Lesson 3 for additional practice.

13F
Compose Sentences

Read the sentences below. From the list at the left, choose the word that best completes the sentence. Use all words. Key the word and tap the ENTER key.

desk
fell
held
sad
salad
sale
seeds
she
shed
shelf

1. Why are you so _____?
2. He _____ down the stairs.
3. She planted the grass _____.
4. Jack _____ the baby.
5. Did the _____ end on Saturday?
6. The antique _____ is quite expensive.
7. The lawn mower is in the _____.
8. When did _____ leave?
9. The book is on the _____.
10. What did you put in the _____?

COLLABORATION

 **checkpoint** Trade places with a classmate. Check your classmate's answers.

Workbook and Worksheet Basics

Data Files:

df 72a worksheet
df 72b last

In Lesson 72, you will:

72A *Learn about workbooks, worksheets, and worksheet parts.*

72B *Open and close* **Excel**; *open, save, and close a workbook.*

72C *Move around in a worksheet.*

72D *Enter and align labels and values.*

72E *View and print gridlines and headings.*

72A

Workbooks, Worksheets, and Worksheet Parts

Excel is a popular spreadsheet program. In *Excel*, a spreadsheet file is called a **workbook**. Each workbook contains one or more **worksheets**, usually with related data. Worksheets can be added to a workbook. Worksheets also can be deleted from a workbook.

A worksheet contains columns, rows, and cells. Columns run up and down a worksheet. Each column has a heading (letters from *A* to *Z*, *AA* to *AZ*, and so on) running left to right across the worksheet. Rows run across a worksheet. Each row has a heading (a number such as 1, 2, or 3). The row headings run down the left side of the worksheet. A cell is formed where a column and row cross. Cells are where information is keyed. A worksheet is shown in Figure 11.1. It contains many parts that you used with other software.

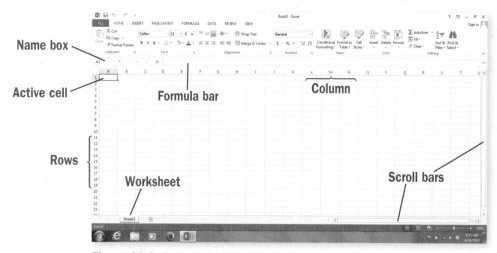

Figure 11.1 *Excel worksheet*

Refer to Figure 11.1 as you read about the basic parts of a worksheet screen in the following list.

Name box: Identifies the active cell by the letter of the column and the number of the row it intersects. It also identifies the range of cells being selected.

Formula bar: Displays the contents of the active cell and is used to create or edit text or values. It may be expanded or contracted by clicking the single arrow at the right edge of the bar.

Lesson 14

New Keys i and r

Learning Outcomes

In Lesson 14, you will:

- *Learn reach technique for **i** and **r**.*
- *Combine **i** and **r** smoothly with home keys.*

14A

Warmup

Instant Message

Tap and release each key quickly.

Key each line twice.

Home keys

1 a f d s k j ; l ask fad all dad sad fall lass jj ;

h/e

2 j h ha has had ash hash d e led fed fled sled fell

All keys learned

3 she had a sale; ask a lad; she sells jade; a lake;

DS

14B

New Keys i and r

Follow the plan for learning new keys shown on page 85. Key each line twice. If time permits, key lines 7–9 again.

i Right middle finger

Learn i

1 k i|ki ki|is is|if if|ill ill|aid aid|kid kid|hail
2 ki ki|like like|jail jail|file file|said said|dial
3 if a kid; he did; a lie; if he; his file; a kid is

Learn r

r Left index finger

4 f r|fr fr|far far|her her|are are|ark ark|jar jars
5 fr fr|jar jar|red red|her her|lark lark|dark dark;
6 a jar; a rake; read a; red jar; hear her; are free

Combine i and r

7 ride ride|fire fire|risk risk|hire hire|hair hairs
8 her hair; hire her; a fire; is she fair; is a risk
9 a ride; if her; is far; red jar; his are; her aide

Double-space (DS) between lesson parts.

Chapter 11   Worksheets

Lessons 72–77

Spreadsheet software is a computer program used to record, report, and analyze data in worksheets. You can use it to add, subtract, divide, and multiply numbers. You can use formulas and functions to find answers. Spreadsheet software solves repetitive math problems correctly, quickly, and easily. Also, it allows you to use charts to show data graphically.

One reason to use spreadsheet software is that when a number in a problem is changed, all related "answers" are changed for you. For example, you can quickly see how the amount of money you earn from selling candy bars goes up or down by changing the number sold or the selling price in the formula.

In this chapter, you will create worksheets. You will edit and format them so they are correct, attractive, and easy to read. You will use formulas and functions to solve easy, difficult, and repetitive math problems. You will create charts to show information.

© iStockphoto.com/Christopher Futcher

TECHNIQUE TIP
• Keep your wrists low but not resting on the desk.
• Keep your hands and arms steady.

Key each line twice.

Reach review

1 hj ed ik rf hj de ik fr hj ed ik rf jh de ki fr hj

2 he he|if if|all all|fir fir|jar jar|rid rid|as ask

h/e

3 she she|elf elf|her her|hah hah|eel eel|shed shelf

4 he has; had jak; her jar; had a shed; she has fled

i/r

5 fir fir|rid rid|sir sir|kid kid|ire ire|fire fired

6 a fir; is rid; is red; his ire; her kid; has a fir

All keys learned

7 jar jar|deal deal|fire fire|shelf shelf|lake lakes

8 he is; he did; ask her; red jar; she fell; he fled

All keys learned

9 if she is; he did ask; he led her; he is her aide;

10 she has had a jade sale; he said he had a red fir;

MicroType

Use *MicroType* Lesson 4 for additional practice.

14D

Enrichment Activity

Unscramble the letters shown below to create eight words. If you have difficulty, key the letters in different orders to unscramble the words.

1. kas   5. drak

2. arf   6. arek

3. efra   7. kile

4. arde   8. rhei

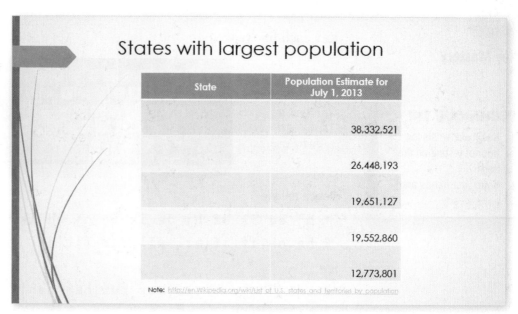

Slide 9

In the left column, insert clip art such as a license plate for states in the following order, top to bottom: California, Texas, New York, Florida, Illinois.

Insert a text box to include the following note beneath the table.

Note: http://en.Wikipedia.org/wiki/
List of U.S. states and territories by population

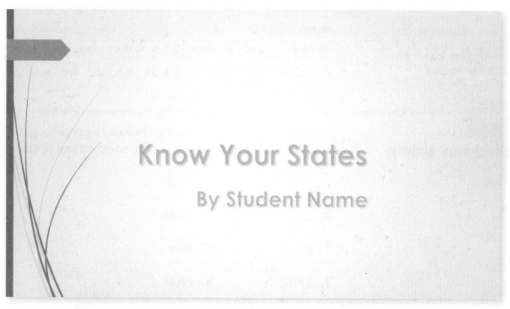

Slide 10

Use WordArt (*Fill – Tan, Accent 1, Outline – Background 1, Hard Shadow – Accent 1*) to create the text.

Change the font size to 40 point for your name.

Review

15A

Warmup

TECHNIQUE TIP

- Keep your wrists low but not touching the keyboard.
- Keep your forearms parallel to the slant of the keyboard.

Key each line twice.

Home keys

1 aa jj ff kk ss ll dd ;; aj fk sl d; dd ff jj ll kk

h/e

2 he fee she ash deed deaf shed held head half easel

i/r

3 fire rile risk hire rail dial rake like raid rider

DS

15B

Space Bar Technique

TECHNIQUE TIP

Quickly space after each word and immediately begin the next word.

Use a down-and-in motion for spacing.

✓ checkpoint

Are you sitting up straight in your chair with your feet on the floor as you key? If not, make an effort to improve your keying position.

Key each line twice.

Short, easy words

1 is as if he hi has ask had are her jar kid lad sad
2 jail half lake sail side rail leaf desk fade flair
3 his like reel fails laser seeks lease hired safari

DS

Short-word phrases

4 he is|if she|a jar|he did|as he is|has had|she did
5 red jar|a lake|red hair|her desk|as a lark|as dark
6 he said|she has had a|here he is|all fall|are free

DS

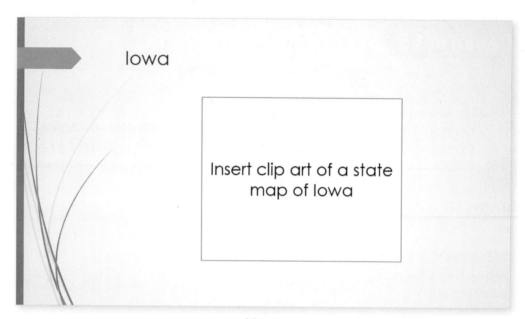

Slide 5

Slide 7

Use *df a3 activity6* for photos.
Resize as necessary and position as shown in illustration.

15C

ENTER Key

TECHNIQUE TIP
Keep up your pace to the end of the line. Tap ENTER quickly and immediately begin the next line.

Key each line twice.

1 if he is;
2 as if she is;
3 he had a fir desk;
4 she has a red jell jar;
5 he has had a lead all fall;
6 she asked if he reads fall ads;
7 she said she reads all ads she sees;
8 his dad has had a sales lead as he said;

DS

15D

Key Mastery

Key each line twice.

h/e

1 he she heel shelf held heed shed heal hire herself
2 he had a sled; she hired a; he has had; she held a

i/r

3 air sir fire liar hair iris ride fair dried desire
4 hire her; she is a risk; his airfare; he fired her

All keys learned

5 he is; he has a red sled; like jade; if he is free
6 is a; he has a jar; a lake; she is safe; fried eel
7 he is free; here she is; she has a jade; like her;
8 he had a; red jars; fire risk; fall ads; sled ride

DS

MicroType

Use *MicroType* Lesson 5 for additional practice.

Slide 8

Convert the bulleted items to SmartArt—Basic Block List.
Change colors to *Colorful – Accent Colors*.

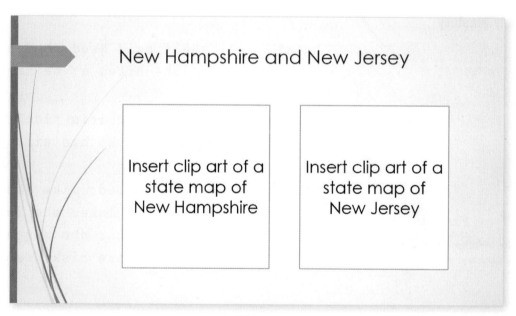

Slide 3

Lesson 16

New Keys o and t

Learning Outcomes

In Lesson 16, you will:
- *Learn reach technique for **o** and **t**.*
- *Combine **o** and **t** smoothly with all other learned keys.*

16A

Warmup

Keep fingers curved and upright.

Key each line twice.

Home row

1 jskj; dlaf; sad fall; had a hall; a fall ad; ask a

3rd row

2 a fire; if her aid; he sees; he irks her; fish jar

All keys learned

3 he had half a jar; as she fell; he sells fir desks

16B

New Keys o and t

o Right ring finger

t Left index finger

Follow the plan for learning new keys shown on page 85. Key each line twice.

Learn o

1 l o|l o|lo lo|do do|of of|so so|old old|fold fold;
2 fork fork|soak soak|hold hold|sold sold|joke joke;
3 a doe; old fork; solid oak door; old foe; oak odor

Learn t

4 f t|f t|it it|fat fat|the the|tied tied|lift lift;
5 ft ft|fit fit|sit sit|hit hit|kite kite|talk talk;
6 lift it; tie the; hit it; take their test; is late

Combine o and t

7 to to|too too|took took|hot hot|lot lot|tort tort;
8 hook hook|told told|fort fort|sort sort|jolt jolt;
9 told a joke; jot or dot; took a jolt; took a look;

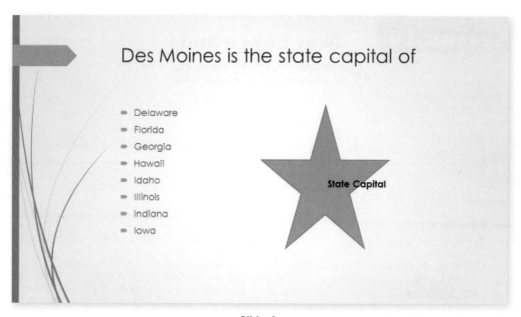

Slide 4

Create the star using Shapes and Text Box.

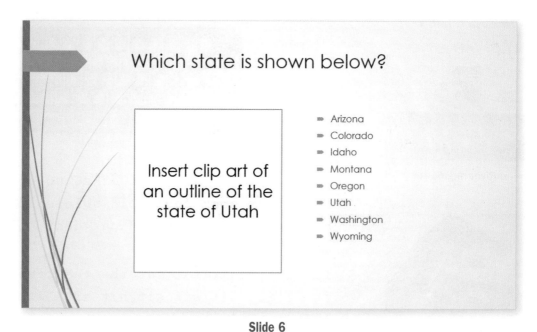

Slide 6

Convert the bulleted items to SmartArt—Vertical Accent List.
Change colors to *Colorful – Accent Colors*.

TECHNIQUE TIP

• Keep your fingers curved and upright.
• Use a down-and-in spacing motion.
• Keep your eyes on the copy as you key.

Key each line twice.

h/e

1 the the|lead lead|held held|hear hear|heart heart;
2 he heard|ask their|here the|has fled|hide the jars

i/t

3 its its|hit hit|tie tie|sit sit|kite kite|fit fit;
4 a tire|a fire|tied to it|it fits|it sits|it is fit

o/r

5 or or|for for|fort fort|oar oar|soar soar|rot rot;
6 three doors|a red rose|for a fort|he rode|for free

Space Bar

7 of he or it is to if do el odd off too are she the
8 off of it|does the|if she|to do the|for the|she is

All keys learned

9 if she is; ask a lad; to the lake; off the old jet
10 he or she; for a fit; if she did; the jar; a salad

MicroType

Use *MicroType* Lesson 6 for additional practice.

16D

Enrichment Activity

Unscramble the letters shown below to create eight words. If you have difficulty, key the letters in different orders to unscramble the words.

1. otd	**5.** aekl
2. tej	**6.** satf
3. erhe	**7.** aodr
4. ierd	**8.** htroe

Slide 1

Search audio online for *patriotic music*. Select *Military Open*.
Start the audio automatically. Hide the audio icon during the slide show.

Slide 2

Convert the bulleted items to SmartArt—Basic Block List.
Change colors to *Colorful – Accent Colors*.

Lesson 17

New Keys n and g

Learning Outcomes

In Lesson 17, you will:
- Learn reach technique for **n** and **g**.
- Combine **n** and **g** smoothly with all other learned keys.

17A

Warmup

Key each line twice.

h/e

1 he has a hoe; he has her heart; her health; he had

o/t

2 took the toad; it is hot; a lot; her toes; dot it;

i/r

3 a tire; it is fair; their jar; their skis; ride it

17B

New Keys n and g

Key each line twice. If time permits, key lines 7–9 again.

n Right index finger

Learn n

1 j n|jn jn|an an|and and|end end|ant ant|land lands
2 jn jn|and and|den den|not not|end end|and and|sand
3 not a train; hand it in; near the end; nine or ten

Learn g

4 f g|fg fg|go go|jog jog|got got|frog frog|get gets
5 fg fg|get get|egg egg|dig dig|logs logs|golf golf;
6 good eggs; eight dogs; a frog; a goat; golf gadget

g Left index finger

Combine n and g

7 gone gone|nag nag|ago ago|gnat gnat|dragon dragons
8 green grass; nine ants; need glasses; ten gallons;
9 go golfing; not again; long ago; ten frogs; a gang

Activity 4
Invitation from Template

Data File:
df a3 activity4

1. Open *df a3 activity4* to create an invitation.

2. Select and insert an appropriate image for the event in the placeholder.

3. Replace [Insert name of school] with **Bedford Middle School**

4. Replace [Insert name of event] with **Baseball Awards Banquet**

5. Replace [Insert brief description] with **Come join us as we celebrate a spectacular season and recognize members of the Bedford Middle School baseball team.**

6. Insert the date as **June 10, 20--** and insert the time as **6:30 to 7:45 p.m.**

7. Replace [Insert contact] with **Head Baseball Coach John Jameson at** john.jameson@bms.net

8. Save the document as *a3 activity4* and close it.

Activity 5
Certificate from Template

Data File:
df a3 activity5

1. Open *df a3 activity5* and make the following changes:

   a. Select **Recipient Name** and change to **Walter Sterling**.
   b. Select **TEAM NAME** and change to **Bedford Middle School Lions—** change the font size to 28 point.
   c. Select **[Signatory name(s)]** and change to **John Jameson**.
   d. Click to select date as **June 10** of the current year.

2. Print the certificate. Save the document as *a3 activity5* and close it.

Activity 6
Presentation

Data Files:
df a3 activity6 clip art
df a3 activity6 photos

1. Create the slides shown below. Use the **Wisp** theme or a similar design. Specific directions are given below each slide.

2. Use Online Pictures for the clip art. Directions for what kind of clips to insert are shown on the slide illustrations. If you don't have Internet access, use *df a3 activity6 clip art*. Use *df a3 activity6 photos* for slide 7.

3. After creating the slides, arrange them by the slide numbers shown beneath each slide.

4. Proofread the text on all slides and correct errors.

5. Save the presentation as *a3 activity6* and close it.

17C

ENTER Key Technique

Tap ENTER quickly and start a new line without pausing.

Key each line twice.

1 here she is;
2 he is at the inn;
3 she goes to ski there;
4 he is also to sign the log;
5 he left the egg on the old desk;
6 he took the old dog to the ski lodge;

 checkpoint   Does your **J** finger remain in place as you tap the ENTER key? If not, make an effort to improve your reach technique.

17D

Key Mastery

TECHNIQUE TIP
Keep your eyes on the copy as you key.

MicroType

Use *MicroType* Lesson 7 for additional practice.

Key each line twice.

n/g

1 gone gone|sing sing|long long|song song|gang gangs
2 sing a song; log on; sign it; and golf; long songs

Space Bar

3 is is|go go|of of|or or|he he|it it|the the|and an
4 if it is a jar|he has a dog|like to go|to do signs

All keys learned

5 an old oak desk; a jade ring; at her side; of the;
6 he goes there at night; she has left for the lake;

7 he took her to the lake; take the hooks off; he is
8 the old jet; sign the list on the; go to the right

17E

Compose Sentences

Read the sentences below. From the list at the left, choose the word that best completes the sentence. Key the word and tap the ENTER key.

desk

hired

lake

long

tires

1. Parker likes to swim at the _____.
2. Owen left his glasses in the _____.
3. The company _____ both of us for the summer job.
4. The _____ on the car need to be replaced.
5. The fish was over 20 inches _____.

1. Open *df a3 activity3* and insert the following replacement text in the appropriate places. Delete unneeded placeholder text.

Bedford Middle School Booster Club

Agenda

May 15, 20--

7:00 p.m.

Type of Meeting: Planning Session

Meeting Facilitator: Shirley Maxton

Invitees: All Booster Club Members

   I. Call to order

  II. Roll call

 III. Approval of minutes from last meeting

 IV. Open issues

      a) Report from Awards Banquet Committee

      b) Selection of banquet menu

  V. New business

      a) Creating invitation for Baseball Awards Banquet

      b) Coordinating volunteers for decorating for banquet

 VI. Adjournment

2. Save the document as *a3 activity3* and close it.

New Keys Left Shift and . (period)

Learning Outcomes

In Lesson 18, you will:

- *Learn reach technique for **Left Shift** and . **(period)**.*
- *Combine **Left Shift** and . **(period)** smoothly with all other learned keys.*

18A

Warmup

Key each line twice.

Reach review

1 rf ol gf ki hj tf nj ed fr lo fg ik jh ft jn a; de

Space Bar

2 as if go at it is in he or to of so do on jet lake

All keys learned

3 a jar; if an; or do; to go; an oak door; she told;

18B

New Keys Left Shift and . (period)

Left Shift *Left little* finger

. (period) *Right ring* finger

TECHNIQUE TIP

To use the Left Shift key:
1. Hold down the Left Shift key with the little finger on the left hand.
2. Tap the letter with the right hand.
3. Return finger(s) to home keys.

Key each line twice. If time permits, rekey lines 7–9.

Learn Left Shift

1 a J|Ja Ja|Ka Ka|La La|Hal Hal|Kal Kal|Jan Jan|Jane
2 Jan did it; Kent took it; Ida said; Jane has a dog
3 I see that Kate is to aid Hans at the Oakdale sale

Learn . (period)

4 l .|1. 1.|fl. fl.|ed. ed.|ft. ft.|rd. rd.|hr. hrs.
5 1. 1.|fl. fl.|hr. hr.|e.g. e.g.|i.e. i.e.|in. ins.
6 a. s. d. f. j. k. l. ;. h. e. i. r. o. t. n. g. o.

Combine Left Shift and . (period)

7 I do. Ian is. Olga did. Jan does. Ken is gone.
8 Hal did it. I shall do it. Kate left on a train.
9 Jan sang a song. Linda read it. Ken told a joke.

Activity 2
Memo from Template

Data File:

df a3 activity2

1. Open *df a3 activity2.* Key **Bedford Middle School** as replacement text in the box at the upper right.

2. Key the following replacement text at the appropriate places:

   TO: Bedford Middle School Baseball Coaching Staff

   FROM: John Jameson, Head Coach

   DATE: April 15, 20--

   SUBJECT: Selection of Most Valuable Player

   Coaches, it is that time of the year again to select the Most Valuable Player for the current baseball season. As in the past, we award the player who exhibits leadership both on and off the field. As a reminder, the following leadership characteristics represent the kind of player we would like to recognize with this award.

   - Ability to gain respect and trust of fellow team members,
   - Dependability,
   - Ability to communicate effectively,
   - Flexibility,
   - Good judgment,
   - Courage, and
   - Honesty.

   Attached is the nomination form. Please turn in your nominations to Coach Jameson by April 22nd.

3. Add appropriate closing lines.

4. Save the document as *a3 activity2* and close it.

18C

ENTER Key Technique

TECHNIQUE TIP
Quickly tap ENTER at the end of each line and immediately begin the next line.

Key each line twice.

1 I like the dog.
2 Janet is at the inn.
3 Jake is to take the test.
4 Hank and Jo left for the lake.
5 Hans took the girls to a ski lodge.
6 Jeff took the old desk to the ski lodge.
7 Jason and Jeff like to listen to those songs.

18D

Key Mastery

SPACING TIP
- Space once after . following abbreviations and initials.
- Space twice after . at the end of a sentence except at the end of a line. There, tap ENTER without spacing.

MicroType

Use *MicroType* Lesson 8 for additional practice.

Key each line twice.

Abbreviations/initials

1 He said ft. for feet; rd. for road; fl. for floor.
2 Lt. Hahn let L. K. take the old gong to Lake Neil.

Short words

3 a an or he to if do it of so is go for got old led
4 go the off aid dot end jar she fit oak and had rod

Short phrases

5 if so|it is|to do|if it|do so|to go|he is|to do it
6 to the|and do|is the|got it|if the|for the|ask for

All letters learned

7 Ned asked Jane. He got the oak door at the lodge.
8 J. L. lost one of the sleds he took off the train.

18E

Enrichment Activity

Unscramble the letters shown below to create eight words. If you have difficulty, key the letters in different orders to unscramble the words.

1. gikn   5. oaltt

2. noij   6. easdk

3. gsoe   7. reith

4. ealt   8. ianga

Warmup Practice

Key each line twice. If time permits, key the lines again.

Alphabet

1 Jack Vance helped Maryann with six bags of quartz.

Figures/Symbol

2 Orlando paid $35,690 on Account #84917 on June 23.

Speed

3 Pamela may go visit with the neighbor by the lake.

gwam 1' | 1 | 2 | 3 | 4 | 5 | 6 | 7 | 8 | 9 | 10 |

Activity 1
Assess Straight-Copy Skill

Key one or two 2' or 3' timed writings on all paragraphs combined. Print, proofread, circle errors, and determine *gwam*.

 all letters used

	gwam	2'	3'

	2'	3'
Stress qualifies as either good or bad depending	5	3
upon the circumstances and ability of people to cope.	10	7
It is good when it has resulted from a pleasant event,	16	11
such as a promotion. In addition, it may increase job	21	14
performance if the pressure is not too great. On the	27	18
other hand, stress is bad when caused by an unpleasant	32	22
event, such as being passed over for a prized promotion.	38	25
Furthermore, it may interfere with the performance of a	44	29
task when the pressure is excessive.	47	32
The major point to recognize is that stress is	5	35
quite normal and will be experienced at times by all.	10	39
Avoiding stress is not an issue, but learning to handle	16	43
day-to-day stress in a proper manner is. A few methods	21	47
that work are taking the time for regular exercise,	27	50
getting enough sleep, and eating well-balanced meals.	32	54
These specific methods relate to personal habits.	37	57
In addition, using some stress reducers that more	42	60
directly relate to the job also will be helpful.	47	63
A good way to reduce stress in the office is to	5	66
use techniques known to improve time management.	10	69
These include analyzing the tasks performed to see	15	72
if all are necessary, judging which ones are most	20	75
important so that priorities can be set, and using	25	78
most of the time to do the jobs that are most important.	31	82
Office workers who do not use these procedures may	36	85
expend considerable energy on less valuable tasks and	41	89
feel stressed when more important ones go unfinished.	47	93

gwam 2' | 1 | 2 | 3 | 4 | 5 |
     3' | 1 | 2 | 3 |

Lesson 19

Review

Learning Outcomes

In Lesson 19, you will:
- Improve use of **Space Bar**, **Left Shift**, and **ENTER**.
- Improve keying speed on words, phrases, and sentences.

19A

Warmup

Key each line twice.

Reach review

1 ki fr lo de jn fg jh ft l. l.lo i.o. r.e. n.g. h.t

Space Bar

2 a as ask|h he hen|n no not|t to too took|d do dot;

Left Shift

3 Kent left. Lana is not here. Jake sang the song.

19B

Key Mastery

Key each line twice.

n/g

1 jn jn|fg fg|slang slang|lingo lingo|jargon jargon;
2 Nate sang eight or nine songs; Lana sang one song.

o/t

3 lo lo|ft ft|to to|foot foot|lots lots|tooth tooth;
4 John has lost the list he took to that food store.

i/r

5 ki ki|fr fr|ire ire|risk risk|ring ring|tire tire;
6 Ida is taking a giant risk riding their old horse.

Left Shift/.

7 Jason K. Hanselt; Katie O. Higgins; Kirk N. Jones;
8 J. L. Johnson is going to Illinois to see her son.

✓ checkpoint

Did you space once after periods following initials?

Employability Skills

Do you know what employers are looking for? Employability skills and characteristics are skills and traits that are attractive to employers. In other words, if you possess these skills and traits, there is a better chance that someone will want to hire you for a job.

1. Working with a partner, use a search engine to research employability skills. You may also use previous Life Success Builder activities for ideas. Together, decide which five skills and characteristics you think are most important to employers.

2. Open *df c10 employability skills*. Follow the directions in the document to create a *PowerPoint* presentation about the skills you chose.

Activity 9

To complete this activity, you will need the Student Interest Survey that you filled out in Career Exploration Portfolio Activity 1. Completing Career Exploration Activities 2–8 would also be helpful but is not mandatory.

1. Review your Student Interest Survey. Note your *second* Career Cluster of interest. Reread its description.

2. Go to http://www.careertech.org. Click the **Career Technical Education** button, and then click **Career Clusters**. Click the name of your second Career Cluster choice near the bottom of the page.

3. Scroll through the categories available within that Career Cluster. Click the Plan of Study **Excel** link under the category you are most interested in to download the file to your system. (Choose the same category, or Pathway, that you used in Activities 3 and 6 if you completed them.)

4. Locate and open the downloaded *Excel* workbook. Read the list of classes you should take in high school to get ready for this career. Then read the list of classes that you should take after high school.

5. Search the Internet to find one or more colleges or technical schools that offer degrees in this career.

6. Use *Word* to write a summary of what you learned in this activity. Save the document as *c10 career 2 skills*, print, and close it.

19C

ENTER Key Technique

TECHNIQUE TIP
Quickly tap ENTER at the end of each line and immediately begin the next line.

Key each line twice.

```
1 Jon has gone to ski;
2 he took a train at eight.
3 Karen asked for the disk;
4 she is to take it to the lake.
5 Joe said he left the file that
6 has the data he needs at the lodge.
7 Janine said she felt ill as the ski
8 lift left to take the girls to the hill.
```

19D

Increase Speed

Key each line twice.

Key words (Think, say, and key the words.)

```
1 is and the if she of air did dog risk forks eight
2 rifle signs their then title ant aisle dials dish
3 shall signal tight shelf rigid right soaks island
```

Key phrases (Think, say, and key the phrases.)

```
4 is to|or do|to it|if he is|to do|it is|of an|if he
5 he did|of the|to all|is for|is a tie|to aid|if she
6 he or she|to rig it|if she did|is to sit|is to aid
```

Key sentences (Tap keys at a brisk, steady pace.)

```
7 Jake is to go to the lake to get her old red skis.
8 Hal asked for a list of all the old gold she sold.
9 Helen said she left the old disk list on his desk.
```

MicroType

Use *MicroType* Lesson 9 for additional practice.

19E

Technique Review

Your techniques are an important part of learning to key. You should continue to work to refine your techniques.

1. Open *df 19e check sheet*. Print the document. Close the file.

2. Work with a classmate. Ask your classmate to key lines 7–9 (above) as you watch for proper techniques. Mark notes on your check sheet. Share your comments with your classmate.

3. Ask your classmate to rate your techniques as you key lines 7–9. Discuss your ratings with your classmate.

COLLABORATION

ACROSS THE CURRICULUM

Academic Connections

Data Files:

df c10 student club
df c10 employee
    benefits
df c10 employability
    skills

Student Clubs

Your school probably has many student clubs and organizations. For example, do you have a chess club? An organization that organizes fund-raisers or community service projects? A social group that plans school dances or events? A ski club? Joining a group is not only fun; it provides other benefits as well.

1. Working with a small group, start *Word* and open *df c10 student club*.

2. Follow the directions in the document to create a *PowerPoint* presentation about student clubs and organizations. In the presentation, explain the benefits of being part of a club or organization. Then use more slides to persuade your audience to join a specific club or organization.

About Business

Employee Benefits

One of the first things people want to know when they are applying for a job is how much they will get paid. While a pay rate is very important, adults also need to consider the employee benefits they will receive. **Employee benefits** are payments made to workers in addition to their salary and are often paid as services, cash, or goods. Insurance, paid vacation, retirement plans, and tuition payments are examples of employee benefits that companies might offer.

1. Use the Internet to find an online job site (such as http://www.Monster.com or http://www.CareerBuilders.com). Find three available jobs for three different careers of your choice. Try to find the following information for each position.

    *   Job title

    *   Name of the company

    *   City and state

    *   Salary

    *   Benefits

    *   Hours (full time or part time)

2. Open *df c10 employee benefits*. Follow the directions in the document to create a *PowerPoint* presentation about the three jobs that you researched.

Lesson 20

New Keys u and c

Learning Outcomes

In Lesson 20, you will:
- Learn reach technique for **u** and **c**.
- Combine **u** and **c** smoothly with all other learned keys.

20A

Warmup

Key each line twice.

Reach review

1 fg jn lo fr ki de l. ft jh gf ij tf nj ed ol rf .l

Space Bar

2 if so to of no go is in it as see are art jet lake

Left Shift

3 Ken has a horse. Jan has a dog. He is going too.

20B

New Keys u and c

Key each line twice. If time permits, rekey lines 7–9.

u Right index finger

c Left middle finger

Learn u

1 j u|ju ju|just just|rust rust|dust dust|used used;
2 ju ju|jug jug|jut jut|turn turn|hug hug|sure sure;
3 turn it; due us; the fur; use it; fur rug; is just

Learn c

4 d c|dc dc|can can|tic tic|catch catch|clock clock;
5 dc dc|ice ice|cat cat|car car|care care|dock docks
6 a can; the ice; she can; the dock; the code; a car

Combine u and c

7 cut cute duck clue cuff cure luck truck curd such;
8 such luck; a cure; to cut; the cure; for the truck
9 Janet and Jack told us to take four cans of juice.

Speed Building

1. Key three 1' timed writings on each paragraph, striving to key more on each timing; determine *gwam*.

2. Key a 2' or 3' timed writing on both paragraphs combined, striving to maintain your highest 1' *gwam*.

A all letters used

	gwam	2'	3'

Taxes are the means used by the government — 4 · 3

to raise money for its expenditures. Taxes have — 9 · 6

never been popular. The legislative branches of — 14 · 9

the government devote a lot of time and energy — 19 · 12

trying to devise a system that requires everyone — 24 · 16

to pay his or her fair and just share. Tax — 28 · 19

assessments are typically based on the benefits — 33 · 22

realized and on an individual's ability to pay. — 38 · 25

Two of the most common taxes are the personal — 42 · 28

income tax and the sales tax. — 45 · 30

The personal income tax is the assessment — 4 · 33

individuals are required to pay on their earnings. — 9 · 36

Employers deduct this tax from employees' — 14 · 39

paychecks. The sales tax is another assessment — 18 · 42

with which the majority of people are familiar. — 23 · 45

It is a tax that is added to the retail price of a — 28 · 48

good or service. While the income tax is an — 33 · 51

assessment based on an individual's ability to pay, — 38 · 55

the general sales tax is based on the benefits a — 43 · 58

person receives. — 45 · 59

gwam 2' | 1 | 2 | 3 | 4 | 5 |
3' | 1 | 2 | 3 |

Key Mastery

TECHNIQUE TIP
- Reach up without moving your hands away from your body.
- Reach down without moving your hands toward your body.

MicroType

Use *MicroType* Lesson 10 for additional practice.

Key each line twice.

3rd/1st rows

1 no to in nut run cue tot cot nun urn ten turn cute
2 Nan is cute; he is curt; turn a cog; he can use it

Left Shift and .

3 Jett had a lead. Kate ate the cake. Lane let us.
4 I said to use Kan. for Kansas and Ore. for Oregon.

Short words

5 if the and cue for end fit rug oak she fur due got
6 an due cut such fuss rich turn dock curl such hair

Short phrases

7 a risk|is fun|to rush|for us|a fit|the dog|such as
8 just in|code it|turn it|cure it|as such|is in luck

All keys learned

9 He told us to get the ice. Juan called her for us.
10 Hal is sure that he can go there in an hour or so.

20D

Critical Thinking Activity

Landov

President Lyndon Johnson

You have learned to key the letters shown below. Notice that only the letters keyed with the right hand are shown as capitals. Key as many U.S. presidents' last names as you can using only these letters.

a c d e f g H I J K L N O r s t U

KEYBOARDING SKILLBUILDING

Warmup Practice

Key each line twice. If time permits, key the lines again.

Alphabet

1 Fran Vasquez put down the six jackets by my glove.

Figure/Symbol

2 The house at 1768 Oak was decreased 15% ($23,490).

Speed

3 Orlando may keep the turkeys in a box by the dock.

gwam 1' | 1 | 2 | 3 | 4 | 5 | 6 | 7 | 8 | 9 | 10 |

Technique Mastery of Individual Letters

Key each line twice, striving to maintain a continuous pace.

TECHNIQUE TIP
Keep your eyes on your textbook as you key each sentence.

A/Z 1 Zach and Anna ate a pizza at the plaza by the zoo.
B/Y 2 Bobby may be too busy to buy Mary a bicycle today.

C/X 3 Chen Xio caught six cod to fix for the six scouts.
D/W 4 Dwight would let Wanda walk the dogs in the woods.

E/V 5 Even Eva had a very heavy box to leave in the van.
F/U 6 Four out of five runners had on fuzzy furry cuffs.

G/T 7 Eight girls tugged on the target to get it higher.
H/S 8 Al's son has his share of those shiny star shapes.

I/R 9 Rick will have their rings shined by Friday night.
J/Q 10 Jacques quit the squad after a major joint injury.

K/P 11 Kip packed a pink backpack and put it on the desk.
L/O 12 Lolita wore the royal blue blouse with gold laces.

M/N 13 Many of those men met in the main entry on Monday.

gwam 1' | 1 | 2 | 3 | 4 | 5 | 6 | 7 | 8 | 9 | 10 |

Improve Keying Technique

1. Key lines 1–5 twice.
2. Take three 30" timed writings on line 5. If you complete the line, key it again.

One-hand words of 2–5 letters

1 no we my be up as on fee you was him get rate pump
2 as oil see act few pop tax mop get kin bee nip red
3 far him hop ilk feed were only card pump case jump
4 lump date pony areas extra after water exact great
5 Give Fred my tax on water after you state my case.

gwam 30" | 2 | 4 | 6 | 8 | 10 | 12 | 14 | 16 | 18 | 20 |

New Keys w and Right Shift

Learning Outcomes

In Lesson 21, you will:
- *Learn reach technique for **w** and **Right Shift**.*
- *Combine **w** and **Right Shift** smoothly with all other learned keys.*

21A

Warmup

Key each line twice.

Reach review

1 fr fg de ju ft jn ki lo dc ki rf l. ed jh ol gf tf

u/c

2 luck used cure such cute cause lunch accuse actual

All letters learned

3 Jefferson just took the huge lead in the election.

21B

New Keys w and Right Shift

w Left ring finger

Right Shift Right little finger

TECHNIQUE TIP
Depress the Shift key, tap the key, and release the Shift key in a quick 1-2-3 count.

Key each line twice. If time permits, rekey lines 7–9.

Learn w

1 s w|sw sw|two two|wet wet|low low|how how|was was;

2 sw sw|were were|what what|snow snow|worker worker;

3 to show; to watch; to win; when we; wash and wear;

Learn Right Shift

4 ;A ;A;|A1 A1;|Dan Dan;|Ann Ann;|Ron Ron;|Gene Gene

5 Chicago; San Diego; Santa Fe; Atlanta; Eau Claire;

6 Richard left for San Diego; Fran left for Chicago.

Combine w and Right Shift

7 Charla and Wanda will watch the show with Willard.

8 We will want to show the award to Walt and Andrew.

9 Wes wished he was in Washington watching the show.

Planets Presentation

In this activity, you will plan, prepare, and deliver a presentation about the planets in our solar system. The purpose of the presentation is to inform your listeners about the planets. The audience will be your classmates.

Data File:

df 71 feedback

1. In a *Word* document, key the name of the presentation. Under the name, key the heading **Purpose**. Under the heading, key two or three goals for your presentation. Key the heading **Audience Profile**. Under the heading, key a bulleted list of four or five points that describe the audience. Save the document as *c10 planets outline*.

2. Do research about the solar system. Your talk should include the names of the planets, their order in relation to the sun, and two or three interesting facts about each planet. Also include basic facts about the sun. Key an outline of the content of the presentation in the *c10 planets outline* document. Save the document again, using the same name.

3. Plan and create a slide show to use in your presentation. You should have at least ten slides (a title slide and a slide for each planet and the sun). Create the slides based on the content of your outline. Find clip art of the planets and include it on the slides. Use an appropriate theme. Save the slide show as *c10 planets*.

4. Practice delivering your presentation using the slides.

5. Deliver the presentation to a group of your classmates. Ask your listeners to complete a feedback form immediately after you give your presentation. (The form is in the file *df 71 feedback*.) Review the completed forms to see how you can improve when giving presentations in the future.

Key Mastery

Space quickly after keying each word.

Key each line twice.

w and Right Shift

1 Dr. Wade works here; Dr. Weeks left two weeks ago.
2 Will Whitt get a watch when his is in town on Wed.

n/g

3 sing a song|long gone|wrong sign|and got|a gallon;
4 Glenda signed the wrong check. Jen is gone again.

Short words

5 is and the she sir for rid cut got rug oak end dog
6 wet red oil ear inn gas ink car on ace look no sea

Short phrases

7 he did|a jet ride|she is|if she can go|take a look
8 as soon as|to go to|if it is|when he is|has done a

All keys learned

 9 Jason and Chuck are going. Laurie thinks she can.
10 Frank worked eight hours; Linda worked four hours.

21D

Spacing with Punctuation

SPACING TIP
Do not space after an internal period in an abbreviation. Space once after each period following initials.

Key each line twice.

1 Dr. Hoag said to use wt. for weight; in. for inch.
2 J. R. Chen has used ed. for editor; Rt. for Route.
3 Sue said Jed Ford got an Ed.D. degree last winter.
4 Use i.e. for that is; cs. for case; ck. for check.

21E

Critical Thinking

MicroType

Use *MicroType* Lesson 11 for additional practice.

In this lesson, you learned the Right Shift key. There are 12 U.S. presidents' names that you can key using the Right Shift key and the letters you have learned that are shown below. See how many of the 12 you can key.

a c d e f g h i j k l n o r s t u w

Before You Move On

Answer these questions to review what you have learned in Chapter 10.

1. Presentations are given for three general purposes. What are those purposes? LO 66A

2. What is an audience profile? Why should you prepare an audience profile when planning a presentation? LO 66B

3. What are the three parts of a good presentation? What does each part do? LO 66C

4. Is reading from a script when you deliver a presentation a good idea? Explain. LO 66C

5. What is a visual aid? LO 66D

6. What does the Slide pane display? What does it allow the user to do? LO 67A

7. What are placeholders? LO 67A

8. What does the Notes pane allow the user to do? LO 67A

9. What is the purpose of the Slide Sorter view? LO 67B

10. What is a theme? LO 68A

11. Describe how to insert online pictures (clip art) in a slide. LO 68B

12. What is the purpose of the Arrange All feature? LO 69C

13. How do you keep the sound icon from appearing on the screen during a presentation? LO 70D

14. Explain how to print six slides vertical to a page. LO 71A

15. List five tips or guidelines you should follow when giving a presentation. LO 71B

Lesson 22

New Keys b and y

Learning Outcomes

In Lesson 22, you will:
- *Learn reach technique for **b** and **y**.*
- *Combine **b** and **y** smoothly with all other learned keys.*

22A

Warmup

Keep fingers curved and upright.

Key each line twice.

Reach review

1 ft. de lo ju sw ki fr dc jn jh l. fg rt ws ol ed.

c/n

2 nice coin cent cane niece dance ounce check glance

All letters learned

3 Jack Elgin had two hits in the first four innings.

22B

New Keys b and y

b Left index finger

y Right index finger

Key each line twice. If time permits, rekey lines 7–9.

Learn b

1 f b f b|fb bf|fib fib|big big|book book|bank bank;
2 fb fb fb|bugs bugs|oboe oboe|label label|bird bird
3 Bob bid; Rob bunted; black rubber ball; brief job;

Learn y

4 j y|jy jy|jay jay|yes yes|eye eye|day day|rye rye;
5 yiy yiy|eye eye|only only|yellow yellow|your yours
6 why did you; yellow cycle; only yesterday; he says

Combine b and y

7 buy buy|boy boy|busy busy|buddy buddy|byway byway;
8 by the bay; you buy a; big burly boy; a yellow bus
9 Bobby went by way of bus to buy the big blue belt.

Animations and Transitions

Slide animations and transitions enhance a slide presentation. Transitions are the visual change between slides. They are used to make the switch between slides interesting and engaging.

To apply transitions between slides, select the slide to which you want to apply the transition. Then click the Transitions tab and select a transition from the Transition to This Slide group.

Animation is used to create interest as slide content appears on the slide. Use animations to make text, graphics, and other objects appear on a slide one at a time. This allows you to control how the information is presented as well as add interest to the presentation. For example, display bullets of text as you discuss each topic rather than displaying all of the bullets when the slide appears. Animations can include a sound effect that plays when an object appears. Also, you can create a motion path for an object, displaying the object in a sequence of locations on the slide. This makes the object appear to be moving on the slide.

To apply animation to objects on a slide:

- Click the **Animations** tab.
- Click the slide containing the object you want to animate.
- Click the object.
- Click the More button on the Animation gallery.
- Click the type of animation you want.

1. Open *df 71 above*, and play the presentation, noting the animations and transitions. Figure 10.26 shows the *Curtains* transition.

Figure 10.26 *Transition using Curtains effect*

2. Open one of the *PowerPoint* presentations you created for this chapter and apply transitions and animations. Close the presentation and *PowerPoint*.

22C

Space Bar Technique

SPACING TIP

Space with a down-and-in motion immediately after each word.

Key each line once.

1 Jason will be able to take the bus to the concert.
2 Gary is to sign for the auto we set aside for her.
3 Rey is in town for just one week to look for work.
4 Ted is to work for us for a week at the lake dock.
5 June said he was in the auto when it hit the tree.
6 Dan has an old car she wants to sell at this sale.

22D

ENTER Key Technique

MicroType

Use *MicroType* Lesson 12 for additional practice.

Key each line once. At the end of each line, quickly tap the ENTER key and start the next line.

1 Gary will hit first.
2 Jan will be the second hitter.
3 Nick will be second and bat after Jason.
4 Roberto will be the center fielder and hit eighth.

gwam 1' | 1 | 2 | 3 | 4 | 5 | 6 | 7 | 8 | 9 | 10 |

22E

Determine Number of Words Keyed

A **standard word** in keyboarding is five characters. These five characters can be letters, numbers, symbols, or spaces. Each group of five characters is shown by the number scale under lines you key. (See scale under line 4 in 22D above.) One measure used to describe keying skill is the number of words you key in a certain amount of time, such as a minute. The number of standard words keyed in 1' is called **gross words a minute** (*gwam*).

1. Key line 4 of 22D again as your teacher times you for 1'. Then follow the steps below to find 1' *gwam* for the timing.

   • Note on the scale the figure beneath the last word you keyed. That is your 1' *gwam* if you key the line partially or only once.

   • If you complete the line once and start over, add 10 to the figure you determined in step 1. The result is your 1' *gwam*.

2. Key line 4 of 22D again as your teacher times you for 30". Then follow the steps below to find 30" *gwam*.

   • Find 1' *gwam* (total words keyed).

   • Multiply 1' *gwam* by 2. The resulting figure is your 30" *gwam*.

Planning and preparing a presentation is only half the task of giving a good presentation. The other half is the delivery. Positive thinking is a must for a good presenter. Prepare and practice before a presentation. This helps you be confident that you can do a good job. Do not worry that the presentation will not be perfect. Set a goal to be a better speaker each time you give a speech, not to be a perfect speaker. Practice the following presentation tips to improve your presentation skills.

- **Know your message.** Knowing the message well allows you to talk with the audience rather than read to them.

- **Look at the audience.** Make eye contact with one person briefly (for two or three seconds). Then move on to another person.

- **Know how to use the visuals.** Practice using the visual aids you have chosen for the presentation. Glance at each visual as you display it. Then focus on the audience.

- **Vary the volume and rate at which you speak.** Slow down to emphasize points. Speed up on points you know are familiar to your audience.

- **Look confident.** Stand erect and show that you want to communicate with the audience.

- **Let your personality come through.** Be natural; let the audience know who you are. Show your enthusiasm for the topic you are presenting.

- **Use gestures and facial expressions.** A smile, frown, or puzzled look, when appropriate, can help communicate your message. Make sure your gestures are natural.

71C

Deliver a Presentation

1. Open *70 school presentation* that you worked on in Lesson 70.

2. Add notes to the slides to create notes pages that are appropriate to use as audience handouts. Print the notes pages. Click the **Spelling** button on the Review tab in the Proofing group to check the spelling. Proofread and correct all errors. Save the file as *71 school presentation*.

3. Review the information you have prepared for the presentation. Decide which information will be presented by each team member. Practice delivering the presentation.

4. Deliver the presentation to the class or to a group of classmates. At the beginning of the presentation, give the audience copies of *df 71 feedback* from your data files. Ask each listener to complete the form immediately after your presentation. Also give the listeners the handouts before you begin the presentation.

5. With your teammates, review the feedback forms completed by the listeners. List points on which the team did particularly well. List ways you can improve when giving presentations in the future.

Lesson 23

Review

Learning Outcomes

In Lesson 23, you will:
- *Improve spacing, shifting, and entering.*
- *Increase keying control and speed.*

23A

Warmup

Key each line twice.

Reach review

1 ton only beat teen week rich used nice count B. J.

b/y

2 buy yes boy year obey eyes been yield debate Bobby

All letters learned

3 Jason knew the gift you held was for Dr. Jacobson.

23B

Space Bar and Shift Keys

Key each line twice.

Space Bar (Space immediately after each word.)

1 in by we so do the and run yet ink low jet fun can

2 in the|when he|if she will|run to|yes you|can be a

3 Lance take a look at her car to see what is wrong.

4 Janet lost both of the keys to the car in the lot.

Shift keys (Hold down Shift key; tap key; quickly return finger(s) to home keys.)

5 Dr. Alou; Jose K. Casey; Sue A. Finch; Jon B. Bins

6 Della and I went to France in June to see her dad.

7 Roger and Carlos went to Salt Lake City on Friday.

8 The San Francisco Giants were in town on Thursday.

SPACING TIP
Space with a down-and-in motion immediately after each word.

 **checkpoint** Do you reach up to keys without moving your hands away from your body?

1. Start *Word*. Open *df 71 fenwick dance notes*. This file contains the notes Ms. Fenwick would like included with the first five slides.

2. Open *70 fenwick dance* that you worked with in Lesson 70.

3. On slide 1, display the Notes pane and key the notes for slide 1 as shown in Figure 10.24.

Text keyed in Notes pane

Figure 10.24 *Notes pane*

4. Continue keying the notes for slides 2–5.

PP   View/Presentation Views/Notes Page

5. To see how the notes pages look, follow the path at the left to display Notes Page view. Click the **Next Slide** or **Previous Slide** button several times to view all of the notes pages. Go to slide 1 and play the show. Notice that the notes do not display.

Instant Message

You may want to print a sample slide or notes page in color to place in your portfolio.

6. To print handouts, click the **File** tab. Choose **Print**. Select a printer if necessary.

7. Key the slides to be printed (**1-5**) as shown in Figure 10.25. Use the down arrow in each box to select the number of slides per page (**6 Slides Vertical**), sides to print on (**Print One Sided**), the orientation (**Landscape Orientation**), and the color of the print (**Grayscale**).

Instant Message

The *Pure Black and White* print option uses the least amount of ink.

8. Click the **Print** button to print the handout page.

9. Save the presentation as *71 fenwick dance* and close it.

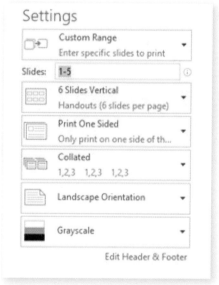

Figure 10.25 *Handouts print options*

Check Speed

KEYING TIP Keep the insertion point moving steadily across each line (no pauses).

Key each line once double-spaced. Key a 20" timed writing on each line. Your rate of gross words a minute (*gwam*) is shown below the lines.

1 I will see her.

2 Janet has a new job.

3 Jack will go to the lake.

4 Karl is to go skiing with her.

5 Kara has two old oak doors to sell.

6 Faye and I took the test before we left.

7 Jessie said she will be in school on Tuesday.

8 Jay will go to the city to work on the road signs.

gwam 20" | 3 | 6 | 9 | 12 | 15 | 18 | 21 | 24 | 27 | 30 |

23D

Speed Building

TECHNIQUE TIP
- Keep your fingers curved and upright.
- Space quickly without pausing between words.

Key each line once.

1 Judy had gone for that big ice show at Lake Tahoe.

2 Jack said that all of you will find the right job.

3 Cindy has just left for work at the big ski lodge.

4 Rudy can take a good job at the lake if he wishes.

5 Rob saw the bird on the lake by the big boat dock.

6 Ted knew the surf was too rough for kids to enjoy.

23E

Critical Thinking

COLLABORATION

MicroType

Use *MicroType* Lesson 13 for additional practice.

Work with another student to complete this activity. Unscramble the letters shown below to create eight words. Work as quickly as you can. Raise your hand when you have all eight words.

1. cush   5. oohtt

2. kjeo   6. eehcr

3. gornw   7. wstae

4. kieal   8. ydnboe

Delivering a Presentation

Learning Outcomes

Data Files:

df 71 fenwick
    dance notes
df 71 feedback

In Lesson 71, you will:

71A Add notes to a presentation.
71B Learn about presentation delivery.
71C Deliver a presentation.

71A

Create Notes

Notes, if used properly, can help the beginning speaker feel more comfortable giving the presentation. Speakers who are comfortable and relaxed tend to deliver a natural, polished presentation. Notes should not be used to read to the audience. They should highlight the main points of the talk and remind you of what you want to say about each slide.

Notes can be added to slides using the Notes pane in Normal view. You also can key notes in Notes Page view. Notes do not display when you play a slide show. However, you can print the notes on notes pages. A notes page shows the slide and the notes below the slide. Use the notes to help you remember details as you give the presentation. You also can use the printed notes pages as handouts for the audience. The top portion of a notes page is shown in Figure 10.23. Note that the font size of the notes was increased from Calibri 12 to 16 to make it easier for the presenter to use the notes during the presentation.

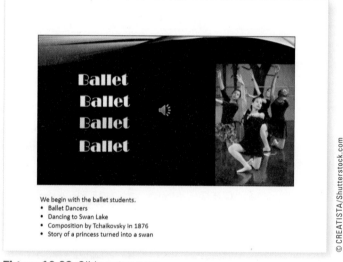

Figure 10.23 *Slide notes page*

To key notes, click the Notes button on the status bar to display the Notes pane. Key the note for the slide. Format the note text as needed. For example, you can apply bold, change the font size, change the text alignment, or create a bulleted list. After keying the note for the first slide, click the Next Slide button and key the note for the second slide. You may want to click and drag the top border of the Notes pane to make the Notes pane larger. This makes entering notes easier and does not affect the slide.

New Keys m and x

Learning Outcomes

In Lesson 24, you will:

- Learn reach technique for **m** and **x**.
- Combine **m** and **x** smoothly with all other learned keys.

24A

Warmup

Key each line twice.

Reach review

1 fg jy lo fr jn de sw ft ki jh fb dc ju by us if ow

b/y

2 by bay buy big yes boy buy bit try bury ruby byway

All letters learned

3 Beth can win the gold if she will just key faster.

24B

New Keys m and x

Key each line twice. If time permits, rekey lines 7–9.

*m **Right index** finger*

*x **Left ring** finger*

Learn m

1 j m|jm jm|jams jams|make make|mail mail|most most;
2 jm jm|me me|may may|moon moon|grim grim|mean meant
3 to them; meet me; make a mark; mail it; mean to me

Learn x

4 s x|sx sx|six six|fix fix|exit exit|extend extend;
5 sx sx|six six|tax tax|hex hex|fix fix|exact exact;
6 to excel; to exile; an exit; by six; an excise tax

Combine m and x

7 mix fox six jam men box hoax coax maxim axle taxi;
8 to fix; mix it; six men; make an exit; make a box;
9 Maxine Cox took the exit exams in Texas on Monday.

3. Use the Internet to learn three facts about each of the following presidents:

- Abraham Lincoln
- Thomas Jefferson
- Franklin D. Roosevelt
- Theodore Roosevelt

4. For each president listed, create a slide similar to the one you created for President Washington. (Use bulleted lists for your facts, rather than a SmartArt diagram.)

5. When you have completed the slides, rearrange them. Place the title slide first and the table slide second. Place the slides about the presidents next. Arrange those slides in order by years served in office.

6. Save the presentation as *70 presidents* and close it.

Activity 2

1. Start *Word*. Open *68 school outline* that you created in Lesson 68.

2. Now that you have had time to think about your school presentation, review the outline that you and your teammates composed. Add two or more sub points for each main topic in your outline.

3. Open *df 70 effective slides* to learn more about using bulleted lists.

4. Start *PowerPoint*. Open *68 school presentation* that you created in Lesson 68. Insert a second slide with the title **Today's Presentation**. Working from your outline, key a bulleted list identifying what your presentation will cover.

5. Insert additional slides and key the main points and sub points of your presentation. Consider changing some of the bulleted lists to SmartArt diagrams. Include a slide with a table that presents some information about your school. For example, you might show the number of male and female students at each grade level.

6. Add appropriate online pictures or pictures your team has taken to at least two slides.

7. Enhance your presentation with animations and transitions (see the *Above and Beyond* feature on page 335).

8. Save the presentation as *70 school presentation* and play it. Discuss with your teammates ways to improve the presentation. Make the necessary changes and save the presentation again. Close *PowerPoint*.

Key Mastery

TECHNIQUE TIP
- Reach up without moving your hands away from your body.
- Reach down without moving your hands toward your body.

MicroType

Use *MicroType* Lesson 14 for additional practice.

Key each line twice.

3rd/1st rows

1 men box but now cut gem rib ton yet not meet mired
2 cub oxen torn went time were note court worn owned

Short words

3 and own she box fix city duck held hair name their
4 art gas face honk milk draw junk aware extra start

Short phrases

5 you want|if she is|one of the|that is|they are not
6 make the call|for all the|and is|able to|they may;

All keys learned

7 Jacki is now at the gym; Lexi is due there by six.
8 Stan saw that he could fix my old bike for Glenda.

24D

Spacing with Punctuation

SPACING TIP
Do not space after an internal period in an abbreviation such as Ed.D.

Key each line twice.

1 He has an Ed.D. in music; I have an Ed.D. in math.
2 She may send a box c.o.d. to Ms. Cox in St. Louis.
3 Maxine will take a boat to St. Thomas in December.
4 Maria used Wed. for Wednesday and Mon. for Monday.

24E

Critical Thinking

Arizona
California
Connecticut
Florida
New York
Pennsylvania
South Dakota
Texas
Wyoming

Key the sentences below. From the list at the left, choose the word that best completes the sentence. Do not key the numbers.

1. Mount Rushmore is located in _____.
2. The Devils Tower is located in _____.
3. San Antonio is located in _____.
4. The Statue of Liberty is located in _____.
5. San Francisco is located in _____.

Insert/Media/Audio

TIP To remove a sound from a slide, select and delete the sound icon.

1. In *70 fenwick dance*, double-click slide 4 to return to Normal view. You will find and add an audio file to this slide.

2. Follow the path at the left and click **Online Audio**. In the Office.com Clip Art (Royalty-free sound clips) box, key **ballet** in the search box and tap ENTER. Select the **Ballerina** sound clip. Click **Insert**. If you do not have online access, use the sound clips on slide 2 of *df 69 fenwick dance*.

3. The sound clip appears in the middle of the screen. Click the icon if necessary to display the Audio Tools Playback tab. Click the down arrow to the right of Start in the Audio Options group and select **Automatically** so that the music begins to play when the slide appears on the screen. See Figure 10.21.

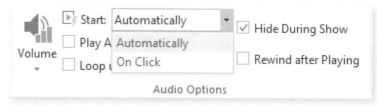

Figure 10.21 *Automatic start option*

4. Click the **Hide During Show** checkbox so that the sound icon doesn't appear on the screen when the slide is displayed. See Figure 10.21.

5. Click slide 7 in the thumbnail pane and search online for the *Jazz Theme* sound clip using **jazz** as your search word. Insert the audio clip and start the sound automatically. Hide the icon during the slide show.

6. On slide 9, insert a tap dance sound clip. It should start automatically and the icon should be hidden during the slide show.

7. Run the presentation to hear the sounds you added. Then close the presentation.

70E

Add Content to Presentations

Instant Message

One good source of information about U.S. presidents is the White House website at http://www.whitehouse.gov /history/presidents.

Activity 1

1. Open *69 presidents* that you worked with in Lesson 69.

2. Insert a new slide at the end of the presentation. Use the Title and Content layout. Create the slide with the table shown in Figure 10.22.

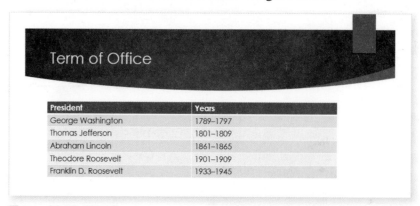

Term of Office

President	Years
George Washington	1789–1797
Thomas Jefferson	1801–1809
Abraham Lincoln	1861–1865
Theodore Roosevelt	1901–1909
Franklin D. Roosevelt	1933–1945

Figure 10.22 *Slide 3*

Lesson 25

New Keys p and v

Learning Outcomes

In Lesson 25, you will:
- *Learn reach technique for **p** and **v**.*
- *Combine **p** and **v** smoothly with all other learned keys.*

25A

Warmup

Key each line twice.

One-hand words

1 gate link face moon extra hook base join beef milk

Phrases

2 if you will|take a look|when they|join us|to see a

All letters learned

3 Jo Buck won a gold medal for her sixth show entry.

25B

New Keys p and v

Key each line twice. If time permits, rekey lines 7–9.

p Right little *finger*

v Left index *finger*

Learn p

1 ; p ;p|pay pay|put put|apt apt|kept kept|pack pack
2 ;p ;p|pain pain|paint paint|paper paper|soap soap;
3 a plan; a party cap; pick a place; a pack of paper

Learn v

4 f v f v|via via|live live|have have|vote vote|save
5 vf vf|van van|visit visit|liver liver|voice voice;
6 five vans; have a visit; very valid; vim and vigor

Combine p and v

7 pave hive open save plan jive soap very pain votes
8 apt to vote; pick a vase; pack the van; five pans;
9 Pam has a plan to have the van pick us up at five.

Rearrange Slide Order

View/Presentation
Views/Slide Sorter

As you review your slides, you may find that you want them to be in a different order. Slides can be rearranged in the **Slide Sorter** view or in the thumbnail pane. To rearrange slides, click and drag a slide to a new location. Slide Sorter view is shown in Figure 10.20.

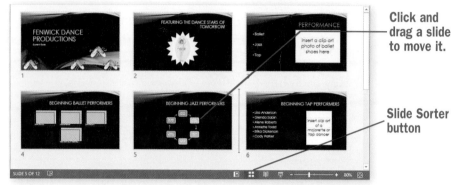

Click and drag a slide to move it.

Slide Sorter button

Figure 10.20 *Slide Sorter view*

1. In *70 fenwick dance*, display the slides in Slide Sorter view.

2. Rearrange the slides in the following order:

   1 **Fenwick Dance Productions**   7 **Beginning Jazz Performers**

   2 **Featuring the Dance Stars of**   8 **Advanced Jazz Performers**
     Tomorrow

   3 **Performance**   9 **Beginning Tap Performers**

   4 **Ballet Ballet Ballet Ballet**   10 **Advanced Tap Performers**

   5 **Beginning Ballet Performers**   11 **Competition Team Placement**

   6 **Advanced Ballet Performers**   12 **Fenwick Award Winners**

3. Copy the first slide and paste it following the last slide.

4. Save the presentation.

 checkpoint Compare the order of your slides with those of a classmate. Make changes if needed.

Add Sound to Slides

Music and other sounds can enhance your presentation. You can add music and sound files from your computer or from online sources. You also can record sounds to use in a presentation. When you use sounds, make sure they are appropriate. The sound, also called an audio, should not be overbearing or distracting. Sound can be used to introduce a topic, build excitement, or provide a transition between topics.

A computer must have speakers and a sound card to play music and sounds. You must have a microphone to record sounds. When music or sounds are added to a slide, a sound icon appears on the slide. You can hide the sound icon if you do not want it to appear when the show is played. You can set sounds to start automatically when the slide displays or to start on a mouse click.

25C

Key Mastery

TECHNIQUE TIP

- Reach up without moving your hands away from your body.
- Reach down without moving your hands toward your body.

Key each line twice.

Reach review

1 jn fr ki ft lo dc jh fg ju fb fv ;p sx jm de jy sw

2 just dear sweat jump fever decade injury swat hush

3rd/1st rows

3 born none mix bore curve more noon bunny comb vice

4 open exit were none trip crop brown money pine pin

Short phrases

5 go to a|they may keep|with your|and the|it will be

6 very much|sure to|a big|make a|too much|to view it

All letters learned

7 Kevin does a top job on your flax farm with Craig.

8 Dixon flew blue jets eight times over a city park.

25D

Shift and ENTER Key Technique

TECHNIQUE TIP

Keep eyes on copy as you shift and as you tap the ENTER key.

Key each line once. At the end of each line, quickly tap the ENTER key and immediately start the next line.

1 Dan took a friend to the game.

2 Jan had a double and a single.

3 Bob and Jose Hill will sing a song.

4 Sam and Jo took the test on Monday.

5 Laura sold her old cars to Sandra Smith.

6 Nicky left to play video games with Tim.

gwam 30" | 2 | 4 | 6 | 8 | 10 | 12 | 14 | 16 |

25E

Critical Thinking Activity

MicroType

Use *MicroType* Lesson 15 for additional practice.

1. To key the names of 13 U.S. states, you have to know the letter *m*. How many of the 13 states can you key?

2. Only three U.S. state names include the letter *p*. How many of them can you key?

3. Only five U.S. state names include the letter *v*. Can you key them?

TIP Click the **Undo** button to reverse an action.

To insert a table on a slide, use the Insert Table button in a content placeholder. You can then select the number of rows and columns for the table. Tables are formatted by default with a table style similar to those you learned to apply to *Word* tables. You can change table formats using the Table Tools Design and Format tabs.

In this activity, you will create a slide with a table to show the Fenwick award winners.

1. In *70 fenwick dance*, click the last slide in the thumbnail pane and then insert a new Title and Content layout slide.

2. In the title placeholder, key **Fenwick Award Winners**.

3. Click the **Insert Table** icon in the content placeholder. The Insert Table dialog box will appear as shown in Figure 10.19. Key **2** in the Number of columns box. Key **6** in the Number of rows box. Click **OK**.

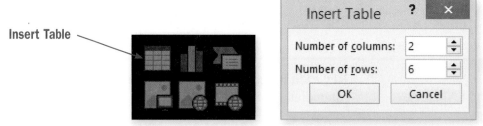

Figure 10.19 *Insert Table icon and Insert Table dialog box*

4. Key the following data in the table. Apply bold and center alignment to the column heads. Use left alignment for the first column and center alignment for the second column.

Student(s)	Award
David Seavers	All-Around Top Male Performer
Rebecca Eastwick	All-Around Top Female Performer
Julia Fleming	Top Jazz Performer
Maria Fernandez	Most Improved Jazz Performer
Joy Ashby & Kent Smyth	Best Pair Performers

5. Click in the first column. On the Table Tools Layout tab, click in the **Column Width** box and key **4.3"** to reduce the width of the first column. Then center the table horizontally on the slide.

PP Table Tools Design/ Table Styles

6. Change the table style to **Light Style 2–Accent 6**.

7. Save the presentation.

Lesson 26

New Keys q and , (comma)

Learning Outcomes

In Lesson 26, you will:

- *Learn reach technique for q and , (comma).*
- *Combine q and , (comma) smoothly with all other learned keys.*

26A

Warmup

Key each line twice.

All letters learned

1 six buy jam ask dog call vote down fork crop there

p/v

2 five pups; to vote; pay for; very plain; her plan;

All letters learned

3 Jacki Farve played six games on Thursday with Ben.

26B

New Keys q and , (comma)

q Left little finger

, (comma) Right middle finger

SPACING TIP
Space once after . used as punctuation.

Key each line twice. If time permits, rekey lines 7–9.

Learn q

1 a q a q|aqua aqua|quote quote|quad quad|quit quits
2 aq|queen queen|quake quake|equip equip|quick quick
3 a square; the quote; a quart; to acquire; is equal

Learn , (comma)

4 k , k , k, k, ,k,|a,b c,d e,f g,h i,j k,l m,n o,p,
5 Monday, Tuesday, Wednesday, Thursday, and Saturday
6 Rob took Janet, Pam, Seth, and Felipe to the game.

Combine q and , (comma)

7 Key the words quit, squad, square, and earthquake.
8 I have quit the squad, Quen; Raquel has quit, too.
9 Quit, quiet, and quaint were on the spelling exam.

Adding Graphics and Tables to Slides

Data File:

df 70 effective slides

Learning Outcomes

In Lesson 70, you will:

70A *Create graphics using shapes.*
70B *Create a slide with a table.*
70C *Rearrange slide order.*
70D *Add sound to slides.*
70E *Add content to presentations.*

70A

Create Graphics Using Shapes

In Chapter 8, you learned to insert shapes from the Shapes gallery. You can use the same procedures to add shapes to *PowerPoint* slides.

1. Open *69 fenwick dance* that you worked with in the last lesson. Insert a new slide following slide 1. Use the Title Only layout. Insert the slide title shown on Figure 10.18.

2. Use the Shapes feature to select and draw a 16-Point Star shape. Set the size of the star to 4.5" height and 4.5" width. Change the fill to white and remove the outline.

Figure 10.18 *Slide 2 in the Fenwick Dance presentation*

COLLABORATION

3. Open *df 69 fenwick graphics*, copy the photo shown in Figure 10.18, and paste it on the slide. Resize the picture to 3.6" high, and center it over the star as shown in the figure.

4. Save the presentation as *70 fenwick dance*.

 checkpoint Ask a classmate to review your slide and offer comments for improvement.

26C

Key Mastery

TECHNIQUE TIP
Reach up without moving your hands away from your body.

Key each line twice. If time permits, key lines 7–8 again.

Double letters

1 add egg ill books access three effect otter cheese
2 Betty and Ross will help cook the food for dinner.

q/comma

3 Marquis, Quent, and Quig were quite quick to quit.
4 Quin, Jacqueline, and Paque quickly took the exam.

Short phrases

5 a box|if the call|when you go|if we can|look for a
6 if we go|it is our|up to you|do you see|she took a

All letters learned

7 Jevon will fix my pool deck if the big rain quits.
8 Verna did fly quick jets to map the six big towns.

26D

Practice

Key each line twice. Try to key the line faster the second time.

Adjacent keys

1 df io sa lk er jk re po ds uy ew ui sa jh gf mn cv
2 Erin never asked Wes Ash to save paper; Perry did.

Long direct reaches

3 ym ec rb nu rg vr ny br mu ice nylon mug any dumb;
4 Bryce must bring the ice to the curb for my uncle.

MicroType

Use *MicroType* Lesson 16 for additional practice.

Double letters

5 doll less food good noon call roof pool wall meet;
6 Ann will seek help to get all food cooked by noon.

26E

Critical Thinking

Thomas Jefferson

John F. Kennedy

Franklin Roosevelt

George Washington

Woodrow Wilson

1. Key the sentences below. From the list at the left, choose the name that best completes the sentence. Do not key the numbers.
2. Use the Internet to learn about these five U.S. presidents. Record the years that each person was president, his birth state, and his home state.

1. *The president who drafted the Declaration of Independence was _____.*
2. *The president who was commander in chief of the Continental Army prior to becoming president was _____.*
3. *The president who called for new civil rights legislation in the 1960s was _____.*
4. *The president who held office when Pearl Harbor was attacked in 1941 was _____.*
5. *The president when the United States entered into World War I was _____.*

69D

Create a Presentation with Multiple Layouts

In this activity, you will begin creating a presentation about U.S. presidents. You will include a title slide and a slide with a bulleted list and a picture. You will then convert the bulleted list to a SmartArt diagram.

1. Start a new presentation. For the presentation title, key **My Favorite Presidents**. For the subtitle, key **By** and your name.

2. From the Themes group on the Design tab, choose a theme for the presentation. Apply the theme to the slide.

3. Insert a Two Content layout slide. In the title placeholder, key **President Washington**. For the first bullet item in the left content placeholder, key **First President**. For the second bullet item, key **Commander of the Continental Army**. Key a third bullet item about President Washington. If necessary, search the Internet to find more information about this president.

4. Click the **Online Pictures** icon in the right content placeholder. Search for a picture of President Washington. Resize the graphic, if needed.

5. Convert the bulleted list on slide 2 to SmartArt using the Vertical Bullet List. Change the colors to **Colorful–Accent Colors**.

6. Save the presentation as *69 presidents* and close it.

21st Century Skills

Media Literacy

At some point in your academic and professional careers, you will have to speak in front of a group or give an oral presentation. Your ability to communicate orally is one of the most important and valuable skills you will be able to apply at school, on the job, and in countless social situations. To deliver an effective presentation, consider the following:

- Plan your presentation by conducting research on your audience and gathering information and materials that support your topic. Prepare an attention-getting introduction, organize your main points, and develop a clear conclusion.

- Practice your presentation either in front of a mirror or with a small group of family and friends. If possible, record your presentation so you can identify areas for improvement.

- Deliver your presentation in an engaging manner. Do not read to the audience; instead, talk to them using an appropriate tone, make eye contact, and be aware of nonverbal body language, such as posture, gestures, and facial expressions.

Think Critically

1. What are the key factors to giving an effective oral presentation?

2. Discuss an instance when you had to give an oral presentation or when you were an audience member for another individual's presentation. Was the presentation a success, or do you think it could have been improved? Explain your answer.

Lesson 27

Review

Learning Outcomes

In Lesson 27, you will:

- *Learn to key block paragraphs.*
- *Improve keying technique and speed.*

27A

Warmup

Key each line twice.

All letters learned

1 Jared helped Maxine quickly fix the big wood vase.

Shift keys

2 Jake and Kathy went to New York City on Wednesday.

Easy

3 Pamela may hang the signs by the door in the hall.

27B

Block Paragraphs

Key each paragraph once. Tap ENTER only at the end of the paragraph. Double-space between the paragraphs; then key the paragraphs again at a faster pace.

Paragraph 1

You already know that you can use the Enter key to space down and start a new line. If you don't use the Enter key, the insertion point will continue on the same line until it reaches the right margin. Then it will automatically space down to the next line.

Paragraph 2

Later in the textbook you will learn how to adjust the right and left margins to vary the line length. As you make the line length smaller, the margins become larger. As you make the line length larger, the margins become smaller.

Instant Message

The paragraphs at the right are called "block" paragraphs. This is because all lines begin evenly at the left margin.

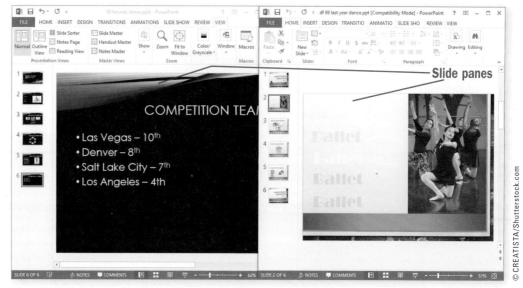

Figure 10.16 *Arrange All feature displays both presentations at the same time.*

TIP Click the Slide pane of the presentation you want to make active.

PP View/Window/ Arrange All

1. With *69 fenwick dance* open, open *df 69 last year dance*. Follow the path at the left and use the Arrange All feature to display both files on the screen as shown in Figure 10.16.

2. You will copy slide 2 from last year's presentation and paste it at the end of this year's presentation. Click slide 2 in the thumbnail pane of last year's presentation. Copy the slide (CTRL + C) and paste (CTRL + V) it after the last slide in the thumbnail pane of this year's presentation (*69 fenwick dance*).

Notice that the design automatically becomes the same as the file you are pasting the slide in.

3. Move the picture to position it as shown in Figure 10.17.

Figure 10.17 *Slide design change*

4. Use the same procedure to copy and paste slides 3, 4, and 5 from last year's presentation to the end of this year's presentation. Apply the Title and Content layout to slides 8, 9, and 10 in this year's presentation. Change the font size of the bulleted items on slide 10 to 32 point.

5. Save the *69 fenwick dance* presentation. Close both files.

Key a 30" timed writing on each line. Your rate in gross words a minute (*gwam*) is shown below the lines.

1 She owns all of the lake land.
2 The man with the sign may aid them.
3 I may make my goal if I work with vigor.
4 Six of the girls may make a bid for the gown.
5 Laurie and Orlando may make the map of the island.

| gwam 30" | 2 | 4 | 6 | 8 | 10 | 12 | 14 | 16 | 18 | 20 |

27D

Build Speed

Key each line twice.

1 I may have six quick jobs to get done for low pay.
2 Vicky packed the box with quail and jam for Jason.
3 Max can plan to bike for just five days with Quig.
4 Jim was quick to get the next top value for Debby.
5 Jack B. Manly requested approval for extra weight.
6 Jacque may have plans for the big dance next week.

| gwam 1' | 1 | 2 | 3 | 4 | 5 | 6 | 7 | 8 | 9 | 10 |

MicroType

Use *MicroType* Lesson 17 for additional practice.

27E

Critical Thinking

1. Key the sentences below. From the list at the left, choose the name that best completes the sentence. Do not key the numbers.

2. Use the Internet to learn about these five U.S. presidents. Record the years that each person was president, his birth state, and his home state.

Ulysses S. Grant

Warren G. Harding

Andrew Jackson

Abraham Lincoln

Ronald Reagan

1. _____ was a military commander in the Civil War prior to becoming president of the United States.

2. _____ was the only president to serve in two wars, the Revolutionary War and the War of 1812.

3. The Teapot Dome scandal took place when _____ was U.S. president.

4. He was an actor prior to becoming a public official. The president whose nicknames include "The Gipper" and "The Great Communicator" was _____.

5. This president had no formal education. His nicknames include "Honest Abe" and "Illinois Rail Splitter." The name of this president was _____.

Figure 10.14 *Bulleted list converted to SmartArt diagram*

5. Use the Convert to SmartArt feature to convert slide 4 to the Block Cycle SmartArt as shown at the left in Figure 10.15.

6. Change the color of the blocks in the diagram to those shown at the right in Figure 10.15 by clicking the center of the graphic to select it. Click the **SmartArt Tools Design** tab. Click the **Change Colors** button in the SmartArt Styles group and select the first choice (**Colorful–Accent Colors**) under the category name *Colorful*.

Figure 10.15 *Slide with SmartArt*

7. Save the presentation.

69C

Copy and Insert Slides from Another Presentation

In this activity, you will work with two files. Some of the slides that were used in last year's production can be used again this year. Rather than recreating the slides, they can be copied from last year's file and placed in this year's file.

To open and view two or more files at the same time (see Figure 10.16), use the Arrange All feature. This feature is located in the Window group on the View tab.

Lesson 28

New Keys z and : (colon)

In Lesson 28, you will:

- *Learn reach technique for **z** and **:** (**colon**).*
- *Combine **z** and **:** (**colon**) smoothly with all other learned keys.*

28A

Warmup

Key each line twice.

All letters learned

1 Max was a big star when he played for Jack Vasque.

Shift keys

2 Ramon Santos; Karl Jones; Kate Van Noy; Sue McMan;

Easy

3 Jan and Bob may work with the maid on the problem.

28B

New Keys z and : (colon)

*z **Left little** finger*

*: (colon) **Right little** finger + **Left Shift***

SPACING TIP

Space twice after : used as punctuation.

Key each line twice. If time permits, rekey lines 7–9.

Learn z

1 a z az za za|zap zap|zoo zoo|zone zone|azure azure
2 zip zip|zinc zinc|quiz quiz|zera zero|Zelda Zelda;
3 speed zone; a zigzag; a zoology quiz; puzzle size;

Learn : (colon)

4 ; : : ;: :; :;|a:b c:d e:f g:h i:j k:l m:n o:p q:r :
5 To: From: Date: Subject: To: Jason Kummerfeld
6 To: Max Tobin|From: Jerry Cole|Dear Mr. Maxwell:

Combine z and : (colon)

7 Please key these words: amaze, seize, and zigzag.
8 Zane read: Shift to enter: and then space twice.
9 Roz, use these headings: City: State: ZIP Code:

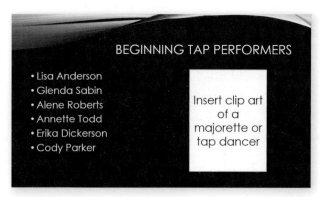

Figure 10.12 *Two-content slide with bulleted list*

8. Create slide 6 using the Title and Content layout. Insert the text shown in Figure 10.13. Then locate an online graphic using the keyword **prize** and place one or more copies of the graphic on the slide to create an interesting appearance.

Figure 10.13 *Title and content slide*

9. Save the presentation as *69 fenwick dance*.

69B

Convert Bulleted Lists to SmartArt

SmartArt is a *PowerPoint* feature that can be used to enhance your presentation. Too many bulleted lists can become boring to your audience. With a few clicks, bulleted lists can be changed to SmartArt diagrams.

1. In *69 fenwick dance*, go to slide 3 and position the insertion point in the bulleted list.

2. On the Home tab, click the down arrow of the **Convert to SmartArt** button shown at the right.

3. Then click **More SmartArt Graphics**. In the left pane, select **Office.com**. Finally, select **Picture Frame** (shown at right) and click **OK**. Your slide should look similar to Figure 10.14.

4. To complete the slide, insert dance graphics from Online Pictures or copy and paste graphics from *df 69 fenwick graphics* in the SmartArt picture placeholders.

Key Mastery

TECHNIQUE TIP
Use curved, upright fingers.

MicroType

Use *MicroType* Lesson 18 for additional practice.

Key each line twice. If time permits, key lines 5–6 again.

q/z

1 quiz quartz amaze quote Amazon mosque muzzle quick

2 Zane amazed us all on the quiz but quit the squad.

x/comma

3 six, box, tax, axle, next, extra, exhibit, example

4 Lexi, Rex, and Felix went to Texas to the exhibit.

v/m

5 move save moon visit imply valve most vain improve

6 Melvin, Kevin, or Matt drove the van to Las Vegas.

28D

Key Block Paragraphs

1. Key each paragraph once. Tap ENTER only at the end of the paragraph.

2. Key a 1' timed writing on each paragraph. Use the numbers and dots above the words to determine *gwam*. Each dot indicates one additional word. For example, if you key to the end of *average* in line 1, you have keyed nine words.

Paragraph 1

```
      •     2     •     4     •     6     •     8     •
The space bar is used frequently.  On average,
   10    •    12    •    14    •    16    •    18    •
every fifth or sixth stroke is a space when you
   20    •    22    •    24    •    26    •    28    •
key.  If you use good techniques, you will be able
   30    •    32    •    34
to increase your speed.
```

Paragraph 2

```
      •     2     •     4     •     6     •     8     •    10
Just keep the thumb low over the space bar.  Move
   •    12    •    14    •    16    •    18    •    20
the thumb down and in quickly towards the palm of
   •    22    •    24    •    26    •    28    •
your hand to get the prized stroke you need to
   30    •    32
build top skill.
```

PP | Insert/Text/WordArt

TIP Delete the title placeholder after you position the WordArt graphic: click the outside border of the placeholder and tap DELETE.

TIP Click Online Pictures on the Insert tab and use **ballet** or **dance** for the search word. If Online Pictures is not available, copy the photo of pink ballet slippers from *df 69 fenwick graphics*.

Online Pictures

3. Select the WordArt style **Gradient Fill – Bright Green, Accent 1, Reflection**, and key **PERFORMANCE** in ALL CAPs. Click and drag the WordArt into the location of the title placeholder as shown in Figure 10.10. In the content placeholder (*Click to add text*), key **Ballet** and tap ENTER. Key **Jazz** and tap ENTER. Key **Tap** and click outside the placeholder. Change the font size to 36 point. Insert an extra line after *Ballet* and *Jazz*.

4. Insert an online picture of ballet shoes in the location shown in Figure 10.10. Size the picture to fit the space.

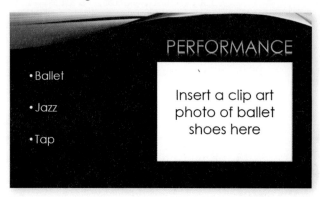

Figure 10.10 *Slide with bulleted list and WordArt*

5. Insert slide 3 using the Title and Content layout. Enter the title and performers in the placeholders as shown in Figure 10.11. Change the bulleted list font size to 32 point for the names of the performers.

Figure 10.11 *Slide with bulleted list*

6. Insert slide 4 with **Beginning Jazz Performers** for the title. The performers are **Jenny Carlson, Ashton Kennedy, Melissa Bliss, Charles Tanner, Pedro Ramirez**, and **Sandra Steiner**. Place each performer on a separate line. Change the font size to 32 point for all performers and for bulleted items in all additional slides that you create.

7. Create slide 5 shown in Figure 10.12 using the Two Content layout. Insert the text in the left content placeholder. Click the **Online Pictures** icon in the right content placeholder. Use **majorette** for your search word and insert a picture of a dancer with a top hat on a starry background. Notice that the picture is automatically sized and positioned at the location of the content placeholder.

Lesson 29

New Keys CAPS LOCK and ?

Learning Outcomes

In Lesson 29, you will:

- *Learn reach technique for **CAPS LOCK** and ?.*
- *Combine **CAPS LOCK** and ? smoothly with all other learned keys.*

29A

Warmup

Key each line twice.

Alphabet

1 Jack P. Hildo may buy five quartz rings next week.

x/z

2 excess zebra fixture zoology exact zest extra zero

Easy

3 Jay is to turn to the right when the signal turns.

gwam 1' | 1 | 2 | 3 | 4 | 5 | 6 | 7 | 8 | 9 | 10 |

29B

New Keys CAPS LOCK and ?

CAPS LOCK Left *little* finger

? (question mark) Right *little* finger + Left Shift

SPACING TIP

Space twice after a question mark at the end of a sentence.

The **CAPS LOCK** key is used to key a series of capital letters. To key capital letters, tap the CAPS LOCK key. Key the letters that are to appear in capitals. Then tap the CAPS LOCK key again to turn off this feature.

Key each line twice. If time permits, rekey lines 7–9.

Learn CAPS LOCK

1 Put CUBS and CARDS and METS and EXPOS on the sign.

2 OHIO STATE plays INDIANA on Wednesday or Thursday.

3 Microsoft is MSFT; Intel is INTC; Coca Cola is KO.

Learn ? (question mark)

4 ; ? ; ? ;?|g?h i?j k?l m?n o?p q?r s?t u?v w?x y?z

5 Who? Who? What? What? When? When? Why? Why?

6 Ask who? Are you sure? What time? Where is she?

Combine CAPS LOCK and ?

7 What symbol is DIS? What symbol is YHOO? Did he?

8 What does CPA stand for? What does CFO stand for?

9 Did your mother use NB, NE, or NEBR. for NEBRASKA?

Lesson 69

Inserting and Formatting Slides

Learning Outcomes

In Lesson 69, you will:

69A *Insert slides and choose layouts.*
69B *Convert bulleted lists to SmartArt.*
69C *Copy and insert slides from another presentation.*
69D *Create a presentation with multiple layouts.*

Data Files:

*df 69 fenwick
graphics
df 69 last year
dance*

69A

**Insert Slides and
Choose Layouts**

TIP To change the layout of an existing slide, click the slide, click the Slide Layout button on the Home tab, and then select the new layout.

You can add slides to a presentation as you develop it. Slides are available in several different layouts. You can choose the layout that will work best for the content of the slide. For example, if you want to include a bulleted list, insert a slide using the Title and Content layout. Examples of slide layouts are shown in Figure 10.9.

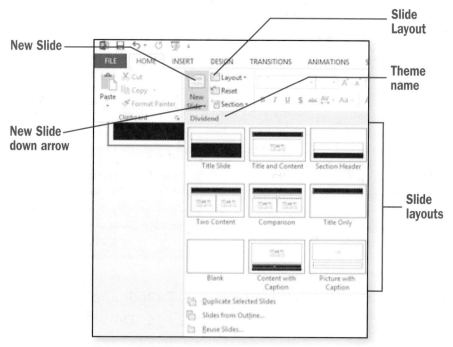

Figure 10.9 *Slide layout options*

To insert a new slide, click the down arrow of the New Slide button. From the gallery of layouts, click the layout you want for the new slide.

In this activity you will insert additional slides into the presentation.

1. Open *68 fenwick dance* that you worked with in the last lesson.

2. On the Home tab, click the **New Slide** down arrow. Click **Title and Content** in the Slide Layout gallery. Slide 2 is added to the presentation.

PP Home/Slides/New Slide

Key Mastery

TECHNIQUE TIP
Use curved, upright fingers.

MicroType

Use *MicroType* Lesson 19 for additional practice.

Key each line twice. If time permits, key lines 5–6 again.

z/v

1 David and Zack Valdez zipped through both quizzes.
2 Vizquel, Alvarez, Chavez, and Gonzalez have voted.

q/p

3 Quincy quickly put the papers next to the puppies.
4 Paul quickly keyed: quiz, opaque, parquet, equip.

x/c

5 Carl Drexler stood next to Connie Cox and Tex Cey.
6 Rex Cain and Max Carr paid the extra tax for Carl.

29D

Key Block Paragraphs

Key each paragraph once. Tap ENTER only at the end of the paragraph. Key a 1' timed writing on each paragraph. Determine your *gwam*.

Paragraph 1

```
        •    2    •    4    •    6    •    8    •
Before long you will key copy that is written in
10   •   12   •   14   •   16   •   18   •
script.  Script copy is copy that is written with
20   •   22   •   24   •   26   •   28   •
pen or pencil.  With practice, you will be able
    30   •   32   •   34   •
to key script at a rapid rate.
```

Paragraph 2

```
        •    2    •    4    •    6    •    8    •   10
A rough draft is a draft that is not yet in final
    •   12   •   14   •   16   •   18   •
form.  It is where the writer can get his or her
20   •   22   •   24   •   26   •   28   •
thoughts down on paper.  After the rough draft is
30   •   32   •   34   •   36   •   38   •
completed, it is ready to be edited.  It may take
40   •   42   •   44   •   46   •   48
several edits before it is put in final form.
```

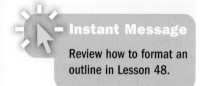

Instant Message

Review how to format an outline in Lesson 48.

4. Insert a page break to begin a new page. Working as a team, develop the main points for the presentation. Remember that the goal is to acquaint new students and their parents with your school and the advantages it offers. Key the main points in an outline.

5. You will develop the sub points for the outline later. Give the outline an appropriate title and format it correctly. Save the document as *68 school outline*. Print the document.

6. Start *PowerPoint* and open a new, blank presentation. Create a title slide for the presentation. On the title slide, include the name of your school and the date. Select and apply a theme. Add appropriate clip art (such as a school logo) if you like.

7. Save the presentation as *68 school presentation* and close it.

Digital Citizenship and Ethics

© mama_mia/Shutterstock.com

The computer has become a storage place for much of our important data and information, whether it's a five-page essay for English class, hundreds of family and personal photos, or detailed records of bank and financial transactions. Responsible digital citizens recognize the need to protect not only their data and personal information, but also access to their computer and its resources. Following are measures you can take to ensure your digital security:

- Maintain up-to-date antivirus software, anti-spyware, and firewalls, which are hardware devices or programs that help protect against unauthorized access to your computer.

- Limit access to your data as well as your online activity by setting strong passwords. Use different passwords for different accounts, change the passwords frequently, and store the passwords in a safe place away from your computer.

- Develop a comprehensive schedule to conduct maintenance checks and back up your files on a regular basis.

As a class, discuss the following:

1. What are the characteristics of a strong password?

2. What tasks should be included in a computer maintenance check?

3. What methods for backing up your data do you use at home?

Lesson 30 | New Keys TAB and BACKSPACE

Learning Outcomes

In Lesson 30, you will:

- *Learn reach technique for **TAB** and **BACKSPACE**.*
- *Combine **TAB** and **BACKSPACE** smoothly with all other learned keys.*

30A

Warmup

Key each line twice.

Alphabet

1 Quig just fixed prize vases he won at my key club.

CAPS LOCK

2 Find ZIP Codes for the cities in WYOMING and IOWA.

Easy

3 It may be a problem if both girls go to the docks.

gwam 1' | 1 | 2 | 3 | 4 | 5 | 6 | 7 | 8 | 9 | 10 |

30B

New Key BACKSPACE

BACKSPACE Right
little finger

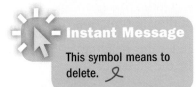

Instant Message

This symbol means to delete. ℓ

The **BACKSPACE** key is used to delete characters. You should key the BACKSPACE key with your right little finger. Keep your index finger anchored to the **J** key as you tap BACKSPACE. Tap the BACKSPACE key once for each letter to be deleted. Then return the finger to the **;** key. When you hold down the BACKSPACE key, letters to the left of the insertion point will be deleted until the BACKSPACE key is released.

Use the BACKSPACE key to edit the sentence as instructed.

1. Key the following.

   The delete

2. Use the BACKSPACE key to make the change shown below.

   The ~~delete~~ backspace

3. Continue keying the sentence as shown below.

   The backspace key can be

4. Use the BACKSPACE key to make the change shown below.

   The backspace key ~~can be~~ is

If you use a button in a content placeholder to insert a picture, the picture will be sized automatically to fit in the placeholder. If you use the Pictures or Online Pictures command on the Insert tab to insert an image, it will appear in the middle of the slide at a default size. You can then resize it and move it to the desired location.

The title slide for your Fenwick Dance Productions presentation looks more professional with the theme applied. In this activity, you will make it even more attractive by inserting pictures.

1. In *68 fenwick dance*, use the Pictures command to insert *df 68 ballet shoes*.

2. Insert the graphic on the slide and position it where the green and blue "ribbons" meet, as shown in Figure 10.8. Adjust the height of the graphic to 1.6". Use the Copy and Paste commands to make three copies of the image. Adjust the height of the copied images to 1.4". Place the copied images near the bottom of the slide as shown.

TIP Click the **Pictures** button on the Insert tab, navigate to the location of your data files, and select the desired picture file.

Pictures

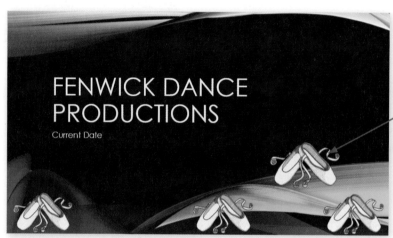

Position the first graphic here.

Figure 10.8 *Clip art images added to slide*

3. Click the **Slide Show** button to see how the slide looks. Save the presentation using the same name, *68 fenwick dance*, and close it.

68C

Create a New Presentation

COLLABORATION

The principal of your school would like you and two of your classmates to develop a presentation. The goal of the presentation is to acquaint new students with your school. The audience will be new students and their parents.

1. Work with two classmates to complete this activity. In a *Word* document, key **SCHOOL PRESENTATION** at the top of the page.

2. Leave one blank line and then key the heading **Purpose**. Under this heading, key three or four goals that you want to accomplish with this presentation.

3. Leave one blank line and key the heading **Audience**. Under this heading, create a bulleted list. Include several points that describe the audience for the presentation. Review Lesson 66 if needed.

5. Continue keying the sentence as shown below.

```
The backspace key is used to fix
```

6. Use the BACKSPACE key to make the change shown below.

```
The backspace key is used to f̶i̶x̶ make
```

7. Continue keying the sentence shown below.

```
The backspace key is used to make changes.
```

30C

New Key TAB

TAB Left little finger

SOFTWARE TIP
Click the **Show/Hide ¶** button in the Paragraph group of the Home tab to display nonprinting characters. TAB appears as a right arrow (→).

The **TAB** key is used to move the insertion point to a specific location on the line. For example, TAB can be used to indent the first line of a paragraph. Word processing software has preset tabs called *default* tabs. Usually, the first default tab is set 0.5" to the right of the left margin. This tab setting is used to indent paragraphs as shown below.

Key each paragraph once. If time permits, key them again.

```
Tab → The tab key is used to indent blocks of copy such
as these.

Tab → It should also be used for tables to arrange data
quickly and neatly into columns.

Tab → Learn how to use the tab key by touch; doing so
will add to your keying skill.

Tab → Tap the tab key very quickly. Begin keying the
line immediately after you tap the tab key.
```

30D

TAB and BACKSPACE

TECHNIQUE TIP
When you use the BACKSPACE key, keep the index finger anchored to the **J** key.

Key each paragraph once. Use the BACKSPACE key to correct errors as you key. If time permits, key the paragraphs again.

```
Tab → George Washington was the first president of the
United States.  Before becoming president, he played a
key role in helping the colonies gain their freedom.

Tab → Washington was the commander of the Continental
Army.  Much has been written about the winter he and
his army spent at Valley Forge.
```

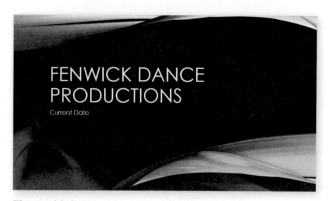

Figure 10.6 *Title slide with Vapor Trail theme*

5. Save the presentation as *68 fenwick dance*.

In Chapter 8, you learned to insert graphics in flyers, brochures, and newsletters. In this chapter, you will use the same procedures for inserting graphics in presentation slides. You can use Online Pictures to locate and insert clip art, or the Pictures command to insert picture files. Use the Shapes and WordArt commands to add other graphics. A slide with a photo, clip art, WordArt, and a star shape is shown in Figure 10.7.

Figure 10.7 *Slide with graphics*

You can use the buttons in a content placeholder, shown below, to insert pictures and other objects such as SmartArt diagrams, charts, and tables.

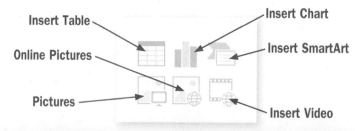

30E

Check Speed

Instant Message

The **E** icon means that the difficulty level of this timed writing is *easy*.

MicroType

Use *MicroType* Lesson 20 for additional practice.

Key each paragraph once. Double-space between paragraphs. Key a 1' timed writing on each paragraph and then determine *gwam*.

 all letters used

```
        •    2    •    4    •    6    •    8    •
     How you key is just as vital as the copy you
   10   •   12   •   14   •   16   •   18   •
work from or produce.  What you put on paper is a
   20   •   22   •   24   •   26   •   28
direct result of the way in which you do the job.
        •    2    •    4    •    6    •    8    •
     If you expect to grow quickly in speed, take
   10   •   12   •   14   •   16   •   18   •
charge of your mind.  It will then tell your eyes
   20   •   22   •   24   •   26   •   28   •
and hands how to work through the maze of letters.
```

30F

Critical Thinking

Delaware

Lake Michigan

Lake Superior

Mt. McKinley

Mt. Rainier

Rhode Island

Vermont

Wyoming

Yellowstone National Park

Zion National Park

Key the sentences below. From the list at the left, choose the word or words that best complete the sentence. Do not key the numbers.

1. The oldest national park in the United States is _____.
2. The highest mountain peak in the United States is _____.
3. The largest lake in the United States is _____.
4. The smallest state is _____.
5. The state with the least population is _____.

© Zack Frank/Shutterstock.com

Enhancing Slides

Data File:

df 68 ballet shoes

Learning Outcomes

In Lesson 68, you will:

68A *Select and apply a theme.*

68B *Add graphics.*

68C *Create a presentation with a theme and graphics.*

68A

Select and Apply a Theme

If you and your classmates decided that the title slide created for Lesson 67 looks plain, you are right. In this lesson, you will learn to make your slides more interesting. One way to make a slide more interesting is to apply a theme. A **theme** is a set of design elements that can be applied to slides. A theme includes elements such as the background, font, font size, and color scheme. Themes give the slides a professional look.

In this activity, you will select and apply a theme to enhance the appearance of your slide.

1. Open *67 fenwick dance* that you created in the last lesson.

2. Click the **Design** tab on the ribbon. Various themes display in the Themes gallery, as shown in Figure 10.5. Point to a sample design to see the name of the theme. The slide in the Slide pane will display the theme to which you are pointing. Move the pointer to several themes to preview how they will look with your title slide. Move the pointer back to the Slide pane. Notice how the slide returns to its original format.

Figure 10.5 *Slide designs in the Themes gallery*

3. To see additional themes, click the More down arrow to the right of the last theme. Choose a theme that you find interesting. To apply the theme, click it. Notice that the title slide now has the theme that you clicked. Your title slide will keep that theme until you change it by clicking a different theme.

4. Click the **Vapor Trail** theme. Your title slide should look like the one in Figure 10.6. This theme is simple yet elegant. The theme also complements the content (dance productions) of the presentation.

21st Century Skills

© wavebreakmedia/Shutterstock.com

Civic Literacy All of us are members of a community, whether it's a small town, suburban neighborhood, or large municipality. Being a member of any type of community comes with certain rights and responsibilities.

As a U.S. citizen, you are given basic constitutional rights, such as freedom to practice any religion you choose or freedom to assemble and protest government policies. But you also have responsibilities as a citizen. These include obeying laws, paying taxes, and participating in elections. Even if you are not subject to paying taxes or old enough to vote or drive, you can show your civic-mindedness in other ways. For example, you can:

- Perform community service, such as picking up trash or planting trees.
- Support political candidates and issues you feel strongly about.
- Identify ways to stay informed and understand governmental processes.

Think Critically

1. In groups, brainstorm issues that affect your community. This could be a local issue, such as downsizing the police force or restricting the use of skateboards in public parks, or a national issue, such as changing the federal income tax rate.

2. As a group, select the one issue that you think is most important. Then create a plan of action for how you would support the issue or bring about change. Would you organize a rally or protest? Send letters to your congressional representatives? Hand out flyers? Present your plan to the class.

View a PowerPoint Presentation

TIP Click the **Slide Show** button to play the show, or tap F5.

Before learning how to create a presentation, become familiar with *PowerPoint* by looking at a presentation that has already been created.

1. Start *PowerPoint*. Open *df 67 american*.

2. Look at the parts of the *PowerPoint* screen labeled in Figure 10.2. Find each part on your computer screen. Note the subtitle placeholder box on slide 1.

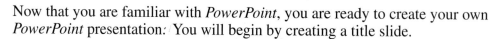

Instant Message The Slide Size is currently set for Widescreen, which is the *PowerPoint* 2013 default size. To adjust the size to Standard, click the Design tab, click the down arrow on Slide Size in the Customize group, and then select Standard. Choose to maximize the slide content or ensure that it fits in the new size.

3. To play the slide show, click the **Slide Show** button near the lower-right corner of the *PowerPoint* window.

4. After viewing the title slide, click the left mouse button or tap the ENTER, Space Bar, or right arrow key to go to the next slide. (Tap the left arrow key to go to a previous slide. To end a show before viewing all of the slides, tap ESC.) You may need to click several times on a slide to see all elements appear. Note the different types of content on the slides, including text, graphics, charts, and diagrams. One slide has a sound effect applied. End the slide show to return to Normal view.

5. Click the **Slide Sorter** button on the status bar to see the slides in this view.

6. Close the presentation. Exit *PowerPoint* (click the **Close** button in the upper-right corner) or continue with the next activity.

Create a Title Slide

TIP If you are continuing from an earlier activity, close any open presentations, click the **File** tab, click **New**, and then click **Blank Presentation** to open a new blank presentation.

Now that you are familiar with *PowerPoint*, you are ready to create your own *PowerPoint* presentation. You will begin by creating a title slide.

1. Start *PowerPoint*. Click **Blank Presentation**. Click inside the placeholder box labeled *Click to add title*. Key **Fenwick Dance Productions** for the title of your presentation.

2. Click inside the subtitle placeholder. Key the current date in this box.

3. You will add other slides later. Save the presentation as *67 fenwick dance*.

4. Click the **Slide Show** button to view the slide.

COLLABORATION

checkpoint Working with two classmates, compare the title slide you just created with the one from the *df 67 american* presentation. Discuss which one looks better and why. Close the presentation.

Before You Move On

Answer these questions to review what you have learned in Chapter 3.

1. Describe how you should arrange your work area. LO 11A

2. List five points that describe proper keying position. LO 11B

3. What are the home keys for the left hand? What are the home keys for the right hand? LO 11C

4. Tap the ENTER key with your _____ finger. LO 11E

5. Space _____ after a semicolon used as punctuation. LO 13C

6. When keying, keep your wrists low but not _____ the keyboard or desk. LO 11B

7. Keep your _____ on the copy as you key. LO 12A

8. How many times should you space after a period at the end of a sentence? LO 18D

9. To key a capital of the letter *P*, hold down the _____ key. LO 18B

10. To key a capital of the letter *S*, hold down the _____ key. LO 21B

11. The number of standard words keyed in 1' is called _____ (*gwam*). LO 22E

12. To key a series of capital letters, use the _____ key. LO 29B

13. How many times should you space after a question mark at the end of a sentence? LO 29B

14. Word processing software has preset tabs called _____ tabs. LO 30C

15. When you hold down the _____ key, letters to the left of the insertion point will be deleted. LO 30B

- The Notes pane allows you to key notes about the slide.
- The **Previous Slide** and **Next Slide** buttons display the previous or next slide in the Slide pane.
- The **view buttons** allow you to view the slides in several different ways depending on what you are doing.

67B

PowerPoint Views

PP View/Presentation Views

PowerPoint has different views that help you work with slides in different ways. Normal view is shown in Figure 10.2. This view is used for creating and editing slides. Slide Sorter view, Figure 10.3, displays thumbnails of the slides. This view is used to display several slides at a time and to sort or rearrange slides.

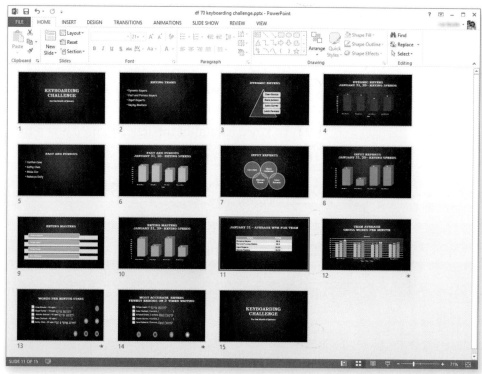

Figure 10.3 *PowerPoint* window in Slide Sorter view

Slide Show view is used to play the slide show. Each slide fills the screen, and you can see the features and sounds applied to slides.

These views can be accessed by clicking the view buttons (shown in Figure 10.4) on the status bar at the bottom of the *PowerPoint* screen.

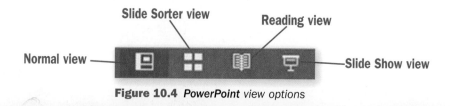

Figure 10.4 *PowerPoint* view options

ACROSS THE CURRICULUM

Academic Connections

Data Files:

df c3 volcanoes
df c3 economy and resources
df c3 goals

Science: Volcanoes

You may know that volcanoes can erupt in oceans to form new islands. In fact, volcanoes have created much of our earth's surface. Have you heard of Mount St. Helens? It is located in the state of Washington. It is the most active volcano on Earth. Mauna Loa is found in Hawaii. It is the largest volcano on our planet. It is even taller than Mount Everest.

What you might not know is that volcanoes exist on other planets as well. A volcano called Olympus Mons, found on Mars, may be the largest volcano in our solar system. It is over 16 miles high! The planets Mercury and Venus also have volcanoes, but those on Mercury don't seem to be erupting anymore. Our own moon has inactive volcanoes, and scientists believe that volcanoes exist on some of the moons of Jupiter, Saturn, and Neptune.

1. Start *Word* and open *df c3 volcanoes*.

2. Read the document to learn more about volcanoes. Answer the questions.

3. Save the document as *c3 volcanoes*, print, and close it.

About Business

COLLABORATION

Economy and Resources

The **economy** is the way a country manages its money and resources in order to buy, produce, and sell goods. **Resources** are materials that are used to make products. They can come from nature, can be provided by people's work, or can be man-made. Consider a bicycle. Its frame might be made from the natural resource titanium. A person who designs the style of the bicycle provides a human resource. The path that a biker rides on could be a man-made resource.

In some countries, the government owns or controls most of its resources. They may also determine what products are made. In the United States, however, we have a **market economy**. That means that consumers' demands often determine the products that are made.

That does not mean that our government plays no role in our economy. Our government does own and control some of our resources. They also pass laws that affect what companies can sell. For example, medicines must be approved by the U.S. Food and Drug Administration. Drugs that are not approved cannot be legally sold. A city government may pass rules about the type of companies it allows in their area. For example, they may ban a company that uses dangerous chemicals.

1. Open *df c3 economy and resources*.

2. Work with one or two classmates to discuss and answer the questions. You may use your own knowledge to provide examples, or you may search the Internet for ideas.

3. Save the document as *c3 economy and resources*, print, and close it.

PowerPoint Basics

Data File:
df 67 american

Learning Outcomes

In Lesson 67, you will:

67A *Learn about **PowerPoint** features.*

67B *Learn about **PowerPoint** views.*

67C *View a **PowerPoint** presentation.*

67D *Create a title slide.*

67A

PowerPoint Features

PowerPoint shares many features with *Word* and other *Office* applications. *PowerPoint* uses the ribbon interface that organizes commands in groups. It has a title bar, window control buttons, zoom controls, and a status bar similar to those you have seen in *Word*.

Features that help you to work with slides are shown in Figure 10.2. These features are described after the figure.

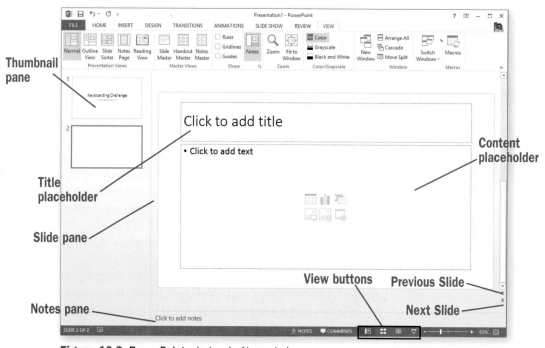

Figure 10.2 *PowerPoint* window in Normal view

- The **thumbnail pane** displays small images of the slides that have been created. You can click a thumbnail to select a slide.

- The **Slide pane** displays the current slide.

- **Placeholders** are boxes with dotted borders that are part of most slide layouts. These boxes hold title and body text or objects such as charts, tables, and pictures.

Goal Setting

Whether or not you know it, you've probably set goals for yourself in the past. Have you worked hard to earn good grades at school? Have you played hard at practices so that you can improve how you play a sport? Do you practice playing an instrument so that you can master a difficult song? If so, you probably had a goal in mind. Setting goals can motivate you, and achieving goals can make you feel good about yourself.

In this activity, you will analyze goals and set some new goals. As you will learn, goals should be specific, measurable, achievable, realistic, and time specific.

1. Open *df c3 goals*.

2. Read the tips for setting goals and complete the table. Be sure to add ways to improve the goals. Then, set your own goals for the time spans given.

3. Save the document as *c3 goals*, print, and close it.

Career Exploration Portfolio

Activity 2

To complete this activity, you will need the Student Interest Survey that you filled out in Career Exploration Portfolio Activity 1.

1. Look on the last page of your survey and note your top Career Cluster of interest. Find its description on the last two pages of the survey and read it.

2. Go to http://www.careertech.org. Click the **Career Technical Education** button, then click **Career Clusters** in the list at the right. Scroll down on the Career Clusters page and click the link for your top Career Cluster. On the web page for your Career Cluster, click the PDF link following Career Cluster Frame in the information near the top of the page. Read the list of careers in the document and pick one or two in which you are interested. Make a note of the category (called a Pathway) of the career(s) you choose. You will need to know the Pathway in a future activity.

3. Use the Internet to find out specific duties of the career(s) that you chose. You may look for other information that interests you as well.

4. Use *Word* to write a summary of what you learned. Save the document as *c3 career 1 details*, print, and close it.

Online Resources:

ngl.cengage.com/c21jr3e

COLLABORATION

With two or three other students, plan the content for a presentation to your principal and teachers at a faculty meeting. The purpose of the presentation is to persuade the principal and teachers to offer a first aid training program for students. The course will be free to students, so the school will have to pay the instructor and any other costs related to the course. The course will be offered after school one afternoon each week for six weeks.

1. Start *Word* and open a new, blank document.

2. Create an outline covering the points you want to make at the presentation to the principal and faculty. Make sure to include an introduction, body, and conclusion in the outline. Limit the number of points covered in the body to four or five.

3. Enter two or more supporting points under each main point. Choose only the most important information.

4. Consider the order in which the information is presented. Should any data be moved earlier or later in the presentation? If yes, move the data.

5. Give the outline an appropriate title and format it correctly. (Review how to format an outline in Chapter 5.) Save the document as *66 outline*. Print the outline and then close the document.

 **checkpoint** Exchange your outline with another group. Have them review your outline for content (introduction, body with necessary points to persuade principal and faculty, and conclusion), format, and correct spelling. Make corrections if needed.

66D

Evaluate Visual Aids

After creating the content for a presentation, consider visual aids you can use to help achieve your goals. A **visual aid** is something you show the audience to help them understand your message. A visual aid can be a sign or poster, perhaps with a drawing or photo. It can be an object, such as a tool you are describing in your presentation.

However, the most common visual used for presentations is the electronic slide created with presentation software. Text, pictures, clip art, screenshots, shapes, SmartArt, and charts can be included on slides.

1. Start *Word* and open a new, blank document.

2. Consider visual aids you might need for your first aid presentation. You may want to include clip art or photos that relate to first aid, shapes such as block arrows to emphasize important points, SmartArt diagrams that show the progress of lessons in the course, and so on.

3. Key a list of your ideas, relating visual aid ideas to specific parts of your outline if possible.

4. Save the document as *66 visual aids*, print, and close it.

Lessons 31–46

Numbers—how would people communicate without them? Numbers tell time, dates, distances, and amounts. They allow you to see how much you must pay for a new computer game. They let you give an exact street address. They tell you how to reach a friend on a cell phone. They let you know how you scored on an exam. They tell you how much a gallon of gas costs and how many miles per gallon your vehicle gets.

Numbers let people learn and share information in a precise way. Because numbers are precise, keying them accurately is important. In this chapter, you will learn to key numbers using both the top row of the keyboard and the numeric keypad. You also will learn to key the keyboard symbols.

17990,00

2744,24
2744,24
17990,00
17990,00

17990,00

,00
.890,00

241,02
288,31   241,02
288,31   .580,00
1.890,00 1.580,00
1.890,00

1.890,00   1.580,00
2.000,00   1.580,00
           1.580,00

460,

© Julija Sapic/Shutterstock.com

- Is the audience likely to be open to new ideas? If not, you will need to be persuasive with the remarks you make during your presentation.

- Are the members of the audience listening by choice, or are they required to attend your talk? If they are required to attend, you will need to create interest in your topic and be more entertaining than if they are there because of their interest in the topic.

Points such as these will affect how you approach your presentation.

Figure 10.1 *Consider your audience when planning a presentation.*

1. Start *Word* and open *df 66 profile*. Print the document and then close the file.

2. Read the description of a presentation and complete a profile for the audience.

66C

Create an Outline

After you have considered the purpose and audience, choose the main points you will cover in the presentation. All of the main points should help you accomplish the goals of the presentation. Use the main points of your presentation to create an outline. Then add supporting points for each main point. Do not view the outline as being final when you are creating it. Think of it as a starting point that can be changed or rearranged as needed.

As you develop the outline, keep in mind that a good presentation has three parts. The **introduction** tells listeners what your talk will be about. The **body** of the presentation gives the main and supporting points. The **conclusion** gives a summary of the points presented and tells the listeners again what action you want them to take.

As a beginning presenter, you may find it helpful to write every word you plan to say in the presentation. This allows you to think through each point carefully. It gives you time to express ideas in complete sentences. However, you should not read from a script when you deliver a presentation. Instead, use brief notes or the contents of slides to help you remember the points you want to discuss.

New Keys 8 and 1

Learning Outcomes

In Lesson 31, you will:

- Learn reach technique for **8** and **1**.
- Improve skill on straight-copy sentences.
- Learn to key rough-draft copy.

31A

Warmup

Key each line twice.

Alphabet

1 Virgil Quin has packed twenty boxes of prize jams.

Space Bar

2 to be able|it is the|if I go|to see the|when it is

Easy

3 When she got such a profit, she paid for the land.

gwam 1'| 1 | 2 | 3 | 4 | 5 | 6 | 7 | 8 | 9 | 10 |

31B

New Keys 8 and 1

Key each line twice. If time permits, rekey lines 7–9.

8 Right middle finger

1 Left little finger

TECHNIQUE TIP

Keep the fingers not being used to tap the number key anchored to the home keys.

Learn 8

1 k 8 k 8|kk 88 kk 88|k8k k8k|88k 88k|8k8 8k8|k8 k8;

2 Add the figures 8 and 888. Only 8 of 88 finished.

3 Felipe lives at 88 Pine; Oscar lives at 88 Spruce.

Learn 1

4 a 1 a 1|aa 11 aa 11|a1a a1a|11a 11a|1a1 1a1|a1 a1;

5 Key the figures 11 and 111. Read pages 11 to 111.

6 Travis keyed 1 instead of 11; I keyed 111, not 11.

Combine 8 and 1

7 His time was 8 min. 1 sec.; mine was 8 min. 8 sec.

8 June 18 was the day Ricardo Santo biked 181 miles.

9 Jane keyed 818 and 181; Michael keyed 811 and 118.

Lesson 66

Planning an Oral Presentation

Learning Outcomes

Data Files:

df 66 purpose
df 66 profile

In Lesson 66, you will:

66A *Determine the purpose of a presentation.*

66B *Develop an audience profile.*

66C *Create an outline.*

66D *Evaluate visual aids.*

66A

Determine the Purpose of a Presentation

A **presentation** is a talk or speech given to inform, persuade, and/or entertain. Good presentations do not just happen—they need a great deal of planning and preparation. You have probably heard that "Those who fail to plan, plan to fail." That saying is particularly true with oral presentations. When planning a presentation, you need to consider the:

- Purpose of the presentation

- Audience for the presentation

- Content of the presentation

- Visual aids for the presentation

Before planning and preparing a presentation, you must know the purpose of the presentation. What are the goals you want to accomplish with it? Is your goal to inform or entertain? Do you want the people who hear the presentation to take some action? Do you want them to have different ideas or opinions after hearing the presentation? Answering those questions will help you determine your goals.

1. Start *Word.* Open *df 66 purpose.* Print the document and then close the file.

2. Read the descriptions of presentations in the left column of the document. In the right column, write one or more goals you think the speaker would want to accomplish with the presentation.

66B

Develop an Audience Profile

As you plan a presentation, you should consider the audience. The **audience** consists of the people who will listen to your talk (Figure 10.1). You need to develop a **profile** (description) of your audience.

To develop an audience profile, list some things you know about the people who will hear your talk. Answer questions such as these:

- Does the audience know a lot or a little about the topic you will discuss? If they know a lot about the topic, you can skip basic information and move on to more advanced points.

- How many and how old are the people in the audience? You would not use the same words to talk to a third-grade class as you would to talk to a group of parents.

Rough-Draft Copy

Proofreaders' Marks

∧ = insert
= add space
∼ = transpose
ℐ = delete
⌒ = close up
≡ = capitalize
lc = lowercase

Study the proofreaders' marks shown at the left and in the sentences. Key each sentence double-spaced, making all handwritten changes.

1 Rough draft is ∧work with hand⌒written change∧.   *keyed copy*ℐ ... ˢ

2 Special marks∧used to show changes∧made.   *are* ... *to be*

3 ∧Read a sentence not∧ing changes; then key∧it.   *First, lc* ... ℐ ... #∧

4 ∧Check to see∧if you made∧the changes correctly.   *Next, lc* ... *that*ℐ ... *all of* ... ℐ

5 Read rough draft∧a bit ahead of∧keying point.   *slightly* ... *the* ... ⌒

6 Doing∧this ℐ will help∧make∧the change∼ right.   *so* ... *you to* ... *all*

7 You∧will key often from script and∧draft.   *soon* ... *rough*

 checkpoint   Did you make each correction indicated by a proofreaders' mark?

31D

Balanced-Hand Sentences

TECHNIQUE TIP
Keep your fingers curved and upright.

Key each line twice.

1 Jane is to pay for the eight audit forms for them.
2 Rich is to go to the lake to fix the signs for us.
3 I may go to the city to do the work for the firms.
4 Profit is a problem for the big firms in the city.
5 The eight maps may aid them when they do the work.

| gwam 30" | 2 | 4 | 6 | 8 | 10 | 12 | 14 | 16 | 18 | 20 |

31E

Timed Writing

 all letters used

MicroType

Use *MicroType* Numeric Keyboarding Lesson 1 for additional practice.

Key a 1' timed writing on each paragraph.

```
            •    2    •    4    •    6    •    8    •
     Keep in home position all of the fingers not
   10    •   12    •   14    •   16    •   18    •
being used to strike a key.  Do not let them move out
 20    •   22    •   24    •   26    •   28    •
of position for the next letters in your copy.
            •    2    •    4    •    6    •    8    •
     Prize the control you have over the fingers.
   10    •   12    •   14    •   16    •   18    •   20
See how quickly speed goes up when you learn that you
       •   22    •   24    •   26    •   28    •
can make them do just what you expect of them.
```

UNIT 4 Computer Applications

Chapter 10 — Presentations

Lessons 66–71

The focus of Chapters 5–9 was on learning word processing skills to communicate through written documents. The focus of this chapter is on learning presentation skills to communicate orally. You will begin by learning how a good oral presentation is developed. You will identify the purpose of a presentation, profile the audience, develop the content, and consider visual aids that will help you get your message across. You will use presentation software to create visual aids to enhance your presentation. After creating the presentation, you will practice delivering it prior to actually giving the presentation. Finally, you will receive audience feedback on your delivery to help you improve your speaking ability.

© Maxim Blinkov/Shutterstock.com

Lesson 32

New Keys 9 and 4

Learning Outcomes

In Lesson 32, you will:
* *Learn reach technique for 9 and 4.*
* *Learn to key from script copy.*

32A

Warmup

Key each line twice.

Alphabet

1 Have my long quiz boxed when Jack stops by for it.

Space Bar

2 to do it | go to the | and to do | if she is | he may work

Easy

3 Title to all of the lake land is held by the city.

gwam 1' | 1 | 2 | 3 | 4 | 5 | 6 | 7 | 8 | 9 | 10 |

32B

New Keys 9 and 4

Key each line twice. If time permits, rekey lines 7–9.

9 Right ring *finger*

4 Left index *finger*

Learn 9

1 1 9 1 9 | 11 99 11 99 | 191 191 | 991 991 | 919 919 | 19 19;

2 My baseball number is 9; my football number is 99.

3 There were 999 racers; only 9 of the 999 finished.

Learn 4

4 f 4 f 4 | ff 44 ff 44 | f4f f4f | 44f 44f | 4f4 4f4 | f4 f4;

5 He read pages 4 to 44. Janet has 44 extra points.

6 Tim added 4, 44, and 444. Jason scored 44 points.

Combine 9 and 4

7 Jay scored 44 of the 99 points; Joe had 49 points.

8 Is his average .449 or .494? Today it is at .449.

9 She keyed a 49 rather than a 94 in the number 494.

Creating a Professional Document

As you've learned, creating professional documents is important, especially when an employer or customer will see them. Since *Word* makes it so easy to format documents, you can quickly make documents for your own use. In this activity, you will create two cover pages—one for your own customer records and one for your Career Exploration Portfolio.

1. Create a cover page using the Ion design in Quick Parts. Replace the existing text with your own name and the company name that you used in the first *About Business* activity in this chapter (business cards). Change the document title to **Client Information** and key the subtitle of **Current and Potential Customers**. Save the document as *c9 client cover page*.

2. Create a second cover sheet using a format of your choice. Save it as *c9 cep cover page*. Replace the text as appropriate for your Career Exploration Portfolio. Save, print, and close both cover sheets.

Career Exploration Portfolio

Online Resources:

ngl.cengage.com/c21jr3e

Activity 8

To complete this activity, you will need the Student Interest Survey that you filled out in Career Exploration Portfolio Activity 1. Completing Career Exploration Activities 2–7 would also be helpful but is not mandatory.

1. Review your Student Interest Survey. Note your *first* Career Cluster of interest. Reread its description.

2. Go to http://www.careertech.org. Click the **Career Technical Education** button, and then click **Career Clusters**. Click the name of your first Career Cluster choice.

3. Scroll through the categories available within that Career Cluster. Click the Plan of Study **Excel** link under the category you are most interested in to download the file to your system. (Choose the same category, or Pathway, that you used in Activities 2 and 5 if you completed them.)

4. Locate and open the downloaded *Excel* workbook. Read the list of classes you should take in high school to get ready for this career. Then read the list of classes that you should take after high school.

5. Search the Internet to find one or more colleges or technical schools that offer degrees in this career.

6. Use *Word* to write a summary of what you learned in this activity. Save the document as *c9 career 1 skills*, print, and close it.

32C

Handwritten Copy (Script)

Key each line twice.

1 *Script is copy that is written with pen or pencil.*
2 *Copy that is written poorly is often hard to read.*
3 *Read script a few words ahead of the keying point.*
4 *Doing so will help you produce copy free of error.*
5 *Leave proper spacing after punctuation marks, too.*
6 *With practice, you can key script at a rapid rate.*

32D

Keying Technique

TECHNIQUE TIP
• Reach up without moving hands away from you.
• Reach down without moving hands toward your body.

Key each sentence twice.

ol/lo

1 ol lo loaf cold sold hold lock loan fold long load
2 Lou told me that her local school loans old locks.

za/az

3 za az zap adz haze zany lazy jazz hazy maze pizzas
4 A zany jazz band played with pizzazz at the plaza.

ik/ki

5 ik ki kit ski kin kid kip bike kick like kiwi hike
6 The kid can hike or ride his bike to the ski lake.

ws/sw

7 ws sw was saw laws rows cows vows swam sways swing
8 Swin swims at my swim club and shows no big flaws.

32E

Keying Technique

Spacing technique

MicroType

Use *MicroType* Numeric Keyboarding Lesson 2 for additional practice.

Key each line twice. If time permits, key the lines again.

Alphabet

1 no best rose very extra zest open queen cast water
2 Robert or Peter will answer their seven questions.

Space Bar

3 at for the and big all how sad fan got jet ask log
4 Tom and Jake may walk to the city to buy the ball.

Shift and number keys

5 March 4; May 18; June 9; July 19; April 18; May 14
6 Jan, Fay, and I went to New York City on March 23.

Number sentences

7 Chi had scores of 81, 94, 84, and 91 on the exams.
8 Key 1894 and 1948; now key 19, 84, 18, 48, and 18.

ACROSS THE CURRICULUM

Academic Connections

Data Files:

df c9 sales receipt
    instructions
df c9 sales receipt
    template
df c9 business card
    instructions
df c9 business card
    template
df c9 resume
    instructions
df c9 resume
    template

Math: Sales Receipts

Businesses use sales receipts to list products and services that customers buy from them. A sales receipt often shows the quantity and description of a product as well as its price. It can provide information on whether a customer paid with cash, credit, or a check. Sales receipts are useful to keep records and when a customer needs to return an item.

1. Start *Word* and open *df c9 sales receipt instructions*.

2. Read the instructions in the document to open a template and create a sales receipt.

About Business

Promoting Your Own Business: Business Cards

Business cards are a great way to promote your business. They usually display your name, company name, and phone number. Customers can store them in a convenient place so that they can easily contact you when they need your services.

1. Open *df c9 business card instructions*.

2. Read the instructions in the document to open a template and create business cards for a real or fictional company.

Life Success Builder

Develop a Resume

A resume is a document that tells the story of you—the skills and qualifications that make you the best candidate for a job.

Your resume must capture the reader's attention quickly. It can show what job you are seeking, how you are qualified for a job, and how your experiences make you right for the position.

1. Open *df c9 resume instructions*.

2. Read the instructions in the document to open a template and create a resume for yourself.

New Keys 0 and 5

Learning Outcomes

In Lesson 33, you will:
- *Learn reach technique for 0 and 5.*
- *Improve skill at keying copy with numbers.*

33A

Warmup

Key each line twice.

Alphabet

1 Aquela Javicz kept the new forms by the tax guide.

?

2 Where is Yuri? Who can say? Is he to go with us?

Easy

3 They may cut the fish down by the end of the dock.

gwam 1' | 1 | 2 | 3 | 4 | 5 | 6 | 7 | 8 | 9 | 10 |

33B

New Keys 0 and 5

Key each line twice. If time permits, rekey lines 7–9.

0 Right little finger

5 Left index finger

Learn 0

1 ; 0 ; 0|;; 00 ;; 00|;0; ;0;|00; 00;|0;0 0;0|0; 0;0

2 Reach from the ; to the 0. The license was 00H00.

3 Kia keyed 000 after the decimal; Tonya keyed 0000.

Learn 5

4 f 5 f 5|ff 55 ff 55|f5f f5f|55f 55f|5f5 5f5|5f 5f;

5 Ken had 55 points on the quiz; Jay also scored 55.

6 Of the 55 exhibits, only 5 won grand prize awards.

Combine 0 and 5

7 Debra told us the number was 505.550, not 550.505.

8 Lance hit .500 during July and .505 during August.

9 Orlando bought 500 pounds of grain on September 5.

1. Key three 1' timed writings on each paragraph, striving to key more on each timing; determine *gwam*.

2. Key a 2' or 3' timed writing on both paragraphs combined, striving to maintain your highest 1' *gwam*.

A all letters used

	gwam	2'	3'
Austria is a rather small country located		4	3
between Germany and Italy. It is about three		9	6
times the size of Vermont. The most recognized		14	9
city in this country is Vienna. Over the years		18	12
this city has been known for its contributions to		23	15
the culture in the region. It is particularly		28	19
known in the area of performing arts. Another		33	22
place that has played an important part in the		38	25
exquisite culture of the area is the city of		42	28
Salzburg.		43	29
Salzburg is also recognized as a great city		4	32
for the performing arts. This city is known for		9	35
music. Just as important, however, is that the		14	38
city is the birthplace of Wolfgang Amadeus		18	41
Mozart. Mozart was one of the greatest composers		23	44
of all time. Perhaps, no other composer had an		28	47
earlier start at his professional endeavors than		33	50
did Mozart. It is thought that he began playing		38	53
at the age of four and began composing at the age		43	56
of five.		44	57

gwam 2' | 1 | 2 | 3 | 4 | 5 |
3' | 1 | 2 | 3 |

33C

Keying Numbers

TECHNIQUE TIP
Reach up without moving your hands away from your body.

Key each line twice.

1 Mario dialed 594.1880 instead of dialing 495.1880.
2 He drove 598 miles one day and 410 miles the next.
3 He bowled 98, 105, and 94 the last time he bowled.
4 Orlando said the odometer read 58,940 on March 15.

✓ **checkpoint** Do your fingers remain curved when you reach to the top row?

33D

Speed Forcing Drill

TECHNIQUE TIP
Reach out with little finger and tap the ENTER key quickly. Return your finger to its home key.

Key a 30" timed writing on each line. Your rate in *gwam* is shown below the lines.

1 Jane left.

2 He paid for us.

3 Joel did their wash.

4 Jo may be here next week.

5 Kent went to the game with me.

6 Did the man make the signs for her?

7 Paul may be able to take the exam later.

8 Jason got a new computer before he left town.

9 Felipe was able to key six words faster this week.

| gwam | 30" | 2 | 4 | 6 | 8 | 10 | 12 | 14 | 16 | 18 | 20 |

✓ **checkpoint** Did you keep your eyes on the copy as you keyed each line?

KEYBOARDING SKILLBUILDING

Warmup Practice

Key each line twice. If time permits, key the lines again.

Alphabet

1 Dr. Kopezy will give Jacques the exam before noon.

Figure/Symbol

2 They received 25% ($164.87) off their order #8390.

Speed

3 Rodney kept the shamrock in the box by the mantel.

gwam 1' | 1 | 2 | 3 | 4 | 5 | 6 | 7 | 8 | 9 | 10 |

Improve Keying Technique

Key each line twice, striving to maintain a continuous pace.

TECHNIQUE TIP
Quickly space after each word and immediately begin keying the next word.

TECHNIQUE TIP
As you key, all movement should be in your fingers as you make the reach to the third row and the bottom row. Your hands and arms should not be moving.

Space Bar

1 and the but can may when them lake high find were;
2 Stan may do the work for the six men on the audit.

SHIFT keys

3 Idaho (Boise) Minnesota (St. Paul) Ohio (Columbus)
4 Sam was sure that the capital of Oregon was Salem.

Adjacent keys

5 buy fire went said ruin were same tree open walked
6 We opened a shop by the same spot as Sandy Merton.

3rd row

7 to yet peer quit were pout pepper terror tire rope
8 Our pups were too little to take to your pet show.

Bottom row

9 extinct, zebra, moving, van, numb, moon, vacation
10 Zeno had a six-month smallpox injection on Monday.

gwam 1' | 1 | 2 | 3 | 4 | 5 | 6 | 7 | 8 | 9 | 10 |

Speed Forcing Drill

Key three 30" timed writings on each line, striving to key more on each attempt.

1 Ann and I had a perfect score.
2 The drive to Atlanta takes an hour.
3 Charles attended the Olympics in Athens.
4 My first jump was longer than my second jump.
5 Dan has checked his answers to the problems again.

gwam 30" | 2 | 4 | 6 | 8 | 10 | 12 | 14 | 16 | 18 | 20 |

Key each paragraph once. Double-space between paragraphs. Key a 1' timed writing on each paragraph; determine *gwam*. Record your best timing.

 all letters used

```
         •    2    •    4    •    6    •    8    •
    You must realize by now that learning to key
  10    •   12    •   14    •   16    •   18    •
requires work.  However, you will soon be able to
  20    •   22    •   24    •   26    •   28    •
key at a higher speed than you can write just now.
         •    2    •    4    •    6    •    8    •
    You will also learn to do neater work on the
  10    •   12    •   14    •   16    •   18    •
computer than you can do by hand.  Quality work at
  20    •   22    •   24    •   26    •   28    •
higher speeds is a good goal for you to have next.
```

MicroType

Use *MicroType* Numeric Keyboarding Lesson 3 for additional practice.

33F

Team Activity

COLLABORATION

1. At the keyboard, compose a brief message about a current event. If you have access to the Internet, use it before composing your message to learn about events that are taking place in the news. After keying your message, print it and give it to one of your classmates.

2. Proofread the keyed message that you received from your classmate. Edit it using the proofreaders' marks shown on p. 129. Return the edited copy to the student who keyed it.

3. When your message is returned, make the corrections shown on the edited copy. Print the final copy.

 Instant Message When writing your message, remember the five *W*s. Tell the Who, What, Where, When, and Why related to the event.

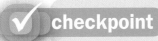 **checkpoint** Does your message include the five *W*s related to the event?

A list of the items available to us is attached. All items can be delivered and installed before school starts in late August.

At your next department meeting, please decide what furniture and equipment we can use. I need to confirm the items we want with AnTech personnel before the end of May.

3. Add appropriate closing lines.

4. Save the memo as *c9 memo* and close it.

Birthday Card from Template

1. Using template *df 63c birthday* or a birthday card template that you choose, design a birthday card for one of your relatives.

2. Save the card as *c9 birthday* and close it.

Invitation from Template

1. Using template *df 63b invitation* or an invitation template that you choose, design an invitation to a party that you will host.

2. Save the document as *c9 invitation* and close it.

Report Cover Page from Building Block

1. Start a new, blank document. Using a predesigned cover page of your choice from the Building Blocks Organizer, prepare a report cover page using the following information:

   • Use **Athletic Training** as the report title.

   • Use **Education Required, Working Conditions, and Employment Opportunities** as the report subtitle.

   • Insert your name as the writer.

   • Insert **Career Explorations** as the course name.

   • Insert the current date.

2. Save the cover page as *c9 cover page* and close it.

New Keys 7 and 3

Learning Outcomes

In Lesson 34, you will:

- *Learn reach technique for 7 and 3.*
- *Improve skill at keying copy with numbers.*

34A

Warmup

Key each line twice.

Alphabet

1 By solving the tax quiz, Jud Mack won first prize.

CAPS LOCK

2 Did you OK this show for ABC, for NBC, or for CBS?

Easy

3 He may do all the work if he works with good form.

gwam 1'| 1 | 2 | 3 | 4 | 5 | 6 | 7 | 8 | 9 | 10 |

34B

New Keys 7 and 3

Key each line twice. If time permits, rekey lines 7–9.

7 Right index *finger*

3 Left middle *finger*

Learn 7

1 j 7 j 7|jj 77 jj 77|j7j j7j|77j 77j|7j7 7j7|7j 7j;

2 Of the 77 computers, 7 are connected to a printer.

3 The highest score on the March 7 exam was only 77.

Learn 3

4 d 3 d 3|dd 33 dd 33|d3d d3d|33d 33d|3d3 3d3|3d 3d;

5 Dr. Ho used only 33 of the original 333 questions.

6 She scheduled quizzes on January 3 and on April 3.

Combine 7 and 3

7 Melanie scored only 73 on the July 3 exam, not 77.

8 Sandra answered 37 of the 73 questions in an hour.

9 Jessie bowled 73, Mike bowled 77, and I bowled 73.

Before You Move On

Answer **True** or **False** to each question to review what you have learned in Chapter 9.

1. A template is a master copy of a set of predesigned styles for a particular type of document. LO 63A

2. When you open a template, you are opening a copy of the template, not the template itself. LO 63A

3. You can use a template that you have created, one that is installed on your computer, or one that you can download from Microsoft Office Online. LO 63A

4. When working with a template, you cannot delete placeholder text. LO 63A

5. A memo is a written message that is usually sent from a person in one business to a person in another business. LO 64A

6. The four heading lines of a memo are TO, FROM, ENCLOSURE, and DATE. LO 64A

7. Memos do not use closing lines for reference initials, copies, and so on. LO 64A

8. In some templates, it is possible to pick a date from a calendar. LO 65B

9. A facsimile is a document that is sent over standard telephone lines. LO 65B

10. Various predesigned documents in the Building Blocks Organizer can be accessed by using the Quick Parts feature. LO 65C

Applying What You Have Learned

Memo from Template

1. Open *df 64a memo*. Key your school name as replacement text in the box at the upper right.

2. Key the following replacement text at the appropriate places:

   TO: Science Teachers

   FROM: Josephine Tillman, Principal

   DATE: April 15, 20--

   SUBJECT: Science Furniture and Equipment Donation

   AnTech Laboratories has up-to-date science laboratory furniture and equipment that it can donate to our school. We believe that our science teachers and students will derive great benefits from what AnTech is offering.

34C

TAB Key

TIP Click the **Show/Hide ¶** button to see the TAB characters on your screen.

¶   Show/Hide ¶ Button

Key each line twice single-spaced. Double-space between sets of lines.

1	5	tab →	10	tab →	394	tab →	781	tab →	908
2	9	tab →	45	tab →	703	tab →	185	tab →	731
3	4	tab →	81	tab →	930	tab →	507	tab →	405
4	7	tab →	30	tab →	585	tab →	914	tab →	341
5	3	tab →	79	tab →	485	tab →	180	tab →	789

34D

Keying Technique

TECHNIQUE TIP
Keep your wrists low but not resting on the keyboard.

MicroType

Use *MicroType* Numeric Keyboarding Lesson 4 for additional practice.

Key each line twice. Key 1' timings on lines 2, 4, and 6.

Letter response

1 milk milk|extra extra|pink pink|wage wage|oil oil;

2 Edward saw a deserted cat on a crate in my garage.

Word response

3 burn burn|hand hand|duck duck|rock rock|mend mend;

4 The eight signs are down by the lake by the docks.

Combination response

5 with only|they join|half safe|born free|goal rates

6 Dave sat on the airy lanai and gazed at the puppy.

gwam 1' | 1 | 2 | 3 | 4 | 5 | 6 | 7 | 8 | 9 | 10 |

34E

Timed Writing

Key each paragraph once. Double-space between paragraphs. Key a 1' timed writing on each paragraph; determine *gwam*.

 all letters used

     •   2   •   4   •   6   •   8   •

Are you one of the people who often look from

  10   •   12   •   14   •   16   •   18   •

the copy to the screen and down at your hands? If

  20   •   22   •   24   •   26   •   28   •

you are, you can be sure that you will not build a

  30   •   32   •   34   •   36   •   38   •

speed to prize. Make eyes on copy your next goal.

     •   2   •   4   •   6   •   8   •

When you move the eyes from the copy to check

  10   •   12   •   14   •   16   •   18   •

the screen, you may lose your place and waste time

  20   •   22   •   24   •   26   •   28   •

trying to find it. Lost time can lower your speed

  30   •   32   •   34   •   36   •   38   •

quickly and in a major way, so do not look away.

1. Start a new, blank document.

2. Click **Quick Parts** in the Text group on the Insert tab as shown in Figure 9.11.

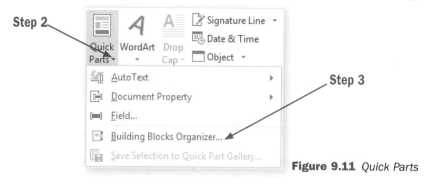

Figure 9.11 *Quick Parts*

3. Click **Building Blocks Organizer**. In the Building Blocks gallery, select the **Whisp** cover page. Click **Insert**.

4. Key **USING BUILDING BLOCKS** to replace the title placeholder text.

5. Click the placeholder text for the subtitle. Tap DELETE twice to delete the text and the content control panel.

6. Click the **[Date]** placeholder text. Click the down arrow and select **Today** to insert the current date.

7. Key your name to replace the name (or text) that appears in the last line of text.

8. Key the name of your course to replace the company name.

9. Save the cover page as *65c cover page* and close it.

21st Century Skills

COLLABORATION

Creativity and Innovation

Being a creative thinker and communicating ideas with others are important skills, whether you are in the classroom, on the job, or in a social situation. When you are willing to suggest and share ideas, you demonstrate your originality and inventiveness. When you are open and responsive to the ideas and perspectives of others, you show consideration and cooperation.

In teams of three to four, develop a class newsletter using a *Word* template. The newsletter should include a minimum of three articles and at least two graphics. Article ideas include recent projects, field trips, guest speakers, upcoming tests or assignments, study tips, teacher profiles, or student achievements. Divide duties as necessary.

Think Critically

1. Creativity can mean a lot of different things. How do you define creativity?

2. What idea creation techniques do you think work best for groups? What about for you individually?

3. What positive things can you learn from an idea that "flops"?

© Amir Ridhwan/Shutterstock.com

Lesson 35 — New Keys 6 and 2

Learning Outcomes

In Lesson 35, you will:

- *Learn reach technique for **6** and **2**.*
- *Improve skill at keying copy with numbers.*

35A

Warmup

Key each line twice.

Alphabet

1 Wade Javey quickly found extra maps in the gazebo.

Spacing

2 am to|is an|by it|of us|an oak|is to pay|it is due

Easy

3 I am to pay the six men if they do the work right.

gwam 1' | 1 | 2 | 3 | 4 | 5 | 6 | 7 | 8 | 9 | 10 |

35B

New Keys 6 and 2

Key each line twice. If time permits, rekey lines 7–9.

6 Right index *finger*

2 Left ring *finger*

Learn 6

1 j 6 j 6|jj 66 jj 66|j6j j6j|66j 66j|6j6 6j6|6j; 6j

2 There were 66 entries. All 66 competed yesterday.

3 He said 76 trombones. I said that is not correct.

Learn 2

4 s 2 s 2|ss 22 ss 22|s2s s2s|22s 22s|2s2 2s2|2s; 2s

5 Of the 222 items, Charlton labeled 22 incorrectly.

6 The 22 girls may play 2 games against the 22 boys.

Combine 6 and 2

7 Monique has gone 262 miles; she has 26 more to go.

8 March 26, August 26, and October 26 are the dates.

9 Just 26 more days before Gilberto is 26 years old.

1. Open *df 65b fax.* Insert the following replacement text and new text in the appropriate places:

To: Mrs. Rita Greenwood	From: Insert your name
Fax: 727-555-0122	Pages: Six
Phone: 727-555-0129	Date: Pick today's date (click the text, select the down arrow, and select Today)
Re: Johnson Street Proposal	CC: None

2. Key an **X** in the **For Review** box.

3. In the Comments section, key **I'll call you on Friday to set up an appointment to discuss the proposal**.

4. Save the fax cover page as *65b fax* and close it.

65C

Cover Pages and Quick Parts

A **cover page** (or title page) is frequently prepared for reports. The cover page generally includes the report title, the name and title of the writer, the name of the writer's school or organization, and the date of the report. You can create a new cover page each time you need one. You can choose a professional-looking cover page from the gallery of predesigned cover pages in the Building Blocks Organizer and then add your information in the same way you inserted text in a template. Figure 9.10 shows a predesigned cover page named Whisp that will be used in this lesson.

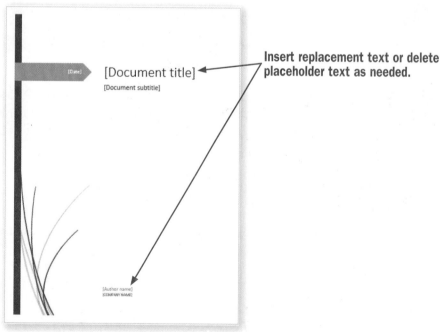

Insert replacement text or delete placeholder text as needed.

Figure 9.10 *Whisp cover page from Quick Parts*

35C

Keying Numbers

TECHNIQUE TIP
Keep your forearms parallel to the slant of the keyboard.

Key each line twice.

Straight copy

1 Jose moved from 724 Park Lane to 810 State Street.

2 Marcos was 3 minutes and 56 seconds behind Carlos.

Rough draft

3 Mrs. kendall siad the practice willbe June 30.

4 Flihgt Nos. 3875 leave at 6:45 a.m. on Octobre 13.

35D

Timed Writing

Key each paragraph once. Double-space between paragraphs. Key a 1' timed writing on each paragraph.

 all letters used

```
       •      2      •      4      •      6      •      8
        Success does not mean the same thing to
   •      10     •     12     •     14     •     16     •     18
everyone.  For some, it means to get to the top at
   •      20     •     22     •     24     •     26     •     28
all costs:  in power, in fame, and in income.  For
   •      30     •     32     •     34     •     36     •     38
others, it means just to fulfill their basic needs
   •      40     •     42     •     44     •     46     •
or wants with as little effort as required.
          •      2      •      4      •      6      •      8      •
        Most people fall within the two extremes.  They
10     •     12     •     14     •     16     •     18     •
work quite hard to better their lives at home, at
20     •     22     •     24     •     26     •     28     •
work, and in the social world.  They realize that
30     •     32     •     34     •     36     •     38     •
success for them is not in being at the top but
40     •     42     •     44     •     46     •     48     •
rather in trying to improve their quality of life.
```

MicroType

Use *MicroType* Numeric Keyboarding Lesson 5 for additional practice.

35E

Compose Sentences

Key each sentence once. Use words of your choice to complete the sentences.

1 My favorite president is _____.

2 My favorite actor/actress is _____.

3 My favorite city is _____.

4 My favorite food is _____.

5 My favorite thing to do is _____.

Meeting Facilitator: Mr. Eric Littleford

Invitees: All math and science teachers

   I. Call to order

  II. Roll call

 III. Approval of minutes from last meeting

 IV. Open issues

      a) Selection of math textbooks

      b) Review of science teacher applications and resumes

      c) Selection of Science Fair judges

  V. New business

      a) Interview dates for teacher applicants

      b) Selection of science textbooks

 VI. Adjournment

2. Save the agenda as *65a agenda* and close it.

65B

Fax Cover Page Template

Fax, short for **facsimile**, is a technology that sends a document using standard telephone lines or a special Internet connection. Along with the faxed document, the sender generally sends a **fax cover page** that includes the name of the recipient, the fax and regular telephone numbers of the recipient, the name of the sender, the number of pages being sent, a brief description of the document, and comments. Figure 9.9 shows the fax template that will be used in this lesson.

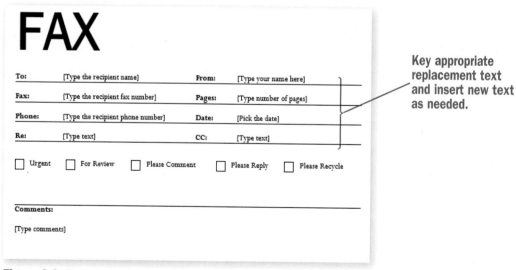

Figure 9.9 *Fax cover page template*

New Keys /, $, and @

Learning Outcomes

In Lesson 36, you will:
- *Learn reach technique for /, $, and @.*
- *Combine /, $, and @ with other keys.*

36A

Warmup

Key each line twice.

Alphabet

1 Jack Vasquez may work for Bill Pagel the next day.

Spacing

2 When did you see the girls go to the lake to work?

Easy

3 She owns the big dock, but they own the lake land.

gwam 1' | 1 | 2 | 3 | 4 | 5 | 6 | 7 | 8 | 9 | 10 |

36B

New Keys / and $

*/ **Right little** finger*

*$ **Left index** finger + Right Shift*

Key each line twice.

Learn / (diagonal)

1 ; / ; /|;; // // ;;|;/; /;/|/p; /p/|/;p /;p|p/; /;

2 He keyed the date as 05/17/05 instead of 05/17/06.

3 Toua added 3 3/4 and 4 1/2 and came up with 8 1/4.

Learn $ (dollar sign)

4 f $ f $|f rr $$ f rr $$|f r $ f r $|r$f r$f|$fr $f

5 $102.93 and $48.76 and $547.29 and $9.86 and $1.03

6 I owed $502.78 for February and $416.39 for March.

SPACING TIP Do not space between a figure and the / or the $.

Lesson 65

Templates: Agendas, Fax Cover Pages, and Report Cover Pages

Data Files:

df 65a agenda
df 65b fax

Learning Outcomes

In Lesson 65, you will:

65A *Use an agenda template.*

65B *Use a fax cover page template.*

65C *Use Quick Parts to create report cover (title) pages.*

65A

Agenda Template

An **agenda** is a list of things to be done or actions to be taken, usually at a meeting. The agenda is normally distributed before the meeting to all who are invited to the meeting so they can be prepared to address each of the agenda items. The agenda also provides the date, time, and place of the meeting. Figure 9.8 shows an agenda template that will be used in this lesson.

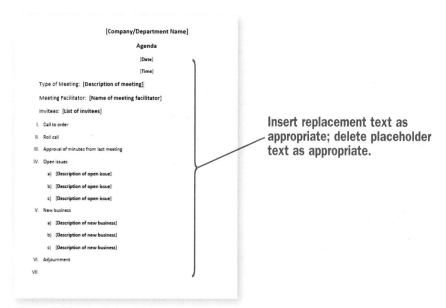

Figure 9.8 *Agenda template*

1. Open *df 65a agenda* and insert the following replacement text in the appropriate places. Delete unneeded placeholder text.

Math and Science Department Meeting
Agenda
March 15, 20--
2:15 p.m.

Type of Meeting: Monthly Department Meeting

36C

Keying Technique

Key each line twice.

Double letters

1 cook ball green puzzle pepper waffle access quarry

2 Dallas or Minnesota plays Tennessee in four weeks.

One-hand words

3 hook cart noun look agree radar pupil state hookup

4 we are|no regrets|only degree|dress up|pink garage

Shift keys

5 We had delegates from Ohio, Texas, Iowa, and Utah.

6 The New York Yankees play the New York Mets today.

`gwam` 15" |　4　|　8　|　12　|　16　|　20　|　24　|　28　|　32　|　36　|　40　|

36D

New Key @

@ Left ring finger + Right
Shift

Key each line twice.

Learn @ (at sign)

1 s @ s @|ss @@ ss @@| s@s s@s|@s@ @s@|5 @ 25 5@ 25;

2 yorkmb@nyu.edu, smithj@charter.net, jonesjc@ku.edu

3 50 shares of PEP @ $81.57; 25 shares of INTC @ $24

Combine /, $, and @

4 The sale for 30 @ $14 or $27 each ends on 9/28/16.

5 Kelly purchased 2 1/2 lbs. @ $6 per pound for $15.

6 I sold 16 @ $149 per chair on 07/30/15 for $2,384.

36E

Keying Script

TECHNIQUE TIP
Keep up your pace to the
end of the line. Tap ENTER
quickly and begin the new
line without a pause or stop.

Key each line twice.

1 *Try to increase your speed on each of these lines.*

2 *Keying each word letter by letter takes very long.*

3 *Keying some of the words as words increases speed.*

4 *Keeping the eyes on the copy also increases speed.*

5 *Keep your fingers upright and curved to go faster.*

6 *Quickly tap the ENTER key at the end of each line.*

the school library, and purchasing a banner that can be used to welcome students back to school each fall. The Give-Back Committee, chaired by Annie Sexton, will study all three options and report back at the May meeting.

VI. <u>Adjournment</u>—Marcie Holmquist adjourned the meeting at 3:35 p.m.

Minutes submitted by: Jerry Finley, Secretary

2. Save the memo as *64b ford minutes* and close it.

Digital Citizenship and Ethics

Peter Alvey People / Alamy

An addiction is a physiological or psychological dependence on something that is harmful. You have likely heard of serious addictions, and perhaps even heard others joke about being addicted to something not so serious, like chocolate or car racing.

Internet addiction—psychological dependence on the online experience—is on the rise, and health experts are warning users about the long-lasting physical and psychological problems it can cause. Signs of Internet addiction include:

- Preoccupation with the Internet; that is, thinking about previous online activity or being anxious for the next online activity.

- Feeling the need to use the Internet more and more frequently.
- Staying online longer than intended and trying to conceal use of the Internet.
- Feeling agitated, restless, and irritable when cutting back on Internet usage.

As a class, discuss the following:

1. What physical and psychological problems can Internet addiction lead to?
2. What can you do to avoid becoming an Internet addict?

36F

Speed Forcing Drill

TECHNIQUE TIP
Keep your eyes on the text as you key.

MicroType

Use *MicroType* Numeric Keyboarding Lesson 7 for additional practice.

Key two 20" timed writings on each line.

1 Pamela is to do the work.

2 He may go with me to the lake.

3 Jo may go to the city with the man.

4 Jay may make a profit for the six firms.

5 Helen may go to the island for the oak shelf.

6 He paid the eight men for their work on the forms.

gwam 20"	3	6	9	12	15	18	21	24	27	30

✓ **checkpoint** Do your fingers remain curved when you reach to the top row?

36G

Enrichment Activity

Unscramble the letters shown below to create eight words. If you have difficulty, key the letters in different orders to unscramble the words.

1. lehfs   5. esrds

2. reetn   6. daoty

3. dpnuo   7. crota

4. erneg   8. csaib

Lesson 37

New Keys %, –, and +

Learning Outcomes

In Lesson 37, you will:

- *Learn reach technique for %, –, and +.*
- *Combine %, –, and + with other keys.*

37A

Warmup

Key each line twice.

Alphabet

1 Marjax made five quick plays to win the big prize.

Figures

2 Miguel told us to add 187, 369, 420, 215, and 743.

Easy

3 It is right for the man to aid them with the sign.

gwam 1'	1	2	3	4	5	6	7	8	9	10

Activity 2

1. Open *df 64b minutes*. Using the template, key the following as replacement text at the appropriate places. Delete placeholder text that is not needed.

Ford Middle School Science Club
Meeting Minutes
April 2, 20--

I. <u>Call to order</u>—Key **President Marcie Holmquist, Science Club, 2:45 p.m., April 2, 20--**, and **Room 214** at the appropriate places.

II. <u>Roll call</u>—Jerry Finley, Secretary, conducted a roll call. All officers, 23 members, and the faculty sponsor were present.

III. <u>Approval of minutes from last meeting</u>—Jerry Finley, Secretary, read the minutes and they were approved as read.

IV. <u>Open issues</u>

   a) There will be five teams of four members each for the candy sale that begins on May 1.

   b) Bill Eaton will organize a team of volunteers to remove the litter on Holt Road. The Rotary Club will provide adult supervision, equipment, and supplies.

   c) The officers recommended that the Club help sponsor an international student this coming year. The officers' recommendation was approved.

V. <u>New business</u>

   a) President Holmquist appointed the Nominating Committee (Sissy Erwin, Roberta Shaw, and Jim Vance). They are to present a slate of officers at the May meeting.

   b) Three suggestions for a give-back gift were discussed. The possibilities include planting a tree near the parking lot, donating one or more reference books to

37B

New Keys % and –

% **Left index** finger + Right Shift

– **Right little** finger

Key each line twice.

Learn % (percent sign)

1 f % f %|ff %% ff %%|f%f f%f|%%f %%f|%8% %f%|%f; %f

2 You will give 5%, 10%, or 15% off all sales today.

3 About 45% voted yes to the increase; 55% voted no.

Learn – (hyphen)

4 ; - ; -|;; -- ;; --|;-; ;-;|--; --;|-;- ;-;|-;- -;

5 Rebecca rated each film 1-star, 2-star, or 3-star.

6 She has 1-, 2-, and 3-bedroom apartments for rent.

37C

Keying Technique

Keep fingers curved and upright.

TECHNIQUE TIP

Tap ENTER quickly and begin the new line without a pause or stop.

Key each line twice.

Double letters

1 little mall three buffet root quizzed mammal grass

2 Barrett will go off to Mississippi in three weeks.

Balanced hands

3 worn keys paid name their handy laugh sight island

4 Dixie may visit the big chapel by the dismal lake.

Shift keys

5 St. Paul, MN|San Diego, CA|Las Vegas, NV|New York,

6 Dr. Chi was in Boise, Idaho, on Monday and Friday.

gwam 15" | 4 | 8 | 12 | 16 | 20 | 24 | 28 | 32 | 36 | 40 |

II. Roll call

Jim Holman, Secretary, conducted a roll call. Thirteen members were present.

III. Approval of minutes from last meeting

Jim Holman, Secretary, read the minutes from the last meeting. The minutes were approved as read.

IV. Open issues

a) Samantha Earl, Fundraising Chair, reported that her committee recommends that our chapter sell candles to raise money to support our members who will compete at the state level. Her committee recommends that we partner with Better Candles since they offer a wide assortment of very good candles. Better Candles will give us 50 percent of the sales. The committee's recommendation was accepted.

b) Madeline Barry reported that our chapter sponsor, Ms. Dearborn, has gained permission to have our members represent our chapter in all team and individual competitive events this year.

V. New business

a) Madeline Barry suggested that our FBLA chapter use the Membership Brochure Template that the national office provides to attract new members. Since the club is a new club, many classmates do not know the membership benefits of FBLA. The members agreed to have Maria Velman and Jack Imhoff download the template and add our information to it. They will distribute the brochure at the next meeting.

VI. Adjournment

Madeline Barry adjourned the meeting at 2:50 p.m.

Minutes submitted by: Jim Holman, Secretary.

2. Save the document as *64b minutes* and close it.

*+ **Right little** finger + Left Shift*

Key each line twice.

Learn + (plus)

1 s; + ; +|;; ++ ;; ++|1 + 2 + 5 is 8|5 + 6 + 9 is 20
2 If you add 30 + 15 + 17 + 8 + 19, you will get 89.
3 Tom and Jay added 6 + 17 + 39 and came up with 62.

Combine +, %, and −

4 It cost $100 − a 25% discount + 5% tax for $78.75.
5 My coupon was for 30% off + an additional 10% off.
6 Determine the answer for 30% of 100 + 12 − 6 + 54.

Digital Citizenship and Ethics

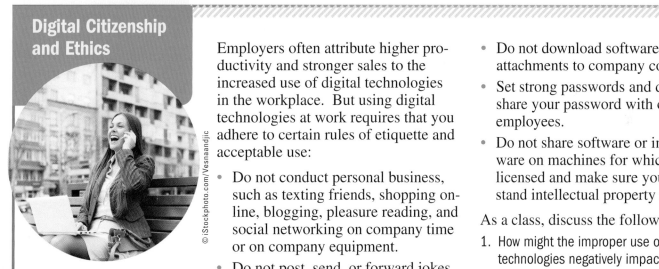

Employers often attribute higher productivity and stronger sales to the increased use of digital technologies in the workplace. But using digital technologies at work requires that you adhere to certain rules of etiquette and acceptable use:

- Do not conduct personal business, such as texting friends, shopping on-line, blogging, pleasure reading, and social networking on company time or on company equipment.

- Do not post, send, or forward jokes, personal photos, or any other material that could be offensive to others.

- Do not post confidential or sensitive information about your employer on a social networking page or in other public forums.

- Do not download software or email attachments to company computers.

- Set strong passwords and do not share your password with other employees.

- Do not share software or install software on machines for which it is not licensed and make sure you understand intellectual property rights.

As a class, discuss the following:

1. How might the improper use of digital technologies negatively impact worker productivity?

2. Every worker at some point needs to make or take a personal call during normal business hours. What is the best way to handle this?

If a memo has reference initials or enclosure, attachment, or copy notations, align them at the left margin and tap ENTER once after keying each part.

3. Add your initials as reference initials, an enclosure notation, and a copy notation indicating that Maria Castillo received a copy of the memo.

4. Save the memo as *64a memo* and close it.

Meeting Minutes Template

Meeting minutes serve as a historical record of what was discussed and decided at a meeting of an organization or a group of people. The secretary of an organization, or someone else who is appointed to take minutes, has the responsibility of recording the discussions and actions during a meeting and then preparing written minutes that will be distributed and approved at the next meeting. Figure 9.7 shows a template that you will use to prepare written meeting minutes.

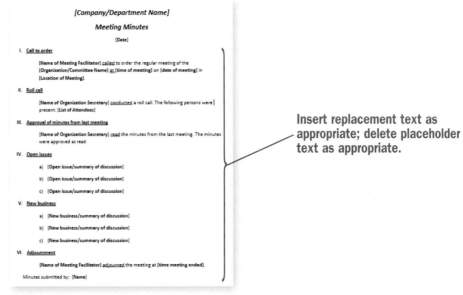

Insert replacement text as appropriate; delete placeholder text as appropriate.

Figure 9.7 *Meeting minutes template*

Activity 1

1. Open *df 64b minutes*. Using the template, key the following as replacement text at the appropriate places. Delete placeholder text that is not needed.

Thomas Middle School FBLA

Meeting Minutes

October 12, 20--

I. Call to order

Insert **Madeline Barry, President, Thomas Middle School FBLA, 2:25 p.m., October 12, 20--**, and **Room 303** at the appropriate places.

TECHNIQUE TIP
Having your chair adjusted
to the correct level will
reduce the risk of repetitive
stress injury (RSI). The
chair should be at a height
so that your arms are
parallel to the keyboard.

Key each paragraph once. Key a 1' timed writing on each paragraph. Key a 2'
timed writing on paragraphs 1 and 2 combined.

 all letters used   gwam 1' 2'

	1'	2'
Each president since George Washington has	9	4
had a cabinet. The cabinet is a group of men and	19	9
women selected by the president. The Senate must	29	14
approve them. It is the exception rather than the	39	19
rule for the president's choice to be rejected by	49	24
this branch of the government. In keeping with	58	29
tradition, most of the cabinet members belong to	68	34
the same political party as the president.	77	38
The purpose of the cabinet is to provide advice	9	43
to the president on matters pertaining to the job	19	48
of president. The person holding the office, of	29	53
course, may or may not follow the advice. Some	39	58
presidents have frequently utilized their cabinet.	49	63
Others have used it little or not at all. For	59	68
example, President Wilson held no cabinet meetings	69	73
at all during World War I.	74	75

MicroType

Use *MicroType* Numeric
Keyboarding Lesson 8 for
additional practice.

gwam 1' | 1 | 2 | 3 | 4 | 5 | 6 | 7 | 8 | 9 | 10 |
2' | 1 | 2 | 3 | 4 | 5 |

The report about one of my career interests is almost finished. An outline of the report is attached. Jim Carney worked with me on this report. We will be ready to give a seven- to ten-minute presentation in class next Friday. We will use the attached slides when we give the report.

As you suggested, we met with our guidance counselor, Mr. Duncan. He helped us find local colleges offering programs that will help us prepare for the career we are pursuing. We will include that information in our presentation.

3. Add an attachment notation and a copy notation indicating that Jim Carney received a copy.

4. Save the memo as *64a career memo* and close it.

Activity 2

1. Open *df 64a memo*. In the box at the upper right, key **Kentworth Enterprises** as the name of the company.

2. Key the following replacement text at the appropriate places:

TO: All Employees
FROM: Ms. Gerry Palko, Administrative Support
DATE: [Insert current date]
SUBJECT: INTEROFFICE MEMOS

When formatting memos for distribution within our company, please follow the format guides given below.

Use the default font, line spacing, and spacing after paragraphs. Use a 2-inch top margin on page 1 and the default top margin for other pages, if needed. Use the default settings for the left, right, and bottom margins.

Memos have four heading lines. The first line names the recipient (TO:). Whom the memo is from (FROM:) is listed next. The date the memo is being sent (DATE:) and what the memo is about (SUBJECT:) follow. All heading words (TO, FROM, DATE, and SUBJECT) are keyed in all caps. They are aligned at the left margin. Tap ENTER once after keying each line. The information following the heading words is aligned about 1 inch from the left margin. A tab setting can be used to align the information.

The paragraphs of the memo begin at the left margin. They are not indented. Tap ENTER once after each paragraph.

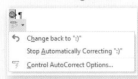

TIP When you key the memo in Activity 2, each instance of ":)" may automatically change to a smiley face (☺). You can correct this by tapping BACKSPACE one time, or you can change the AutoCorrect feature to prevent this from happening.

To change the AutoCorrect feature:

1. Hover the pointer over the correction; a small blue rectangle will appear at the left edge of the word.
2. Move your mouse to the rectangle.
3. Click the AutoCorrect Options button that appears and choose one of the options shown in Figure 9.6.

↻ Change back to ":)"
    Stop Automatically Correcting ":)"
⌐ Control AutoCorrect Options...

Figure 9.6 *AutoCorrect Options button*

New Keys #, &, and !

Learning Outcomes

In Lesson 38, you will:
- *Learn reach technique for #, &, and !.*
- *Combine #, &, and ! with other keys.*

38A

Warmup

Key each line twice.

Alphabet

1 Nate will vex the judge if he backs my quiz group.

Figures

2 See Fig. 19 and 20 on page 48 or Fig. 37 on p. 56.

Easy

3 The six girls in the sorority may pay for the bus.

gwam	1'	1	2	3	4	5	6	7	8	9	10

38B

New Keys # and &

Key each line twice.

 # Left middle finger +
Right Shift

Learn # (number/pounds)

1 d E # d E #|d # d #|d#d d#d|#d3# #d3#|D e #; D e #
2 Orders #673, #677, and #679 still need to be done.
3 Checks #841, #842, and #845 are still outstanding.

Learn & (ampersand)

4 j U & j U &|j & j &|j&j j&j|&j7& &j7&|J u &; J u &
5 Sanchez & Johnson; Barns & Kennedy; Scott & Fitzer
6 I went to the law firm of Matsui & Alou on Friday.

& Right index finger +
Left Shift

Templates: Memos and Meeting Minutes

Data Files:

df 64a memo

df 64b minutes

Learning Outcomes

In Lesson 64, you will:

64A *Use a memo template.*

64B *Use a meeting minutes template.*

64A

Memo Template

Memos are written messages used by people in an organization. Memos are sometimes called *interoffice memos*. For example, your school principal might write a memo to your teacher about a staff meeting. A memo is shown in Figure 9.5. Refer to it as you read about the parts of a memo.

Memos have four heading lines and a body. The paragraphs in the memo are called the *body*. The memo heading lines tell the:

- Name of the person to whom the memo is written.
- Name of the person who is writing the memo.
- Date the memo is written.
- Subject of the memo.

Memos, like letters, may contain reference initials, enclosure and attachment notations, and copy notations after the body. Figure 9.5 shows a memo template you will use in this lesson.

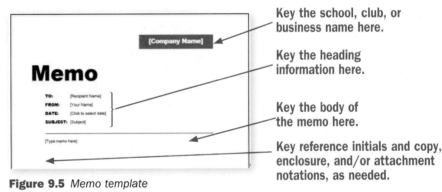

Figure 9.5 *Memo template*

Key the school, club, or business name here.

Key the heading information here.

Key the body of the memo here.

Key reference initials and copy, enclosure, and/or attachment notations, as needed.

Activity 1

1. Open *df 64a memo*. Key your school name as replacement text in the box at the upper right.

2. Key the following replacement text at the appropriate places:

TO: [Your teacher's name]

FROM: [Your name]

DATE: [Insert current date]

SUBJECT: CAREER INTEREST

38C

Speed Forcing Drill

Key two 20" timed writings on each line.

1 Dick may lend us the map.

2 The firm kept half of the men.

3 Lana may go to the lake with Helen.

4 If the city pays, Elena may do the work.

5 Vivian may do the problems for the six girls.

6 Hal may go with me to make the signs for the city.

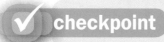

gwam 20" | 3 | 6 | 9 | 12 | 15 | 18 | 21 | 24 | 27 | 30 |

✓ **checkpoint** Did you tap ENTER quickly and begin the new line without a pause or stop?

38D

New Key !

! *Left little* finger + Right Shift

Key each line twice. If time permits, rekey lines 4–6.

Learn ! (exclamation point)

1 a ! a ! |a! a! a!| !a! !a! |No! No!|Absolutely!|Ohh!

2 Leave two spaces after ! at the end of a sentence.

3 That is great news! She won! She won! Terrific!

Combine #, &, and !

4 Order #824 was for Bay & Cey and their 500 guests!

5 Check #38 was from Brown & Smith, not Cray & Retz!

6 Wow! Check #208 from Sebo & Day was for $100,000!

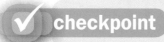

Templates can be used to create award certificates to recognize friends or family members who have completed a special program or subject or who have performed at an excellent level by doing outstanding community service, getting high grades, and so on. Perhaps you want to use a template to present members of a school club with a certificate of membership that they can put in their scrapbook. Figure 9.4 shows a certificate template you will use in this lesson.

Figure 9.4 *Certificate template*

Activity 1

1. Open *df 63d certificate* and make the following changes:
   a. Select **WORLD'S BEST** and change to **NEWTON'S TOP**.
   b. Select **NAME/TITLE** and change to **WEB PAGE DESIGNERS**—change the font size to 48 point.
   c. Select **[Recipient name here]** and change to **Todd Elcore and Mary Popp**.
   d. Select **[Your text here]** and change to **Expertise and Creativity**.
2. Print the certificate. Save the certificate as *63d certificate* and close it.

Activity 2

1. Open *df 63d award* and make the following changes:
   a. Select **[Member Name]** and replace it with **Sarah Milanovich**.
   b. Select **[Organization Name]** and replace it with **Future Business Leaders of America**.
   c. Select **[date]** and replace it with **September 15, 20--**.
   d. In the line above the signatures, change **[day]** to **15th** and **[Month, Year]** to **September, 20--**.
2. Save the certificate as *63d award* and close it.

Key each paragraph once. Double-space between paragraphs. Key a 1' timed writing on each paragraph. Key a 2' timed writing on paragraphs 1 and 2 combined.

 all letters used

	gwam	1'	2'

	1'	2'
Who was Shakespeare? Few would question that	9	5
he was the greatest individual, or at least one of	19	10
the greatest individuals, ever to write a play.	29	15
His works have endured the test of time. Produc-	39	19
tions of his plays continue to take place on the	49	24
stages of theaters all over the world. Shakespeare	59	30
was an expert at creating comedies and tragedies,	69	35
both of which often leave the audience in tears.	<u>79</u>	39
Few of those who put pen to paper have been	9	44
as successful at creating such prized images for	19	49
their readers as Shakespeare. Each character he	28	54
created has a life of its own. It is entirely	38	58
possible that more middle school and high school	48	63
students know about the tragedy that Romeo and	57	68
Juliet experienced than know about the one that	67	73
took place at Pearl Harbor.	<u>72</u>	75

MicroType

Use *MicroType* Numeric Keyboarding Lesson 9 for additional practice.

gwam	1'	1	2	3	4	5	6	7	8	9	10
	2'		1		2		3		4		5

1. You now know how to key every letter of the alphabet. Working with a classmate, compose a sentence that includes every letter of the alphabet. Use only one proper noun. After you are finished, check the sentence to make sure it is grammatically correct.

2. Key the sentence as many times as you can until all students have finished.

e. [insert location] to **Newton Middle School, Room 204**.

f. [insert name] to **Mrs. Pauline Gettens**.

2. Save the document as *63b open house* and close it.

A big selection of greeting card templates is available for you to send as friendship, thank-you, holiday, get well, and sympathy cards. You also can use templates to send congratulations, welcome, and farewell cards. Figure 9.3 shows a greeting card template you will use in this lesson.

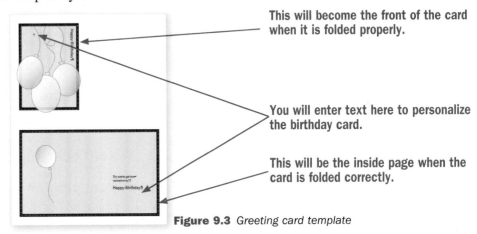

This will become the front of the card when it is folded properly.

You will enter text here to personalize the birthday card.

This will be the inside page when the card is folded correctly.

Figure 9.3 *Greeting card template*

Activity 1

1. Open *df 63c birthday*. Key **To Our Favorite Teacher** where the insertion point is blinking in the section that will become the front of the birthday card.

2. Click the text in the section that will become the right inside page of the birth-day card to select the text box. Tap ENTER after *Birthday* and change the font to 11-point Georgia.

3. At that point, key **and wishes for many more to come from your favorite class**.

4. Print the card and fold it properly. Save the card as *63c birthday* and close it.

Activity 2

1. Open *df 63c apology*. Key the following text where a personal message is to be inserted.

   I'm sorry I had to miss your birthday party. My cousin who was visiting from out of town had an accident, and I needed to go to the emergency room with him. He wasn't released in time for me to attend.

2. Change the font to 10-point Arial.

3. *Optional:* Change the clip art in this card by clicking it, deleting it, and insert-ing another piece of appropriate clip art. Follow the instructions at the left to rotate the picture.

4. Save the card as *63c apology* and close it.

TIP

1. Select the object you want to rotate.
2. On the Drawing Tools Format tab, click **Rotate** in the Arrange group.
3. Select **Flip Vertical**.

New Keys (,), =, and *

Learning Outcomes

In Lesson 39, you will:

- *Learn reach technique for (,), =, and *.*
- *Combine (,), =, and * with other keys.*

39A

Warmup

Key each line twice.

Alphabet

1 Wusov amazed them by jumping quickly from the box.

Figures

2 The addresses were 1847 Oak, 203 Joy and 596 Pine.

Easy

3 Vivian may handle all the forms for the big firms.

gwam 1' | 1 | 2 | 3 | 4 | 5 | 6 | 7 | 8 | 9 | 10 |

39B

New Keys (and)

Key each line twice.

*(**Right ring** finger + Left Shift*

*) **Right little** finger + Left Shift*

Learn ((left parenthesis)

1 l o (l o (| l (l ((| (l (l | l(o(l(o(| 19(19 (| (l(o(

2 (1, (2, (3, (4, (5, (6, (7, (8, (9, (10, (11, (12,

3 The shift of 9 is (. Use the l finger to key (9(.

Learn) (right parenthesis)

4 ; p) ; p) | ;) ;) |);); | ;)p) ;)p) | ;0) ;0) |);) p)

5 1), 2), 3), 4), 5), 6), 7), 8), 9), 10), 11), 12),

6 The shift of 0 is). Use the ; finger to key)0).

Templates are available for several kinds of events, including birthday parties, holiday parties, school open houses, family reunions, and pool parties. If no appropriate template is available for your event, you can use a generic template that you modify to meet your needs. Figure 9.2 shows a party invitation template that you will use in this lesson.

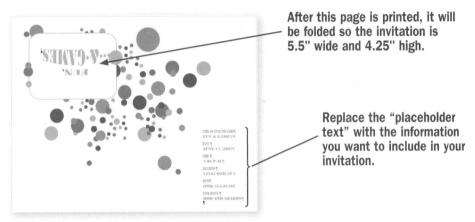

After this page is printed, it will be folded so the invitation is 5.5" wide and 4.25" high.

Replace the "placeholder text" with the information you want to include in your invitation.

Figure 9.2 *Invitation template*

Activity 1

1. Start *Word*. Open *df 63b invitation*.

2. To change the date to March 15 of this year, select **June 17, 2014** and key or select the desired date. *Note:* There is no need to use a Shift key or the CAPS LOCK key or to format the text as you key the replacement text since this template has predesigned font styles, colors, and sizes.

3. To change the time, select **7:00** and key **4:15**.

4. To change the location, select **12345 Oak St.** and key **145 Harris Lane**.

5. To change the RSVP, select **(808) 555-0156** and key **(919) 555-0125**.

6. To list yourself as the host, select **Bob and Sharon** and key your name.

7. Print the invitation and fold it in half lengthwise and then in half widthwise so it is 5.5" high and 4.25" wide. *Fun and Games* should appear as the front cover with the party information appearing as the inside right page.

8. Save the invitation as *63b invitation* and close it.

Activity 2

1. Open *df 63b open house* and make the following replacements in the template by clicking the placeholder text and keying the desired text:

   a. [insert name] to **Mrs. Pauline Gettens**.

   b. [insert phone number or email address] to **gettens.p@net.com**.

   c. [insert date] to **October 12, 20--**.

   d. [insert time] to **7:15 p.m. to 8:30 p.m.**

Keying Numbers

Key each line twice.

1 My next games are on May 19 and 20.

2 Beth spent $378,465 on the project.

3 Helen paid $4,378 for 150 shares of USB.

4 Johan paid $8,692 for 100 shares of IBM.

5 The dates were June 18, June 30, and July 27.

6 Gomez was hitting .459 on Thursday, April 26.

New Keys = and *

*= **Right little** finger*

Key each line twice.

Learn = (equal sign)

1 ; = ; =|;; == ;; ==|;=; ;=;|=;= =;=|ac = b ac = b;

2 a = b = c = d = e = f = g = h = i = j = k = l = m;

3 = 1 = 2 = 3 = 4 = 5 = 6 = 7 = 8 = 9 = 10 = 11 = 12

Learn * (asterisk)

4 k * k *|*K* *K*|k I * k I *|ki* ki*|*k; *k;|*.* *.

5 *abc* *def* *ghi* *jkl* *mno* *pqr* *stu* *vwx yz*

6 *1* *2* *3* *4* *5* *6* *7* *8* *9* *10* *11* *12*

Combine (,), =, and *

7 Does (5 * 8) + (2 * 7) = 54? What about (6 * 13)?

8 If x = 15 and y = 10, what does (x * y - x) equal?

9 It should have been (x = 6 * 3), not (x = 16 * 3).

* *Right middle* finger +
Left Shift

Templates: Invitations, Greeting Cards, and Certificates

Data Files:

df 63b invitation
df 63b open house
df 63c birthday
df 63c apology
df 63d certificate
df 63d award

Learning Outcomes

In Lesson 63, you will:

63A *Learn about **Word** templates.*
63B *Use an invitation template.*
63C *Use a greeting card template.*
63D *Use a certificate template.*

63A

Learn about Word Templates

A **template** is a master copy of a set of predefined styles for a particular type of document. A template may contain text and formatting for margins, line spacing, colors, borders, styles, and themes. A template contains **placeholder text** that you replace with your own text.

When you open a template, a new document opens that is based on the template you selected. That is, you are opening a copy of the template, not the template itself. You key and format in that new document, using the text and formats that were built into the template in addition to adding, deleting, or making changes. Your changes are saved to the copy of the template, and the template is left in its original state. Therefore, one template can be used over and over again.

Normally, you select templates from those that are installed on your computer, templates you can download from Microsoft Office Online, or templates you have created and saved. Figure 9.1 shows some of the template options that display when you open *Word*. However, in this chapter, you will use documents that have been saved as template data files rather than selecting templates in *Word* or online.

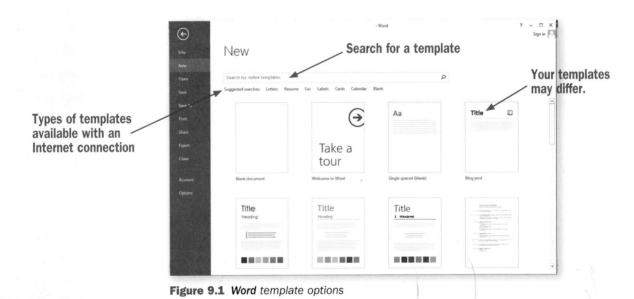

Figure 9.1 *Word* template options

Key each paragraph once. Key a 1' timing on each paragraph. Key two 2' timings on the paragraphs. Determine *gwam* on each.

 all letters used

	gwam	1'	2'

The Bill of Rights includes the changes to   9   4

the Constitution that deal with human rights of   18 9

all people. The changes or amendments were to   28 14

improve and correct the original document. They   37 19

were made to ensure the quality of life and to   47 23

protect the rights of all citizens.   <u>54</u> 27

One of the changes provides for the right to   9 31

religious choice, free speech, and free press.   19 36

Another addresses the right to keep and bear fire-   29 41

arms. Another deals with the rights of the people   39 46

with regard to unreasonable search and seizure   48 51

of person or property. Two others deal with the   58 56

right to an immediate and public trial by a jury   68 61

and the prevention of excessive bail and fines.   <u>77</u> 66

MicroType

Use *MicroType* Numeric Keyboarding Lesson 10 for additional practice.

Lessons 63–65

Do you prepare invitations to birthday parties or design greeting cards for friends and family members? Do you need to prepare cover (title) pages for the reports you write? Do you prepare the minutes of committee or club meetings? Do you need to write to others in your school? If you answered "yes" to one or more of those questions, you will find that learning to use templates is beneficial for these and other tasks that you do frequently.

A template saves you time since you use it as a starting point rather than creating every document from scratch. For example, if you attend weekly club meetings and have to create an agenda for each meeting, starting with a template that is formatted and has much of the repetitive text already in place will save you time. All you need to do is change the details that differ from week to week.

© Andresr/Shutterstock.com

Lesson 40 | New Keys ', ", and \

Learning Outcomes

In Lesson 40, you will:

- *Learn reach technique for ', ", and \.*
- *Combine ', ", and \ with other keys.*

40A

Warmup

Key each line twice.

Alphabet

1 Zeb or Jack Gore explained why seven of them quit.

Figures

2 Felipe wrote Check Numbers 268, 297, 304, and 315.

Easy

3 A neighbor paid the men to fix the bicycle for us.

gwam 1' | 1 | 2 | 3 | 4 | 5 | 6 | 7 | 8 | 9 | 10 |

40B

New Keys ' and "

Key each line twice.

' Right little finger

" Right little finger + Left
Shift

Learn ' (apostrophe)

1 ; ' ; '|;; '' ;; ''|;'; ;'';|'p' 'p'|'0' '0'|'9' '9

2 isn't, aren't, can't, don't, you're, what's, let's

3 Isn't the rock 'n' roll troupe performing tonight?

Learn " (quotation mark)

4 ; " ; "|;; "" ;; ""|;"; ;";|"p" "p"|"0" "0"|"9" "9

5 Tom said, "I can fix it." Janet said, "So can I."

6 I think the theme for "2005" was "New Beginnings."

 Instant Message On your screen, apostrophes and/or quotation marks may look different
from those shown in these lines. Even if they look different, the marks serve the same purpose.

Data Files:

df a2 activity6
df a2 picture2

1. Open *df a2 activity6*. Change the orientation to Landscape and set margins to Narrow.

2. Key the information below after the last paragraph.

3. Use Title style to format the document title and Heading 1 style for the side headings.

4. Arrange the text below the document title in three columns separated by vertical lines. Hyphenate the text.

5. Insert the following text box between the last line of the *Club Fair* section and the *Art Club* side heading. Use a 10-point font. Use a light blue shape fill, a 2¼-point weight shape outline, and a gray Glow shape effect.

> This year's Club Fair will be held on Monday, September 11, from 1 p.m. to 3 p.m.

6. Insert *df a2 picture2* near the right side of the paragraph describing the Golf Club. Size it so it is about 1" wide and use Tight to wrap the text around it.

7. Balance the columns so they are nearly equal in length. Adjust space above the first side heading if necessary so columns align at the top.

8. Spell-check, proofread, and correct any errors. Save the document as *a2 activity6*; print and close it.

Newspaper

Students who are outgoing, dedicated, and willing to commit their time and energy to produce an online newspaper are invited to join. Students write/edit for several sections of the paper including editorials, news, features, sports, etc. The staff meets at least twice a month after school until 4:30 p.m.

Student Council

Student Council is the student government organization for Newtown Middle School. The Executive Council of the Student Council is made up of four officers and five senators, all 8th graders who are elected the previous May. In the fall, each grade elects five representatives to the Student Council.

The major goals of the Student Council are to serve the middle school community, to support the principals and guidance counselors with various programs, to organize and participate in annual all-school service projects, and to develop leadership skills through programs provided by the state's Association of Student Councils.

Keying Technique

Use a down-and-in spacing motion.

Key each line twice.

Letter response

1 acres onion bread puppy trade jump saved oil faces
2 are we|my best|minimum tax|are graded|best regards
3 Carter ate a plump plum tart in a cafe on a barge.

Word response

4 problem right eight bugle shake world cubic mangle
5 is the|eight girls|go to the|if they are|go to the
6 The key is to make the right sign for all of them.

Combination response

7 box base dusk milk half secret kept best make jump
8 refer to|the average|the award|city tax|big garage
9 Carter and Edward saw the bread and ate all of it.

gwam 20" | 3 | 6 | 9 | 12 | 15 | 18 | 21 | 24 | 27 | 30 |

40D

**New Key **

\ *Right little* finger

Key each line twice.

Learn \ (backslash)

1 ; \ ; \|C:\ C:\|D:\Tests\Unit 1 D:\Test 12\Unit 23
2 He mapped the drive to access \\spss 25\deptdir56.
3 The complete file name is C:\Unit 1\Lsn 14\Part A.

Combine \, ', and "

4 Wasn't a \ "backslash" used for ASCII programming?
5 Isn't a "\" used to indicate "left" in a language?
6 Didn't Joan mistakenly use a "/" instead of a "\"?

Activity 4
Convert Text to Table

Data File:
df a2 activity4

1. Open *df a2 activity4* and convert it to a table.
2. Apply AutoFit Contents to set column widths.
3. Center-align the main heading, column headings, and columns 3 and 4.
4. Apply an appropriate style; center the table horizontally and vertically.
5. Save the table as *a2 activity4*; print and close it.

Activity 5
Flyer

Data File:
df a2 picture1

1. Open a new, blank document to create a flyer that will fit attractively on 8.5" × 11" paper. Use WordArt, text boxes and/or shapes, and the picture file *df a2 picture1* in the flyer.
2. Include the information below in your flyer.
3. Save the flyer as *a2 activity5*; print and close it.

Scholarships for College Sophomores, Juniors, and Seniors

The Forde Foundation plans to award five $2,000 scholarships to deserving alumni of Forde High School who will be continuing their college education during the upcoming school year.

Eligibility Requirements

Applicants must continue their education as a full-time student at an accredited trade/technical school or a two- or four-year college or university. Applicants must be a graduate of Forde High School and have a current home address within the Forde School District.

Application Procedure and Due Date

- Obtain an application at www.fordefndtn.org
- Complete the application as directed.
- Mail the completed application, an up-to-date personal resume, a college transcript showing all courses completed and cumulative grade point average, and a copy of your upcoming fall semester course schedule by July 10 to:

Ms. Jamie Dominic
FF Scholarship Chair
4810 Smokey Road
Newman, GA 30263-4510

Key each paragraph once. Key a 1' timed writing on each paragraph. Key a 2' timed writing on paragraphs 1 and 2 combined.

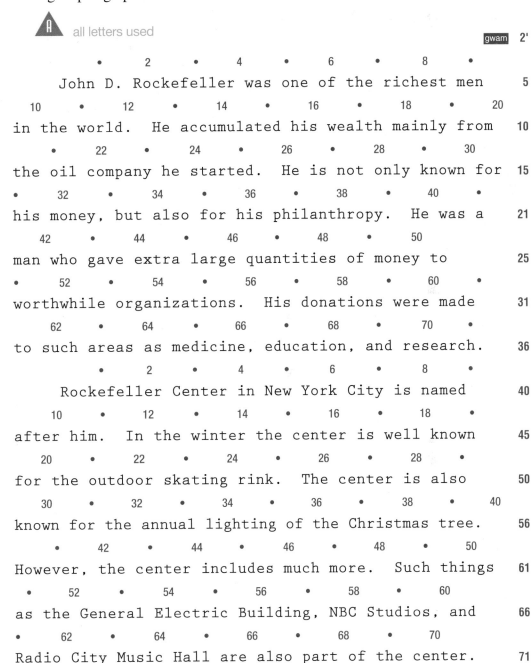

A all letters used

gwam 2'

```
         •      2      •      4      •      6      •      8      •
        John D. Rockefeller was one of the richest men        5
   10    •     12     •     14     •     16     •     18     •     20
in the world.  He accumulated his wealth mainly from         10
         •     22     •     24     •     26     •     28     •     30
the oil company he started.  He is not only known for        15
   •     32     •     34     •     36     •     38     •     40     •
his money, but also for his philanthropy.  He was a          21
   42     •     44     •     46     •     48     •     50
man who gave extra large quantities of money to              25
   •     52     •     54     •     56     •     58     •     60     •
worthwhile organizations.  His donations were made           31
   62     •     64     •     66     •     68     •     70     •
to such areas as medicine, education, and research.          36
         •      2      •      4      •      6      •      8      •
        Rockefeller Center in New York City is named         40
   10    •     12     •     14     •     16     •     18     •
after him.  In the winter the center is well known           45
   20    •     22     •     24     •     26     •     28     •
for the outdoor skating rink.  The center is also            50
   30    •     32     •     34     •     36     •     38     •     40
known for the annual lighting of the Christmas tree.         56
   •     42     •     44     •     46     •     48     •     50
However, the center includes much more.  Such things         61
   •     52     •     54     •     56     •     58     •     60
as the General Electric Building, NBC Studios, and           66
   •     62     •     64     •     66     •     68     •     70
Radio City Music Hall are also part of the center.           71
```

gwam 2' | 1 | 2 | 3 | 4 | 5 |

MicroType

Use *MicroType* Numeric
Keyboarding Lesson 11 for
additional practice.

1. Open a new, blank document. Create the table shown below using the following information.

   a. Insert a 5 × 9 table grid. Set width for column 1 to 1.5"; columns 2, 3, and 4 to 0.8"; and column 5 to 1".

   b. Bold the main heading and column headings; use Align Center for the main heading and column headings.

   c. Use left alignment for entries in column 1; center alignment for entries in columns 2 and 3; and right alignment for entries in columns 4 and 5.

SCCL Investment Club First Quarter Portfolio Report				
Stock		**Shares**	**Current**	**Current**
Company	**Symbol**	**Owned**	**Share Price**	**Stock Value**
Hershey Company	HSY	210	$104.25	$21,892.50
McDonald's	MCD	178	103.39	18,403.42
Nike	NKE	265	75.40	19,981.00
Range Resources	RRC	130	87.23	11,339.90
3D Systems	DDD	90	68.57	6,171.30
Coca-Cola	KO	164	38.32	6,284.48

2. Add a row at the bottom of the table and key the information in it as shown below:

Current Portfolio Value	**$84,072.60**

3. Center the table horizontally and vertically and add a 3-point outside border around the table. Shade the first and last row of the table using a light color.

4. Save the table as *a2 activity2*; print and close it.

Data File:

df a2 activity3

1. Open *df a2 activity3* and make the following changes:

   a. Delete the Derek Stanton row and add this row at the bottom:

Fred Gaskin	6	208	724	95	819

   b. Change row heights to 0.4".

   c. Delete columns 4 and 5.

   d. Sort the table by Total Sales in descending order.

   e. Insert a row at the top and key this as a main heading: **Top Sellers by Grade and Room**.

   f. Center the table vertically and horizontally; apply an appropriate style and then apply Align Center to all cells.

2. Save the table as *a2 activity3*; print and close it.

Lesson 41

New Keys _, [,], <, and >

Learning Outcomes

In Lesson 41, you will:

- *Learn reach technique for _, [,], <, and >.*
- *Combine _, [,], <, and > with other keys.*

41A

Warmup

Key each line twice. If time permits, key the lines again.

Alphabet

1 Jake Win placed first by solving the complex quiz.

Figures

2 The June 15 quiz covered pages 289 and 307 to 426.

Easy

3 The signs by the downtown spa may work for us too.

gwam 1' | 1 | 2 | 3 | 4 | 5 | 6 | 7 | 8 | 9 | 10 |

41B

New Keys [,], and _

[*Right little* finger

] *Right little* finger

_ *Right little* finger + Left Shift

Key each line twice.

Learn [(left bracket)

1 ; [; [|;; [[;; [[|[a [b [c [d [e [f [g [h [i [j;
2 [k [1 [m [n [o [p [q [r [s [t [u [v [w [x [y [z [;

Learn] (right bracket)

3 ;] ;] | ;;]] ;;]] | red] blue] green] black] gold]
4 1] 2] 3] 4] 5] 6] 7] 8] 9] 10] 11] 12] 13] 14] 15]

Learn _ (underline)

5 ; _ ;_|_a_ _a_|_an_ _an_|_ and_ _and_|_the_ _the|_;
6 _is_ _is_|_can_ _can_|_saw_ _saw_|_ was_ _was_|low_
7 _his_ _his_|_man_ _man_|_lake_ _lake_|_red_ _red_;

Assessment 2 Tables and Desktop Publishing

Warmup Practice

Key each line twice. If time permits, key the lines again.

Alphabet

1 Jim won the globe for six quick sky dives in Napa.

Figures/Symbol

2 My May 17 bill should be $45.39 instead of $62.80.

Speed

3 She is to go to the city with us to sign the form.

gwam 1' | 1 | 2 | 3 | 4 | 5 | 6 | 7 | 8 | 9 | 10 |

**Activity 1
Assess Straight-Copy
Skill**

Key one or two 2' timed writings on both paragraphs combined. Print, proofread, circle errors, and determine *gwam*.

 all letters used

gwam 2'

Before choosing a career, learn as much as	4
you can about what individuals in that career do.	9
For each job classification, there are job	13
qualifications that must be met. Analyze these	18
tasks carefully in terms of your personality	23
and what you like to do.	26
Many of today's jobs require more formal	30
education or training after high school. The	34
training may be very specialized. This requires	39
intensive study or interning for a year or two.	44
You must decide if you are willing to expend so	49
much time and effort.	51
After you have chosen a career to pursue,	56
discuss the choice with parents, teachers, and	60
others. Such people can help you design a plan	65
to help you achieve your goals. Keep the plan	70
flexible and change it whenever necessary.	74

gwam 2' | 1 | 2 | 3 | 4 | 5 |

41C

Keying Numbers

Key each line twice.

1 I was 13 years old in 2005, not 14.
2 Only 98 of the 1,367 kids finished.
3 My phone number was changed to 175-8369.
4 I took 420 feet of pipe for the project.
5 Mr. Dean ordered 140 computers on October 25.
6 He received the bill for $136,786 on April 9.

gwam 20" | 3 | 6 | 9 | 12 | 15 | 18 | 21 | 24 | 27 |

41D

New Keys < and >

Key each line twice.

> Right ring *finger +*
Left Shift

Learn > (greater than sign)

1 1 > 1>|L>1 L>1|1.> 1.>|15 > 10 15 > 10|3 > 2 3 > 2
2 26 > 25; 108 > 98; a + b is > b + c; 128 + a > 133
3 Use the symbol (>) for greater than (A > C + 8/2).

Learn < (less than sign)

4 k < k <|k,< k,<|k<b, k<b,|1 < 2 1 < 2|2 < 3 2 < 3;
5 16 < 17 < 18 < 19 < 20; 36 < 37 < 38 < 39 < 40 < X
6 Use this symbol (<) for less than. He said a < b.

< Right middle *finger +*
Left Shift

Combine <, >, _, [, and]

7 Use [square brackets], <pointy brackets> or _____.
8 Did he use _ [underline key] or the <Ctrl U> keys?
9 [a > b] [b < d] therefore [a > _]; the answer is d

Organizing a Community Event

In this activity, you will create a newsletter about recycling.

1. Start a new, blank *Word* file.

2. Research facts about recycling. Find out items that can be recycled, how to recycle, and why you should recycle.

3. Create a newsletter to convince your community to participate in a recycling event. Use either Portrait or Landscape orientation and use more than one column. Use other elements that you've learned to improve its appearance.

4. Save the document as *c8 recycling*, print, and close it.

Activity 7

To complete this activity, you will need the Student Interest Survey that you filled out in Career Exploration Portfolio Activity 1. Completing Career Exploration Activities 2–6 would also be helpful but is not mandatory.

1. Review your Student Interest Survey and note your *third* Career Cluster.

2. Go to http://www.careertech.org. Click the **Career Technical Education** button, then click Career Clusters to open the Career Clusters page. Click your third Career Cluster choice.

3. Scroll through the categories available within that Career Cluster. Click the Knowledge & Skills Statements **Excel** link under the category you are most interested in to download it to your system. (Choose the same category, or Pathway, that you used in Activity 4 if you completed it.)

4. Locate the downloaded file on your system and open it. Scroll down and read the knowledge and skill statements for this career.

5. Think about the knowledge and skills you have gained from classes at school, after-school activities, and other experiences. Do they match any of the knowledge and skills listed in this file? If not, how can you gain them?

6. Use *Word* to write a summary of what you discovered. Save the document as *c8 career 3 skills*, print, and close it.

Online Resources:

ngl.cengage.com/c21jr3e

Key each paragraph once. Double-space between paragraphs. Key a 1' timed writing on each paragraph. Key a 2' timed writing on paragraphs 1 and 2 combined.

A   all letters used

gwam 2'

	•	2	•	4	•	6	•	8	•	

Whether you are an intense lover of music or — 5

	10	•	12	•	14	•	16	•	18	•

simply enjoy hearing good music, you are more than — 10

	20	•	22	•	24	•	26	•	28	•

likely aware of the work completed by Beethoven, — 15

	30	•	32	•	34	•	36	•	38	•

the German composer. He is generally recognized as — 20

	40	•	42	•	44	•	46	•	48	•

one of the greatest composers ever to live. Much — 25

	50	•	52	•	54	•	56	•	58	•

of his early work was influenced by those who wrote — 30

60	•	62	•	64	•	66

music in Austria, Haydn and Mozart. — 33

	•	2	•	4	•	6	•	8

It can be argued whether Beethoven was a — 38

•	10	•	12	•	14	•	16	•	18

classical or romantic composer. This depends upon — 43

•	20	•	22	•	24	•	26	•

which period of time in his life the music was — 47

28	•	30	•	32	•	34	•	36	•	38

written. His exquisite music has elements of both. — 53

•	40	•	42	•	44	•	46	•	48

It has been said that his early works brought to a — 58

•	50	•	52	•	54	•	56	•	58

conclusion the classical age. It has also been — 63

•	60	•	62	•	64	•	66	•

stated that Beethoven's later works started the — 67

68	•	70	•	72

romantic age of music. — 70

MicroType

Use *MicroType* Numeric Keyboarding Lesson 12 for additional practice.

gwam 2' | 1 | 2 | 3 | 4 | 5 |

ACROSS THE CURRICULUM

Data Files:

df c8 staying healthy

df c8 being your own boss

COLLABORATION

Social Studies: Create a Travel Flyer

Flyers are often used in advertising. They can be used to sell a product, attract interest to a show, or advertise a fund-raiser. In this activity, you are going to use *Word* to create a flyer to encourage people to visit a state of your choice.

1. With a partner, choose a state and research a few facts about it. You may want to find the capital city, the population, history facts, a map, and things to do.

2. Start a new, blank *Word* file. Create a flyer about the state. Include formatted WordArt and text boxes. Also include a shape with text in it, clip art, and pictures.

3. Save the document as *c8 state flyer*, print, and close it.

Science: Staying Healthy

Newsletters often inform people on various topics. Your dentist might send out newsletters to update you and your parents on the latest dental tips. Your local library might create a newsletter to let people know about new books and services that they provide. In this activity, you will create a newsletter to provide tips on staying healthy.

1. Open *df c8 staying healthy*.

2. Read the document and then apply Landscape orientation. Change the text to appear in two or three columns. Then finish your newsletter by adding section breaks as needed; a title using WordArt or a text box; headings above each topic using WordArt, text, or text boxes; auto hyphenation; and appropriate clip art or pictures. Adjust margins as necessary to fit the text on one page.

3. Save the document as *c8 staying healthy*, print, and close it.

COLLABORATION

Promoting Your Business: Creating a Flyer

An **entrepreneur** is a person who starts his or her own business. In this activity, you will discover some of the advantages and disadvantages of becoming an entrepreneur. You will also create a flyer for a business.

1. Open *df c8 being your own boss*.

2. Work with one of your classmates to discuss and answer the questions.

3. After you answer the questions, create a flyer as instructed. Then save the document as *c8 being your own boss*, print, and close it.

Repetitive Stress Injury

Repetitive stress injury (RSI) is a result of repeated movement of a particular part of the body. A familiar example is tennis elbow. Of more concern to keyboard users is a form of RSI called **carpal tunnel syndrome (CTS)**.

CTS develops gradually. CTS can cause numbness or pain in the hand, wrist, elbow, or shoulder. It also can make gripping objects difficult. Computer users can reduce the risk of developing CTS by taking these precautions:

- Position the keyboard directly in front of your chair. Keep the front edge of the keyboard even with the edge of the desk.

- Place the monitor about 18 to 24 inches from your eyes, with the top edge of the display screen at eye level.

- Use a proper chair and sit up correctly. Keep your feet flat on the floor while you are keying. Sit erect and as far back in the seat as possible.

- Keep your arms near the side of your body in a relaxed position. Your wrists should be parallel to the keyboard. They should not rest on the desk or the keyboard.

- Keep your fingers curved and upright over the home keys. Tap each key lightly, using the fingertip.

- If keying for a long period of time, take short rest breaks.

Using proper keying position helps avoid CTS.

© franksiteman.com 2007

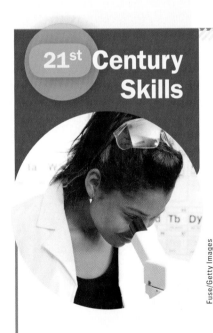

Fuse/Getty Images

21st Century Skills

Initiative and Self-Direction

Initiative and self-direction are important skills and attributes to attain as you develop as a student and as a person. These skills and attributes will help you succeed in any task you set out to do in the course of your personal and professional life, including learning keyboarding and computer applications.

Taking initiative means making the decision to do something—a job, a project, a specific task—without needing to be prompted by someone else. It means you don't need to have a teacher, parent, or friend tell you that you must do something. You see what needs to be done and you do it.

Self-direction means you are able to guide yourself and motivate yourself through the various steps of a job, project, or task. You make good decisions about what needs to be done next, and if necessary, you push yourself to do it.

As with any other skill, learning to keyboard properly requires a certain amount of initiative and self-direction.

Think Critically

1. What prompted you to want to learn keyboarding and computer applications?

2. Now that you have worked through the first chapters of this book, how do you think you can demonstrate initiative and self-direction as you learn these skills?

3. Describe some ways in which you have demonstrated initiative and self-direction at home, at school, or on a job.

1. Key three 1' timed writings on each paragraph, striving to key more on each timing; determine *gwam*.
2. Key a 2' timed writing on both paragraphs combined, striving to maintain your highest 1' *gwam*.

A   all letters used   gwam 1' 2'

       •   2   •   4   •   6   •   8

You are nearly at the end of your computer   8   4

   •   10   •   12   •   14   •   16   •   18

applications class. The keyboarding skill level   18   9

   •   20   •   22   •   24   •   26   •

you attained is much better now than when you   27   14

 28   •   30   •   32   •   34   •   36   •

were given keying instruction for the first time.   37   19

 38   •   40   •   42   •   44   •   46   •

During the early period of your training, you   47   24

     48   •   50   •   52   •   54   •   56   •

were taught to key the letters of the alphabet as   57   29

    58   •   60   •   62   •   64   •   66   •

well as the figures by touch. During the initial   67   34

    68   •   70   •   72   •   74   •   76

time of learning, the emphasis was placed on   76   38

     •   78   •

keying technique.   <u>79</u>   40

       •   2   •   4   •   6   •   8

After you learned to key the alphabet and   8   44

   •   10   •   12   •   14   •   16   •

the figures, your next job was to learn how to   17   49

 18   •   20   •   22   •   24   •   26   •

format documents. The various types of documents   27   54

 28   •   30   •   32   •   34   •   36   •

you learned to format included letters, tables,   37   59

    38   •   40   •   42   •   44   •   46

and reports. During this time of training, an   46   64

 •   48   •   50   •   52   •   54   •   56

emphasis also was placed on increasing the rate   56   69

   •   58   •   60   •   62   •   64   •   66

at which you were able to input. You should now   66   74

   •   68   •   70   •   72   •

recognize the value of a keying skill.   <u>74</u>   78

gwam 1' | 1 | 2 | 3 | 4 | 5 | 6 | 7 | 8 | 9 | 10 |
2' | 1 | | 2 | | 3 | | 4 | | 5 |

Numeric Keypad 4, 5, 6, 0

Learning Outcomes

In Lesson 42, you will:

- *Learn numeric keypad operating position.*
- *Learn to access the Calculator program.*
- *Learn reachstrokes for 4, 5, 6, and 0.*

42A

Numeric Keypad Operating Position

© franksiteman.com 2007

Position yourself at the keyboard as shown at the left. Sit in front of the keyboard with the book at the right—body erect, both feet on the floor.

Curve the fingers of your right hand and place them on the numeric keypad. Use the little finger for the ENTER key as indicated in Figure 4.1. To key the numbers, place the:

- Index finger on **4**.
- Middle finger on **5**.
- Ring finger on **6**.
- Thumb on **0**.

 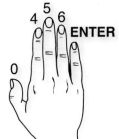

Figure 4.1 *Home keying position for numeric keypad*

42B

Access the Calculator

Use the Calculator on your computer to learn and practice the numeric keypad. Follow the instructions below to access the Calculator.

1. Start *Windows* if necessary.

2. Display the Charm bar and click the **Search** charm.

3. Key **Calculator** in the Search box. Then select the first **Calculator** in the list of search results.

4. The Calculator window will open, as shown in Figure 4.2.

Figure 4.2 *Calculator*

KEYBOARDING SKILLBUILDING

Warmup Practice

Key each line twice. If time permits, key the lines again.

Alphabet

1 Jack Betz will give us the equipment for six days.

Figure/Symbol

2 I paid Invoice #508 ($346.79 with a 12% discount).

Speed

3 The chair by the chapel in the city is an antique.

gwam 1' | 1 | 2 | 3 | 4 | 5 | 6 | 7 | 8 | 9 | 10 |

Improve Keying Technique

Key each line twice, striving to maintain a continuous pace.

TECHNIQUE TIP
Think, say, and key the words as words, not letter by letter.

Balanced-hand words

1 auto burn dusk kept form half rich pale sign maid;

2 panel quake; right shelf chair; eight elbow giant;

3 enrich handle eighty bushel chapels turkey suspend

Balanced-hand phrases

4 by the end|pay the man|if they fix the|go to work

5 make the sign|right problem|key to the map|to risk

6 with the neighbor|work with the city|sign the maps

Balanced-hand sentences

7 Pay the girl by the city dock for the six bushels.

8 The girls paid for their gowns for the big social.

9 The city officials kept the fox in the big kennel.

10 Jay and Hal may go with us to visit the neighbors.

gwam 30" | 2 | 4 | 6 | 8 | 10 | 12 | 14 | 16 | 18 | 20 |

Speed Forcing Drill

Key a 30" timed writing on each line, striving to key more on each attempt.

TECHNIQUE TIP
Keep your eyes on the copy as you reach out with your little finger and tap the ENTER key quickly.

1 He is to go with us.

2 Jay and I kept both pens.

3 Diane may work on their forms.

4 Orlando may go with me to the dock.

5 Jane and I may fix the signals for Kent.

6 Glen owns the lake land down by the big dock.

7 Helen is to go to the lake with the men to fix it.

gwam 30" | 2 | 4 | 6 | 8 | 10 | 12 | 14 | 16 | 18 | 20 |

Home Keys 4, 5, 6, and 0

TIP You may need to tap the NUM (NUMBER) LOCK key (located above the 7 on the numeric keypad).

TECHNIQUE TIP

- Tap each key quickly with the tip of the finger.
- Keep the fingers curved and upright.
- Use the side of the right thumb to tap the 0 similar to the way you tap the Space Bar.

MicroType

Use *MicroType* Numeric Keypad Lesson 1 for additional practice.

Use the Calculator to complete the addition drills shown below.

1. Key the first number with the proper finger(s) and tap the + key with the little finger of the right hand.

2. Key the next number and tap the + key.

3. After entering the last black number in the column and tapping the + key, verify your answer with the answer shown in color.

4. Tap ESC on the main keyboard to clear the number. Then do the next problem.

Drill 1

A	B	C	D	E
4	5	6	4	6
4	5	6	5	4
8	10	12	9	10

Drill 2

A	B	C	D	E
44	55	44	45	56
55	66	66	46	45
99	121	110	91	101

Drill 3

A	B	C	D	E
45	54	46	44	64
56	64	65	56	46
64	56	45	65	55
165	174	156	165	165

Drill 4

A	B	C	D	E
40	40	60	506	504
50	60	50	406	406
60	50	40	540	560
150	150	150	1,452	1,470

Drill 5

A	B	C	D	E
54	504	405	605	450
50	605	506	406	406
56	406	604	540	605
160	1,515	1,515	1,551	1,461

 **checkpoint** Did you check each answer against the book?

Newsletter

1. Open *df c8 newsletter*.

2. Set top, bottom, and side margins to 0.75". Use Landscape orientation.

3. Tap ENTER two or three times to insert space at the top of the document. Create WordArt for the text **Strategies for Success**. Position the WordArt as the main title at the top of the page and center it horizontally. Format it using Times New Roman font.

4. Place the pointer to the left of the *R* in *Reputation* in the first section heading and insert a Continuous section break after the title.

5. Arrange the text below the WordArt in three columns.

6. Format all text in 12-point Times New Roman font. Format the section headings in 14-point bold and left-align them.

7. Insert a text box between the first and second paragraphs. Set the height of the text box to 0.5" and the width to 2.5". Format it using a 1½-point border and a blue fill. Use the Top and Bottom text wrap option.

8. Key the following text in the text box. Change the font to bold, 10-point Times New Roman and center the text in the text box.

   ## A bad reputation can result from one mistake.

9. Place a copy (Copy/Paste) of the text box after the last line of the *Reputation and Choice* section. Delete the existing text and key the following text in the text box, formatting it the same as the other text box.

   ## Choices you make destroy or enhance your reputation.

10. Place another copy of the text box after the last line of the first paragraph of the *Learning about People* section. Delete the existing text and key the following text in the box, formatting it the same as the previous text boxes.

    ## Relating well to others is a major challenge.

11. Create another text box after the last paragraph of the *Learning about People* section. Delete the existing text and key the following text in the box, formatting the text the same as the other text boxes. Change the height of this text box to 0.3".

    ## Learn from experienced workers.

12. Hyphenate the text.

13. Insert a Continuous section break after the last paragraph to balance the columns.

14. Make needed formatting adjustments, spell-check the document, and proofread carefully. Correct all errors.

15. Save the document as *c8 newsletter*. Print the document and then close it.

TIP Review the line endings. If a word in a text box is hyphenated, tap SHIFT + ENTER before the hyphenated word to make the whole word appear on the next line.

Numeric Keypad 7, 8, 9

Learning Outcomes

In Lesson 43, you will:

- *Learn reachstrokes for 7, 8, and 9.*
- *Combine the 7, 8, and 9 keys with other keys.*

43A

Warmup

Use the Calculator to complete the addition drills shown below.

A	B	C	D
4	56	406	440
5	45	504	506
6	64	650	605
15	165	1,560	1,551

43B

New Keys 7, 8, and 9

7 Index finger
8 Middle finger
9 Ring finger

Drill 1   7

A	B	C	D	E
577	607	747	667	756
774	575	70	75	707
757	740	675	757	574
2,108	1,922	1,492	1,499	2,037

Drill 2   8

A	B	C	D	E
808	680	884	458	800
484	584	480	684	68
586	868	856	880	548
1,878	2,132	2,220	2,022	1,416

Drill 3   9

A	B	C	D	E
459	954	496	944	964
596	609	965	596	469
964	596	459	659	595
2,019	2,159	1,920	2,199	2,028

Drill 4 All numbers learned

A	B	C	D	E
409	740	695	509	594
507	964	570	476	807
608	850	409	840	560
1,524	2,554	1,674	1,825	1,961

MicroType

Use *MicroType* Numeric Keypad Lesson 2 for additional practice.

Before You Move On

Answer these questions to review what you have learned in Chapter 8.

1. Desktop publishing uses _____ with text to make a good visual impression. CO

2. Decorative text that you create in *Word* with predesigned font colors, shapes, and other effects is called _____. LO 59A

3. A drawing object that is a container for text or graphics is a(n) _____. LO 60A

4. One of the small squares that appears on the border of a selected graphic and can be used to change its size is called a(n) _____. LO 60B

5. List five things you should do to make a flyer communicate a good visual message. LO 60D

6. The ready-made objects and lines that can be accessed from *Word*'s Illustrations group are called _____. LO 61A

7. The Pictures command is used to find pictures located on your _____. LO 61B

8. When you change the height of a picture, the _____ feature will change the width as well. LO 61B

9. Describe what *Word*'s Columns feature does. LO 62A

10. To balance text in two or more columns, insert a(n) _____ section break at the end of the last column. LO 62A

Applying What You Have Learned

Data Files:

df c8 fitness
df c8 newsletter

Flyer

1. Open *df c8 fitness*.

2. Using the text and picture, design a flyer. You decide the layout, but do the following:
   - Cut/paste or rekey the text in the data file as needed.
   - Use one font with appropriate sizes, styles, effects, and color.
   - Format the picture appropriately.
   - Use text boxes and/or shapes with borders and shading.
   - Use WordArt.

3. Spell-check the document and proofread carefully. Correct all errors.

4. Save the document as *c8 fitness*; print and close it.

Lesson 44

Numeric Keypad 1, 2, 3

Learning Outcomes

In Lesson 44, you will:

- *Learn reachstrokes for **1**, **2**, and **3**.*
- *Combine the **1**, **2**, and **3** keys with other keys.*

44A

Warmup

Use the Calculator to complete the addition drills shown below.

A	B	C	D
549	596	406	740
670	408	809	596
486	758	750	805
1,705	1,762	1,965	2,141

44B

New Keys 1, 2, and 3

*1 **Index** finger*
*2 **Middle** finger*
*3 **Ring** finger*

Drill 1 1

A	B	C	D	E
171	916	147	415	156
814	151	811	611	417
151	110	901	718	901
1,136	1,177	1,859	1,744	1,474

Drill 2 2

A	B	C	D	E
202	289	722	290	256
425	524	208	724	728
726	262	526	282	249
1,353	1,075	1,456	1,296	1,233

Drill 3 3

A	B	C	D	E
453	453	303	734	368
396	309	963	583	493
363	396	357	639	735
1,212	1,158	1,623	1,956	1,596

Drill 4 All numbers learned

A	B	C	D	E
429	710	195	325	914
537	264	570	176	827
608	350	432	840	360
1,574	1,324	1,197	1,341	2,101

WP Page Layout/Page
Setup/Orientation

✓ checkpoint

View the line endings in each
column. Were hyphens inserted
at the end of several lines? Is
the document title centered over
all of the columns?

1. Open *df 62c design*. Set the side margins to 0.5".

2. To set the page orientation to Landscape, follow the path at the left and select **Landscape**. (See Figure 8.18.)

3. Insert a Continuous section break at the beginning of the paragraph following the title, *Document Design*.

4. Arrange the text in the section beneath the title in three columns with vertical lines between the columns. If needed, delete the blank line at the top of the first column to align its text with the vertical position of the text in columns two and three.

5. Hyphenate the text in the three columns.

6. Select the text in the three columns and justify it.

7. Insert a Continuous section break at the end of the document to balance the columns.

8. Save the document as *62c design*; print and close it.

Figure 8.18 *Page Orientation*

62D

Newsletter with Pictures and Text Wrapping

WP Picture Tools Format/
Arrange/Wrap Text

1. Open *df 62d conference*. Change the page orientation to Landscape.

2. Insert a Continuous section break at the beginning of the paragraph after the title.

3. Format the text below the title in two columns with a vertical line between them. Adjust spacing so both columns begin at the same vertical position. Balance the columns.

4. Click between words that are near the center of the *Special Events* paragraph. Insert the picture file *df 62d golfer*. Resize it so its height is 1".

5. To wrap the text tightly around the picture, follow the path at left to open the Wrap Text options. Select the **Tight** option shown in Figure 8.19.

6. Nudge or drag the picture as needed so it is in the center of the text below the first line of text.

7. Click in the *Program* paragraph in the first column about 1" inch to right of center and on line 1. Insert the picture *df 62d speaker*. Resize it to 1" high.

8. To position the picture in the upper-right portion of the *Program* paragraph, select **Square** from the Wrap Text options. Drag and nudge the picture so it is aligned at the right margin with its top aligned with the top of the text in line 1.

9. Spell-check, proofread, and correct errors. Save the document as *62d conference*; print and close it.

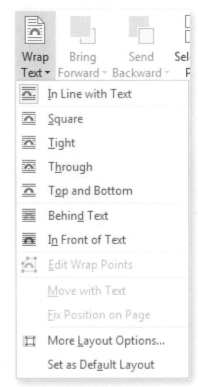

Figure 8.19 *Wrap Text options*

Using the Calculator, work with a classmate to solve the math problems shown below.

1. Parker wrote five checks this week. Check No. 216 was for $38.91, Check No. 217 was for $l7.42, Check No. 218 was for $56.20, Check No. 219 was for $3.95, and Check No. 220 was for $16.74. What was the total amount of the five checks?

2. Karen bought items costing $1.98, $3.65, $2.74, $2.05, $.97, $3.68, and $1.40. What was the amount she owed excluding tax?

3. Kimberly accumulated these points during this grading period for quizzes (10, 10, 8.5, 9.5, 7, and 8), projects (48, 25, 16, 23, and 17), and tests (90, 95, and 87). How many points did she accumulate for quizzes? For projects? For tests? How many total points did she accumulate this grading period?

MicroType

Use *MicroType* Numeric Keypad Lesson 3 for additional practice.

4. Tim, Jane, Chen, and Felipe each bowled three games. Tim's scores were 98, 175, and 126. Jane's scores were 127, 145, and 129. Felipe's scores were 145, 127, and 140. Chen's scores were 136, 114, and 169. What were the total pins for each person, and what were the total pins for their team?

Lesson 45

Subtraction and Multiplication

Learning Outcomes

In Lesson 45, you will:

- *Learn subtraction on the numeric keypad.*
- *Learn multiplication on the numeric keypad.*

45A

Warmup

Use the Calculator to complete the addition drills shown below.

A	B	C	D
102	938	476	517
289	304	560	976
854	391	208	645
1,245	1,633	1,244	2,138

WP *Continuous Break*
Page Layout/Page
Setup/Breaks

6. To balance the text in two columns, click at the end of the last sentence. Follow the ***Continuous Break*** path at the left. In the Section Breaks list, click **Continuous**, as shown in Figure 8.15. The text should now be in two nearly equal columns.

7. Save the document as *62a career fair* and close it.

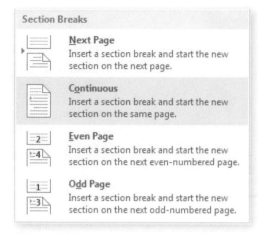

Figure 8.15 *Continuous break*

62B

Three-Column Document

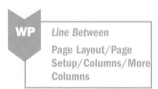
WP *Line Between*
Page Layout/Page
Setup/Columns/More
Columns

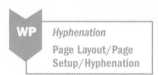
WP *Hyphenation*
Page Layout/Page
Setup/Hyphenation

COLLABORATION

In this activity, you will change the number of columns in a document from two to three and insert a vertical line between the columns.

1. Open *62a career fair* that you created earlier. Follow the ***Line Between*** path at the left. Select three columns from the Presets as shown in Figure 8.16.

2. To insert a vertical line between the columns, click the **Line between** checkbox as shown in Figure 8.16.

3. Hyphenate the text by using the ***Hyphenation*** path at the left. Select the **Automatic** option as shown in Figure 8.17.

4. Save the document as *62b career fair*; print and close it.

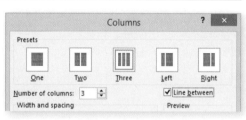

Figure 8.16 *Insert Line between*

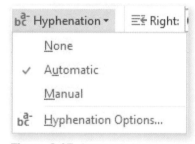

Figure 8.17 *Automatic hyphenation*

checkpoint Compare your printed document with a classmate's document. If they are different, determine why. Make corrections if necessary.

62C

Multi-Column Document in Landscape Orientation

Word documents can be designed with one of two page orientations. **Portrait orientation** places a document on the page with the short side of the paper at the top. **Landscape orientation** places a document on the page with the long side of the paper at the top. Portrait orientation is used for documents such as letters and reports. It is the default setting in *Word*. Landscape orientation may be used for wide tables, newsletters, and flyers.

Subtraction

Use the Calculator to complete the subtraction drills shown below. Key the first number and tap the – key. Key the second number and tap the ENTER key.

Drill 1

	A	B	C	D	E
	907	872	614	730	756
	- 489	- 312	- 459	- 583	- 621
	418	560	155	147	135

Drill 2

	A	B	C	D	E
	509	847	625	913	810
	- 293	- 764	- 501	- 264	- 398
	216	83	124	649	412

– **Little** finger

Multiplication

Use the Calculator to complete the multiplication drills shown below. Key the first number and tap the * key. Key the second number and tap the ENTER key.

Drill 3

	A	B	C	D	E
	96	75	84	40	132
	× 40	× 46	× 73	× 28	× 19
	3,840	3,450	6,132	1,120	2,508

Drill 4

	A	B	C	D	E
	405	697	803	467	371
	× 208	× 50	× 32	× 140	× 62
	84,240	34,850	25,696	65,380	23,002

* **Ring** finger

WP *First-Line Indent*
Home/Paragraph
dialog box launcher/
Indentation

3. To automatically indent the first line of each paragraph 0.25", follow the *First-Line Indent* path at the left. Choose **First line** from the Special list and, if necessary, key **0.25"** in the By box as shown in Figure 8.13.

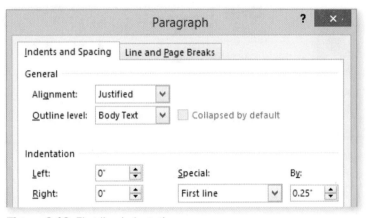

Figure 8.13 *First-line indentation*

WP *Columns*
Page Layout/Page
Setup/Columns

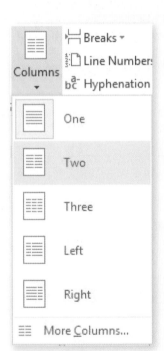

Figure 8.14 *Columns gallery*

4. Format the document for two columns of equal width by following the *Columns* path at the left to open the Columns gallery (see Figure 8.14 at the left). Select two columns as shown.

5. Key the following text. The text will appear only in the first column.

Career Fair

The Career Fair will be held May 15 from 9 a.m. to 12:30 p.m. It will be in Room 214. Next week you will get a list of the employers who are coming. Each employer represents a different career. Therefore, there will be a variety of careers for you to explore.

You are urged to speak to as many of the employers as possible. Be sure to take notes about the education needed for each career. Also, ask them what they like and dislike about the career they represent. You will need to get the signature of each employer on the notes you take. Give the notes and signatures to your instructor.

Remember to act appropriately during the Career Fair. Use good grammar and speak clearly without using slang to make a favorable first impression. You should have an up-to-date resume to show the employers. This will quickly tell them your interests and the subjects you are taking.

Math Problems

COLLABORATION

MicroType

Use *MicroType* Numeric Keypad Lesson 4 for additional practice.

Using the Calculator, work with a classmate to solve the math problems shown below.

1. Owen bought four cups @ 3.98 each, six plates @ $4.50 each, and four saucers @ $4.25 each. How much was the purchase Owen made? How much was the total purchase before tax? How much was the total purchase with a 5% sales tax included?

2. Miles missed 12 points on the first exam, which was worth 125 points. He lost 23 points on the second exam, which was worth 150 points, and he lost 15 points on the third exam, which was also worth 150 points. What were the total points available on the three exams? What were the total points that Miles got on the three exams?

3. One of the plates Owen purchased (problem 1) was chipped. He decided to return the damaged plate. How much did the dishes cost him after the return of the damaged plate? Include the 5% sales tax in the total cost.

4. During the week, Sharon purchased five beverages @ $1.50 each, three sandwiches @ $3.25 each, two cups of soup @ $1.98 each, three bags of chips @ $.90, and two desserts @ $1.25 each. How much did Sharon spend this week if there is no tax on the food she purchased?

Lesson 46

Division

Learning Outcomes

In Lesson 46, you will:

- *Learn division on the numeric keypad.*
- *Learn to complete math problems on the numeric keypad.*

46A

Warmup

Use the Calculator to complete the addition problems shown below.

A	B	C	D
821	673	276	401
309	540	809	823
547	189	305	576
1,677	1,402	1,390	1,800

21st Century Skills

Health Literacy The state of your physical and mental health greatly impacts your ability to build and strengthen the skills you will employ in all areas of your life. Through physical well-being, you keep your body strong and have a high energy level. When you are physically healthy, you are alert and can focus clearly on schoolwork, job tasks, and other responsibilities. You have the energy and stamina to participate in the activities you want and need to do and achieve your goals.

Through mental well-being, you have a positive, open-minded attitude and engage in activities that stimulate your intellect. When you are mentally healthy, you are confident and have high self-esteem. You can communicate well with others, make decisions, and think critically.

Think Critically

1. What can you do to contribute to your physical and mental well-being? List at least three things for each.

2. List at least three risky behaviors that could threaten your physical or mental health.

3. In a new word processing document, design a one-page flyer that illustrates your responses to questions 1 and 2 above. Insert clip art and other graphics as desired. Save and print the flyer as directed by your instructor.

© Monkey Business Images/Shutterstock.com

Lesson 62

Multi-Column Documents

Data Files:

df 62c design
df 62d conference
df 62d speaker
df 62d golfer

Learning Outcomes

In Lesson 62, you will:

62A *Create a document using Columns, Justify alignment, and First-line Indent.*
62B *Create a three-column document using Line between and Hyphenation.*
62C *Create a three-column document using Landscape orientation.*
62D *Prepare a newsletter using pictures and text wrap.*

62A

Two-Column Document

Documents such as brochures and newsletters often have text in two or more columns on a page. The columns may be equal or unequal in width and length. A page may have a different number of columns. For example, a heading may be one column, and two or more columns of text may be below it. The text within the multiple columns often uses Justify alignment and is hyphenated.

1. Open a new, blank document. Key **Career Fair** in bold on the first line and center the text. Tap ENTER.

2. Set the alignment to Justify (Home/Paragraph/Justify).

Division

/ Middle finger

Use the Calculator to complete the division drills shown below. Key the dividend and tap the / key. Key the divisor and tap the ENTER key. Round answers to two decimal places.

Drill 1

A	B	C	D	E
120.6	79	90.33	119	70.8
5/603	11/869	6/542	8/952	10/708

Drill 2

A	B	C	D	E
21.65	64.49	197.51	95.56	134.58
23/498	79/5,095	43/8,493	62/5,925	67/9,017

Math Problems

COLLABORATION

Instant Message

A deposit is an addition to a bank account. A check or service charge is a subtraction from a bank account.

MicroType

Use *MicroType* Numeric Keypad Lesson 5 for additional practice.

Using the Calculator, work with a classmate to solve the math problems shown below.

1. Rebecca made four deposits last month. They were for $37.28, $15.91, $45.76, and $50.37. How much money did she deposit for the month?

2. Sarah bought two CDs for $15.99 each. She bought two video games for $59.95 and $49.75. The state sales tax is 5.5%. How much did she spend?

3. Yukio is paid each week. His last four checks were for $49.78, $35.97, $53.76, and $28.73. What did he average per week over this period?

4. Antonio is paid $6.25 per hour. Last week he worked 4 hours on Monday, 3½ hours on Tuesday, 5 hours on Wednesday, 2 hours on Thursday, and 4½ hours on Friday. How much did he make last week?

5. At the end of last month, Brandon had an ending bank balance of $153.37. During the month, he made one deposit for $97.68. He wrote five checks ($7.98, $15.83, $38.53, $17.21, and $49.76). His service charge this month was $3.25. What is his current balance after recording these amounts?

checkpoint Compare your answers with a classmate's answers. If they do not agree, do the problem again to find the correct answer.

4. Select the bottom left picture and format and size it as you choose. Position it in the middle center.

5. Save the document as *61b laptops* and close it.

61C

Flyer

1. Open a new, blank document to create a flyer that will fit attractively on 8.5" × 11" paper.

2. Insert *df 61c picture* (a picture file) into the document at the top center. Size and format it as desired.

3. Key **WMS Student Government** as WordArt below the picture. Size and format the WordArt appropriately.

4. Insert a text box to hold the following information and format the text and the text box appropriately.

President: Kim Chung
Vice President: Tess O'Malley
Secretary: Tom Habib
Treasurer: Gloria Perez
Historian: Marci Kelleran

5. Select and insert a shape and key **Thanks to all who voted** inside the shape. Format the shape appropriately.

6. Make any positioning and sizing adjustments to arrange the information attractively on the page.

COLLABORATION

7. Save the flyer as *61c flyer*; print and close it.

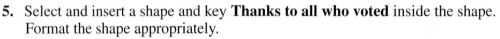

✓ **checkpoint** Ask one or two classmates to critique your flyer. Make any changes you believe will improve the visual message.

61D

Design a Flyer

1. Working with one or two classmates to complete this activity, design a flyer your teacher can use to tell others about the value of this course. Review the guidelines on page 269 for creating flyers. Include some of the following points in your flyer:

   • The name of the course

   • The activities you enjoy

   • Important things you have learned

   • Reasons others should take the course

   • The computer software you use

   • Ways the course helps you in other courses or activities

COLLABORATION

2. Use WordArt, pictures, or other graphics to make the flyer attractive.

3. Save the document as *61d flyer*; print and close it.

Before You Move On

Answer these questions to review what you have learned in Chapter 4.

1. When keying numbers, where should you keep the fingers not being used to tap the number key? LO 31B

2. What does the proofreaders' mark for transpose mean? LO 31C

3. What is the proofreaders' mark for delete? For close up? LO 31C

4. Another name for handwritten copy is _____. LO 32C

5. To make TAB characters display on the screen, click the _____ button. LO 34C

6. When keying, keep your forearms _____ to the slant of the keyboard. LO 35C

7. Do not _____ between a figure and the / or the $ sign. LO 36B

8. You should keep your _____ on the copy as you key. LO 36F

9. What is carpal tunnel syndrome (CTS)? Follows 41E

10. List three precautions you can take to help prevent CTS. Follows 41E

11. Describe home-keying position for the numeric keypad. LO 42A

12. When using the Calculator, you may need to tap the _____ key (located above the 7 on the numeric keypad). LO 42C

13. When using the numeric keypad, use your _____ to tap the 0 key. LO 42A

14. List the steps for using the Calculator to do a subtraction problem. LO 45B

15. The key used for multiplication on the numeric keypad is the _____. LO 45C

TIP The ratio of width to height for a picture is called *aspect ratio*. By default, *Word* locks aspect ratio so that changing one dimension of the picture automatically changes the other a corresponding amount.

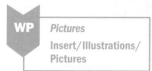

WP *Online Pictures*
Insert/Illustrations/
Online Pictures

WP *Pictures*
Insert/Illustrations/
Pictures

TIP Clip art and pictures you find on the Internet may be copyrighted. Read and follow the acceptable-use guidelines for clip art and pictures you find online.

Many of the features on the Picture Tools Format tab operate the same as or similar to those on the Drawing Tools Format tab that you used with WordArt, text boxes, and shapes. One difference is that when you size a picture, you need only change the width or height. When the width or height is changed, the other dimension automatically is changed to maintain the proper ratio of height to width.

To insert a picture that is stored on your computer or one that you are connected to, select Pictures from the Illustrations group to open the Insert Picture dialog box and navigate to the location of the picture file. To find and insert a picture from an online source such as Office.com Clip Art, select Online Pictures. In the Insert Pictures dialog box, you can select and use an online source to search.

Activity 1

1. Open a new, blank document and insert a picture by doing one of the following:

   - If you are permitted to search the Internet for pictures, follow the ***Online Pictures*** path at the left, and then use an online service to find a picture of a penguin. Insert the desired picture.

   - To find a picture of penguins on your computer, follow the ***Pictures*** path at the left, and then look in the folder where your data files are stored for *df 61b penguins* (a picture file). Select the picture and then click **Insert**.

2. Select the picture to display the Picture Tools Format tab. Click the tab if necessary to display commands.

3. Change the Shape Width setting in the Size group to 3". Notice that the Shape Height setting changed automatically to maintain the proper aspect ratio.

4. Change the picture's position to top center using the Position feature in the Arrange group.

5. Move the picture down about 1" by dragging or nudging it.

6. Scroll through the built-in picture styles in the Picture Styles group and select a style that you like.

7. Save the document as *61b penguins* and close it.

Activity 2

1. Open *df 61b laptops*. It contains three pictures that are left-aligned at the top, middle, and bottom.

2. Select the top left picture and do the following:
   a. Change its height to 2".
   b. Format it using a built-in style that does not have a border.
   c. Position it at the top right.

3. Select the left center picture.
   a. Change its width to 2".
   b. Format it using your choice of Picture Border and Picture Effects options.
   c. Position it at the bottom right.

KEYBOARDING SKILLBUILDING

Warmup Practice

Key each line twice. If time permits, key the lines again.

Alphabet

1 Before leaving, Jexon quickly swam the dozen laps.

Figure/Symbol

2 Our tax increased by 12.7% ($486); we paid $3,590.

Speed

3 Hal and I may go to the social held on the island.

gwam 1' | 1 | 2 | 3 | 4 | 5 | 6 | 7 | 8 | 9 | 10 |

Improve Keying Technique

Key each line twice, striving to maintain a continuous pace.

TECHNIQUE TIP
Keep your eyes on the copy.

Balanced-hand words

1 go if am us to by of he an so is do it go me be or
2 is and the may did man due big for box but oak six
3 with when make such work city down they them their

Balanced-hand phrases

4 big box|pay for|and the|own them|to the end|he may
5 if they|make a|the right|by the|wish to|when did I
6 sign the|for them|make them|when is|and then|to it

Balanced-hand sentences

7 Nancy and I may go to the city for the audit form.
8 Enrique may make a map of the island for the firm.
9 Orlando may work with the men on the bus problems.

gwam 30" | 2 | 4 | 6 | 8 | 10 | 12 | 14 | 16 | 18 | 20 |

3. Use the Shape Outline feature to select a color of your choice and then set the border weight to 2¼ point.

4. Use the Shape Fill to choose an appropriate fill color.

5. If desired, use the Shape Effects to add formatting changes.

6. Right-click inside the shape. Select **Add Text** from the shortcut menu and key **First Aid Station** at the blinking insertion point.

7. Select the text on the shape. Choose a desired font color and change the font to 14-point Arial.

8. Position the cross at the middle center of the document.

9. Save the document as *61a first aid* and close it.

Activity 2

1. Open a new document. Access the Shapes gallery. Select the 5-Point Star shape from the Stars and Banners group.

2. Set the size for the star at 5" tall by 5" wide. Position the shape at the middle center of the document. Format the star as desired.

3. Add this text to the shape: **Be a Star!** Use a font, font size, and font color of your choice.

4. Save the document as *61a star* and close it.

61B

Insert and Format Pictures

Pictures, including **clip art**, can be inserted or copied into a document. Clip art is ready-made drawings and photography. You can get pictures from files stored on your computer or from online sources. If you use pictures from the online sources, you must be careful not to violate copyright laws. *Word*'s Pictures and Online Pictures features can help you locate pictures for your documents.

When you select a picture, the Picture Tools Format tab will open (see Figure 8.12), and you can use the features on it to format, position, and size your picture. In this lesson, you will use features in the Picture Styles, Arrange, and Size groups to make these changes.

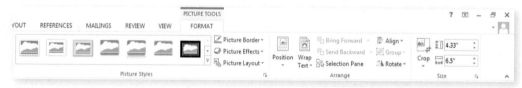

Figure 8.12 *Picture Styles, Arrange, and Size groups*

TECHNIQUE TIP
Reach out with your little finger and tap the ENTER key quickly. Return your finger to its home key.

1 Pamela may be able to go.
2 You can see the next game too.
3 Mike will be out of town on Friday.
4 Shawn and I can take the exam next week.
5 Nancy will bring your new computer next week.
6 The new version of the video game will be on sale.

gwam 30" | 2 | 4 | 6 | 8 | 10 | 12 | 14 | 16 | 18 | 20 |

Speed Building

1. Key three 1' timed writings on each paragraph, striving to key more on each timing; determine *gwam*.

2. Key a 2' timed writing on both paragraphs combined, striving to maintain your highest 1' *gwam*.

LA all letters used

	gwam	1'	2'
When saying hello to someone is the correct		8	4
thing to do, make direct eye contact and greet the		19	10
person with vitality in your voice. Do not look		28	14
down or away or speak only in a whisper. Make the		39	20
person feel happy for having seen you, and you		48	24
will feel much better about yourself.		56	28
Similarly, when you shake hands with another		9	33
person, look that person in the eye and offer a		18	38
firm but not crushing shake of the hand. Just a		28	53
firm shake or two will do. Next time you meet a		38	58
new person, do not puzzle over whether to shake		47	63
hands. Quickly offer your hand with confidence.		57	68

gwam 1' | 1 | 2 | 3 | 4 | 5 | 6 | 7 | 8 | 9 | 10 |
2' | 1 | 2 | 3 | 4 | 5 |

Lesson 61 — Shapes, Pictures, and Flyers

Data Files:

df 61b penguins
df 61b laptops
df 61c picture

Learning Outcomes

In Lesson 61, you will:

61A Create and format shapes.
61B Insert and format pictures.
61C Create a flyer.
61D Design a flyer.

61A

Create and Format Shapes

Shapes are ready-made objects such as rectangles, circles, lines, curves, stars, and banners available in the Illustrations group on the Insert tab. Figure 8.10 shows some of the categories of shapes that are available. Each category contains a variety of shapes from which you can choose the desired shape.

When you select a shape from the gallery, your pointer changes to a cross. Use the cross to draw the shape as you did to draw a text box.

Once the shape has been drawn, the Drawing Tools Format tab appears as it did with WordArt and text boxes. You can modify a selected shape by changing it to a different shape; adjusting the size, border color and thickness, and fill color; and adding text to the shape.

Use features in the Insert Shapes, Shape Styles (see Figure 8.11), and Size groups to modify the appearance of a shape.

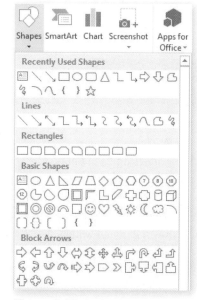

Figure 8.10 *Available shapes in the Shapes gallery*

Figure 8.11 *Insert Shapes and Shape Styles groups*

Activity 1

In this activity, you will create a cross similar to the one illustrated at the left. You will set the size for the shape, select a Shape Outline (border) color and width, apply a Shape Fill color, and add text to the shape.

1. Open a new, blank document. Follow the path at left and select the **Cross** shape in the Basic Shapes group.

2. Draw a Cross shape that is about 1" high and 1" wide. Select the shape and use the Size feature to set the height to 1.1" and width to 1.5".

WP Insert/Illustrations/Shapes

ACROSS THE CURRICULUM

Academic Connections

Data Files:

df c4 symbols
df c4 payroll
df c4 sales tax
df c4 earnings

Language Arts: Symbols

Not all symbols can be keyed using the keyboard. However, as you will learn in this activity, *Word* and other programs allow you to create symbols such as copyright © and trademark ™ symbols.

1. Start *Word* and open *df c4 symbols*.

2. Read the instructions in the document and create the symbols.

3. Save the document as *c4 symbols*, print, and close it.

Math: Payroll

Before you get a job, you should learn to calculate your pay. This way, you can make sure you are receiving the right amount. You may be paid an hourly rate called a *wage*. You are likely to receive a higher hourly rate for overtime—the number of hours you work beyond a regular workweek. Most employers pay an overtime rate if you work more than 40 hours in one week. Some employers pay overtime if you work more than 8 hours in one day.

In this activity, you will learn how to calculate regular pay, an overtime hourly rate, and total overtime pay. You will also learn about gross pay and net pay.

1. Open *df c4 payroll*.

2. Read the document to learn more payroll terms. Follow the directions to calculate payroll items and key your answers to the questions. Be sure to show your work.

3. Save the document as *c4 payroll*, print, and close it.

About Business

COLLABORATION

Business and Government

Businesses and governments affect each other. Governments can affect businesses by passing laws. For example, the government sets the lowest hourly pay that a company can pay its employees. This is called the **minimum wage**. Governments also forbid companies from selling unsafe products.

Likewise, businesses affect the government. They pay taxes that help support the programs and activities of the government. Taxes that businesses pay may also help run your school. You will learn more about taxes in this activity.

1. Open *df c4 sales tax*. Complete the problems and key your answers in the document.

2. Compare your answers with a classmate. If your answers are different, find and fix those that are incorrect.

3. Save the document as *c4 sales tax*, print, and close it.

Flyers do not follow a standard format like letters and reports. You can be creative when designing and laying out a flyer. Your flyer should send an effective visual message and should persuade readers to take the action you want.

In this activity, you will use WordArt and text boxes to prepare a flyer using applicable guidelines from the previous page.

1. Open *df 60d flyer.*

2. Select the WordArt at the top. Change the text to a 48-point font size and set its width at 6.5". You decide all other formatting features using features from the WordArt Styles group. Adjust the height to fit your formatted WordArt.

3. Center-align the text in each text box. Use at least an 18-point font size for the text. Align the left text box at or near the left margin and the right text box at or near the right margin. Make each text box height and width the same or nearly the same and position them so the top of each is at the same vertical position. Format the text boxes using features from the Shape Styles group.

4. Key **WMSCC Wants You!** as WordArt below the text boxes. You decide all formatting features.

5. Insert the following text in a text box below the WordArt you inserted. You decide all formatting features.

> For more information, contact Mrs. Keller in Room 303 or come to the information meeting on Tuesday, September 14, in the Information Technology Room 210.

6. Reposition the WordArt and text boxes vertically as needed to make the flyer attractive and easy to read. *Reminder:* Use the positioning tools—dragging, nudging, and Position options—as needed.

7. Save the document as *60d flyer*; print and close it.

✓ **checkpoint**

Form groups of four or five, have each person in a group show his/her flyer, and then identify one that the group believes sends the strongest visual message.

Digital Citizenship and Ethics

Online auction sites such as eBay, uBid, and Bidz.com enable individuals and companies to buy and sell products using electronic bidding. While this form of digital commerce can be convenient, you should understand all sides of these transactions.

- Researching online merchants will help you identify the "best deal" and minimize the risk of making an unwise purchase.

- Online purchases can run up credit card debt. If you cannot pay your bills, you can ruin your credit rating.
- Providing personal information to insecure sites can make you vulnerable to Internet scams and identity theft.

As a class, discuss the following:

1. How can irresponsible online purchasing practices lead to poor credit ratings?
2. How can you use an online auction site as a tool for comparison shopping?

Dirk Enters/imageBROKER / Alamy

Reading Earning Statements

You have already learned about gross pay and net pay. You learned that employers take deductions out of your pay. Taxes are one of the deductions. They go to various government agencies. If you receive benefits such as insurance, you may have to pay a portion of that cost too. In this activity, you will work with an earnings statement and take a closer look at deductions.

1. Open *df c4 earnings*.

2. Study the earning statements and answer the questions following it.

3. Save the document as *c4 earnings*, print, and close it.

Activity 3

1. Look on the last page of your survey and note your *second* Career Cluster of interest. Find its description on the last two pages of the survey and read it.

2. Go to http://www.careertech.org. Click the **Career Technical Education** button, then click **Career Clusters** in the list at the right. Scroll down on the Career Clusters page and click the link for your second Career Cluster. On the web page for your Career Cluster, click the **PDF** link following Career Cluster Frame in the information near the top of the page. Read the list of careers in the document and pick one or two you are interested in. Make a note of the category (called a Pathway) of the career(s) you choose. You will need to know the Pathway in a future activity.

3. Use the Internet to find out specific duties of the career(s) that you chose. You may look for other information that interests you as well.

4. Use *Word* to write a summary of what you learned. Save the document as *c4 career 2 details*, print, and close it.

Online Resources:

ngl.cengage.com/c21jr3e

Format a Text Box

Once a text box is inserted into your document, you can format it using the features available on the Drawing Tools Format tab that displays when a text box is selected. In this activity, you will use features in the Shape Styles group shown in Figure 8.9 to select a preformatted style (the Shape Styles gallery), change or add shading to the text box (Shape Fill), change or delete the border (Shape Outline), and add effects to the text box (Shape Effects).

Figure 8.9 *Shape Styles group*

WP Drawing Tools
Format/Shape Styles

1. Open *df 60c text box* and select the first text box.

2. Use the path at the left to display the Shape Styles gallery in the Shape Styles group. Select a style from the gallery.

3. Adjust the text box width to 2.5" and then adjust its height to accommodate the text. Center the text box horizontally.

4. Format the bottom text box by selecting a:
   a. Desired text box shade from the Shape Fill options.
   b. 3-point border in a desired color from the Shape Outline options.
   c. Desired shape effect from the Shape Effects options.

5. Change the width to 2.5" and adjust the height as needed to accommodate the text.

6. Save the document as *60c text box* and close it.

Flyers

A **flyer** is an announcement or advertisement usually intended for wide distribution. A flyer is usually one page with large text and graphics. People create flyers for many purposes. Flyers are used to announce activities in a school or community. Flyers may tell people how to register for a soccer, football, or baseball team. They may provide information about a school meeting or party. People use flyers to announce yard sales, apartment rentals, and items for sale. You may make flyers to ask for help in finding a lost pet or piece of jewelry.

When you design a flyer, make sure you create a strong visual message. The flyer should:

- Be colorful so it attracts the attention of those who see it.

- Have ample white space so it is easy to read.

- Use pictures that relate to the subject of the flyer.

- Use all capital letters sparingly because they are difficult to read.

- Use fonts that are easy to read.

- Use only one or two fonts. (You can use bold, italic, and different sizes to vary the appearance of the fonts you use.)

UNIT 3

Word Processing, Desktop Publishing, and Document Formatting

Chapter 5   Reports

Lessons 47–50

Reports, reports, reports! Everybody wants one—your science teacher, your math teacher, your English teacher. A **report** is a document that gives facts, ideas, or opinions about one or more topics. A review of a library book you have read is an example of a report. A summary of a science project you created is another example of a report. In this chapter, you will learn to use word processing software to format reports. **Format** means to place text on a page so that it looks good and is easy to read.

The reports will be arranged in standard format or the MLA format. *MLA* stands for *Modern Language Association*. School reports are often prepared using this format.

When you write reports, you may quote information from other sources. For example, you might include a quote from a magazine article. You will learn the in-text method of citing sources for quoted material. You also will learn how to format a page that lists all of the works cited in a report. An outline of a report is another report part that you will learn to format.

© Solphoto/Shutterstock.com

Draw and Size a Text Box

WP *Draw*

Insert/Text/Text Box/
Draw Text Box

TIP A selected text box has **sizing handles** (small squares). To increase or decrease width or height, move the pointer over a sizing handle at the top, bottom, or side of the text box. When the pointer changes to a two-sided arrow, click on the square and drag to adjust the box size. To increase or decrease height and width at the same time, drag a corner sizing handle.

WP *Size*

Drawing Tools
Format/Size/Shape
Height and/or Shape
Width

If you choose, you can use the Draw Text Box option to create a text box from scratch instead of using a built-in one. Once it is drawn, the size of a text box can be changed to fit the text and space, and it can be moved to the desired position. A text box may have **borders** and/or **shading**—the default settings are a single-line border and no shading (fill) as shown in Figure 8.7.

> The Draw Text Box option was used to create this text box. It uses the default font and border. The Size feature was used to adjust its size.

Figure 8.7 *Drawn text box with default settings*

1. Open a new, blank document. Center your name on line 1, key the text **Draw Text Box** on line 2, and then tap ENTER.

2. Follow the *Draw* path at the left to select **Draw Text Box**. The insertion point will change to a cross. Move the cross about 1" or 2" to the left of and below the centered text. Click and drag to the right and then down until the text box you are drawing is about 3" wide and 2" tall to accommodate the text to be keyed in it. Release the mouse button. A text box will appear, and the blinking insertion point inside the text box indicates where text will be inserted when you begin keying.

3. Key the following text in the text box. The text will wrap automatically to the next line. Do not tap ENTER after the paragraph is keyed.

This text box has a single-line border and no shading, which are the default settings. I keyed text into the text box, changed the size of the text box, and horizontally centered it. In the next activity, I will learn to change the format of a text box.

4. The text box should still be selected. To resize the text box so its height and/or width are appropriate to its contents and the space it will occupy, increase or decrease the Shape Height and Shape Width settings (see the *Size* path at the left) in the Size group as needed (see Figure 8.8). For this activity, the text box is to be 3" wide; the height should be enough to accommodate the text (1.5").

Shape Height ——
Shape Width ——
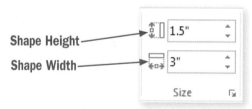

Figure 8.8 *Shape Height and Shape Width*

5. If needed, move the text box so it is horizontally centered below the second line of text.

6. Save the document as *60b text box* and close it.

MLA Reports

Learning Outcomes

In Lesson 47, you will:

47A Learn about line spacing and selecting text.

47B Use paragraph alignment commands.

47C Apply font settings from the Home tab.

47D Insert page numbers in headers and footers.

47E Learn about MLA format reports.

47F Compose an MLA report.

Data Files:

df 47a report
df 47a select
df 47b report
df 47c font
df 47d report

47A

Line Spacing and Selecting Text

WP Home/Paragraph/
Line and Paragraph
Spacing

TIP Line spacing of 1.0 is also called single spacing. Line spacing of 2.0 is also called double spacing.

Line spacing is the amount of blank space between lines of text. The default setting for *Word 2013* is 1.08 spacing. **Paragraph spacing** is the amount of space before or after a paragraph. The default setting for *Word 2013* is 8 points of blank space after a paragraph. You can choose the line spacing and amount of blank space before and after paragraphs by clicking the down arrow next to the Line and Paragraph Spacing button in the Paragraph group on the Home tab. (See Figure 5.1.) The Add Space Before Paragraph and Remove Space After Paragraph choices can be used to add and remove blank space that is inserted whenever the ENTER key is tapped.

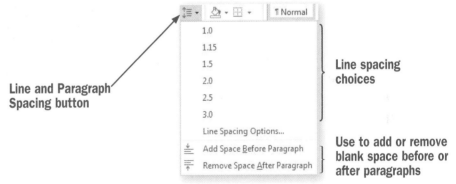

Figure 5.1 *Line and paragraph spacing choices*

When you are creating a document, you may want to **select** text to change the text in some way. For example, you might change the line spacing or size of the text. To do so, you must first select the text. An example of selected text is shown in Figure 5.2. To select text, click and drag the mouse pointer over the text. You can delete selected text by tapping the DELETE key. You can replace selected text by keying new text.

> You need to select text to change it. Selected text appears highlighted on the screen.
> Selected text look like this.

Figure 5.2 *Highlighted selected text*

Lesson 60 | Text Boxes and Flyers

Data Files:

df 60c text box
df 60d flyer

In Lesson 60, you will:

60A *Use a built-in text box.*

60B *Draw and size a text box.*

60C *Format a text box.*

60D *Use WordArt and text boxes to create a flyer.*

60A

Preformatted Text Boxes

A **text box** is a container for text or graphics. Text boxes are used to call the reader's attention to specific text or graphics. They also are used to position several blocks of text on a page. You can choose a preformatted text box or draw your own.

In this activity, you will use a preformatted (built-in) text box. The text box shown in Figure 8.6 was created by selecting SimpleText Box from the Built-in text box gallery. It has a border and contains placeholder text that will be replaced with text you key.

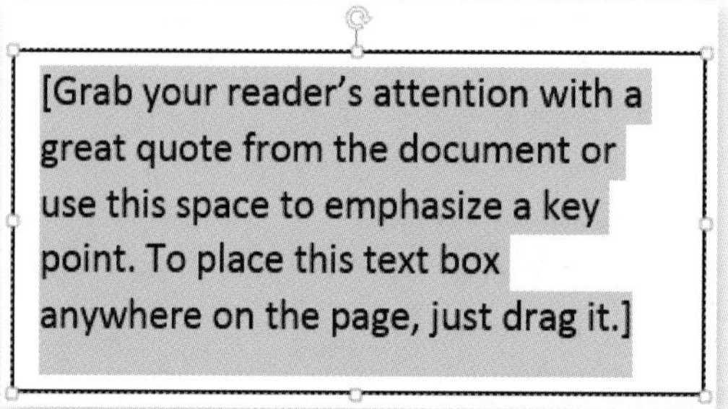

[Grab your reader's attention with a great quote from the document or use this space to emphasize a key point. To place this text box anywhere on the page, just drag it.]

Figure 8.6 *Built-in Simple Text Box*

WP Insert/Text/Text Box

1. Open a new, blank document.

2. Display the Text Box gallery using the path at the left. Select the **Simple Text Box** from the Built-in section of the gallery. A horizontally centered, preformatted text box will appear, the text box will be selected, and the placeholder text will be highlighted.

3. Begin keying the following text in the text box—the placeholder text will be deleted, the text box will be resized, and text will wrap automatically to the next line. Do not tap ENTER after the paragraph is keyed.

This text box has a single-line border and no shading. When I begin keying, the placeholder text is removed and the text box is resized automatically to fit the amount of text I key in the text box.

4. Position the text box at the top left. *Hint:* Text box objects can be positioned or moved the same ways as WordArt objects.

5. Save the document as *60a text box* and close it.

1. Start *Word.* Open the document *df 47a report.*

2. Select the title and the paragraphs of the report and change line spacing to 2.0. (See Figure 5.1 on the previous page.) Notice that there is more blank space between the paragraphs than between the lines within a paragraph in the document.

TIP To learn other ways to select text, open *df 47a select.* Practice the ways to select text described in the document.

3. Delete the extra space between the paragraphs by using the Remove Space After Paragraph feature. (See Figure 5.1 on the previous page.) The report should now be double-spaced with no extra blank space after the paragraphs.

4. Select **School** in the title and change it to all capitals.

5. Begin the document at or near the 2" line. If the word *AT* is not displayed on the bottom status bar as shown in Figure 5.3, follow the instructions in the Tip at the left.

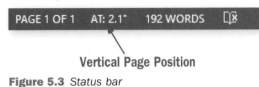

PAGE 1 OF 1   AT: 2.1"   192 WORDS

Vertical Page Position

Figure 5.3 *Status bar*

TIP If the Vertical Page Position indicator is not displayed on your status bar, right-click the status bar and select **Vertical Page Position**.

6. Save the document as *47a report* and close it.

47B

Paragraph Alignment Commands

WP Home/Paragraph

Paragraph alignment refers to how text is placed on a page. In word processing terms, a **paragraph** is any amount of text that is keyed before the ENTER key is tapped. A paragraph can be one word or several words or lines. Paragraphs can be aligned before or after text is keyed.

Figure 5.4 shows the toolbar buttons used to set alignment. Each button also shows how text will be placed on the page. **Align Left** starts all lines of the paragraph at the left margin. Align Left is the default paragraph alignment. **Align Right** ends all lines at the right margin. **Center** places an equal (or nearly equal) space between the text and each side margin. **Justify** starts all lines at the left margin and ends all full lines at the right margin.

Align Left   Center   Align Right   Justify

Figure 5.4 *Alignment buttons*

1. Open *df 47b report.*

2. Use Center to format the title.

3. Use Align Left to format the first two paragraphs of the body.

4. Use Justify to format the third and fourth paragraphs.

5. Save the document as *47b report* and close it.

WP Drawing Tools
Format/WordArt
Styles/Text Fill,
Text Outline, or Text
Effects

Once WordArt is created, it can be selected and edited. You can edit its words by using the features in the Font group on the Home tab as you do with other text. If you want to change the WordArt style, the text fill, the text outline, or the text effects, you can use the features in the WordArt Styles group shown in Figure 8.4. Other features on the Drawing Tools Format tab can also be used to change the WordArt.

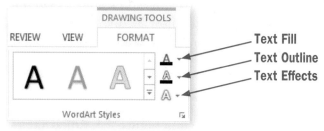

Figure 8.4 *WordArt Styles group*

1. If needed, open *59b wordart* and select **WordArt Example 1**.

2. Delete *My* from the text and then key **Revised** at the end of the text. Using the Font group on the Home tab, change the font to Times New Roman; and if necessary, reposition the WordArt at the top right.

3. From the WordArt Styles group, use the Text Fill button to select a dark red fill color and use the Text Outline button to select a black outline for the text.

4. From the Text Effects list (see Figure 8.5), select **Transform** and then select the **Triangle Up** or **Triangle Down** option (3rd and 4th styles in row 1 of Warp).

5. Save the document as *59c wordart*; do not close.

6. Using WordArt Example 2 and WordArt Example 3, select colors that you want from the Text Fill and Text Outline options. For Example 2 text effects, select **3-D Rotation** and then apply one of the Parallel options. For Example 3 text effects, select **Transform** and then apply the Circle style from the Warp list.

7. Save the document as *59c wordart* and close it.

Figure 8.5 *Text Effects list*

COLLABORATION

1. Open a new, blank document.

2. Using your school name and school colors, create WordArt that is positioned at the top center.

3. Save the document as *59d school*; print and close it.

✓ **checkpoint** Form groups of four or five, have each person in a group show his/her WordArt, and then identify one that the group believes is most appropriate for your school.

Font Settings

WP Home/Font

TIP The Format Painter can be used to copy formats to another place or to multiple places in a document. Access the Format Painter in the Clipboard group on the Home tab. Click the **Format Painter** button once to copy the format to another place; double-click it to copy the format to multiple places.

The default font settings for *Word 2013* are Calibri (font type), 11 points (font size), and black (font color). Each of these font settings in addition to others (strike-through, superscript, subscript, and text highlight color) can be changed by using features in the Font group on the Home tab. Font default settings are frequently changed to make text attractive, to make it easy to read, or to contain a specific attribute. Figure 5.5 shows the various features in the Font group. Additional font features may be chosen by clicking the dialog box launcher arrow and selecting from the available options. The changes can be made before or after text is keyed.

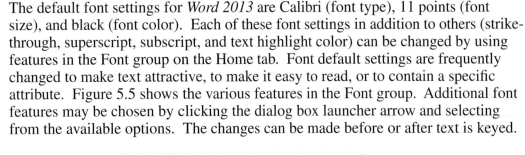

Figure 5.5 *Font features*

1. Open *df 47c font* and move your pointer over each feature in the Font group on the Home tab to display and read the name and description of each feature.

2. Follow the directions in the file to use the font features in the Font group on the Home tab.

3. Save the document as *47c font* and close it.

Page Numbers in Headers and Footers

WP Insert/Header & Footer/Page Number

TIP To exit a header or footer, double-click outside the header or footer area.

A **header** is text (such as a title, name, page number, date, etc.) printed in the top margin of a page. Letters, tables, and reports that are longer than one page often contain a header. A **footer** is similar to a header, except the information is placed at the bottom of the page.

You can insert a **page number** into the header or footer by selecting an option in the Page Number feature in the Header & Footer group on the Insert tab (see Figure 5.6), or you can format your own.

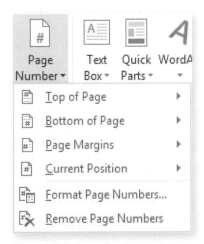

Figure 5.6 *Page Number options*

Position WordArt

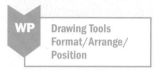

WP | Drawing Tools Format/Arrange/Position

TIP To nudge an object, hold down the CTRL key while pressing an arrow key.

WordArt can be moved like any other object. You can reposition it by dragging it, or you can use the Position feature (see Figure 8.3) to choose from a variety of vertical and horizontal positions.

To drag a selected object, move the pointer over the object's perimeter and click and drag it to the desired position when the four-headed arrow appears. Holding down the Shift key as you drag will move the object horizontally or vertically in a straight line. Once you move it near the desired location, you can nudge it to the desired position (see Tip at the left).

To use the Position feature, select the WordArt and click the Position button in the Arrange group on the Drawing Tools Format tab to display the various horizontal and vertical options (see Figure 8.3). Select the desired position.

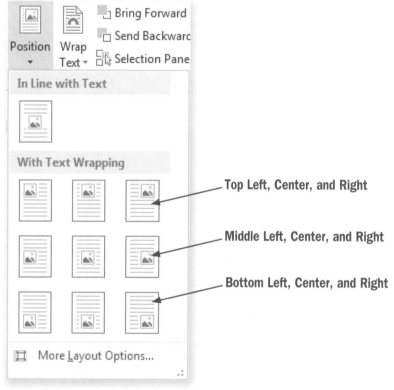

Figure 8.3 *Position options*

1. If needed, open *59a wordart*.

2. Select **WordArt Example 1** and position it at the top right.

3. Select **WordArt Example 3** and position it at the bottom center.

4. Select **WordArt Example 2** and position it in the middle center.

5. Select **WordArt Example 1** and drag or nudge it so it ends near the 6" point on the horizontal Ruler.

6. Preview the document to see if the WordArt objects are aligned correctly. Save the document as *59b wordart*, but do not close it.

1. Open *df 47d report*. Format the text with Line Spacing 2.0 and remove any extra space after the paragraphs. Replace 20-- with the current year.

2. Access the Page Number options (Insert/Header & Footer/Page Number) and select Plain Number 3 from the Top of Page options. Key your last name beginning at the blinking cursor that is to the left of the page number, and then tap the Space Bar once to insert a space between your last name and the page number. Double-click outside the header to exit it.

3. Insert a footer that uses the Plain Number 2 style for the page numbers. Exit the footer area.

4. Save the document as *47d report* and close it.

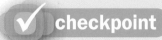

Review your document. Both pages should have your last name and page number right-aligned as a header and a number centered as a footer.

47E

MLA Style Report

TIP To close an application, you can also right-click its title bar icon and select Close from the pop-up menu that appears.

Your teachers may have you use a certain format when you write a report. In this lesson, you will learn to use a format suggested by the MLA (Modern Language Association). The MLA format is used in many schools. A sample report is shown on p. 176.

For MLA report format, all margins are 1". The writer's last name and the page number appear in a header. The name and page number are right-aligned in the header area. Line spacing of 2.0 with 0 points after paragraphs is used for all lines (except the header). Report heading lines appear at the top of the report on separate lines and are aligned at the left margin. The headings are the writer's name, teacher's name, subject name, and date (day/month/year style). The report title comes after the headings and is centered. The first lines of paragraphs are indented 0.5".

1. In a new, blank document, key the report on the next page in MLA format as shown. Insert the writer's last name and page number right-aligned in a header.

2. Proofread the report and correct any errors. Save the document as *47e report* and close it.

COLLABORATION

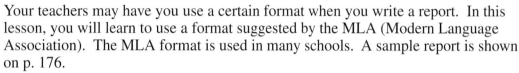

Exchange reports with a classmate. Check each other's report to see if MLA-style guidelines were followed.

47F

Compose an MLA Report

1. Open a new, blank document. Compose a short report (one to two pages) about yourself. Format the report in MLA style.

2. Use your name, your teacher's name, your class name, and the current date for the headings. Key your name and the word **Autobiography** for the title. For the body:

   • Tell about when and where you were born.

   • Talk briefly about your parents, brothers and sisters, or other family members.

   • Describe your physical appearance and your personality.

   • Talk about your interests or hobbies.

   • Name one or two jobs that you might like to have in the future.

3. Save the document as *47f report* and close it.

WordArt

In Lesson 59, you will:

59A *Create WordArt.*
59B *Position WordArt.*
59C *Edit WordArt.*
59D *Create, position, and format WordArt.*

59A

Create WordArt

> **TIP** WordArt can also be created after the text has been keyed. To use this method, key the text for the WordArt, select it, access the WordArt gallery, and select the desired style.

WordArt is a feature that allows you to change text into a graphic. Use the WordArt gallery to apply predesigned font colors, shapes, and other effects to text for a decorative effect.

To create WordArt, click the desired WordArt style (see Figure 8.1) from the WordArt gallery in the Text group on the Insert tab.

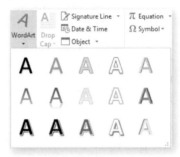

Figure 8.1 *WordArt style gallery*

After a style is selected, a WordArt text box will open and display sample text (see Figure 8.2). Replace the sample text to create your WordArt.

Figure 8.2 *WordArt text box*

WP Insert/Text/WordArt

1. Open a new, blank *Word* document.

2. Use the path at the left to access the WordArt gallery shown in Figure 8.1.

3. Select a style that you choose. Replace the text in the WordArt text box with **My WordArt Example 1** and then click outside the text box to deselect it.

4. Move your pointer about 0.5" below your WordArt and then double-click to position the insertion point in a new paragraph where WordArt will be inserted. Using a different style from the WordArt gallery, insert **My WordArt Example 2**.

5. Using a different style from the WordArt gallery, insert **My WordArt Example 3** about 0.5" below the second WordArt example.

6. Save the document as *59a wordart*, but do not close it.

1" top, bottom, and side margins

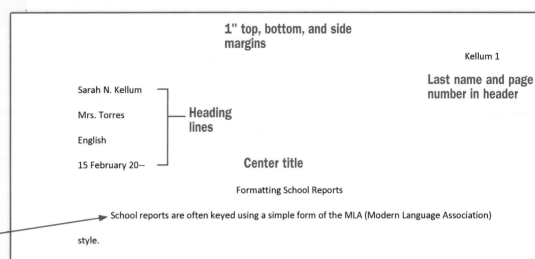

Kellum 1

Last name and page number in header

Sarah N. Kellum

Mrs. Torres ⎤ **Heading lines**

English

15 February 20-- ⎦

Center title

Formatting School Reports

Line spacing 2.0 with 0 point space after for all lines and 0.5" indent on first lines of paragraphs → School reports are often keyed using a simple form of the MLA (Modern Language Association) style.

The top, bottom, left, and right margins on all pages are 1 inch. Right-align a page number in a header on each page. The writer's last name should come before the page number.

Double-space the entire report. The report heading lines begin 1 inch from the top of the page. Left-align and double-space the report heading lines. They include the writer's name, teacher's name, subject name, and date (day/month/year style) on separate lines.

Center the report title below the date. The title is keyed using rules for capitalizing and punctuating titles. The report title may be keyed in a slightly larger font size to make it stand out. However, it should not be underlined or placed in quotation marks.

Report in MLA Format

Chapter 8 Desktop Publishing

Lessons 59–62

Everyone sees and uses flyers, brochures, and newsletters. You may have read a flyer giving details about an upcoming dance. You may have received a brochure when you had your school picture taken, explaining the different buying options. Your principal may send a newsletter to parents to keep them informed of what is happening in your school.

All of these documents use **desktop publishing (DTP)**. DTP is closely related to word processing. Both require similar skills, but DTP requires additional skills. These new skills are needed to design and lay out documents that do not follow a standard format like letters and reports. Also, DTP uses **graphics** with text to make a good visual impression. The graphics you will learn in this chapter include WordArt, text boxes, shapes, and pictures. You will learn to insert, resize, position, and format graphics to deliver an effective message.

Datacraft Co Ltd/Getty Images

Outlines and MLA Reports with Citations

Learning Outcomes

Data Files:

df 48b report
df 48c outline
df 48d indents
df 48f sources

In Lesson 48, you will:

48A *Learn about bulleted and numbered lists.*
48B *Insert a bulleted list in an MLA report.*
48C *Make an outline using the numbered list feature.*
48D *Learn about paragraph indents.*
48E *Insert a manual page break.*
48F *Format an MLA report with citations.*
48G *Research a topic and prepare a report in MLA format.*

48A

Bulleted and Numbered Lists

WP Home/Paragraph/
Bullets or Numbering

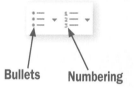

Bullets   Numbering

TIP You can apply bullets or numbering to text that has already been keyed. Select the items for the list. Click the Bullets or Numbering button in the Paragraph group on the Home tab.

Bulleted and numbered lists are used for a variety of reasons. You may want to prepare an outline for your report using one of the list features. Or you may want to create a list in a document. For example, you might list steps for doing a task such as baking a cake. Outlines and lists can be formatted with bullets or numbers. **Bullets** are characters or graphics (squares, circles, pictures) that appear before each item in the list. Use bullets for a list when the items can be in any order.

Other lists have a number before each item in the list. Use a numbered list when the items need to be in a certain order. For example, when baking a cake, you would not list the step for putting the cake in the oven before the steps for adding the flour, milk, and eggs.

The Bullets and Numbering features (see buttons at the left) allow you to select styles for bullets or numbering from lists in a library. The Bullet and Numbering Libraries are shown in Figure 5.7. Note that some styles for an ordered (numbered) list use letters.

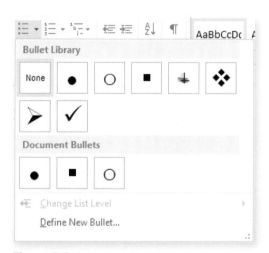
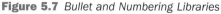
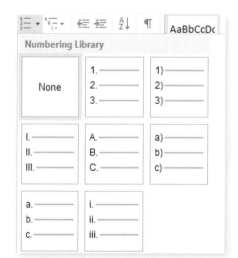

Figure 5.7 *Bullet and Numbering Libraries*

Asking for a Reference

The information on your job application may lead an employer to take a closer look at you. If someone is thinking about hiring you, they may then ask for references. A **reference** is someone who knows you and can tell an employer what kind of person you are.

1. Open *df c7 references*. Save the document as *c7 references*.

2. Use the instructions in the data file to create a table that lists four possible references. Format the table as directed. Then convert a copy of the table to text. Answer questions 1 and 5 and key your answers in the document.

3. Follow step 6 to write a letter to ask someone to serve as a reference for you. Save, print, and close your documents.

Career Exploration Portfolio

Online Resources:

ngl.cengage.com/c21jr3e

Activity 6

To complete this activity, you will need the Student Interest Survey that you filled out in Career Exploration Portfolio Activity 1. Completing Career Exploration Activities 2–5 would also be helpful but not mandatory.

1. Review your Student Interest Survey. Note your *second* Career Cluster of interest. Reread its description.

2. Go to http://www.careertech.org. Click the **Career Technical Education** button, then click Career Clusters to open the Career Clusters page. Click your second Career Cluster choice.

3. Scroll through the categories available within that Career Cluster. Click the Knowledge & Skills Statements **Excel** link under the category you are most interested in to download it to your system. (Choose the same category, or Pathway, that you used in Activity 3 if you completed it.)

4. Locate the downloaded workbook on your system and open it. Scroll down and read the knowledge and skill statements for this career.

5. Think about the knowledge and skills you have gained from classes at school, after-school activities, and other experiences. Do they match any of the knowledge and skills listed in this file? If not, how can you gain them?

6. Write a summary of what you discovered through this activity. Save the document as *c7 career 2 skills*, print, and close it.

1. In a new, blank document, key the following text and then tap ENTER.

   I need to take these three books home this evening:

2. Choose a bulleted list from the Bullet Library and then key the following three words. Tap ENTER after each word.

   Math

   English

   Science

3. To end the bulleted list, tap the BACKSPACE key as needed to move the insertion point to the left margin.

4. Key this text below the last bulleted item and then tap ENTER.

   These are my homework priorities for this weekend:

5. Choose a numbered list from the Numbering Library and key the following three lines. Tap ENTER after each line.

   Write a draft of my English theme.

   Do end-of-chapter math problems.

   Begin science project.

6. Tap BACKSPACE as needed to end the numbered list and move the insertion point to the left margin.

7. Key your name beginning at the insertion point. Save the document as *48a lists* and close it.

48B

MLA Report with Bulleted List

1. Open *df 48b report*. Format the document in correct MLA style. Use your name as the person writing the report. Create an appropriate header. Change 20-- to the current year in the report heading.

2. Change the numbered list to a bulleted list.

3. Check the format. Proofread carefully. Make corrections as needed. Save the document as *48b report* and close it.

48C

Outline Using the Numbering Feature

WP   Home/Paragraph/
Numbering
Home/Paragraph/
Decrease Indent or
Increase Indent

An **outline** is a document that gives the main points of a subject. Outlines are helpful in planning and organizing reports. Frequently, they are prepared using the Numbering or Multilevel List feature. The Multilevel List button is to the right of the Numbering button. In this lesson, you will use the Numbering feature to prepare an outline that has multiple levels.

To move from one level to another within your outline, you can use the Decrease Indent or Increase Indent features. (See Figure 5.8.) You also can move to different levels by using the TAB key or the SHIFT + TAB keys. Tapping the TAB key will move you to a lower level. Tapping the TAB key while pressing the SHIFT key will move you to a higher level in your outline.

Figure 5.8 *Decrease and Increase Indent*

ACROSS THE CURRICULUM

Academic Connections

Data Files:

df c7 bank form
df c7 profits
df c7 application
  instructions
df c7 electronic
  application
df c7 references

Math: Reconcile a Checking Account

When you keep money in a checking account, you should keep accurate records. A **check register** is the form on which you write information each time you make a transaction. When you write a check, make a deposit, or withdraw money, you should write it in your check register.

Your bank will send you a statement each month. The **bank statement** is a report that lists all of your transactions for the month. You should compare your check register to the bank statement.

1. Start *Word*. Open the document *df c7 bank form*. Read the information about bank statements and review the example.

2. Follow the instructions to complete the two activities.

3. Save the document as *c7 bank form*, print, and close it.

About Business

Calculating Profits

Most businesses try to predict future sales. Managers compare sales to costs and expenses to figure out if the business will make a profit. Sometimes sales are lower than expected. This may be due to the economy, competition, or other factors. When sales are low, some companies try to increase profits by reducing expenses or lowering the price of their products.

1. Open *df c7 profits*.

2. Follow the steps in the data file to help a bike company set prices.

3. Save the document as *c7 profits* and close it.

Life Success Builder

Filling out a Job Application

When you apply for a job, you usually have to fill out a job application. An application asks for your name, address, age, and other basic information. Most applications also ask about your experience.

1. Open *df c7 application instructions*.

2. Read the information and instructions in the data file. Use it to complete the electronic application provided.

Activity 1

1. In a new, blank document, key the text below as an outline. Use default margin settings. Center the outline title. Use a numbered list with Roman numerals for the outline topics and Decrease and Increase Indents to move from one level to another.

2. Proofread your outline and correct any misspelled words and formatting errors. Save the document as *48c outline1* and close it.

Computer Graphics

   I. Introduction

  II. Computer charts

     a. Bar charts

        i. Vertical bar

       ii. Horizontal bar

     b. Circle charts

        i. Whole circle

       ii. Exploded circle

     c. Line charts

        i. Without shaded areas

       ii. With shaded areas

Activity 2

1. Open *df 48c outline*. Select all the text in the document. Choose a numbering style from the Numbering Library to format the text as an outline.

2. Use Decrease Indent and Increase Indent as needed to show that *Breakfast* and *Lunch* are at the first level; *cereal, toast, orange juice, sandwich, chicken soup,* and *apple* are at the second level; and the remaining items are at the third level.

3. Check the format of the outline and make any necessary changes. Save the document as *48c outline2* and close it.

Key a 30" timed writing on each line, striving to key more on each attempt. Your *gwam* is shown below the lines.

TECHNIQUE TIP
Keep your eyes on the copy as you reach out with your little finger and tap the ENTER key quickly.

1 Paula went out for track.
2 Jan told me to see that movie.
3 Which search engine did Carmen use?
4 Paul bought the video game last weekend.
5 Sandy had a meeting with Mr. Sanchez at noon.
6 My coach told me to be ready for a difficult game.

gwam 30" | 2 | 4 | 6 | 8 | 10 | 12 | 14 | 16 | 18 | 20 |

Speed Building

1. Key three 1' timed writings on each paragraph, striving to key more on each timing; determine *gwam*.

2. Key a 2' timed writing on both paragraphs combined, striving to maintain your highest 1' *gwam*.

A all letters used

gwam 1' 2'

	1'	2'
We live and learn in an information age where	9	5
expert computer skills are extremely important.	19	10
Your teachers have probably told you that every	28	14
year. Your school has included this technology	38	19
course in your studies so you can acquire these	47	24
important skills to use at school, home, and	56	28
play so you can be more productive.	64	32
Many people believe that having an ability to	9	37
key by touch is just as important as learning to	19	42
write with a pen or pencil. Touch keyboarding is	29	47
an amazing skill that rewards you every time you	38	52
use a keyboard to enter information. This skill	48	57
enables you to be more efficient when you use	57	62
software to write papers, compose e-mail messages,	68	68
and so on.	70	69

gwam 1' | 1 | 2 | 3 | 4 | 5 | 6 | 7 | 8 | 9 | 10 |
     2' | 1 | 2 | 3 | 4 | 5 |

21st Century Skills

CuriousCatPhotos/Alamy

Media Literacy Think about the various ways you receive information. In addition to classroom lectures and studies, you might watch a television show, listen to a radio broadcast, browse the Web, or read a magazine. As you process the information you receive daily, you form impressions and make interpretations and judgments. Consciously—or subconsciously—the many messages you process every day influence the decisions you make and have a significant impact on the way you live your life.

Think Critically

1. Think of an advertisement you have recently seen or heard. Where did you see or hear the ad? What was being advertised? How did the ad influence your opinion of the advertiser? Would you make a purchase based on the ad?

2. Write a short report about one of your favorite products (e.g., a brand of clothing or shoes or a favorite food or drink). Include at least three paragraphs that identify the product, who makes it, the target market, the format in which you saw it advertised (print, broadcast, Web, etc.), and the key features of the product that convinced you to buy it. Save the document as directed by your instructor.

3. Share the report with your class. As a class, discuss the appeal of the product and why consumers with different demographic characteristics (such as age, gender, race, income level, etc.) would or would not buy it.

48D

Paragraph Indents

WP Home/Paragraph/ Paragraph dialog box launcher

In an MLA report, long quotes (four or more keyed lines) are indented 1" from the left margin to make them stand out from the rest of the report body. You can indent the paragraph by using the Increase Indent feature or by setting the left indentation in the Indents and Spacing options in the Paragraph dialog box shown in Figure 5.9. You can see an example of an indented quote on page 182.

In an MLA report, the list of references used is titled Works Cited. In other report styles, it may be titled References or Bibliography. The list of works cited is formatted using the **hanging indent** feature. The hanging indent format moves all lines except the first line away from the left margin. You can see an example of a hanging indent on page 182. With this indent style, the authors' names stand out and are easier to find. The options on the Indents and Spacing tab in the Paragraph dialog box shown in Figure 5.9 can be used to set these special indents.

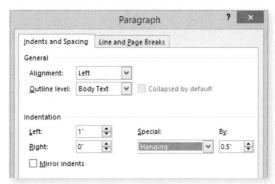

Figure 5.9 *Paragraph dialog box*

KEYBOARDING SKILLBUILDING

Warmup Practice

Key each line twice. If time permits, key the lines again.

Alphabet

1 Wesley Van Jantz quickly proofed the biology exam.

Figure/Symbol

2 On 08/13/07 Jorge paid invoice #291 for $2,358.64.

Speed

3 Pamela may hand signal to the big tug by the dock.

gwam 1' | 1 | 2 | 3 | 4 | 5 | 6 | 7 | 8 | 9 | 10 |

Technique Mastery of Individual Letters Keying Technique

Key each line twice, striving to maintain a continuous pace.

TECHNIQUE TIP
Fingers should be curved and upright.

N No one knew Nathan N. Nevins was not here at noon.

O I told Jose and Brook not to mop the floors today.

P Philippe paid for the pepper and paprika for Pepe.

Q Quinton quit questioning the adequacy of the quiz.

R Carrie, correct the two problems before departing.

S Steven and I saw Sam at Sally's session on Sunday.

T Tim bottled the water after talking with the maid.

U He urged us to put the rugs under the four trucks.

V Vivian Von Vogt took the vivid van to the village.

W Will Wesley work on the walnut wall for two weeks?

X The tax expert explained the tax exam's existence.

Y Jay may be ready to pay you your money on Tuesday.

Z Zelda was puzzled by the sizzling heat at the zoo.

gwam 30" | 2 | 4 | 6 | 8 | 10 | 12 | 14 | 16 | 18 | 20 |

1. Open *df 48d indents* from your data files.

2. This document contains part of a report. Select the second paragraph of the report, which is a long quote. Indent this paragraph by setting the Left indentation to 1" on the Indents and Spacing tab of the Paragraph dialog box as shown in Figure 5.9.

3. Move to the next page of the document. This is a Works Cited page. Select all of the entries after the title and use a 0.5" hanging indent for the entries as shown in Figure 5.9.

4. Save the document as *48d indents* and close it.

48E

Manual Page Breaks

WP Page Layout/Page Setup/Breaks

TIP A manual page break can also be inserted by holding the CTRL key down while tapping ENTER.

TIP Refer to the status bar at the lower-left corner of the screen. This bar shows the page you are on and the total pages in the document. PAGE 3 OF 3

Two types of **page breaks** are used to signal the end of a page. The software places *automatic* page breaks when the current page is full. You can enter a *manual* page break when you want to begin a new page before the current page is full. Manual page breaks, referred to as Page in Figure 5.10, remain where are inserted unless they are deleted.

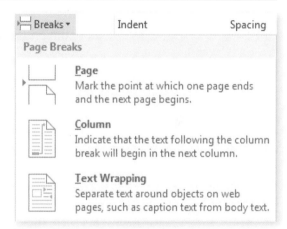

Figure 5.10 *Page break options*

1. In a new, blank document, key the following line and then enter a manual page break at the end of the line.

   This text is line 1 on page 1.

2. Key the following line and then enter a manual page break at the end of the line.

   This text is line 1 on page 2.

3. Key the following line.

   This text is line 1 on page 3.

4. The insertion point should be at the end of line 1 of page 3. Look at the status bar. It should show **PAGE 3 OF 3**.

5. Revise the text on page 3 to read:

   This text is also on page 2.

6. Delete the manual page break by placing the insertion point at the beginning of the last line of text you revised. Tap the BACKSPACE key twice to delete the manual page break. The last two lines of text should now appear on the second page. Close the document without saving.

5. Insert a row at the top, merge the cells, and key the following main heading:

SUPER GIANT CORPORATION UNITS SOLD

6. Change the height of row 1 to 0.5" and the height of rows 2–7 to 0.3".

7. Apply a table style to make the table attractive and easy to read.

8. Right-align all numbers and center-align main and column headings. Vertically center all cell entries. Center the table horizontally and vertically on the page.

9. Save the document as *c7 table1* and close it.

Create and Format a Table

1. Open *df c7 list*.

2. Convert the list to a table using the tabs as the separators and AutoFit Contents.

3. Sort the list by last name and then first name, both in ascending order.

4. Insert a row at the top and key **BATTING AVERAGES** as a centered main heading.

5. Apply an appropriate table style and make formatting changes so that the table is attractive and easy to read. Center the table horizontally.

6. Save the document as *c7 table2* but do not close it.

7. Sort *c7 table2* by Average in descending order.

8. Save the document as *c7 table3* and close it.

TIP In step 7, since the table includes two header rows (a main heading and column heading), select only the rows you want sorted (rows 3-9); then perform the sort. Otherwise, the software recognizes the main heading as the header row and includes the column headings in the sort.

Works Cited Page Using Indents and Manual Page Breaks

In an MLA report, notes are placed in the body to mark material taken from other sources. These notes are called citations. For example, in a report that you write, you might quote from a magazine article. You should cite (give information about) where this material came from.

Citations are placed in parentheses in the report body. The following model shows an example of an in-text citation. Citations include the name(s) of the author(s) and page number(s) of the material.

Quotes of up to three keyed lines are placed in quotation marks. Long quotes (four or more keyed lines) are left-indented 1", as shown in the model. Summarized material is not put in quotation marks.

Lillian Jackson Braun is a popular mystery writer. Many people enjoy reading her books about an amateur detective and his cats. The cats, Koko and Yum Yum, know how to make themselves at home anywhere.

Indent long quotes 1"
It was their first night in the cabin by the creek. Qwilleran placed the cats' blue cushion on one bunk. They settled down contentedly, while he retired to the other bunk. Sometime during the night, the arrangement changed; in the morning Qwilleran was sharing his pillow with Yum Yum, and Koko was snuggled in the crook of his knee. (Braun 123) ◄—— **In-text citation**

All references cited in a report in MLA style are listed on a separate page. This page is the last page of the report. It is called the Works Cited page. An example of a Works Cited page is shown in the following model.

1" top and side margins
Title centered

Anderson 3

Writer's name and page number in header

Works Cited

Ackerman, Jennifer. "Cranes." National Geographic Apr. 2004: 44.

0.5" hanging indent for paragraphs —►
Anson, Chris M., and Robert A. Schwegler. The Longman Handbook for Writers and Readers,
3rd ed. New York: Addison-Wesley Educational Publications, Inc., 2003.

Braun, Lillian Jackson. The Cat Who Went Up the Creek. New York: Jove Books, 2003. **Line Spacing 2.0 for all lines**

Hoggatt, Jack P., and Jon A. Shank. Applied Computer Keyboarding. 6th ed. Cincinnati:
South-Western Cengage Learning, 2009.

"Mesa Verde." National Park Service. 13 July 2004 http://www.nps.gov/meve/index.htm.

At least 1" bottom margin

Before You Move On

Answer **True** or **False** to each question to review what you have learned in Chapter 7.

1. Table rows run horizontally, and columns run vertically. LO 55A

2. The place where a row and a column cross each other is called a subrow. LO 55A

3. To select an entire table, click the Table Move handle. LO 56B

4. When AutoFit Contents is used, the table grid may have varying column widths, but none will be narrower than 1 inch. LO 55B

5. Center tables vertically by selecting Center in the Layout tab of the Page Setup dialog box. LO 56A

6. Cells in adjacent rows and cells in adjacent columns can be merged. LO 56B

7. Rows can be added above or below existing rows. LO 56C

8. All row heights in a table must be the same size. LO 57A

9. The default placement for data in a cell is left and top alignment. LO 57A

10. Only table columns with numbers can be sorted. LO 58A

Applying What You Have Learned

Data Files:

df c7 table1
df c7 list

Revise and Format a Table

1. Open *df c7 table1*.

2. Add a column at the right and key the following information in that column.

April
504
605
589
1698

3. Add a row after Helen Goins and key the following information. Then correct the totals in row 6.

Jim Jones	582	631	768	604

4. Make column A 1.3" and columns B–E 1".

This page should have the same margins and header as the report body. The title, Works Cited, is centered at the top of the page. Line Spacing 2.0 is used for all lines on the Works Cited page. The works are placed in alphabetical order by author's last names, if known. If the author is not known, use the title of the work. A hanging indent is applied to the paragraphs.

1. Open *df 48f sources*. Add a header for the writer's last name and the page number.

2. Insert (**Anson and Schwegler 619**) as a citation at the end of the third sentence between the end quotation mark and the period.

3. Insert (**Hoggatt and Shank 169**) as a citation between the last word in the final sentence and the period.

4. Review the format of a Works Cited page on the previous page and then create a Works Cited page using the following two sources and the MLA style.

Anson, Chris M., and Robert A. Schwegler. <u>The Longman Handbook for Writers and Readers</u>, 3rd ed. New York: Addison-Wesley Educational Publications, Inc., 2003.

Hoggatt, Jack P., and Jon A. Shank. <u>Applied Computer Keyboarding</u>, 6th ed. Cincinnati: South-Western Cengage Learning, 2009.

5. Your Works Cited page should look similar to the model on page 182 (but with only two Works Cited entries). Save the document as *48f sources* and close it.

✓ checkpoint

Did you place the period after the in-text citations? Is your Works Cited page on a separate page? Does page 2 have a header with the page number? Is Line Spacing 2.0 used for all lines?

48G

MLA Report with Works Cited

☞ Instant Message

Enter **national parks** or the park name in a search engine to find information on the Internet.

1. Do research and write a report about a U.S. national park. Find information about national parks in your local library or on the Internet. Then choose a park. In your report, you should include information such as:

   • The park location.

   • A general description.

   • Primary attractions.

   • Other interesting information.

2. Use at least two sources of information about the park. Note the reference information for each source.

3. Format the report in MLA style. Use an appropriate header, an appropriate title, and appropriate report headings. Write at least three paragraphs for the body. Include at least two in-text citations. Create a Works Cited page as the last page of the report. List all of the sources you used.

4. Proofread carefully and correct any errors or make necessary revisions to your text. Save the document as *48g report* and close it.

COLLABORATION

✓ checkpoint Trade papers with a classmate. Ask your classmate to proofread your paper and mark errors you may have missed. Make corrections if necessary.

6. Format the table using an appropriate table style. Apply **Heading 1** style to the main heading and **Heading 2** style to the column headings. Center-align the main and column headings. Center the table horizontally and vertically.

7. Insert the following information at an appropriate place in the table.

```
Flogg         Martha      Harding       102.13
Sanchez       Corina      Harding       101.14
```

8. Change the height of rows 3–10 to 0.3".

9. Save the document as *58d table*. Print and close it.

COLLABORATION

 **checkpoint** Compare your table to a classmate's table. Is the sort correct? Were the rows inserted at the proper point? Is the table attractive and easy to read? Are there any errors?

58E

Research and Design a Table

COLLABORATION

1. Working with another student, choose ten first names for people. Do research in your local library or on the Internet to find the meaning of each name. Enter **first name meanings** or similar search terms in a search engine to find information on the Internet. Try to find similar information about each name so that you can report your findings in a table.

2. Design a table to report your research findings. The table should have a title, column headings, and cell entries to show each name and the information you learned about the name.

3. Key the information in the table and format the table to make it attractive and easy to read.

4. Save the document as *58e table*. Print and then close the document.

Lesson 49 Reports in Standard, Unbound Format

Data Files:

df 49a report
df 49d report

Learning Outcomes

In Lesson 49, you will:

49A *Use the Spelling & Grammar feature.*
49B *Learn the Different First Page feature.*
49C *Apply different styles to text.*
49D *Learn about standard, unbound report formats.*
49E *Format a standard, unbound report with references.*

49A

Spelling and Grammar

WP   Review/Proofing/
     Spelling & Grammar

Errors in a document can distract the reader, so it is important that you produce error-free documents. The Spelling & Grammar feature can assist you in proof-reading. This feature compares the words you have keyed with words in the software's dictionary. As you key, a red wavy line appears under words not listed in the dictionary. A blue wavy line appears under words or phrases that have potential grammar, style, and contextual errors. You can correct these errors as you key by right-clicking a word above the wavy line and selecting one of the options on the shortcut menu that opens (shown in Figure 5.11 at the left). If you prefer to make all corrections when you are finished keying, you can use the options in the Spelling task pane (shown in Figure 5.11 at the right), which appears when you click the Spelling & Grammar button in the Proofing group on the Review tab.

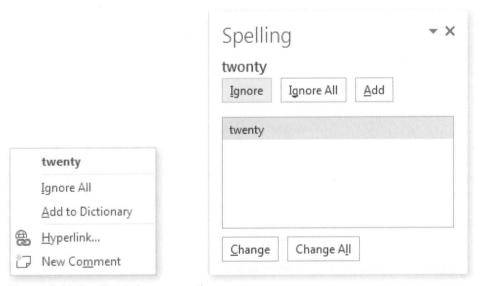

Figure 5.11 *Spelling & Grammar options*

Convert a Table to Text

WP · Table Tools Layout/
Data/Convert to Text

You can convert a table into text that is separated by tabs, commas, or other separators by using the **Convert to Text** feature.

1. Open *df 58a table2*.

2. To convert the table to text, click a cell in the table. Follow the path at the left to the Convert to Text button and click it to open the Convert Table to Text dialog box shown in Figure 7.17.

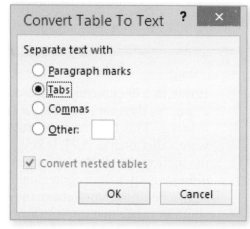

Figure 7.17 *Convert Table to Text dialog box*

3. Click the radio button for Tabs if necessary. Click **OK**; the list should appear as a four-column list with 16 rows.

4. Save the document as *58c text* and close it.

58D

Sort and Convert

1. Open a new, blank document. Set Left Tabs at 3", 4.5", and 6".

2. Key the following list, using the TAB key to move across each row.

```
Last          First        School        Time
Belardus      Colleen      York          100.13
Davis         Kylie        Harris        100.72
Flogg         Martha       Jamestown     103.83
McLaughlin    Sarah        York          104.12
Toth          Jessica      Harris        103.45
Vernon        Andrea       Jamestown     102.69
```

3. Convert the text to a four-column table. AutoFit the table to its contents.

4. Sort the table by School in ascending order and then by Time in descending order.

5. Insert a row at the top of the grid, merge the cells, and key the following as a main heading:

GIRLS 100-YARD BUTTERFLY RESULTS

1. Open *df 49a report*. Scroll through the text to see the red and blue wavy lines beneath text that the word processor has indicated as incorrect. All names are spelled correctly.

2. "Correct" the two words in the first paragraph by right-clicking them and using the shortcut menu that appears.

3. Use the Spelling task pane to "correct" the remaining errors.

4. Proofread the document and correct any errors that Spelling & Grammar did not detect.

5. Save the document as *49a spell* and close it.

TIP Since Spelling & Grammar does not detect all possible errors, you must proofread carefully after using the feature and correct any undetected errors.

49B

Different First Page

WP Header & Footer Tools Design/Options/ Different First Page

When you format a report in MLA style, page numbers are right-aligned in a header and included on each page. In other report styles, the page number is not shown on the first page and page numbers may appear at the top or bottom of the page aligned at the left, at the right, or centered.

When the page number (or header or footer) is not to appear on the first page, click in the header or footer area to display the Header & Footer Tools Design tab, and select Different First Page in the Options group (shown in Figure 5.12).

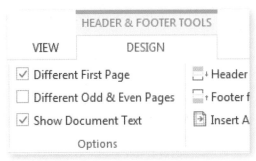

Figure 5.12 *Different First Page option*

1. Open *49a spell*.

2. Insert a page number centered at the bottom of each page.

3. Do not display the page number on page 1.

4. Verify that the page number does not appear on page 1 but that it does appear on page 2. Save the document as *49b page* and close it.

TIP Choose **Number** for the Type when sorting by column R. Choose **Text** when sorting by the Last Name column.

COLLABORATION

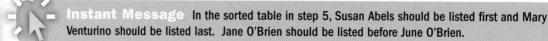

Instant Message In the sorted table in step 5, Susan Abels should be listed first and Mary Venturino should be listed last. Jane O'Brien should be listed before June O'Brien.

6. Save the document and keep it open.

7. Sort the data by column R (runs) in descending order and then by the Last Name column in ascending order.

8. Save the document as *58a sort2*. Print and close the document.

**checkpoint** Compare your *58a sort2* with that of a classmate. If the data are not sorted correctly, identify what is wrong and sort the table again.

Table Sorts 3 and 4

1. Open *df 58a table2*.

2. Sort the data by School in ascending order and then by Last in ascending order.

3. Save the document as *58a sort3* and leave it open.

4. Sort the data by School in ascending order and then by Points in descending order.

5. Save the document as *58a sort4* and close it.

58B

Convert Text to a Table

WP Insert/Tables/Table/ Convert Text to Table

Another way to create a table is to convert text that is separated by a tab, a comma, or another separator character into a table. For example, if you have a list of first names, last names, and birth dates separated by tabs and want to convert the list into a table, you can use the **Convert Text to Table** feature. In this case, *Word* recognizes the tab as the separator and will divide the text into columns. The new paragraph mark at the end of each line will be used to begin a new row.

1. Open *df 58b list*.

2. To convert the text to a table, select the text and then follow the path at the left to open the Convert Text to Table dialog box shown in Figure 7.16.

3. If necessary, key **3** in the Number of columns box in the Table size section; choose **AutoFit to contents** in the AutoFit behavior section; and choose **Tabs** in the Separate text at section if it is not already selected. Click **OK**. The list should appear as a three-column table with 11 rows.

4. Save the document as *58b table* and close it.

Figure 7.16 *Convert Text to Table dialog box*

Home/Styles

Styles are collections of format settings for font, font size, color, paragraph spacing, alignment, and so on that are named and stored together in a style set. The default style set for *Word 2013* is named Word 2013, and the default style is named Normal. Each style set contains styles for a title, subtitle, various headings, and so on that can be quickly applied to text in a document to make it attractive and easy to read. Styles can be selected from the Styles gallery in the Styles group on the Home tab. (See Figure 5.13.)

Figure 5.13 *Styles gallery*

To see if you like how your text will appear with a specific style before you apply it, point to the thumbnail of the style you want. A live preview shows your text formatted with that style. If you like the style, click its thumbnail to apply the style to the selected text. You can then apply this style to other text you want to format the same way. Figure 5.14 shows text formatted using the Normal (default font style), Heading 1, and Title styles.

- The Normal style uses Calibri 11-point black font, 1.08 line spacing, and 8-point spacing after paragraphs.

- The Heading 1 style uses Calibri Light 16-point blue font and 12-point spacing before paragraphs.

- The Title style uses Calibri Light 28-point black font and 0-point spacing after paragraphs.

Style Name	Style Example
Normal	This is keyed using Normal style
Heading 1	This is keyed using Heading 1 style
Title	This is keyed using Title style

Figure 5.14 *Style examples*

If the style you want is not displayed as a thumbnail in the gallery, use the More button to display additional choices.

You can choose a different style set, color choices, and fonts by clicking options in the Document Formatting group on the Design tab.

1. Open *49b page*.

2. Format the report title in Title style.

3. Format the side headings in Heading 1 style. *Note:* You can use the Format Painter to quickly copy the format of the first side heading to each of the other side headings.

4. Save the document as *49c styles* and close it.

Sort and Convert Tables

Learning Outcomes

Data Files:

df 58a table1
df 58a table2
df 58b list

In Lesson 58, you will:

58A *Sort data in a table.*

58B *Convert text to a table.*

58C *Convert a table to text.*

58D *Sort and convert.*

58E *Research data and design a table.*

58A

Sort in Tables

Sort means to arrange or group items in a particular order. You can sort information in a table in ascending or descending order. **Ascending** order means A to Z for words. For numbers, ascending order means from the lowest to the highest number. **Descending** order means Z to A for words. For numbers, descending order means from the highest to the lowest number. You can sort information in the entire table or selected information in one or more columns.

Table Sorts 1 and 2

1. Open *df 58a table1.* Save the document as *58a sort1.*

WP Table Tools Layout/
Data/Sort

2. Click a cell in the table. Follow the path at the left to the Sort button. Click the **Sort** button to open the Sort dialog box shown in Figure 7.15.

Select a column to sort by

Select a column to sort by

Select to use a header row

Select a sort order

Select a sort order

Figure 7.15 *Sort dialog box*

3. If necessary, select **Last Name** from the Sort by drop-down list. This will cause the data to be sorted first by the person's last name. Text should appear for the Type. Select **Ascending** for the sort order if it is not already selected.

4. Select **First Name** in the first Then by box. This will cause the data to be sorted next by the person's first name. Text should appear for the Type. Select **Ascending** for the sort order if it is not already selected.

5. Click the radio button by *Header row* if it is not already selected. This option means that the first row in your table contains column headings that will not be included in the sort. Click **OK**.

Short reports are often prepared without covers and binders. If they are more than one page, a paper clip or staple in the upper-left corner usually holds them together. These reports are called **unbound reports** and are frequently formatted using a **standard format**.

The standard format for your reports will use the following:

Margins. Use the default margin settings on all pages and begin page 1 and the reference page at or near the 2" vertical position.

Page numbering. Do not number the first page; insert a centered page number in a footer or a right-aligned page number in a header for the second and subsequent pages.

Line spacing. Use the defaults (1.08 line spacing and 8 points of blank space after each paragraph).

Styles. Use Title style for the report title and Heading 1 style for the side headings in the default (Word 2013) style set.

Textual citations. Key textual citations in parentheses in the body of the report at the point where the credit for paraphrased or quoted material is given. Quotations that are fewer than four keyed lines are enclosed in quotation marks. Long quotations that occupy four or more keyed lines are indented 0.5" from the left margin.

Reference list. Key and format *References* in Title style near the 2" vertical position. Key each reference using a 0.5" hanging indent style. Use the same line spacing that is used for the report body. Number the reference list page in the same manner that page 2 and subsequent pages are numbered.

A model of the standard, unbound format is shown on page 188.

Digital Citizenship and Ethics

© Monkey Business Images/Shutterstock.com

COLLABORATION

You've probably used the Internet to gather information for a school project, or maybe you visit websites as part of your classroom learning, or perhaps you've accessed an online tutorial to learn about effective study habits or how to write better essays. E-learning, or online education, has become a popular and accessible way for learners at all levels to take classes and further their academic pursuits. Many colleges and universities now offer online degree programs, and businesses often use online and computer-based training for employees.

E-learning offers many advantages, including:

- Flexible scheduling, which enables learners to complete coursework when it's convenient for them.
- Self-paced learning, which allows participants to learn at their own pace as long as coursework is turned in by the due date.
- No transportation costs or hassles, as you typically work from your home computer.

As a class, discuss the following.

1. How have you used e-learning at home or in school within the last six months?
2. What are some drawbacks of taking online courses?

WP Table Tools Design/
Table Styles/Shading

6. To add shading to row 1, follow the path at the left to open the shading options from the Shading drop-down list. Select a light color from the Theme Colors or Standard Colors (shown in Figure 7.14) that you like. Row 1 should be shaded.

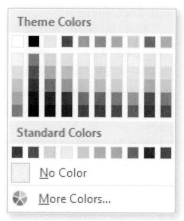

Figure 7.14 *Shading colors*

7. Save the document as *57b table2*. Print it but do not close it.

8. Experiment with applying borders and shading to other cells, rows, and columns in the table. Close the table without saving changes.

Digital Citizenship and Ethics

© Monkey Business Images/Shutterstock.com

Blogs are a common way for Web users to share their opinions, ideas, products, and services. A blog, which is derived from the words *Web log*, is an online personal journal or log typically written and maintained by an individual (referred to as a blogger). A blog consists of regular entries of commentary that often deal with issues that are sensitive to the blogger.

Blogs are easy to set up and enable just about anyone to write what they think and bring their opinions to the forefront for all to read. A feature of many blogs is the ability for readers to respond to content on the site with their own comments and thoughts, thus providing a forum that promotes dialog among people with a common interest. All blogs allow postings to be linked to other blogs, creating a network of blogs called the blogosphere. Some of the most popular blogs are *Mashable*, *TechCrunch*, and *The Huffington Post*. As a class, discuss the following:

1. What opportunities do blogs provide for education and collaboration?
2. What are some drawbacks of blogs?

1.08 line spacing with 8 points of space after paragraphs

Default 1" margins

Title style; title is keyed at or near the 2" vertical position

Internet Etiquette

What kind of Internet user are you? Are you the same kind of person on the Internet as you are when you meet face-to-face with a friend? Do you have respect for other people's time? Do you respect their privacy? Do you abuse the power the Internet gives you?

Rules of the Road ← **Heading 1 style**

Several informal "rules of the road" are being created as more and more people communicate with one another on the Internet. The rules are called "netiquette." Netiquette covers the dos and don'ts of online communication. It includes the guidelines everyone should follow to be courteous to others. By using the rules, you will help yourself look good and avoid wasting other people's time and energy (Netiquette Basics, 2014).

Don't Use Capital Letters

When corresponding on the Internet, do not use all caps. Use all caps only to draw the reader's attention to one or a few words. Those who use proper netiquette are likely to interpret an internet message that is keyed in ALL CAPS as "shouting" and rude. Those interpretations can affect how your message is received (NetworkEtiquette.net, 2014).

Don't Be Offensive

A good question to ask yourself when you are communicating on the Internet is, "Would I say this to the person if we were communicating face to face?" If you answer "No", then you need to revise the message and proofread it as often as needed until you can answer "Yes" to the question (Netiquette, 2014).

***References* is keyed at or near the 2" vertical position**

References ← **Title style**

Hanging indent

Netiquette. "The Core Rules of Netiquette." http://www.albion.com/netiquette/rule1.html (5 January 2014).

"Netiquette Basics." http://www.livinginternet.com/i/ia_nq_basics.htm (5 January 2014).

NetworkEtiquette.net. "The Rules of Netiquette." http://www.networketiquette.net/netiquette.htm (5 January 2014).

57B

Borders and Shading

WP Table Tools Design/
Borders/Borders

Borders are the printed lines around cells in a table. Borders can enhance the appearance of a table and make it easy to read. By default, tables are printed with a black 0.5-point solid line border around all cells. You can change the color, thickness, and style of the border. You can choose to have the border around all cells in the table or around selected cells. You also can choose to print the table without any borders.

Shading is a colored fill or background that can be applied to cells in a table. Shading also can enhance the appearance of your table and make it easy to read. You can use varying shades of gray or color for shading cells. Shading covers the selected area. It may be applied to the entire table or to selected cells, rows, or columns.

1. Open *57a table2* that you saved earlier in this lesson.

2. Select the table. To format the table without borders, use the path at the left to access the Borders drop-down list. Select No Border from the list as shown in Figure 7.13.

Figure 7.13 *Border options*

3. The table should now appear with no border lines. However, the table gridlines may be displayed. The light gray gridlines that appear on the screen will not print. If the gridlines are not displayed, click a cell in the table and then click the **Table Tools Layout** tab if necessary. In the Table group, click **View Gridlines**. If you want to hide the gridlines on the screen, click **View Gridlines** again.

4. Save the document as *57b table1* and do not close it.

5. To add a border around the main heading, select row 1 of the table. Choose the **Outside Borders** option from the Borders drop-down list. Row 1 should have a border.

1. Open *df 49d report*. Format all text in Calibri 11-point font. Verify that line spacing is set to 1.08 and that spacing after paragraph is set at 8 point.

2. Begin the report title near the 2" vertical position. Format the report title in Title style.

3. Format the four side headings in Heading 1 style.

4. Insert a page break after the last paragraph of the report. Format *References* in Title style near the 2" vertical position on the new page.

5. Format the references in 0.5" hanging indent style.

6. Insert a centered page number in the footer. Do not display the number on the first page.

7. Use Spelling & Grammar to check for and correct errors. Proofread to find additional errors, if any. Save the document as *49d report* and close it.

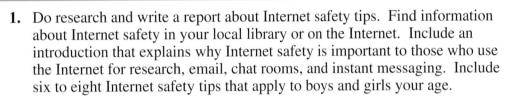

49E

Standard, Unbound Report with References

Instant Message

Enter **Internet safety** tips in a search engine to find information on the Internet.

1. Do research and write a report about Internet safety tips. Find information about Internet safety in your local library or on the Internet. Include an introduction that explains why Internet safety is important to those who use the Internet for research, email, chat rooms, and instant messaging. Include six to eight Internet safety tips that apply to boys and girls your age.

2. Use at least two sources of information. Note the reference information for each source.

3. Format the report in standard, unbound style. Use appropriate styles for the report title and side headings. Include at least two in-text citations. Create a References page as the last page of the report, listing all of the sources you used.

4. Use Spelling & Grammar, proofread carefully, and correct any errors or make necessary revisions to your text. Save the document as *49e report* and close it.

COLLABORATION

 **checkpoint** Trade papers with a classmate. Ask your classmate to proofread your paper and mark errors you may have missed. Make corrections if necessary.

Table 1

1. Open *df 57a table1*.

2. To change the row 1 height, click in row 1 and follow the ***Row Height*** path at the left. Key **0.5** in the Height box as shown in Figure 7.11.

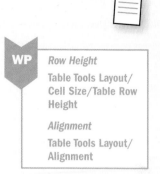

WP *Row Height*

Table Tools Layout/
Cell Size/Table Row
Height

Alignment

Table Tools Layout/
Alignment

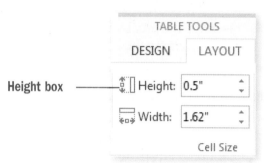

Height box

Figure 7.11 *Change row height.*

3. To change the text alignment, select the cells in row 1. Follow the ***Alignment*** path at the left to display the Alignment options. Click the **Align Center** button shown in Figure 7.12.

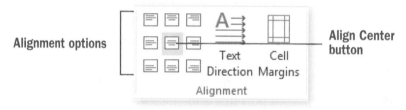

Alignment options

Align Center button

Figure 7.12 *Alignment group*

4. Using the process you used in step 2, set the height for rows 2–6 to 0.3". Set the vertical alignment for the cells to Align Center Left.

5. Save the document as *57a table1* and close it.

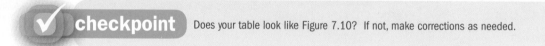

checkpoint Does your table look like Figure 7.10? If not, make corrections as needed.

Table 2

1. Open *df 57a table2*.

2. Change the height of row 1 to 0.7". Change the height of row 2 to 0.5". Change the height of the remaining rows to 0.3".

3. Change the alignment for all rows to Align Center.

4. Save the document as *57b table2*. Print and close the document.

Reports

Learning Outcomes

In Lesson 50, you will:

50A *Learn and use proofreaders' marks.*

50B *Format a standard, unbound report with proofreaders' marks.*

50A

Proofreaders' Marks

Every document you create should be checked carefully. You should make sure it does not have spelling, punctuation, or format errors. **Proofreaders' marks** are letters and symbols used to show the errors or revisions in a document. These marks make it easy for you or someone else to make the changes noted in the copy. Study the following frequently used marks. Other marks are shown in the resource section of the textbook.

Mark	Action Required	Mark	Action Required
¶	Begin a new paragraph	*Cap* ≡	Capitalize
◡	Close up	♀	Delete
∧	Insert	*stet*	Let it stand
lc	Make lowercase	⊏	Move left
⊐	Move right	∩ *tr*	Transpose

1. In a new, blank document, key the following text. Make corrections as indicated by the proofreaders' marks. Proofread to find one error that is not marked.

2. Save the document as *50a proof* and close it.

just how well do you adjust to changes in your life? You should recognize that change is as certain as life and death and taxes. You can not avoid change, but your can adjust to it. How quickly you can do this is a good index of the success you are likely to have in the future years. Can you think of changes that have affected you in the past year? Were you able to adjust to them?

Tables: Changing Row Height, Borders, and Shading

Data Files:

df 57a table1
df 57a table2

Learning Outcomes

In Lesson 57, you will:

57A *Change row height and vertical alignment of cell data.*
57B *Format tables using borders and shading.*

57A

Change Row Height and Vertical Alignment

Row height is the vertical amount of space in a row. Row heights adjust automatically to allow room for text in large font sizes. Row heights also can be set to a certain measurement. The height for row 1 in the table shown in Figure 7.10 is set to 0.5". Rows 2–5 are set to 0.3".

In previous lessons, you changed the horizontal alignment of text in a cell. You also can change the vertical alignment of text in a cell. The text may be aligned at the top, center, or bottom of a cell. Using the options in the Alignment group on the Table Tools Layout tab, you can apply both vertical and horizontal alignments at the same time. For example, you can align text at the bottom and right side of a cell using Align Bottom Right.

By default, text is placed in the upper left of a cell using the Align Top Left alignment. The text in the table shown in Figure 7.10 is set to Align Center Left. In this lesson, you will learn to set row heights to exact measurements and align text in cells vertically.

MEN'S SOCCER WORLD CUP WINNERS

Year	Winner	Final Opponent
1994	Brazil	Italy
1998	France	Brazil
2002	Brazil	Germany
2006	Italy	France
2010	Spain	Netherlands

Figure 7.10 *This table has changed row height and vertically centered cells.*

1. In a new, blank document, key the report on the next two pages in standard, unbound format. Make corrections as indicated by the proofreaders' marks.

2. Save the document as *50b report* and close it.

Hillsdale High School Update

During the past month, Hillsdale High School hired three new teachers. The new teachers, Ms. Anne Hartman, Mr. Terry Nolan, and Ms. Mary Knowles, officially Start begin when school opens this year, but they have been at the high school on a regular basis to prepare their classrooms and courses for the new school year and to meet with the principal and other staff members.

About the New Teachers

Ms. Hartman has a B.S. degree from Clark College, where she majored in biology. Anne taught for three years at at Reynolds High before coming to Hillsdale. She has been very active in her church and community. She resides in Morningside with her husband, Dale, and two daughters, Ashlee and Melanie. Mr. Nolan has a B.A. degree with a major in English. He also has an M.S. degree from Garrett University. Terry taught for six years at Worthington High School before entering the business world, where he worked the last five years for Environmental Services, Inc. Company He and his wife, Sandy, are in the process of moving into the school district.

4. Delete the last three columns (Beginning Amount, Ending Amount, and Gain).

5. Add a row at the top of the table. Merge the cells in row 1. Key the following title in row 1:

STOCK CLUB TOP PERFORMERS

6. Center-align the text in all cells and apply an appropriate table style.

7. Save the document as *56d table* and keep it open. Open *df 56d letter*.

8. Make *56d table* the active window. Click the Table Move handle to select the entire table. Click the **Copy** button in the Clipboard group on the Home tab.

9. Make *df 56d letter* the active window. Click in the letter at the beginning of the second paragraph. Click **Paste** in the Clipboard group. The table should now appear in the letter.

10. Center the table horizontally. Save the letter as *56d letter* and print it. Close *56d letter* and *56d table*.

✓ checkpoint Is the table centered between the margins? Compare your % Gain answers with those of a classmate and correct any answers that are wrong.

21st Century Skills

Information, Communications, and Technology (ICT) Literacy

Today's technology has drastically changed the way we present and exchange information. Through word processing and other types of software applications, we can quickly and easily prepare professional-looking correspondence, reports, tables, and other types of documents.

Being a proficient user of software applications, including word processing, spreadsheet, presentation, and database programs, is an important skill both in the classroom and on the job. Further, knowing how to use these tools to effectively communicate information and ideas will help you succeed in all areas of your life.

© wavebreakmedia/Shutterstock.com

Think Critically

Open a new word processing document and create a table with the following headings. Under each heading, key the information as shown. Insert another row and list at least two types of files you could create with each type of application.

- **Word Processing:** Use to create text documents.
- **Spreadsheet:** Use to create worksheets for recording and calculating data.
- **Presentation:** Use to create multimedia slide shows.
- **Database:** Use to organize and manage data.

Save the document as directed by your teacher.

Ms. Knowles just completed her B.S. degree in Business Education. She returned to Clark College to earn her teaching certification after working at Integrated Computer Systems for the past four years. Mary is a graduate of Hillsdale High, and some may recall that she was a member of the softball team that won a state championship. Ms. Knowies lives with her husband, Ken, and young daughter, Martha, in Millerstown.

Grant Awarded

Mr. Gary Johnson, head of the Science department, will serve as the project director for the $75,000 grant Hillsdale High received from the Morris Foundation, The money will be used to purchase new software for the science laboratories. In addition, the grant supports a series of professional development workshops for the elementary, middle, and high school science teachers. This grant is the second one Hillsdale has received from this foundation during the past six years.

Professional Development

Early in the new school year, Dr. James Jenson, President, Center for the Improvement of Schools, will speak to all of the district's teachers. His presentation will focus on what changes schools need to make to prepare students for a world where business is carried out internationally, communications are instantaneous, and people from various societies must be able to live and work together.

Table 2

1. Open *df 56c table2*. Insert a new column between the Birth Date and Email Address columns. Key the following data in the new column:

Phone Number
614-555-0133
614-555-0179
614-555-0144
614-555-0156
614-555-0184
614-555-0172
614-555-0141
614-555-0166
614-555-0111
614-555-0199
614-555-0139

2. Delete the Email Address column.

3. Delete row 10 (*Yarborough, Pam*) and row 4 (*Guitterez, Maria*). Add a row after row 2 (*Aceto, Jill*). (To add the row, click in row 2 and choose the **Table Tools Layout** tab. In the Rows & Columns group, click **Insert Below**.) Key the following data:

Bauer, Brianne	Left Back	10/14/97	614-555-0163

4. Add a row after row 5 (*Lei, Su*) and key the following data in the new row:

McCoy, Kim	Right Mid	03/01/98	614-555-0118

5. Add a row at the top of the table. Merge the cells in row 1. Using a bold font, key the following main heading in the new row:

TREESDALE ROSTER FOR SOCCER TOURNAMENT

6. Center the page vertically. Save the document as *56c table2* and close it.

56D

Letter with Table

1. Open *df 56d table*.

2. Add a column to the right of column 3 (Room). Key **% Gain** for the column heading.

3. Start the *Calculator* program. Find the percent of gain for each student by dividing the number in the Gain column by the number in the Beginning Amount column. Key the answers in the appropriate cells in the % Gain column. (Round numbers to one decimal place.)

ABOVE and BEYOND

Are you writing a research paper with many references that you will cite in the paper? If so, *Word* has Citations and Bibliography features that you may want to explore on your own. The features are in the Citations & Bibliography group on the References tab, shown in Figure 5.15.

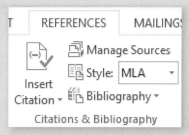

Figure 5.15 *Citations & Bibliography group*

As you conduct your research, you can add sources to a library that *Word* will maintain for you. You add each source by keying information (author, date, title, publication, and so on) into a dialog box that appears when the Insert Citation feature is used. *Word* automatically builds citations on the information you provide and can arrange them in several different style manuals, such as the MLA style manual used in this chapter. When you write your paper, you can use the Insert Citation feature to easily insert a citation in the text—either from the library or from a new source. If necessary, you can preview or edit the entries in your library by using the Manage Sources feature.

When you are ready to create the report bibliography, you can use the Style and Bibliography features to automatically format the entries to meet MLA guidelines or other popular style guidelines and arrange them on your Works Cited or References page. If necessary, you can edit the references.

To learn more about this feature, search *Citations & Bibliography* in *Word's* Help index.

REFRESHMENT STAND STAFFING				
Saturday	8 a.m.-10 a.m.	10 a.m.-11 a.m.	11 a.m.-1 p.m.	
September 5	J. Triponey	M. McKeever	B. Hohn	
September 12	D. Ford | M. Lu	G. Bauer	A. Carr | V. Dee	
September 19	C. Rickenbach		D. Mars | Z. Sia	
September 26	A. Kopolovich		B. Gordon	
October 1	S. Creely | D. Sanchez		M. Nash | R. Janson	
October 8	I. Che | A. Jaso	R. Dolphi	A. Berger	

56C

Add and Delete Rows and Columns

WP Table Tools Layout/ Rows & Columns/ Insert options or Delete options

You can add and delete rows and columns to change your table grid. Rows can be added above or below the row in which you have placed the insertion point in the table. Columns can be added to the left or right of the column in which you have placed the insertion point.

Table 1

1. Open *df 56c table1*.

2. Select row 2 and delete it by following the path at the left to the Delete drop-down list options. Click **Delete Rows** on the list.

3. To add a row below the last row, click in the last cell in the last row. Tap TAB to add a new row to the bottom of the table.

4. Key the following data in the last row:

2010	Spain	Brazil

5. To add a column between the first and second columns, click in column 1 and then follow the path at the left to the Insert options. Click **Insert Right**.

6. Key the following data in the cells in the new column that was inserted:

Site
Mexico
Italy
United States
France
Japan/South Korea
Germany
South Africa

7. To delete the last column, click in the last column. Select **Delete Columns** from the Delete drop-down list.

8. Save the document as *56c table1* and close it.

Before You Move On

Answer these questions to review what you have learned in Chapter 5.

1. A document that gives facts, ideas, or opinions about one or more topics is called a(n) _____. CO

2. The amount of blank space between the text and the edge of the paper is called the _____. LO 47E

3. What line spacing is used for an MLA report? LO 47E

4. What line spacing is used for an unbound report in standard format? LO 49D

5. The style of the letters, figures, symbols, and so on in a document is called the _____. LO 47C

6. A collection of settings for font, font size, color, and so on is called a(n) _____. LO 49C

7. A(n) _____ contains information that appears at the top of pages in a document. LO 47D

8. A(n) _____ contains information that is displayed at the bottom of the page. LO 47D

9. A(n) _____ shows an ordered list of topics to be included in a report. LO 48C

10. When using the _____ feature, you can choose to ignore a possible misspelled word or change it. LO 49A

11. Where should the page number appear on an MLA report? LO 47E

12. What is the name of the page on which sources used in an MLA report are listed? LO 48D

13. Use _____ for a list when the items can be in any order. LO 48A

14. _____ are letters and symbols used to show the errors in a document. LO 50A

6. Key the following data in your table grid. Your grid should match the grid shown here. Format text in the cells as shown.

ELECTED COCAPTAINS					
Team Red		Team White		Team Blue	
Mary	Mark	Jose	Prajakar	Mario	Lynora

7. Use the AutoFit Contents command to change the column widths. Center the table horizontally and vertically on the page.

8. Save the document as *56b table1* and close it.

Table 2

1. Open a new, blank document. Create a table grid with four columns and five rows.

2. Use the Merge Cells and Split Cells commands to make your table grid look like the one shown here. Then key the data in the table as shown. Use center alignment in all cells.

All cells in row 1 were merged into one cell that spans all of the columns.			
These four cells were merged into one cell.		The cell below was split into four cells.	These two cells were merged.
	The cell above was split into two cells.		
			These two cells were merged.

3. Center the page vertically. Save the document as *56b table2* and close it.

Table 3

1. Open a new, blank document. Create a table grid with four columns and eight rows.

2. Merge and split cells and format cell entries as shown in the following table. Then key the data in the table shown below. Use AutoFit Contents to change column widths. Center the table on the page horizontally. Center the page vertically.

3. Save the document as *56b table3*. Proofread and correct errors. Print and then close the table.

Data Files:

df c5 report1
df c5 report2
df c5 report3

Report in Standard, Unbound Format

1. Open *df c5 report1*.

2. Format the report in standard, unbound style. Do not number page 1.

3. Add the following text to the end of the report. Make the changes indicated by the proofreaders' marks.

4. Use Spelling & Grammar to check the document, and proofread the document carefully. Correct all errors.

5. Save the document as *c5 report1* and close it.

Unfortunately, far too many tires are *abandoned* ~~thrown away~~ rather than recycled. Abandoned tires often litter the sides of our rivers and creeks. Many are *found* ~~hidden~~ in our forests. Too often, worn-out tires are stacked in piles that are ugly and provide breeding grounds for pests. These tire piles are fire hazards. If they catch fire, they can burn for weeks, ruining the air. The *heat of the* fire can cause the rubber to decompose into oil. This oil is likely to *dirty* ~~pollute~~ nearby ground and surface water, causing damage to the environment.

The next time you change ~~your~~ tires, even on your bicycle, make sure you dispose *of* them properly. If you can, leave them at the store where you buy the replacement tires. The old tires can be recycled into useful products such as buckets, shoes, mouse pads for computers, and dust pans.

WP Home/Paragraph/
Show/Hide ¶

¶

Use the Show/Hide ¶ button (see icon at left) to display table markers as shown in Figure 7.7. These markers are helpful when moving a table or selecting parts of a table.

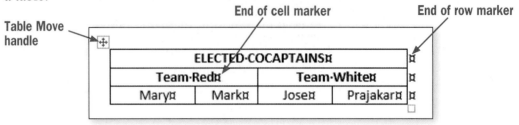

Figure 7.7 *Table markers*

Table 1

1. Open a new, blank document. Insert a table grid with three columns and three rows. Use the Show/Hide ¶ button to display table markers.

2. Using the mouse, point outside the gridlines and to the left of row 1. Click to select the row as shown in Figure 7.8.

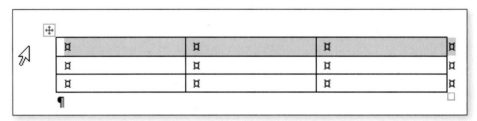

Figure 7.8 *Selected row of cells*

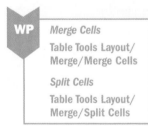

WP *Merge Cells*
Table Tools Layout/
Merge/Merge Cells

Split Cells
Table Tools Layout/
Merge/Split Cells

3. To merge the three cells in row 1, click **Merge Cells** in the Merge group on the Table Tools Layout tab. Row 1 should now have only one cell.

4. To split each cell in row 3 into two cells, select row 3. Click **Split Cells** in the Merge group on the Table Tools Layout tab. The Split Cells dialog box shown in Figure 7.9 will appear.

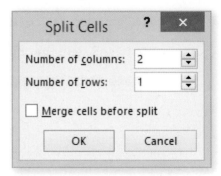

Figure 7.9 *Split Cells dialog box*

5. Key **2** in the Number of columns text box. Key **1** in the Number of rows text box. Remove the check mark from the **Merge cells before split** box. Click **OK**. Row 3 should now have six cells.

Report in MLA Format

1. Open *df c5 report2*. Format the report in MLA style. *Note:* If a side heading appears at the bottom of a page without at least two lines of text below the heading, insert a page break to move the heading (and the line following it, if applicable) to the next page.

2. Create a Works Cited page with the following sources.

3. Use Spelling & Grammar and proofread the document carefully. Correct all errors. Save the document as *c5 report2* and close it.

TIP When you key a URL in a reference, *Word* will automatically format it in blue with an underline.

Works Cited

Fulton-Calkins, Patsy, and Karin M. Stulz. <u>Procedures & Theory for Administrative Professionals</u>, 6th ed. Cincinnati: South-Western, 2009.

Law Dictionary. "What is Occupational Outlook Handbook?" 7 January 2014. <u>http://thelawdictionary.org/occupational-outlook-handbook/#ixzz2oPofpoLF</u>.

University of Waterloo. <u>Career Development eManual</u>. "Self-Assessment." 7 January 2014 <u>http://www.cdm.uwaterloo.ca</u>.

Report in Standard, Unbound Format

1. Open *df c5 report3*. Format the report in standard, unbound format.

2. Use Spelling & Grammar and proofread the document carefully. Correct all errors. Save the document as *c5 report3* and close it.

WP *Horizontal Alignment*
Table Tools Layout/
Table/Properties

4. To center the table horizontally, click in the table and then follow the ***Horizontal Alignment*** path at the left to open the Table Properties dialog box. Click **Center** in the Alignment section as shown in Figure 7.6. After you click **OK**, the table should be centered horizontally between the left and right margins.

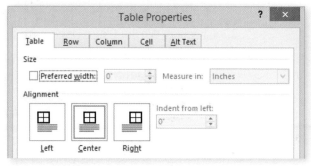

Figure 7.6 *Center alignment*

5. Save the document as *56a table1*. Complete the following CheckPoint and then close the document.

 **checkpoint** Is your table centered vertically and horizontally? Use the Preview screen to check the layout of the document.

Table 2

1. Open *55e table* that you created in Lesson 55.

2. Center-align the main heading. Change the top margin to about 1". Center the table vertically. Center the table horizontally. Use the Preview screen to check the placement.

3. Save the document as *56a table2* and close it.

56B

Select, Merge, and Split Cells

While formatting tables, you can **merge** (join) cells that are next to each other in the same row or the same column. You can use this feature when information in a table needs to span more than one column or row. You can **split** (divide) a cell into two or more cells. Merging and splitting cells allows you to create tables that are more useful or creative than those that use a standard grid.

When you want to merge or split cells in a table, you must first select the cells. You can always click and drag over cells to select them. However, the table below tells how to select parts of a table quickly.

To Select	Move the Insertion Point
Entire table	Over the table and click the Table Move handle
Column	To the top of the column until a solid down arrow appears; then click
Row	To the left area just outside the table until an open arrow appears; then click

Outline for Report

1. In a new, blank document, key the following outline using the Numbering feature and default margin settings.

2. Use Spelling & Grammar, proofread the document carefully, and correct all errors.

3. Save the document as *c5 outline* and close it.

The Ear

I. Parts of the ear

    a. Outer ear

    b. Middle ear

    c. Inner ear

II. How we hear

    a. How sounds reach the inner ear

    b. How the inner ear sends sounds to the brain

III. Care of the ear

    a. Preventing ear infections

        i. Keeping fluids out of the ear

        ii. Cleaning the ear

    b. Preventing ear injury

Tables: Merging and Splitting Cells

Data Files:

df 56c table1
df 56c table2
df 56d table
df 56d letter

Learning Outcomes

In Lesson 56, you will:

56A *Center tables vertically and horizontally.*

56B *Select, merge, and split cells in tables.*

56C *Add and delete rows and columns in tables.*

56D *Insert a table in a letter.*

56A

Table Alignment

Tables are usually centered horizontally on a page. However, they can be aligned at the left or right margin. Tables, like letters and other documents, can be centered vertically on a page. When a table is used in the body of a report or letter, center it between the left and right margins.

Table 1

1. Open *55d table* that you created in Lesson 55. In the steps that follow, you will center the table vertically and horizontally.

2. Center-align the main heading.

3. Change the vertical position of the heading to 1.1". To center the table vertically, use the ***Vertical Alignment*** path at the left to display the Layout tab of the Page Setup dialog box. Select **Center** from the Vertical alignment list in the Page section as shown in Figure 7.5. The table should be centered vertically after you click **OK**.

WP *Vertical Alignment*
Page Layout/Page
Setup dialog box
launcher/Layout tab

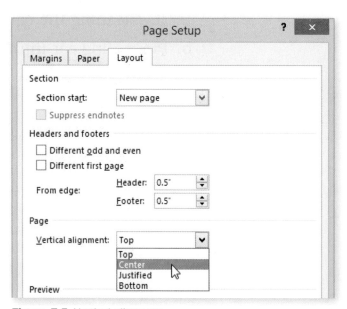

Figure 7.5 *Vertical alignment*

KEYBOARDING SKILLBUILDING

Warmup Practice

Key each line twice. If time permits, key the lines again.

Alphabet

1 Jack Vasquez placed my next bid for the two gowns.

Figure/Symbol

2 With a 20% discount, Invoice #139 totaled $854.76.

Speed

3 Alan and Glen did half of the problems on the bus.

gwam 1' | 1 | 2 | 3 | 4 | 5 | 6 | 7 | 8 | 9 | 10 |

Improve Keying Technique

Key each line twice, striving to maintain a continuous pace.

TECHNIQUE TIP
Keep your fingers curved and upright.

One-hand words

1 in be we as my at no at up was few see you him get
2 were only date case fact area rate free card aware
3 state hook great link water nylon after puppy best

One-hand phrases

4 as far as|you see|we are|at best|were you|best bet
5 erase my debt|my only rate|upon a hill|hook a bass
6 set a date|free bread|extra pulp|only oil|bad debt

One-hand sentences

7 Get him extra tax cards after you set a case date.
8 As you see, you set only my bad debt fees in July.
9 Only a few cards get you great reserved oil rates.

gwam 30" | 2 | 4 | 6 | 8 | 10 | 12 | 14 | 16 | 18 | 20 |

Table Styles

WP Table Tools Design/
Table Styles
Table Tools Design/
Table Style Options

After a table has been inserted, features in the Table Styles group and the Table Style Options group in the Table Tools Design tab can be used to format your table. A table style is a ready-made assortment of colors and borders used to format a table. This feature can be used before or after text is keyed. Also, features in the Styles group in the Home tab can be used to enhance the appearance of the main heading or other text in the table.

1. Open *55b table4* that you completed in 55B.

2. Click in a cell in the table to display the Table Tools Design tab. Click the **Plain Table 4** style (the fifth one in the first row) in the Table Styles group to format your table.

3. Remove the check from the Banded Columns box in the Table Style Options group to shade every other row in your table.

4. To remove the remaining shading in the table, choose the **Table Grid Light** style—the left one in row 1 of the Table Styles gallery.

5. Use options from the Table Styles group and the Table Style Options group to apply formatting that you believe is appropriate for this table.

6. Select the main heading of the table and apply the Heading 1 style from the Styles group on the Home tab to format the main heading.

7. Use the Heading 2 style to format the column headings.

8. Save your document as *55c table* and close it.

55D

Change Table Styles and Heading Styles

1. Open *55b table1* that you completed in 55B.

2. Using features in the Styles, Table Styles, and Table Style Options groups, format the table in an attractive, easy-to-read manner.

3. Save the document as *55d table* and close it.

55E

Design a Basic Table

1. Open a new, blank document. Beginning at or near the 2" vertical position, create the following table. Use AutoFit Contents to set column widths.

2. Using features in the Styles, Table Styles, and Table Style Options groups, format the table in an attractive, easy-to-read manner.

3. Proofread the table and correct all errors. Save the document as *55e table*. Print the table and then close it.

MONTHS OF THE YEAR IN SPANISH AND ENGLISH

English	Spanish	English	Spanish
January	enero	July	julio
February	febrero	August	agosto
March	marzo	September	septiembre
April	abril	October	octubre
May	mayo	November	noviembre
June	junio	December	diciembre

Speed Forcing Drill

Key a 30" timed writing on each line, striving to key more on each attempt. Your *gwam* is shown below the lines.

TECHNIQUE TIP
Reach out with your little finger and tap the ENTER key quickly. Return your finger to its home key.

1 She may be in her office.
2 He forgot to take their money.
3 Benito won first place in his race.
4 I will have him call you when he leaves.
5 Tryouts for the play take place next Tuesday.
6 Jason and Katie plan on going to the lake to swim.

| gwam 30" | 2 | 4 | 6 | 8 | 10 | 12 | 14 | 16 | 18 | 20 |

Speed Building

1. Key three 1' timed writings on each paragraph, striving to key more on each timing; determine *gwam*.

2. Key a 2' timed writing on both paragraphs combined, striving to maintain your highest 1' *gwam*.

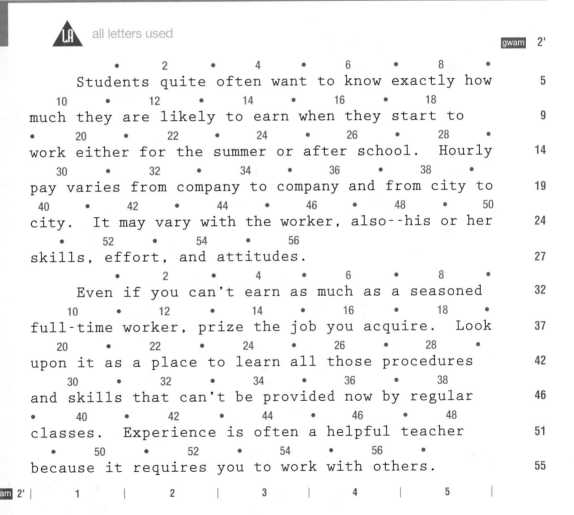

LA all letters used

gwam 2'

```
             •     2     •     4     •     6     •     8     •
         Students quite often want to know exactly how        5
     10      •     12      •     14      •     16      •     18
much they are likely to earn when they start to               9
•     20     •     22      •     24     •     26     •     28     •
work either for the summer or after school.  Hourly           14
     30      •     32      •     34      •     36      •     38     •
pay varies from company to company and from city to           19
 40     •     42     •     44     •     46     •     48     •     50
city.  It may vary with the worker, also--his or her          24
     •     52     •     54     •     56
skills, effort, and attitudes.                                27

             •     2     •     4     •     6     •     8     •
         Even if you can't earn as much as a seasoned         32
     10      •     12      •     14      •     16      •     18     •
full-time worker, prize the job you acquire.  Look            37
     20      •     22      •     24     •     26     •     28     •
upon it as a place to learn all those procedures              42
     30      •     32      •     34     •     36     •     38
and skills that can't be provided now by regular              46
•     40     •     42     •     44     •     46     •     48
classes.  Experience is often a helpful teacher               51
     •     50     •     52     •     54     •     56     •
because it requires you to work with others.                  55
```

| gwam 2' | 1 | 2 | 3 | 4 | 5 | |

Change Column Widths

Column widths can be changed in different ways. In this lesson, you will use the **AutoFit Contents** option in the **AutoFit** feature. AutoFit Contents adjusts the column widths to be just wide enough for all of the contents in a column to fit in the cells. The **AutoFit Window** option in this feature adjusts the column widths to fit within the left and right margins in your document.

Another way to change column widths is by entering numbers in the **Table Column Width** box in the Cell Size group in the Table Tools Layout tab that displays when you click within a table. In this box (shown in Figure 7.4), you can set a column to an exact width, such as 1" or 1.56".

Table 1

1. Open *55a table2* that you created in 55A.

2. Click inside a cell of the table to display the Table Tools Layout tab. In the Cell Size group, click **AutoFit** and choose **AutoFit Contents** as shown in Figure 7.4.

Figure 7.4 *Use AutoFit to adjust column widths.*

3. Note that the table is not centered horizontally after the change in column widths. You will learn to center a table horizontally in a later lesson. Save the document as *55b table1* and close it.

Table 2

1. Open *55a table1* that you created in 55A.

2. Click a cell in column A and change its width to 1.5" by keying **1.5** in the Table Column Width box.

3. Click in a cell in column B and change its width to 1".

4. Use the same procedure to change the width of column C to 1.5" and column D to 1".

5. This table also will not be centered horizontally. Save the document as *55b table2* and close it.

Tables 3 and 4

1. Open the document *df 55b table*. Use the AutoFit Content option to change the column widths. Save the document as *55b table3* and then close it.

2. Open *df 55b table* again. Set the width for columns A and C to 1.6". Set the widths for columns B and D to 0.6". Save the document as *55b table4* and close it.

ACROSS THE CURRICULUM

Academic Connections

Data Files:

df c5 numbers
df c5 organizations
df c5 home-based
    businesses
df c5 job
    discrimination

COLLABORATION

Language Arts: Number Usage

Numbers can be expressed as words (three) or figures (3). In this activity, you will learn some rules about when to write numbers as words and when to write them as figures.

1. Start *Word* and open the document *df c5 numbers*.

2. Read the rules in the Guides. Then read the examples in the Learn lines. Make corrections that are needed in the Practice and Apply lines.

3. Apply the formatting changes given in the instructions near the bottom of the document.

4. Save the document as *c5 numbers*, print, and close it.

Student Organizations: Are They Right for You?

Do your activities go beyond the classroom? Do you take part in any community service projects? Do you help organize any after-school events with your class-mates? Do you belong to any teams, clubs, or music groups? Have you partici-pated in any competitions or held a leadership position?

    If you answered yes to some of these questions, you are probably gaining im-portant skills. You may be learning how to work with others. You may be teaching, leading, or serving others. You are probably showing that you can accept responsi-bility. Employers like to see that you have had these types of experiences.

1. Working with one or two other classmates, open *df c5 organizations*.

2. Follow the directions in the data file to learn more about student organizations and practice your *Word* skills.

3. Save the *c5 organization essay* document that you create in this exercise, print, and close it.

About Business

COLLABORATION

Home-Based Businesses

A **home-based business** is a company that is run out of a person's house. The owner may use a room of his or her house as an office or other type of work space. Home-based businesses are an important part of the economy in the United States.

1. Working with a partner, open *df c5 home-based businesses*.

2. Read the information in the document and follow the directions to learn more about a specific home-based business. Last, create an outline for an essay.

3. Save the document as *c5 home-based businesses*, print, and close it.

FUND-RAISING RESULTS FOR ROOM 202

Name	Amount	Name	Amount
Harry Xidas	$128.23	Mary Henry	$93.66
Julio Clemente	$114.56	Vinnie Werner	$91.42
Kerri Gorski	$106.09	Naomi Quinnones	$89.77
Lawrence Miller	$99.25	Betty Upton	$82.50

6. Select the cells under the column heading in column B (as shown in Figure 7.3 at the left), and change the alignment to Align Right (as shown in Figure 7.3 at the right).

Amount
$128.23
$114.56
$106.09
$99.25

Amount
$128.23
$114.56
$106.09
$99.25

Figure 7.3 *Select cells to apply formatting.*

7. Right-align the cells under the column head in column D.

8. Save the document as *55a table1* and close it.

Table 2

1. Open a new, blank document. Key the table's main heading, shown below, beginning at or near the 2" vertical position.

2. Insert a table grid that is four columns by six rows. Key the data shown below in the cells.

SPRING VALLEY MIDDLE SCHOOL FBLA OFFICERS

Name	Office	Room	Telephone
Jo Longo	President	218	330-555-0110
Bobbi Kite	Vice President	119	330-555-0134
Brent Diaz	Secretary	214	330-555-0159
Katie Verez	Treasurer	101	330-555-0162
Jerry Wilson	Parliamentarian	116	330-555-0177

3. Apply bold and center alignment to the main heading and column headings.

4. Use left alignment for words and right alignment for numbers for the cells in the rows under the column headings.

5. Save the document as *55a table2* and close it.

Life Success Builder

Employment Discrimination

Many companies are required by law to protect their employees from discrimination. They are also not allowed to discriminate against people applying for jobs with their company. **Discrimination** is the unfair treatment of people due to certain factors. These include race, age, religion, disability, gender, and more.

1. Open *df c5 job discrimination*.

2. Follow the directions to go to the U.S. Equal Employment Opportunity Commission website. Write summaries about different types of discriminations as directed and format your document.

3. Save the document as *c5 job discrimination*, print, and close it.

Career Exploration Portfolio

Activity 4

To complete this activity, you will need the Student Interest Survey that you filled out in Career Exploration Portfolio Activity 1.

1. Look on the last page of your survey and note your *third* Career Cluster of interest. Find its description on the last two pages of the survey and read it.

2. Go to http://www.careertech.org. Click the **Career Technical Education** button; then click **Career Clusters** in the list at the right. Scroll down on the Career Clusters page and click the link for your third Career Cluster. On the web page for your Career Cluster, click the **PDF** link following Career Cluster Frame in the information near the top of the page. Read the list of careers in the document and pick one or two you are interested in. Make a note of the category (called a Pathway) of the career(s) you choose. You will need to know the Pathway in a future activity.

3. Use the Internet to find out specific duties of the career(s) that you chose. You may look for other information that interests you as well.

4. Use *Word* to write a summary of what you learned. Save the document as *c5 career 3 details*, print, and close it.

Online Resources:

ngl.cengage.com/c21jr3e

Table Format Guidelines

Refer to Figure 7.1 as you read the following formatting guidelines for tables:

- A **main heading** describes the content of a table. Unless directed otherwise, key the main heading in all capital letters. Apply bold and center-align the heading. The main heading may be keyed as the first row in the table grid, as shown in Figure 7.1, or above the table grid.

- A **column heading** appears at the top of a column and describes the data in the column. Unless directed otherwise, key column headings in bold, capital and lowercase letters, and center-aligned in the column.

- Key data in cells using the default font unless directed otherwise. Data in cells can be aligned left, aligned right, or centered. Usually, numbers are aligned right and words are aligned left or centered.

- Center tables horizontally on the page. Center the table vertically on the page or begin the table at or near the 2" vertical position.

- Tables can be printed with the cell borders showing (the default) or without cell borders showing. Unless directed otherwise, print tables with cell borders showing.

Table 1

1. Start *Word* and open a new, blank document. Complete the following steps to create the table shown after step 5.

2. Beginning at or near the 2" vertical position, key the main heading **FUND-RAISING RESULTS FOR ROOM 202** using bold and center alignment. Tap ENTER once.

3. Select the **Insert** tab, the **Table** drop-down list in the Tables group, and then use your mouse to create a table of four columns and five rows from the Insert Table grid as shown in Figure 7.2. A 4 × 5 table grid will be inserted below the main heading.

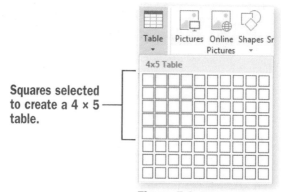

Squares selected to create a 4 × 5 table.

Figure 7.2 *Table grid*

TIP Use the TAB key or an arrow key to move from one cell to another.

4. Key the column headings in row 1, using bold and center alignment. Tap the TAB key one time to move to the next cell in row 1.

5. Key the data in the cells in rows 2–5 as shown in the table. Use the default alignment.

Lessons 51–54

People often need to send written messages to others. They may write to others to thank them for assistance or invite them to an event. People also send messages to make requests, complain, or try to persuade. A message may be created as a text message, an email, or a personal-business letter. In this chapter, you will learn to create email messages and personal-business letters. You also will learn to use features of word processing and messaging software to prepare documents efficiently.

© Mike Flippo/Shutterstock.com

Lesson 55

Basic Tables

Learning Outcomes

In Lesson 55, you will:

55A *Create tables.*
55B *Change widths of columns in tables.*
55C *Use table styles.*
55D *Change table styles and heading styles.*
55E *Design a basic table.*

Data File:

df 55b table

55A

Create a Table

| **WP** | Insert/Tables/Insert Table grid |

Table Format

Tables are used to organize information. Information is arranged vertically in **columns** and horizontally in **rows**. Columns and rows are marked in Figure 7.1. The place where a row and a column cross each other is called a **cell**. Text, numbers, and formulas for calculating amounts can be entered in a cell. When text is keyed in a cell, it wraps within that cell—instead of moving to the next row. A line space is added to a cell each time the text wraps within it. **Gridlines** mark the outline of the area for each cell and are not printed.

Use the TAB key or right arrow key to move from cell to cell in a row and from row to row. To fill in a table, key text in the table cells. (Tapping ENTER will cause a blank line space to be added to the cell.) To move in a filled-in table, use the arrow keys, TAB, or the mouse (click the desired cell).

Text in a table can be formatted (font size, color, alignment, style, and so on) in the same manner as text in the letters and reports you have completed. By default, the **borders** that outline the cells in the table grid as shown in Figure 7.1 will be printed.

	Column A	Column B	Column C	Column D
Row 1	SPRING VALLEY MIDDLE SCHOOL FBLA OFFICERS			
Row 2	**Name**	**Office**	**Room**	**Telephone**
Row 3	Jo Longo	President	218	330-555-0110
Row 4	Bobbie Kite	Vice President	119	330-555-0134
Row 5	Brett Diaz	Secretary	214	330-555-0159
Row 6	Katie Verez	Treasurer	101	330-555-0162
Row 7	Jerry Wilson	Parliamentarian	116	330-555-0177

Left-aligned data   Center-aligned data   Right-aligned data   Cell

Figure 7.1 *Data in a table is arranged in columns and rows.*

Email

Learning Outcomes

In Lesson 51, you will:

51A *Learn email format, addresses, and guidelines and create a message.*
51B *Send an email message to multiple recipients.*
51C *Receive, reply to, forward, and delete email messages.*
51D *Research computer viruses and email threats.*

51A

Email

EM   Home/New/New
     Email

Email (electronic mail) is used quite frequently, partly because of the ease of creating and the speed of sending messages. An email is often delivered in minutes. Many people now use email in place of memos and letters.

To use email, you must have an email account. You also may need to set up an account with an Internet service provider. An Internet service provider (ISP) is a company that provides customer connections to the Internet. Google and Yahoo are popular ISPs.

Email Format

An email includes heading lines and the message body. The heading lines include the:

- Email address of the person(s) receiving the email.

- Email address of the person sending the email.

- Date the email was sent.

- Subject of the email.

The email address of the person receiving the message is keyed in the To box. Use capital and small letters that appear in the addresses given to you. Sometimes a message is sent to more than one person. Separate the addresses with a comma or semicolon and a space. This can vary depending on the program you use.

Always key a subject in the Subject box. Many people delete emails without reading them when the messages do not include subject lines. Subjects are sometimes keyed in all capitals.

A copy of an email can be sent to another person. If a copy is sent, key the address in the Cc box. If a **blind copy** is sent, key the address in the Bcc box. A blind copy is used when you do not want the person receiving the email to know that you have sent the message to another person.

Normally, you do not need to key the sender's name and the date. The software inserts this information.

A file can be attached to an email. This is done using the Attachment feature of the software. Common types of attachments include picture, video, word processing, spreadsheet, and PDF (portable document format) files.

Use the default margins and line spacing to key the paragraphs of the email. Tap ENTER twice after each paragraph to insert one blank line between paragraphs. Align all lines in the body at the left margin.

Lessons 55–58

A **table** is information arranged in rows and columns so that readers can easily understand it. Your textbooks use tables to show information that supports what you are learning. A table may contain dates and events. It may show states and their capital cities. Newspapers often use tables. Tables show the rankings of sports teams and players. Television programs and daily temperatures are usually reported in tables.

Think about how you use tables. Do you have a schedule of classes that shows your subjects, days and times, room numbers, and teacher names? Do you have a to-do list that shows what you plan to do each day? Do you have a list of frequently called phone numbers? In this chapter, you will learn to create tables to show information in a format that is easy to understand.

© Robert Kneschke/Shutterstock.com

Email Addresses

Before you can send an email, you must have an **email address**. Each email address must be different from all others. Otherwise, email could be delivered to the wrong person. An email address contains a username and a domain name separated by the at sign (@). For example:

> Kim@swep.com
>
> Mkim@speakingabout.com
>
> Maria_Bravo@speakingsolutions.com
>
> maria_bravo@corpview.com

Spaces are not used in email addresses. An underline or a period is sometimes used to separate parts of a username.

Email Guidelines

Follow these guidelines for writing emails:

- Be courteous to others in your messages.
- Keep your emails short and to the point, but include all necessary information.
- Place the most important points of the message in the first three or four lines of text.
- Use correct grammar in your messages.
- Use standard punctuation and capitalization in your messages.
- Do not use all caps for whole words. Using all caps is viewed as shouting at the reader and is considered rude. Use bold or italic instead of all caps.
- Proofread your message before sending it.
- Do not send private or personal information by email.
- Remember that in many cases, email is not private. Always assume that someone besides the person to whom you are writing may see the message.

Instructions for using *Microsoft Outlook* are given in this lesson. If you use a different email program, the features will be similar.

1. Start *Outlook.* Click **New Email** (see Figure 6.1 at the left) in the New group on the Home tab to open an email message screen (see Figure 6.2).

Figure 6.1 *New Email message*

TIP If email software is not available, key the emails in this lesson as standard, unbound reports, using the subject line as the report title.

TIP To check Spelling & Grammar in *Outlook*, click the button in the Proofing group on the Review tab.

Figure 6.2 *Outlook new message screen*

Mr. Farrell, are there any specific math, science, and information technology courses that I should complete? Is there any advice you can give me about a specific major I should pursue when I'm in college? I have enclosed a list of the math, science, and IT courses I have taken in middle school and those that are available in our high school.

I appreciate any guidance you can give me. You can respond to me via email at j.hemingford@lscd.edu or text me at 803-555-0130. If you prefer, I could visit your office at a time that is convenient for you on the first Monday, Tuesday, or Wednesday of next month.

Sincerely

Joanne Hemingford

Enclosure

Activity 6
Personal-Business Letter in Modified Block Format

Data File:
df a1 activity6

1. Open *df a1 activity6*. Format the letter in modified block format with indented paragraphs and mixed punctuation.

2. Save the letter as *a1 activity6*.

3. Create a No. 10 envelope with a letter address and a return address.

4. Print the envelope and letter and then close the document.

TIP The date and time the message was sent and your email address will appear in the heading lines when the receiver opens the message.

2. Key the address your instructor gives you in the To box.

3. Key **OPEN HOUSE** in the Subject box.

4. Key the following in the message area.

My parents and I went to the STEM open house on Monday. We learned a lot. We agreed that I should take as many STEM courses as I can before I graduate from high school.

Since I plan to major in engineering in college, we believe that middle and high school science, technology, engineering, and math courses will help me prepare for my college studies.

5. Save the message as *51a email* as shown in Figure 6.3.

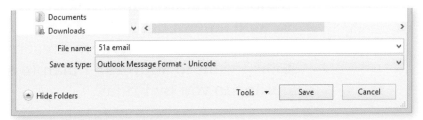

Figure 6.3 *Save As dialog box*

6. Your teacher will tell you whether you should send the email. If permitted, click the **Send** button to send the email. Close the email program.

51B

Send Email to Multiple Recipients

1. Create a new email message.

2. Key the two addresses your teacher gives you in the To box. (Insert a semi-colon and a space between addresses.) Send a copy to the address your teacher gives you.

3. Key **THE STORY OF SCIENCE** as the subject.

4. Key the following as the email message.

Please invite all of your students to a showing of "The Story of Science." This award-winning film will be shown at 7 p.m. at the Civic Center. Dates for the film are Thursday, Friday, and Saturday evenings, March 3-5, 20--.

Students will be admitted without charge on Thursday evening. Tell students they will need to present their school ID card at the door.

Students attending on Friday or Saturday evening must pay $7.50 with a valid school ID card. Students without proper ID and adults will be charged $10.

5. Proofread and correct errors. Save the document as *51b email*.

6. Send the email if your teacher permits it. Close the email program.

Activity 4
Email Message

1. Start *Outlook*. Create a new email message using your teacher's email address in the To box. Include the email address of a classmate in the Cc box.

2. Key **REPORT TOPIC** in the Subject box.

3. Key the email message below. If permitted, send the email. If not, save it as *a1 activity4* and close it.

I have decided to do my report on Gettysburg. I went there last summer on a family vacation and have become very interested in this period of our country's history.

I know there are ample resources available because I have located several books in our school library and various resources on the Internet. Presently, I'm trying to define the topic I want to address. I plan to submit my preliminary outline to you by Friday.

Activity 5
Personal-Business Letter in Block Format

1. Start a new, blank *Word* document and key the letter below in block format with open punctuation.

2. Save the letter as *a1 activity5*, print, and close it.

206 Glenville Drive
Fort Mill, SC 29715-2647
Insert current date to update automatically

Mr. Connor Farrell
Longwell Technologies
7666 Charlotte Highway
Indian Land, SC 29707-4002

Dear Mr. Farrell

Ms. Rita Williams, my technology teacher at Indian Land Middle School, suggested I write to you because of my interest in information technology. She indicated that you serve on our school's technology advisory committee.

I am in the 8th grade and have completed a career exploration project relating to information technology. My next goal is to get advice from people in IT as to the high school courses I should complete.

Receive, Reply to, Forward, and Delete Email

EM   Home/Delete or Respond

COLLABORATION

Once you begin using email, you can quickly accumulate many messages in your email Inbox. As shown in Figure 6.4, you can use features in the Respond group to process the messages. For example, you can use Reply to reply to the sender, Reply All to reply to all who received this email message, or Forward to send the message to another person. You can use features in the Delete group to help you manage your emails.

Figure 6.4 *Delete and Respond groups*

To complete this activity, work with your classmates to send, receive, and forward email. Write down the email addresses of three classmates to use in the activity. Give your email address to three classmates to use in this activity.

1. Open a new email message. Key the address of a classmate in the To box. Key **LEARNING TO USE EMAIL** in the Subject box. For the body of the email, compose and key a paragraph telling some points you have learned about email.

2. With your teacher's permission, send the email.

3. One of your classmates should send you an email. When the message arrives, it will appear in your Inbox folder. An example is shown in Figure 6.5.

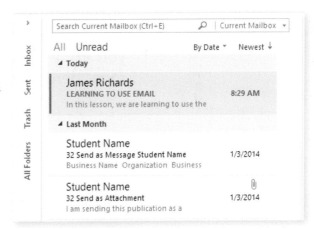

4. Select, open, and read the message.

5. Reply to the message by keying a sentence or two thanking your classmate for helping you learn to use email.

Figure 6.5 *Outlook Inbox*

6. Send the message.

7. Open the LEARNING TO USE EMAIL message you received and forward it to two classmates.

8. Classmates may have replied to your message or forwarded a message to you. If so, select one of these messages and delete it.

9. Deleted messages may be moved to the Deleted Items folder. Click the Deleted Items folder to see if the message has been moved there.

10. Close any open message windows. Close the email program.

the high school student is typically enrolled in a regular class with college students. Other variations may include the college professor teaching the course at the high school or high school students enrolling in summer classes at the college (Getting College Credit in High School: Worth It?).

Because of the variety of and differences among the dual-enrollment programs, colleges may or may not accept the college-level course for AP or AS.

Other Advantages

In addition to the possibility of shortening the time and lessening the costs to earn a college degree, there are other advantages to taking college-level courses in high school. One is that these programs prepare students for the academic rigor of college courses. With this preparation, students are likely to have a better transition to the college classroom, resulting in a more positive experience.

Another advantage is that having AP, IB, and/or dual-enrollment courses noted on your high school transcript or college application shows the college admission personnel that you are willing to challenge yourself academically by taking the most demanding courses.

References

Fox Business. "Getting College Credit in High School: Worth It?" http://www.foxbusiness.com/personal-finance/2012/01/20/getting-college-credit-in-high-school-worth-it/ (15 March 2014).

The Princeton Review. "An Intro to Getting College Credit in High School." 02/09/2011. http://in.princetonreview.com/in/2011/02/an-intro-to-getting-college-credit-in-high-school.html (15 March 2014).

National Association for College Admission Counseling. "Earning College Credit in High School." http://www.nacacnet.org/studentinfo/articles/Pages/EarningCollegeCredit.aspx (15 March 2014).

Protecting Your Computer When Using Email

Email is a terrific form of communication for keeping in touch with family, friends, and business associates. However, using it unwisely may make you and your computer susceptible to spam, phishing scams, viruses, and other online threats.

Here are some basic procedures you can use to protect yourself and your computer.

- Install antivirus software and have it automatically scan all email attachments and downloaded files.

- Never open attachments from people you don't know.

- Beware of spam-based phishing schemes—never click on links in emails.

1. To learn more about threats that can affect your security, access the Internet. Use a search tool to find sites or articles that give information about protecting your security when using email software.

2. Record the name and source information for the article or site. A sample source record is shown below. Open a new *Word* document and key a summary or list of the main points you learned from reading the article. Save the document as *51d summary*.

McAfee. "Top 10 Tips to Protect Your Email." http://home.mcafee.com/advicecenter/?id=ad_eims 6 January 2014.

© Andresr/Shutterstock.com

21st Century Skills

Productivity and Accountability

Email has become one of the most common ways for computer users to communicate, both personally and for business purposes. Although email is considered less formal than other business communications, it is still important to articulate your thoughts and ideas effectively in an email message. You should:

- Write in complete, active sentences.
- Organize using paragraphs and bulleted or numbered lists.
- Proofread and check your spelling.
- Avoid "bells and whistles," such as writing in all caps, inserting emoticons, or using other gimmicks that detract from your message.

Most important, you should always know your audience and understand that your message could be shared either intentionally or by mistake with someone else.

Open a new word processing document, and compose answers to the following questions. Save as directed by your teacher.

1. What perception might you form of a person who sends an email that has spelling and grammatical errors?

2. Under what circumstances in a business setting might email *not* be the best form of communication?

3. Give an example of how you could use email at work to instruct others on a topic.

in 1911 "in recognition of her service to the advancement of chemistry by the discovery of the elements radium and polonium, by the isolation of radium and the study of the nature and compounds of this remarkable element" (Nobel Prize Awarded Women).

In 1935, Irene Joliot-Curie, the daughter of Pierre and Marie Curie, shared the Nobel Prize in Chemistry with her husband, Frederic Joliot, "in recognition of their synthesis of new radioactive elements" (Nobel Prize Awarded Women).

In 1964, Dorothy Crowfoot Hodgkin received the chemistry award "for her determination by X-ray techniques of the structures of important biochemical substances" (Nobel Prize Awarded Women).

The most recent Nobel Prize in Chemistry was awarded to Ada E. Yonath for "studies of the structure and function of the ribosome" (Nobel Prize Awarded Women).

Works Cited

"Nobel Prize Awarded Women." *Nobelprize.org.* Nobel Media AB 2013. Web. 10 Mar 2014.

The World Almanac and Book of Facts, 2011, New York, NY: World Almanac Books, 2011, p. 266.

Activity 3
Standard, Unbound Report

1. Open *df a1 activity3*. Format the text in standard, unbound report format.
2. Format the last paragraph as a long quotation.
3. Key the following text below the long quotation.
4. Save the report as *a1 activity3*, print, and close it.

Data File:
df a1 activity3

Dual-Enrollment Courses

Many high schools have partnered with local two- and four-year colleges to provide college-level courses to high school students. While dual-enrollment programs vary widely, they typically involve the student taking a college-level course at the high school or at the college campus. If the course is taken at the student's high school, it is frequently taught by the high school faculty. If the course is taken at the college campus,

Personal-Business Letters

Data Files:

df 52c paste1
df 52c paste2
df 52d replace1
df 52d replace2
df 52e letter

Learning Outcomes

In Lesson 52, you will:

52A *Format a personal-business letter in block format with open punctuation.*
52B *Format a personal-business letter in block format with mixed punctuation.*
52C *Cut, copy, and paste text.*
52D *Find and replace text.*
52E *Arrange letter parts in correct order.*

52A

Personal-Business Letter

A **personal-business letter** deals with personal matters. For example, you might write this kind of letter to request information for a trip. Your principal might send this kind of letter to congratulate you for winning an award. A letter is considered more formal than an email or text message.

Personal-business letters are often arranged in block format. Block format means that every line of the letter starts at the left margin. Paragraphs, for example, are not indented as they are in many reports. A personal-business letter is shown on page 210.

1. Review the sample letter in the model copy on page 210 and the guidelines for keying letters on pages 208–209.

2. Start a new *Word* document and key the model letter on page 210 using the guidelines shown. *Note: Use Word to create the documents in the remaining activities of this chapter unless directed otherwise.*

3. Save the document as *52a letter* and close it.

Guidelines for a Personal-Business Letter in Block Format

A model of a personal-business letter is shown on page 210. Refer to this model as you read the following information about letter parts and formatting letters.

Margins. Use default margin settings.

Line spacing. Use the default settings (1.08 line spacing with 8 points of space after each paragraph) except where noted below.

Alignment. Begin all lines at the left margin.

Return address. Start the **return address** at or near the 2" vertical position. It consists of a line for the writer's street address and a line for the city, state, and ZIP Code. Use SHIFT + ENTER after keying each line. (See the margin tip at the left.)

Date. Key the month, day, and year on the line below the city, state, and ZIP Code. Use the month/day/year format (*January 4, 2015*). Tap ENTER twice after keying the date.

TIP Holding the Shift key when you tap ENTER inserts a line break that removes the 8 points of space after a paragraph.

1. Start *Word* and open a new, blank document. Key the report below in MLA format. Key your last name and page number as a header. Use your name, your teacher's name, your course name, and the current date for the headings.

2. Save the report as *a1 activity2*, print, and then close it.

Female Nobel Laureates in Physics and Chemistry

The Nobel Foundation was established in 1901 when Alfred B. Nobel (1883-96), inventor of dynamite, bequeathed $9 million so that the interest earned could be distributed to individuals judged to have most benefited humankind in physics, chemistry, physiology or medicine, literature, and promotion of peace (The World Almanac and Book of Facts, 2011, p. 266).

The first woman to receive a Nobel Prize was Marie Curie in 1903. Including her 1903 award, 44 women have received a Nobel Prize 45 times. Between 1901 and 2013, the Nobel Prize in Physics has been awarded 107 times to 195 different individuals, including two women. During the same time period, the Nobel Prize in Chemistry has been awarded 105 times to 165 different individuals, including four women (Nobel Prize Awarded Women).

Female Nobel Laureates in Physics

Marie Curie received the Nobel Prize in Physics in 1903. She shared this award with Pierre Curie, her husband, and Henri Becquerel. These individuals were honored "in recognition of the extraordinary services they have rendered by their joint researches on the radiation phenomena" (Nobel Prize Awarded Women).

Maria Goeppert Mayer and J. Hans D. Jensen shared part of the Nobel Prize in Physics in 1963 "for their discoveries concerning nuclear shell structure" (Nobel Prize Awarded Women).

Female Nobel Laureates in Chemistry

Marie Curie was the first woman to receive the Nobel Prize for Chemistry and the only woman between 1903 and 2013 to receive two Nobel Prizes. She received her award for chemistry

Letter mailing address. The name and address of the person to whom you are writing is called the **letter mailing address**. Key a personal title (*Miss, Mr., Mrs., Ms.*) or a professional title (*Dr., Lt., Senator*) before the receiver's name. Use SHIFT + ENTER to key all lines of the letter mailing address except the last line. Tap ENTER once after keying the last line.

Salutation. A **salutation** is a greeting. Key a salutation, such as *Dear Mr. Smith*, after the letter address. Tap ENTER once after keying the salutation.

Body. The paragraphs or message of a letter is called the **body**. Tap ENTER once after each paragraph in the body.

Complimentary close. Key the **complimentary close** (the farewell for a letter) after the last paragraph. *Sincerely* is an example of a complimentary close. Tap ENTER twice after keying the complimentary close.

Writer's name. Key the writer's name below the complimentary close. A personal title (*Miss, Ms.*) may be used before the name to indicate how a female prefers to be addressed in a response. If a male has a name that does not clearly indicate his gender (*Kim, Leslie, Pat*), the title *Mr.* may precede his name. Tap ENTER once after keying the writer's name.

Reference initials. If the letter is keyed by someone other than the person whose name is keyed as the writer, the initials of the person keying the letter should be placed in lowercase letters at the left margin below the writer's name. Tap ENTER once after keying the **reference initials**.

Copy notation. If someone will receive a copy of the letter, add a **copy notation** after the writer's name (or below the reference initials if they are used). Key **c**, tab to the 0.5" mark, and key the name of the person receiving the copy. Tap ENTER once after keying the copy notation.

Attachment/Enclosure notation. If another document is attached to a letter, add an **attachment notation** to the letter by keying the word *Attachment* below the preceding letter part. If the additional document is not attached, add an **enclosure notation** to the letter by keying the word *Enclosure*.

Punctuation style. Open punctuation style does not use punctuation after the salutation or complimentary close. Mixed punctuation style uses a colon after the salutation and a comma after the complimentary close.

Assessment 1　Reports, Email, and Letters

Warmup Practice

Key each line twice. If time permits, key the lines again.

Alphabet

1 Javy quickly swam the dozen extra laps before Gus.

Figure/Symbol

2 Blake's cell number was changed to (835) 109-2647.

Speed

3 The six men may work down by the lake on the dock.

gwam 1' | 1 | 2 | 3 | 4 | 5 | 6 | 7 | 8 | 9 | 10 |

Activity 1
Assess Straight-Copy Skill

Key one or two 2' timed writings on both paragraphs combined. Print, proofread, circle errors, and determine *gwam*.

 all letters used

gwam 2'

Money is much harder to save than it is to	4
earn. Somebody is always willing to help you	9
spend what you make. If you confuse your needs	14
and wants, you can quickly spend much of it	18
yourself. Often, friends and relations can	23
become an additional major drain if you allow	27
them to assist you.	29
And, of course, many politicians at all	33
levels think that they can spend your money for	38
you much better than you can do it yourself. It	43
is really amazing how ready some are to spend the	48
money of others. At times their motives may be	53
excellent; at other times, just selfish. So	58
beware.	59

gwam 2' | 1 | 2 | 3 | 4 | 5 |

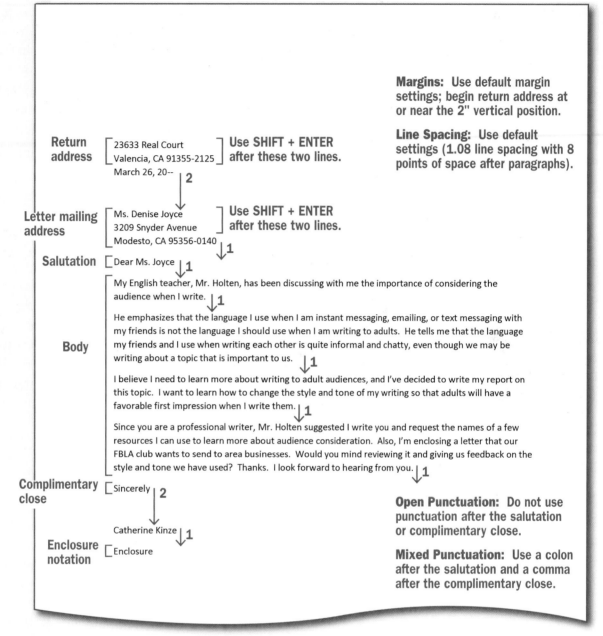

Margins: Use default margin settings; begin return address at or near the 2" vertical position.

Line Spacing: Use default settings (1.08 line spacing with 8 points of space after paragraphs).

Return address
23633 Real Court
Valencia, CA 91355-2125
} Use SHIFT + ENTER after these two lines.
March 26, 20--

↓2

Letter mailing address
Ms. Denise Joyce
3209 Snyder Avenue
Modesto, CA 95356-0140
} Use SHIFT + ENTER after these two lines.

↓1

Salutation
Dear Ms. Joyce ↓1

Body
My English teacher, Mr. Holten, has been discussing with me the importance of considering the audience when I write. ↓1

He emphasizes that the language I use when I am instant messaging, emailing, or text messaging with my friends is not the language I should use when I am writing to adults. He tells me that the language my friends and I use when writing each other is quite informal and chatty, even though we may be writing about a topic that is important to us. ↓1

I believe I need to learn more about writing to adult audiences, and I've decided to write my report on this topic. I want to learn how to change the style and tone of my writing so that adults will have a favorable first impression when I write them. ↓1

Since you are a professional writer, Mr. Holten suggested I write you and request the names of a few resources I can use to learn more about audience consideration. Also, I'm enclosing a letter that our FBLA club wants to send to area businesses. Would you mind reviewing it and giving us feedback on the style and tone we have used? Thanks. I look forward to hearing from you. ↓1

Complimentary close
Sincerely ↓2

Catherine Kinze ↓1

Enclosure notation
Enclosure

Open Punctuation: Do not use punctuation after the salutation or complimentary close.

Mixed Punctuation: Use a colon after the salutation and a comma after the complimentary close.

Personal-Business Letter in Block Format with Open Punctuation

52B

Personal-Business Letter

COLLABORATION

1. Open a new, blank document.

2. Key the letter shown on the next page. Check the spelling and proofread the letter carefully. Correct all errors. Save the letter as *52b letter* and close it.

 **checkpoint** Check the format of a classmate's letter. Have that classmate check the format of your letter. Was mixed punctuation used? Discuss any errors that either of you found and correct them.

Strengths, Values, and Wants

Everyone has personal strengths and values that make him or her unique. This activity will allow you to evaluate your values and skills.

1. Open *df c6 strengths and values* and save it as *c6 strengths and values*. Follow the instructions to have a friend rank you and then rank yourself.

2. Continue to follow the directions in the data file to mark areas you would like to change about yourself. Then summarize each section and write a letter to a potential employer.

3. Close all open documents.

Activity 5

To complete this activity, you will need the Student Interest Survey that you filled out in Career Exploration Portfolio Activity 1. Completing Career Exploration Activities 2–4 would also be very helpful but is not mandatory.

1. Review your Student Interest Survey. Note your *first* Career Cluster of interest. Reread its description.

2. Go to http://www.careertech.org. Click the **Career Technical Education** button, then click Career Clusters to open the Career Clusters page. Click your first Career Cluster choice.

3. Scroll through the categories available within that Career Cluster. Click the Knowledge & Skills Statements **Excel** link under the category you are most interested in to download it to your system. (Choose the same category, or Pathway, that you used in Activity 2 if you completed it.)

4. Locate the downloaded file on your system and open it. Scroll down and read the knowledge and skill statements for this career.

5. Think about the knowledge and skills you have gained from classes at school, after-school activities, and other experiences. Do they match any of the knowledge and skills listed in this file? If not, how can you gain them?

6. Write a summary of what you discovered through this activity. Save the document as *c6 career 1 skills*, print, and close it.

207 Brainard Road
Hartford, CT 06114-2207
May 15, 20--

Mr. Justin A. Alaron
Brighton Life Insurance Co.
I-84 & Route 322
Milldale, CT 06467-9371

Dear Mr. Alaron:

Your job in actuarial science is of great interest to me. I am a student at Milldale School and participate in the Shadow Experience Program (SEP). I learned about actuarial science while researching jobs related to mathematics. Math is my favorite subject, and I have done very well in all of my math classes. Math appears to be one of my strengths.

SEP encourages students to shadow a person who is working in a career field they are exploring. I would like to shadow you for one or two days so that I can learn more about what an actuary does. A brochure with more information about SEP is enclosed.

I can arrange to be with you at your office for one or two days during the coming month. Please send your written response to me so that I can present it to Ms. Michelle Kish, the SEP coordinator. Thank you.

Sincerely,

Ms. Valerie E. Lopez

Enclosure

52C

Cut, Copy, and Paste

WP   Home/Clipboard/
Cut, Copy, or Paste

When you write a report or letter, you may write several drafts or versions of it. You may decide to cut some data that does not fit with the subject. You may decide to move a word, sentence, or paragraph from one place to another. Once you have selected the text you want to cut or move, the **Cut**, **Copy**, and **Paste** features can be used to make these types of changes to a document.

The Cut command removes selected text from a document. The Copy command copies selected text so it can be pasted to another location. The Paste command places text that has been cut or copied into a document. You can access the Cut, Copy, and Paste commands quickly by clicking the buttons in the Clipboard group on the Home tab, as shown in Figure 6.6.

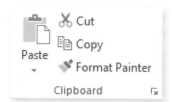

Figure 6.6 *Cut, Copy, and Paste*

ACROSS THE CURRICULUM

Academic Connections

Social Studies: Lewis and Clark

In 1803, President Thomas Jefferson bought a large area of land from France. It was called the Louisiana Purchase. Jefferson hired Meriwether Lewis and William Clark to learn about the land. They were told to gather data about the land, climate, plants, and animals. They were also told to follow the Missouri River to its source and to find the most direct water route to the Pacific.

Data Files:

df c6 museum letter
df c6 copies
df c6 strengths and
values

1. Start *Word* and open the document *df c6 museum letter*.

2. Follow the instructions in the data file to create a personal-business letter. Correct any errors you find and create an envelope.

3. Save the document as *c6 museum letter*. Print the letter and the envelope and then close the document.

About Business

Analyzing Costs and Benefits

Business owners usually have a limited amount of money, so they need to decide how to spend it. For example, should they buy new equipment or spend more on advertising? To help owners make decisions, they can analyze their costs and benefits. A typical approach includes the steps below:

- **Define a problem.** For example, a problem could be stated as, "How do we spend our advertising funds?"
- **Identify the choices available.** Choices could be made to spend money on television, magazines, radio, newspapers, or website ads.
- **Gather data.** Gather data on the costs of each advertising method. Also decide which ads will reach your target customers.
- **Analyze the data.** Compare the expected increase in sales to the cost of each type of advertisement.
- **Make a decision and take action.** If radio and magazine ads cost the least and are most effective, choose to advertise using these methods.

COLLABORATION

1. Open *df c6 copies*.

2. Read the steps in the data file. Follow the instructions to analyze the costs and benefits. After you key your answers, save the document as *c6 copies*, print, and close it.

3. Summarize your decision in an email message. Send it to your instructor and one classmate. Also watch for a similar email from one of your classmates. When you receive it, respond (using Reply All) to tell that student whether you agree with his or her decision.

Activity 1

1. Open the document *df 52c paste1*.

2. Cut the line numbered 1 and paste it at the beginning of the first line.

3. Read the Tip at the left. Drag the line numbered 2 so it follows line 1.

4. Select all four lines. Copy and paste them to the blank paragraph below line 4.

5. Save the document as *52c paste1* and close it.

TIP You also can move text from one place to another by selecting it and dragging it to a new location.

Activity 2

1. Open *df 52c paste2*.

2. Use Cut and Paste to move paragraph 2 to make it paragraph 1.

3. Move the *Don't Be Offensive* heading so that it is above paragraph 4, and move the *Be On Guard* heading so that it is above paragraph 5.

4. Save the document as *52c paste2* and close it.

52D

Find and Replace

WP Home/Editing/Find or Replace

TIP The word you want to find can appear as part of other words. For example, *pay* may appear in *payment*. To prevent this, click the More button and select Find whole words only.

The **Find and Replace** dialog box (see Figure 6.7) can be used to quickly search for a keystroke, word, or phrase in a document and then replace that text with the desired keystroke, word, or phrase. All occurrences of the text in the document can be replaced at one time, or replacements can be made individually (selectively). You can refine this feature by using the More button to display various search and find and replace options. To access the Find and Replace dialog box, choose Replace from the Editing group (see Figure 6.8).

Figure 6.7 *Find and Replace dialog box*

Figure 6.8 *Editing group*

1 Jan left to go home.

2 They won their last game.

3 Kay's test score was terrible.

4 The four games may not be canceled.

5 The hurricane struck Florida on Tuesday.

6 The teacher said Jane could make up the exam.

7 She may be able to catch a later flight on Friday.

gwam 30" | 2 | 4 | 6 | 8 | 10 | 12 | 14 | 16 | 18 | 20 |

Speed Building

1. Key three 1' timed writings on each paragraph, striving to key more on each timing; determine *gwam*.

2. Key a 2' timed writing on both paragraphs combined, striving to maintain your highest 1' *gwam*.

A all letters used

	gwam 1'	2'
• 2 • 4 • 6 • 8		
To move to the next level of word processing	9	5
10 • 12 • 14 • 16 • 18 •		
power, you must now demonstrate certain abilities.	19	10
20 • 22 • 24 • 26 • 28 •		
First, you must show that you can key with good	29	15
30 • 32 • 34 • 36 • 38 •		
technique, a modest level of speed, and a limit on	39	20
40 • 42 • 44 • 46 • 48 •		
errors. Next, you must properly apply the basic	49	25
50 • 52 • 54 • 56 • 58 •		
rules of language use. Finally, you must arrange	59	30
60 • 62 • 64		
basic documents properly.	**64**	35
• 2 • 4 • 6 • 8		
If you believe you have already learned	8	39
• 10 • 12 • 14 • 16 •		
enough, think of the future. Many jobs today	17	44
18 • 20 • 22 • 24 • 26 •		
require a higher degree of keying skill than you	27	49
28 • 30 • 32 • 34 • 36 •		
have acquired so far. Recognize, also, that other	37	54
38 • 40 • 42 • 44 • 46		
styles of letters and reports and more complex	46	59
• 48 • 50 • 52 • 54 • 56		
tables are in common use. As a result, would you	56	64
• 58 • 60 • 62 • 64 •		
not benefit from another semester of training?	**66**	69

gwam 1' | 1 | 2 | 3 | 4 | 5 | 6 | 7 | 8 | 9 | 10 |
2' | 1 | 2 | 3 | 4 | 5 |

checkpoint

How many times does *pay* appear in the document after the replacements have been made? Compare your answer with a classmate's answer.

Activity 1

1. Open *df 52d replace1*. Make the following changes using Find and Replace.
   a. Replace *dairy* with *grocery store*.
   b. Replace all occurrences of *assessments* with *taxes*.
   c. Replace the second and fourth occurrences of *pay* with *earnings*.
   d. Replace social security with Social Security.
2. Save the document as *52d replace1* and close it.

Activity 2

1. Open *df 52d replace2*. Make the following changes:
   a. Change *Rd.* to *Road*.
   b. Change *Str.* to *Street*.
   c. Change *Ave.* to *Avenue*.
   d. Change *Blvd.* to *Boulevard*.
   e. Change *Ln.* to *Lane*.
   f. Change *Dr.* to *Drive* in the street addresses but not the *Dr.* that appears as a personal title.
   g. Change *Miss* to *Ms.*
   h. Change *Ms. Stacey Bethel* to *Mrs. Stacey Bell*.
   i. Change *Ms. Ann Buck* to *Dr. Ann Buck*.

checkpoint

Did you remove the periods after the abbreviations in the street addresses? Did you add the period to *Ms.*? Did you leave *Dr.* as the personal title? Did you add the comma between the city and state?

2. Use Find and Replace to insert a comma after the city name. *Hint:* In the Find what box, tap the Space Bar once and key **TX**. In the Replace with box, key a comma, tap Space Bar once, and key **TX**.

3. Save the document as *52d replace2* and close it.

52E

Personal-Business Letter

COLLABORATION

1. Open *df 52e letter*. The letter parts are identified in red font. Arrange the letter in block format by using Cut and Paste to put the letter parts in the proper order. (Do not delete the text in red.) Use mixed punctuation.

2. Use Find and Replace to make these changes: *plane* to *airplane*, *scattered* to *soft*, and *positive* to *meaningful*.

3. Save the document as *52e letter*, print it, and close it. Exchange letters with a classmate and verify that the letter parts are in the correct order, mixed punctuation has been used, and the format is correct. Make any needed changes.

KEYBOARDING SKILLBUILDING

Warmup Practice

Key each line twice. If time permits, key the lines again.

Alphabet

1 Jasper amazed Hank by quickly fixing two big vans.

Figure/Symbol

2 Tax (451.38) was added to the invoice (#40-62-79).

Speed

3 Laurie may fish off the big dock down by the lake.

gwam 1' | 1 | 2 | 3 | 4 | 5 | 6 | 7 | 8 | 9 | 10 |

Technique Mastery of Individual Letters

Key each line twice, striving to maintain a continuous pace.

TECHNIQUE TIP
Keep your fingers curved and upright.

A Abe ate banana bread at Anna's Cafe at 18 Parkway.

B Bob Abbott bobbled the baseball hit by Barb Banks.

C Cecelia can check the capacities for each cubicle.

D Dan added additional games and divided the squads.

E Emery recently developed three new feet exercises.

F Jeff Florez offered the fifty officials free food.

G Gregg gingerly gave the giggling girl a gold ring.

H Herb shared his half of the hay with his neighbor.

I I will live in Illinois after leaving Mississippi.

J Jay, Jet, and Joy enjoyed the jet ride to Jamaica.

K Kay Kern took the kayak to Kentucky for Kent Kick.

L Will lives in Idaho; Lance Bell lives in Illinois.

M Mary Mead assumed the maximum and minimum amounts.

gwam 30" | 2 | 4 | 6 | 8 | 10 | 12 | 14 | 16 | 18 | 20 |

Digital Citizenship and Ethics

Through texting and instant messaging, users of digital technologies have developed their own form of shorthand or texting slang. For example, most of us are familiar with HRU for "how are you?" and the popular LOL for "laughing out loud." This type of exchange is acceptable between friends and in casual, nonbusiness communications. But more and more, it is finding its way into the professional world.

According to a recent survey of human resource managers, strong written communication skills are essential not only to getting hired but also to advancing. Employers expect workers at every level to be able to string together clear,

coherent thoughts in all forms of written communication. In a competitive job environment, successful digital citizens must be able to distinguish between appropriate writing for personal and professional purposes. They must pay close attention to the quality of their writing and how to use it effectively to reflect their best selves.

As a class, discuss the following:

1. How might the use of texting slang and shorthand in a business situation reflect negatively on an individual's communication skills?
2. What measures can you take now in your daily digital activities to strengthen your written communication skills?

Lesson 53 — Personal-Business Letters and Envelopes

Data Files:
df 53a preview
df 53c letter

Learning Outcomes

In Lesson 53, you will:

53A *Use the Zoom feature.*
53B *Use Print screen options.*
53C *Prepare envelopes.*
53D *Create a personal-business letter and envelope.*

53A

Zoom

WP | View/Zoom

Sometimes having a close-up view of your document is helpful. At other times, you might want to see one or more pages at a reduced size. The various features in the **Zoom group** (see Figure 6.9) on the View tab allow you to see close-up or reduced views of a document.

The Zoom Slider at the lower right on the status bar can be used to zoom in and out while you are viewing a document. The Zoom Slider is shown in Figure 6.10.

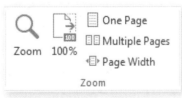

Figure 6.9 *Zoom group*

Figure 6.10 *Zoom Slider*

Personal-Business Letter in Block Format

1. Open a new *Word* document. Key the following personal-business letter in block format. Use mixed punctuation. Save the letter as *c6 letter1*; do not close it.

2. Create and print a No. 10 envelope with return and mailing addresses for the letter. Close *c6 letter1*.

```
853 North Highland Avenue Atlanta, GA 30306-0403
October 15, 20--

Ms. Amy Mazanetz
4505 Ashford Road
Atlanta, GA 30346-0346

Dear Ms. Mazanetz:

Thank you for speaking to our community Service Club. Your points
on the importance of giving back to the community were very well
received. They will help motivate us to do as much service work
as can we.

I enjoyed learning about the projects you have worked on. Our members
plan to adopt at least two of the projects you described. Your
thoughts about what it takes to plan and carry out service
projects will be helpful to us.

Again, thank you for sharing information with our club and
agreeing to work with us in the future.

Sincerely,

Alex Neu Secretary
```

Personal-Business Letter in Modified Block Format

1. Open *c6 letter1* and format it as a modified block letter with open punctuation and indented paragraphs.

2. Save the letter as *c6 letter2* and close it.

Personal-Business Letter in Block Format

1. Open *df c6 letter3*. Format the letter in block format with mixed punctuation. Use a 12-point Times New Roman font. Use your address as the return address. Insert the current date so that it updates automatically.

2. Use Find and Replace to make changes in the letter. Change *Doe* to *Ford*, *June* to *July*, *team* to *squad*, and *games* to *matches*.

3. Correct all spelling and grammar errors. Save the letter as *c6 letter3*.

4. Create a No. 10 envelope. Print the envelope. Close the letter.

1. Open *df 53a preview*.

2. Use the various options in the Zoom group to see the different ways the document can be displayed.

3. Move the Zoom Slider at the bottom right of the status bar to the left and right to see how the size of the document changes.

4. Close the document without saving the changes.

53B

Print Preview and Print Settings

Often, you will want to see the whole page on the screen to check the appearance (margins, spacing, graphics, tables, etc.) prior to printing the document. As you learned in 53A, features in the Zoom group can be used for this purpose. However, you can use the **Print screen** to display one or more pages of the document before you print it. You can use one or more of the options in the Settings list to make changes to margins, page orientation, paper size, etc., prior to printing the document. The Print screen is shown in Figure 6.11.

Figure 6.11 *Print screen*

1. Open *df 53a preview*. Access the Print screen. Preview the document that is displayed.

2. Use various options in the Settings list to see the changes that can be made to the document prior to printing. For example, change the margins, page orientation, paper size, etc.

3. Use the Zoom Slider at the lower-right corner of the Print screen to zoom in and out.

4. Close the document without saving any of the changes you made.

Before You Move On

Answer these questions to review what you have learned in Chapter 6.

1. An email address contains a(n) _____ name and a(n) _____ name separated by the _____ sign. LO 51A

2. What feature in the email software lets a person know that he or she received a copy of the email but the recipient does not know that person received a copy? LO 51A

3. When block format is used in a letter, all lines begin at the _____. LO 52A

4. When a letter is keyed, the line spacing should be set at _____. LO 52A

5. What two *Word* features allow you to see a document on screen in a reduced size? LO 53A & 53B

6. Identify the seven parts that should be included in a personal-business letter. LO 52A

7. Instead of keying a date in a letter, you can use the _____ feature to place the date in the letter. LO 54B

8. When modified block letter format is used, the return address, date, complimentary close, and _____ begin at the _____ mark on the Ruler. LO 54D

9. Use the _____ and _____ features to quickly move text from one place to another in a document. LO 52C

10. Use the _____ feature to locate words in a document and change them to other words. LO 52D

Applying What You Have Learned

Data File:

df c6 letter3

Email Message

1. Open *Outlook*. Key the following information as an email. Use an address provided by your teacher if the message is to be sent. If email software is not available, format the information as a standard, unbound report, using the subject for the report title.

SUBJECT: MATH REASONING SKILLS CHALLENGE

A meeting to discuss the Math Reasoning Skills Challenge has been set. The meeting will be on Tuesday, April 17, in Room 23 at 2:30 p.m. Vice Principal Arlo Rome will join us.

The main purpose of the meeting is to discuss the rules for taking part in this competition. We also will talk about program awards and future meeting dates.

2. Save the document as *c6 email* and close it.

WP | Mailings/Create/
Envelopes

You can use *Word*'s **Envelopes** feature to create envelopes for the letters you have keyed. This feature allows you to choose the size of the envelope, include the return address and delivery address, print the envelope, etc. (see Figure 6.12). The delivery address can be keyed, inserted automatically from the letter file, or inserted from your Address book.

In this lesson, you will learn to create a No. 10 envelope with delivery and return addresses. This is the most frequently used envelope size for letters printed on 8.5" × 11" paper.

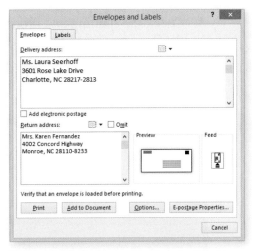

Figure 6.12 *Envelopes and Labels dialog box*

Envelope 1

1. Open *df 53c letter*. Select the lines of the letter mailing address so the letter address will be used to create the delivery address.

2. Use the Envelopes feature to prepare a No. 10 envelope. Confirm that Laura Seerhoff's name and address appear in the Delivery address box.

3. If necessary, remove the check mark from the Return address Omit checkbox. Key the following in the Return address box.

   Mrs. Karen Fernandez
   4002 Concord Highway
   Monroe, NC 28110-8233

4. Click the envelope in the Preview box to verify that a No. 10 envelope is being used.

5. Print the envelope. Close the document without saving the changes.

Envelope 2

1. Open a new, blank document.

2. Use your instructor's name and school address as the delivery address and your name and home address as the return address to prepare a No. 10 envelope.

3. Print the envelope. When it has printed, close the file without saving.

54F

**Modified Block
Personal-Business
Letter**

COLLABORATION

1. Open a new, blank document. Set tabs for a modified block letter with indented paragraphs.

2. Compose a letter to your teacher from you. Use your return address, insert the current date so that it does not update automatically, and address the letter to your teacher at your school's address. For the body of the letter, tell your teacher about a place you would like to visit for a class field trip. Give the name and the location or address. Describe the place. Explain why you think this would be a good place for your class to visit.

3. Check the spelling and proofread the letter carefully. Correct any errors. Use the Preview screen to check the format of the letter.

4. Save the letter as *54f letter*. Print the letter and close it.

 **checkpoint** Exchange papers with a classmate. Proofread and mark any errors you find in the letter. Make corrections to your letter if necessary.

ABOVE and BEYOND

Business Letters

In the previous lessons, you learned to create a personal-business letter. Another type of letter is used often in business. It is called a **business letter**. Business letters are sent from a person in a business to another person. The other person may work within the same business or at another business, or he or she may be a customer or client.

A business letter is the same as a personal-business letter with one difference. A return address is not keyed in a business letter. It is not keyed because business letters are printed on special paper. This paper is called **letterhead** paper. The business name and address are printed on letterhead paper. Letterhead paper often includes the company's phone and fax numbers. Web addresses are often included too.

 To view a business letter, open *df 54 above* in your data files. The file shows a letter keyed on letterhead paper. Notice that the letter contains *jas* before the enclosure notation. This letter part, *jas* in this letter, is called reference initials.

Reference initials are included in a letter when the person keying the letter is not the person whose name appears as the writer. In this letter, Harry Piper is the writer and the person who keyed the letter has the initials *jas*. The use of reference initials helps identify the person who keyed the letter. Reference initials also are used in personal-business letters that are keyed by someone other than the writer.

1. Open a new, blank document. Key the personal-business letter below using block format and open punctuation style.

2. When you are finished, use the Print screen or Zoom to check the format. Save the letter as *53d letter*. Print it.

3. Create and print a No. 10 envelope using the letter mailing address for the delivery address and the writer's name and address for the return address.

4. Save the letter as *53e letter* and close it.

8503 Kirby Dr.
Houston, TX 77054-8220
May 5, 20--

Ms. Jenna St. John, Personnel Director
Regency Company
219 West Greene Road
Houston, TX 77067-4219

Dear Ms. St. John:

Ms. Anne D. Salgado, my teacher, told me about your company's Computer Learn Program. She speaks very highly of your company and the computer program. She thinks I would benefit greatly by taking this course. After learning more about the program, I agree that the course would help me.

I am in the seventh grade at Taft School. I have completed a computer applications course. I learned to use spreadsheets in word processing reports. I also have taken a programming course. It introduced me to Visual Basic and HTML. I developed and maintain a website for my baseball team. A copy of my last grade report is enclosed.

I would like to visit you to talk more about the summer program. Please telephone me at (713) 555-0121 or email me at dougr@suresend.com to suggest a meeting date. I can meet with you any day after school. Thank you.

Sincerely,

Douglas H. Ruckert

Enclosure

TIP When you key an email address in a document, *Word* will automatically format it in blue with an underline.

207 Brainard Road
Hartford, CT 06114-2207
Insert date here

Mr. Glenn Rostello
3480 Martin Drive
North Olmsted, OH 44070-3000

Dear Mr. Rostello

Thank you for your inquiry about the best perennial plants to use along walkways. I have researched this topic and found several low-growing plants that will work well in our area.

Scientific Name	Common Name
Achillea ptarmica	Yarrow
Artemisia	Wormwood
Geranium	Geranium
Oenothera	Evening primrose
Sedum	Stonecrop
Trollius	Globeflower

Each of the above plants is available at our Ohio Street garden center. Anyone who buys plants this month will receive a 10 percent discount. If more than 15 plants are purchased, we will deliver and plant them for a small fee. When we do the planting, the plant has a one-year warranty.

Please say hello to me when you visit our store.

Sincerely

Harry Piper
Owner

Modified Block Personal-Business Letters

Data File:

df 54 above

Learning Outcomes

In this lesson, you will:

54A *Set Left, Right, Center, and Decimal Tabs.*

54B *Insert the date and time.*

54C *Set tabs and insert date and times.*

54D *Key a modified block personal-business letter with indented paragraphs.*

54E *Key a modified block personal-business letter with a list.*

54F *Compose a modified block personal-business letter.*

54A

Tabs

⌊⌋ (L)

Left Tab

⌐

Right Tab

⊥

Center Tab

⊥.

Decimal Tab

Tabs are set locations at which text can be placed. By default, a Left Tab is set every one-half inch on the Ruler and text appears to the right of it as you key if one or more manual tabs have not been set. Other tabs include Right Tabs, Center Tabs, and Decimal Tabs (see tab symbols at left). A Right Tab sets the start position so that text appears to the left of it as you type. Text that is keyed at a Center Tab appears to the left and right of it. A Decimal Tab aligns numbers on a decimal point, and text runs to the left or right depending on its position relative to the decimal point. In this lesson, you will use the Ruler to set manual tabs (see Figure 6.13). Tabs also can be set or formatted using the Tabs dialog box that is accessed from the Paragraph dialog box launched from the Home tab.

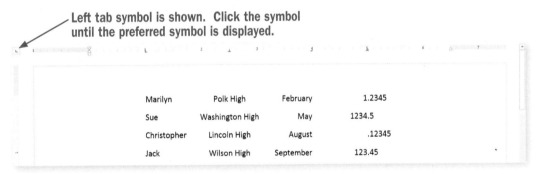

Left tab symbol is shown. Click the symbol until the preferred symbol is displayed.

Marilyn	Polk High	February	1.2345
Sue	Washington High	May	1234.5
Christopher	Lincoln High	August	.12345
Jack	Wilson High	September	123.45

Figure 6.13 *Ruler with tabs*

TIP You can move a tab on the Ruler by clicking and dragging it to the point you choose.
You can delete a tab on the Ruler by clicking and dragging it off the Ruler.

1. Open a new, blank document.

2. Verify that the Ruler is displayed. If not, select **Ruler** in the Show group on the View tab to display it.

3. Set the following tabs on the Ruler: a Left Tab at the 1" mark, a Center Tab at the 2.5" mark, a Right Tab at 4", and a Decimal Tab at 5".

4. Key the following text from left to right, using the TAB key to move from one column to the next. Begin the first column at the Left Tab, second column at the Center Tab, third column at the Right Tab, and fourth column at the Decimal Tab. Tap ENTER at the end of each line. Your copy should look like the copy in Figure 6.13.

Margins, vertical line spacing, and horizontal spacing for a modified block letter are the same as a block letter except as noted.

Set a Left Tab at the 3" mark on the Ruler and begin these lines at that point.

6894 Maddux Drive
Cincinnati, OH 45230-2411
March 6, 20--

Mr. Donald Rosenthal
H & R Specialty Company
876 Neeb Road
Cincinnati, OH 45233-0876

Dear Mr. Rosenthal

Open or mixed punctuation style may be used.

    Your company name was given to me by my math teacher, Miss Laura Eggleston. She spoke with you at the Tri-County Teachers of Mathematics Conference last month.

¶s may be indented 0.5" or blocked at the left margin

    I am the secretary of the Calculus Club. We need to purchase a variety of specialty items for a fund-raiser. We need to raise at least $650 to support the members of the Calculus Club who will participate in the Math Games in May.

    Please send us five copies of your current catalog so that we can review the items you have available and make our selections. We also need a list that shows the current price and the profit margin for each item.

    Please send an email to Miss Eggleston at eggleston@zoom.net if you need more information quickly.

Sincerely

Begin these lines at the Left Tab at the 3" mark on the Ruler.

Cora Nester
Calculus Club Secretary

copy notation ———— c   Miss Eggleston

Personal-Business Letter in Modified Block Format with Indented Paragraphs and Open Punctuation

54E

Modified Block Personal-Business Letter with List

1. Open a new, blank document. Key the following letter in modified block format without indented paragraphs. Use mixed punctuation. Set a Left Tab at 1.5" and a Right Tab at 5" to key the list of plants. Insert the date so that it automatically updates.

2. Check spelling and grammar and proofread the letter carefully. Correct any errors. Save the document as *54e letter* and close the file.

Marilyn	Polk High	February	1.2345
Sue	Washington High	May	1234.5
Christopher	Lincoln High	August	.12345
Jack	Wilson High	September	123.45

5. Save the document as *54a tabs* and close it.

WP | Insert/Text/Date & Time

The **Date & Time** feature is used to insert the date and/or time in a document. This feature can be helpful when you are keying letters and other documents that have dates. You can select the format for the date and time. You can select an option to have the date and time updated automatically each time the file is opened (see Figure 6.14). The Date & Time command is found on the Insert tab in the Text group.

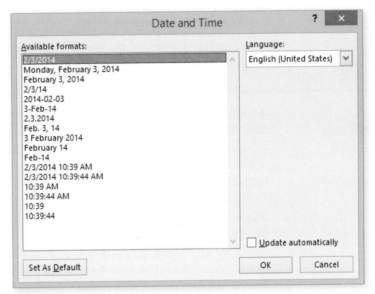

Figure 6.14 *Date and Time dialog box*

1. Open a new, blank document.

2. Use the Date & Time feature to insert today's date on line 1. Choose the format that is used to key the date in letters. Choose to not have the date updated automatically. Tap ENTER twice.

3. Use the Date & Time feature and select the format that will show the month/day/year and time in hours/minutes/seconds. Choose to have the date and time updated automatically. The current date and time should appear in your document. Write the minutes and seconds on a piece of paper so you will remember the time.

4. Save the document as *54b date* and close it.

5. Open *54b date* and look at the time. The time should have been updated to show the time you opened the document. Close the document without saving it.

Set Tabs and Insert Date and Time

Compare your difference to that of a classmate. Who used the least amount of time?

1. Open a new, blank document. Use the Date & Time feature to insert the current date on the first line, using a format you choose. (Do not update automatically.) Tap ENTER twice. Insert the time (including seconds) using a format you choose. (Do not update automatically.) Tap ENTER twice.

2. Key the following text using a Left Tab at 1", Center Tab at 2.5", Decimal Tab at 4", and Right Tab at 5.5".

Mary	Hawthorn	8.046	Cincinnati
Kenneth	Jones	18.03	Orlando
Jan	Leffington	256	Philadelphia
Nancy	Montgomery	.98	Dayton

3. Tap ENTER twice. Insert the time, using the same format you chose in step 1.

4. Subtract the time in step 1 from the time in step 3 to determine the difference. Key the difference two lines below the time.

5. Save the document as *54c practice* and close it.

54D

Modified Block Personal-Business Letter

You have learned to key personal-business letters using block format. In block format, all lines begin at the left margin. In modified block format, certain lines of the personal-business letter begin at or near the center of the page. The lines that begin at or near the center are the return address, date, complimentary close, typed signature, and typed title if it is included.

In addition, the first line of each paragraph may be indented 0.5" in a modified block letter. All other lines begin at the left margin. The spacing before and after the letter parts is the same as for block format.

Refer to the model copy on page 221 to view a personal-business letter arranged in modified block format. Notice the copy notation at the bottom left of the letter. If a copy notation is used, it is placed after the typed name, title, or enclosure notation, whichever is the last part of the letter.

1. Open a new, blank document. Set Left Tabs at 0.5" and 3".

2. Key the model copy on page 221 as a personal-business letter in modified block format with indented paragraphs and open punctuation.

3. Use Find and Replace to change all occurrences of *Calc* to *Calculus*.

4. Use Print Preview to check the accuracy of the format. Proofread and correct all errors. Save the letter as *54d letter* and close it.

Reference Guide

Capitalization Guides

Capitalize

1. The first word of every sentence and complete quotation. Do not capitalize (a) fragments of quotations or (b) a quotation resumed within a sentence.

   Crazy Horse said, "I will return to you in stone."
   Gandhi's teaching inspired "nonviolent revolutions."
   "It is . . . fitting and proper," Lincoln said, "that we . . . do this."

2. The first word after a colon if that word begins a complete sentence.

   Remember: Keep the action in your fingers.
   These sizes were in stock: small, medium, and extra large.

3. First, last, and all other words in titles except articles, conjunctions, or prepositions of four or fewer letters.

   The Beak of the Finch   *Raleigh News and Observer*
   "The Phantom of the Opera"

4. An official title when it precedes a name or when used elsewhere if it is a title of distinction.

   In what year did Juan Carlos become King of Spain?
   Masami Chou, our class president, met Senator Thurmond.

5. Personal titles and names of people and places.

   Did you see Mrs. Watts and Gloria while in Miami?

6. All proper nouns and their derivatives.

   Mexico   Mexican border   Uganda   Ugandan economy

7. Days of the week, months of the year, holidays, periods of history, and historic events.

   Friday   July   Labor Day
   Middle Ages   Vietnam War   Woodstock

8. Geographic regions, localities, and names.

   the East Coast   Upper Peninsula Michigan
   Ohio River   the Deep South

9. Street, avenue, company, etc., when used with a proper noun.

   Fifth Avenue   Wall Street   Monsanto Company

10. Names of organizations, clubs, and buildings.

    National Hockey League   Four-H Club
    Biltmore House   Omni Hotel

11. A noun preceding a figure except for common nouns, such as line, page, and sentence.

    Review Rules 1 to 18 in Chapter 5, page 149.

12. Seasons of the year only when they are personified.

    the soft kiss of Spring   the icy fingers of Winter

Number Expression Guides

Use words for

1. Numbers from one to ten except when used with numbers above ten, which are keyed as figures. Common business practice is to use figures for all numbers except those that begin a sentence.

   Did you visit all eight websites, or only four?
   Buy 15 textbooks and 8 workbooks.

2. A number beginning a sentence.

   Twelve of the new shrubs have died; 48 are doing well.

3. The shorter of two numbers used together.

   fifty 45-cent stamps   150 twenty-cent stamps

4. Isolated fractions or indefinite numbers in a sentence.

   Nearly seventy members voted, which is almost one-fourth.

5. Names of small-numbered streets and avenues (ten and under).

   The theater is at the corner of Third Avenue and 54th Street.

Use figures for

1. Dates and times except in very formal writing.

   The flight will arrive at 9:48 a.m. on March 14.
   The ceremony took place the fifth of June at eleven o'clock.

2. A series of fractions and/or mixed numbers.

   Key 1/4, 1/2, 5/6, and 7 3/4.

3. Numbers following nouns.

   Case 1849 is reviewed in Volume 5, page 9.

4. Measures, weights, and dimensions.

   6 feet 9 inches   7 pounds 4 ounces
   8.5 inches by 11 inches

5. Definite numbers used with percent (%), but use words for indefinite percentages.

   The late fee is 15 percent of the overdue payment.
   The brothers put in nearly fifty percent of the start-up capital.

6. House numbers except house number *One*.

   My home is at 8 Rose Lane; my office is at One Rose Plaza.

7. Amounts of money except when spelled for emphasis (as in legal documents). Even amounts are keyed without the decimal. Large amounts (a million or more) are keyed as shown.

   $17.75   75 cents $775   seven hundred dollars ($700)
   $7,500 $7 million $7.2 million $7 billion

Punctuation Guides

Use an apostrophe

1. As a symbol for *feet* in charts, forms, and tables or as a symbol for *minutes*. (The quotation mark may be used as a symbol for *seconds* and *inches*.)

   12' × 16'   3' 54"   8' 6" × 10' 8"

2. As a symbol to indicate the omission of letters or figures (as in contractions).

   can't   do's and don'ts   Class of '14

3. To form the plural of most figures, letters, and words used as words rather than for their meaning: Add the apostrophe and *s*. In market quotations and decades, form the plural of figures by the addition of *s* only.

   7's   ten's   ABC's   Century 4s   1960s

4. To show possession: Add the apostrophe and *s* to (a) a singular noun and (b) a plural noun that does not end in *s*.

   a woman's watch   men's shoes   girl's bicycle

   Add the apostrophe and *s* to a proper name of one syllable that ends in *s*.

   Bess's Cafeteria   James's hat   Jones's bill

   Add the apostrophe only after (a) plural nouns ending in *s* and (b) a proper name of more than one syllable that ends in *s* or *z*.

   girls' camp   Adams' home   Martinez' report

   Add the apostrophe (and *s*) after the last noun in a series to indicate joint or common possession by two or more persons; however, add the possessive to each of the nouns to show separate possession by two or more persons.

   Lewis and Clark's expedition
   the secretary's and the treasurer's reports

Use a colon

1. To introduce a listing.

   These poets are my favorites: Shelley, Keats, and Frost.

2. To introduce a question or a long direct quotation.

   The question is this: Did you study for the test?

3. Between hours and minutes expressed in figures.

   10:15 a.m.   4:30 p.m.   12:00 midnight

Use a comma (or commas)

1. After (a) introductory phrases or clauses and (b) words in a series.

   When you finish keying the report, please give it to Mr. Kent.
   We will play the Mets, Expos, and Cubs in our next home stand.

2. To set off short direct quotations.

   Mrs. Ramirez replied, "No, the report is not finished."

3. Before and after (a) appositives—words that come together and refer to the same person, thing, or idea—and (b) words of direct address.

   Colette, the assistant manager, will chair the next meeting.
   Please call me, Erika, if I can be of further assistance.

4. To set off nonrestrictive clauses (not necessary to meaning of sentence), but not restrictive clauses (necessary to meaning).

   Your report, which deals with that issue, raised many questions.
   The man who organized the conference is my teacher.

5. To separate the day from the year in dates and the city from the state in addresses.

   July 4, 2005   St. Joseph, Missouri   Moose Point, AK

6. To separate two or more parallel adjectives (adjectives that modify the noun separately and that could be separated by the word *and* instead of the comma).

   The big, loud bully was ejected after he pushed the coach.
   The big, powerful car zoomed past the cheering crowd.
   Cynthia played a black lacquered grand piano at her concert.
   A small red fox squeezed through the fence to avoid the hounds.

7. To separate (a) unrelated groups of figures that occur together and (b) whole numbers into groups of three digits each. (Omit commas from page, policy, room, serial, and telephone numbers.)

   By the year 2015, 1,200 more local students will be enrolled.
   The supplies listed on Invoice #274068 are for Room 1953.

Use a dash

Create a dash by keying two hyphens or one em-dash.

1. For emphasis.

   The skater—in a clown costume—dazzled with fancy footwork.

2. To indicate a change of thought.

   We may tour the Orient—but I'm getting ahead of my story.

3. To emphasize the name of an author when it follows a direct quotation.

   "All the world's a stage. . . ."—Shakespeare

4. To set off expressions that break off or interrupt speech.

   "Jay, don't get too close to the—:" I spoke too late.
   "Today—er—uh," the anxious presenter began.

Punctuation Guides (continued)

Use an exclamation point

1. After emphatic interjections.

   Wow!   Hey there!   What a day!

2. After sentences that are clearly exclamatory.

   "I won't go!" she said with determination.
   How good it was to see you in New Orleans last week!

Use a hyphen

1. To join parts of compound words expressing the numbers twenty-one through ninety-nine.

   Thirty-five delegates attended the national convention.

2. To join compound adjectives preceding a noun they modify as a unit.

   End-of-term grades will be posted on the classroom door.

3. After each word or figure in a series of words or figures that modify the same noun (suspended hyphenation).

   Meeting planners made first-, second-, and third-class reservations.

4. To spell out a word.

   The sign read, "For your c-o-n-v-i-e-n-c-e." Of course, the correct word is c-o-n-v-e-n-i-e-n-c-e.

5. To form certain compound nouns.

   WGAL-TV   spin-off   teacher-counselor   AFL-CIO

Use italic

To indicate titles of books, plays, movies, magazines, and newspapers. (Titles may be keyed in ALL CAPS or underlined.)

   A review of *Runaway Jury* appeared in *The New York Times*.

Use parentheses

1. To enclose parenthetical or explanatory matter and added information.

   Amendments to the bylaws (Exhibit A) are enclosed.

2. To enclose identifying letters or figures in a series.

   Check these factors: (1) period of time, (2) rate of pay, and (3) nature of duties.

3. To enclose figures that follow spelled-out amounts to give added clarity or emphasis.

   The total award is fifteen hundred dollars ($1,500).

Use a question mark

At the end of a sentence that is a direct question. But use a period after requests in the form of a question (whenever the expected answer is action, not words).

   What has been the impact of the Information Superhighway?
   Will you complete the enclosed form and return it to me.

Use quotation marks

1. To enclose direct quotations.

   Professor Dye asked, "Are you spending the summer in Europe?"
   Was it Emerson who said, "To have a friend is to be one"?

2. To enclose titles of articles, poems, songs, television programs, and unpublished works, such as theses and dissertations.

   "Talk of the Town" in the *New Yorker*   "Fog" by Sandburg
   "Survivor" in prime time   "Memory" from *Cats*

3. To enclose special words or phrases or coined words (words not in dictionary usage).

   The words "phony" and "braggart" describe him, according to coworkers.
   The presenter annoyed the audience with phrases like "uh" and "you know."

Use a semicolon

1. To separate two or more independent clauses in a compound sentence when the conjunction is omitted.

   Being critical is easy; being constructive is not so easy.

2. To separate independent clauses when they are joined by a conjunctive adverb, such as *consequently* or *therefore*.

   I work mornings; therefore, I prefer an afternoon interview.

3. To separate a series of phrases or clauses (especially if they contain commas) that are introduced by a colon.

   Al spoke in these cities: Denver, CO; Erie, PA; and Troy, NY.

4. To precede an abbreviation or word that introduces an explanatory statement.

   She organized her work; for example, naming folders and files to indicate degrees or urgency.

Use an underline

To call attention to words or phrases (or use quotation marks or italic).

   Take the presenter's advice: <u>Stand</u> up, <u>speak</u> up, and then <u>sit</u> down.
   Students often confuse <u>its</u> and <u>it's</u>.

Basic Grammar Guides

Use a singular verb

1. With a singular subject.
   Dr. Cho was to give the lecture, but he is ill.
2. With indefinite pronouns (*each, every, any, either, neither, one,* etc.)
   Each of these girls has an important role in the class play.
   Neither of them is well enough to start the game.
3. With singular subjects linked by *or* or *nor,* but if one subject is singular and the other is plural, the verb agrees with the nearer subject.
   Neither Ms. Moss nor Mr. Katz was invited to speak.
   Either the manager or his assistants are to participate.
4. With a collective noun (*class, committee, family, team,* etc.) if the collective noun acts as a unit.
   The committee has completed its study and filed a report.
   The jury has returned to the courtroom to give its verdict.
5. With the pronouns *all* and *some* (as well as fractions and percentages) when used as subjects if their modifiers are singular. Use a plural verb if their modifiers are plural.
   Some of the new paint is already cracking and peeling.
   All of the workers are to be paid for the special holiday.
   Historically, about 40 percent has voted.
6. When *number* is used as the subject and is preceded by *the,* use a plural verb if *number* is the subject and is preceded by *a.*
   The number of voters has increased again this year.
   A number of workers are on vacation this week.

Use a plural verb

1. With a plural subject.
   The players were all here, and they were getting restless.
2. With a compound subject joined by *and.*
   Mrs. Samoa and her son are to be on a local talk show.

Negative forms of verbs

1. Use the plural verb *do* or *don't* with pronoun subjects *I, we, you,* and *they* as well as with plural nouns.
   I do not find this report believable; you don't either.
2. Use the singular verb *does not* or *doesn't* with pronouns *he, she,* and *it* as well as with singular nouns.
   Though she doesn't accept the board's offer, the board doesn't have to offer more.

Pronoun agreement with antecedents

1. A personal pronoun (*I, we, you, he, she, it, their,* etc.) agrees in person (first, second, or third) with the noun or other pronoun it represents.
   We can win the game if we all give each play our best effort.
   You may play softball after you finish your homework.
   Andrea said that she will drive her car to the shopping mall.
2. A personal pronoun agrees in gender (feminine, masculine, or neuter) with the noun or other pronoun it represents.
   Each winner will get a corsage as she receives her award.
   Mr. Kimoto will give his talk after the announcements.
   The small boat lost its way in the dense fog.
3. A personal pronoun agrees in number (singular or plural) with the noun or other pronoun it represents.
   Celine drove her new car to Del Rio, Texas, last week.
   The club officers made careful plans for their next meeting.
4. A personal pronoun that represents a collective noun (*team, committee, family,* etc.) may be singular or plural, depending on the meaning of the collective noun.
   Our women's soccer team played its fifth game today.
   The vice squad took their positions in the square.

Commonly confused pronouns

it's (contraction): it is; it has
its (pronoun): possessive form of it
   It's good to get your email; it's been a long time.
   The puppy wagged its tail in welcome.

their (pronoun): possessive form of they
there (adverb/pronoun): at or in that place; sometimes used to introduce a sentence
they're (contraction): they are
   The hikers all wore their parkas.
   Will they be there during our presentation?
   They're likely to be late because of rush-hour traffic.

who's (contraction): who is; who has
whose (pronoun): possessive form of who
   Who's seen the movie? Who's going now?
   I chose the one whose skills are best.

Confusing Words

accept (vb) to receive; to approve; to take
except (prep/vb) with the exclusion of; leave out

affect (vb) to produce a change in or have an effect on
effect (n) result; something produced by an agent or a cause

buy (n/vb) to purchase; to acquire; a bargain
by (prep/adv) close to; via; according to; close at hand

choose (vb) to select; to decide
chose (vb) past tense of "choose"

cite (vb) use as support; commend; summon
sight (n/vb) ability to see; something seen; a device to improve aim
site (n) location

complement (n) something that fills, completes, or makes perfect
compliment (n/vb) a formal expression of respect or admiration; to pay respect or admiration

do (vb) to bring about; to carry out
due (adj) owed or owing as a debt; having reached the date for payment

farther (adv) greater distance
further (adv) additional; in greater depth; to greater extent

for (prep/conj) indicates purpose on behalf of; because of
four (n) two plus two in number

hear (vb) to gain knowledge of by the ear
here (adv) in or at this place; at or on this point; in this case

hole (n) opening in or through something
whole (adj/n) having all its proper parts; a complete amount

hour (n) the 24th part of a day; a particular time
our (adj) possessive form of "we"; of or relating to us

knew (vb) past tense of "know"; understood; recognized truth or nature of
new (adj) novel; fresh; existing for a short time

know (vb) to be aware of the truth or nature of; to have an understanding of
no (adv/adj/n) not in any respect or degree; not so; indicates denial or refusal

lessen (vb) to cause to decrease; to make less
lesson (n) something to be learned; period of instruction; a class period

lie (n/vb) an untrue or inaccurate statement; to tell an untrue story; to rest or recline
lye (n) a strong alkaline substance or solution

one (adj/pron) a single unit or thing
won (vb) past tense of win; gained a victory as in a game or contest; got by effort or work

passed (vb) past tense of "pass"; already occurred; moved by; gave an item to someone
past (adv/adj/prep/n) gone or elapsed; time gone by

personal (adj) of, relating to, or affecting a person; done in person
personnel (n) a staff or persons making up a workforce in an organization

plain (adj/n) with little decoration; a large flat area of land
plane (n) an airplane or hydroplane

pole (n) a long, slender, rounded piece of wood or other material
poll (n) a survey of people to analyze public opinion

principal (n/adj) a chief or leader; capital (money) amount placed at interest; of or relating to the most important thing or matter or persons
principle (n) a central rule, law, or doctrine

right (adj) factual; true; correct
rite (n) customary form of ceremony; ritual
write (v) to form letters or symbols; to compose and set down in words, numbers, or symbols

some (n/adv) unknown or unspecified unit or thing; to a degree or extent
sum (n/vb) total; to find a total; to summarize

stationary (adj) fixed in a position, course, or mode; unchanging in condition
stationery (n) paper and envelopes used for processing personal and business documents

than (conj/prep) used in comparisons to show differences between items
then (n/adv) that time; at that time; next

to (prep/adj) indicates action, relation, distance, direction
too (adv) besides; also; to excessive degree
two (n/adj) one plus one

vary (vb) change; make different; diverge
very (adv/adj) real; mere; truly; to high degree

waist (n) narrowed part of the body between chest and hips; middle of something
waste (n/vb/adj) useless things; rubbish; spend or use carelessly; nonproductive

weak (adj) lacking strength, skill, or proficiency
week (n) a series of seven days; Monday through Sunday

wear (vb/n) to bear or have on the person; diminish by use; clothing
where (adv/conj/n) at, in, or to what degree; what place, source, or cause

your (adj) of or relating to you as possessor
you're (contraction) you are

Proofreaders' marks are used to mark corrections in keyed or printed text that contains problems and/or errors. As a keyboard user, you should be able to read these marks accurately when revising or editing a rough draft. You also should be able to write these symbols to correct the rough drafts that you and others key. The most-used proofreaders' marks are shown below.

=	Align copy; also, make these items parallel
¶	Begin a new paragraph
cap ≡	Capitalize
⌒	Close up
⅄	Delete
⅄#	Delete space
No ¶	Do not begin a new paragraph
∧	Insert
∧ (comma)	Insert comma
⊙	Insert period
∜	Insert quotation marks
#	Insert space
∨	Insert apostrophe
stet	Let it stand; ignore correction
lc	Lowercase
⌐	Move down; lower
⊏	Move left
⊐	Move right
⌐	Move up; raise
sp	Spell out
↔	Transpose
—	Underline or italic

Email Format and Software Features

Email format varies slightly, depending on the software used to create and send it.

Email Heading

Most email software includes these features:

Attachment: line for attaching files to an email message

Bcc: line for sending copy of a message to someone without the receiver knowing

Cc: line for sending copy of a message to additional receivers

Date: month, day, and year message is sent; often includes precise time of transmittal; usually is inserted automatically

From: name and/or email address of sender; usually is inserted automatically

Subject: line for very brief description of message content

To: line for name and/or email address of receiver

Email Body

The message box on the email screen may contain these elements or only the message paragraphs (SS with DS between paragraphs).

- Informal salutation and/or receiver's name (a DS above the message)
- Informal closing (e.g., "Regards," "Thanks") and/or the sender's name (a DS below the message). Additional identification (e.g., telephone number) may be included.

Special Email Features

Several email features make communicating through email fast and efficient.

Address list/book: collection of names and email addresses of correspondents from which an address can be entered on the To: line by selecting it, instead of keying it.

Distribution list: series of names and/or email addresses, separated by commas, on the To: line.

Forward: feature that allows an email user to send a copy of a received email message to others.

Recipient list (Group): feature that allows an email user to send mail to a group of recipients by selecting the name of the group (e.g., All Teachers).

Reply: feature used to respond to an incoming message.

Reply all: feature used to respond to all copy recipients as well as the sender of an incoming message.

Signature: feature for storing and inserting the closing lines of messages (e.g., informal closing, sender's name, telephone number, address, fax number).

Interoffice Memo

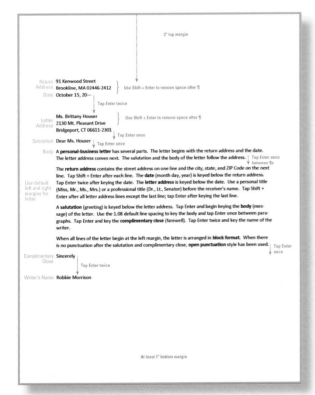

Personal-Business Letter in Block Format with Open Punctuation

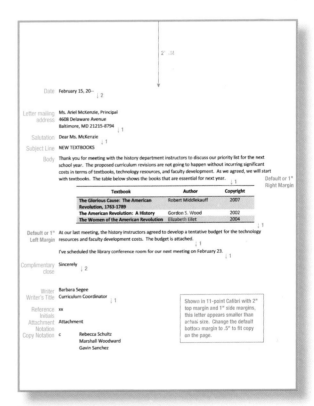

Business Letter in Block Format with Special Features

Letter in Modified Block Format with Postscript

Approximately 2" TM
or Center Vertically

Begin Dateline, Complimentary Close,
Writer's name and title at same tab at
or near the center.

Date — September 15, 20-- ↓1

Mailing notation — FACSIMILE ↓1

Attention line in letter address — Attention Training and Development Department ↓1   } Remove space after paragraph—
Science Technologies ↓1   use Shift Enter to insert Line Break
3368 Bay Path Road ↓1   after first three lines.
Miami, FL 33160-3368 ↓1

Salutation — Ladies and Gentlemen: ↓1

Subject line — MODIFIED BLOCK FORMAT ↓1

Body — This letter is arranged in modified block format. In this letter format the date and closing lines (complimentary close, name of the writer, and the writer's title) begin at or near horizontal center. In block
format all letter parts begin at the left margin. ↓1

Default or 1.25" LM and RM — Mixed punctuation (a colon after the salutation and a comma after the complimentary close) is used in
this example. Open punctuation (no mark after the salutation or complimentary close) may be used
with the modified block format if you prefer. ↓1

The first line of each paragraph may be blocked as shown here or indented one-half inch. If paragraphs
are indented, the optional subject line may be indented or centered. If paragraphs are blocked at the
left margin, the subject line is blocked, too. ↓1

Complimentary close — Sincerely, ↓2

Writer — Derek Alan ↓1   } Remove space after paragraph—
Writer's title — Manager ↓1   use Shift Enter to insert Line Break
                                after name.

Reference initials — DA:xx ↓1

Enclosure notation — Enclosure ↓1

Copy notation — c   Kimberly Rodriquez-Duarte ↓1

Postscript — A block format letter is enclosed so that you can compare the two formats. As you see,
either format presents an attractive appearance.

At least 1" BM

**Letter in Modified Block
Format with Postscript**

Memo with Special Features

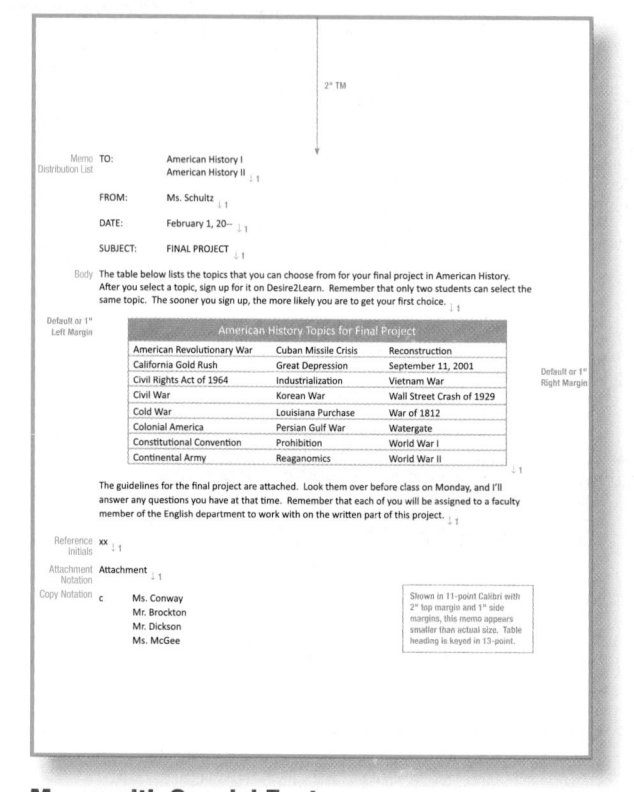

2" TM

Memo Distribution List — TO: American History I
                                American History II ↓1

FROM: Ms. Schultz ↓1

DATE: February 1, 20-- ↓1

SUBJECT: FINAL PROJECT ↓1

Body — The table below lists the topics that you can choose from for your final project in American History.
After you select a topic, sign up for it on Desire2Learn. Remember that only two students can select the
same topic. The sooner you sign up, the more likely you are to get your first choice. ↓1

Default or 1" Left Margin

American History Topics for Final Project		
American Revolutionary War	Cuban Missile Crisis	Reconstruction
California Gold Rush	Great Depression	September 11, 2001
Civil Rights Act of 1964	Industrialization	Vietnam War
Civil War	Korean War	Wall Street Crash of 1929
Cold War	Louisiana Purchase	War of 1812
Colonial America	Persian Gulf War	Watergate
Constitutional Convention	Prohibition	World War I
Continental Army	Reaganomics	World War II

Default or 1" Right Margin

↓1

The guidelines for the final project are attached. Look them over before class on Monday, and I'll
answer any questions you have at that time. Remember that each of you will be assigned to a faculty
member of the English department to work with on the written part of this project. ↓1

Reference Initials — xx ↓1

Attachment Notation — Attachment ↓1

Copy Notation — c   Ms. Conway
                     Mr. Brockton
                     Mr. Dickson
                     Ms. McGee

Shown in 11-point Calibri with
2" top margin and 1" side
margins, this memo appears
smaller than actual size. Table
heading is keyed in 13-point.

Memo with Special Features

Letter in Modified Block Format with Paragraph Indentations and List

Current date

Ms. Valerie E. Lopez
207 Brainard Road
Hartford, CT 06114-2207

Dear Ms. Lopez:

SHADOWING AT BRIGHTON LIFE INSURANCE CO.

I'm pleased that you have chosen Brighton Life Insurance Co. as the place where
you want to complete your shadow experience. I believe that you will learn a great deal
about being an actuary by spending two days at Brighton with me.

To help you prepare for your visit, I have listed some of the things you should
know about actuaries:

- Gather and analyze statistics to determine probabilities of death, sick-
  ness, injury, disability, unemployment, retirement, and property loss.

- Specialize in either life and health insurance or property and casualty insurance; or specialize in pension plans or employee benefits.

- Hold a bachelor's degree in mathematics or a business area, such as actuarial science, finance, or accounting.

- Possess excellent communication and interpersonal skills.

Also, I have enclosed actuarial career information published by the Society of
Actuaries (life and health insurance), Casualty Actuarial Society (property and casualty
insurance), and American Society of Pension Actuaries (pensions). These three associations offer actuaries professional certification through a series of examinations. We can
discuss the societies and the importance of obtaining the professional designations they
offer.

**Letter in Modified Block Format
with Paragraph Indentations and List**

Letter (p. 2) Showing Second-Page Heading

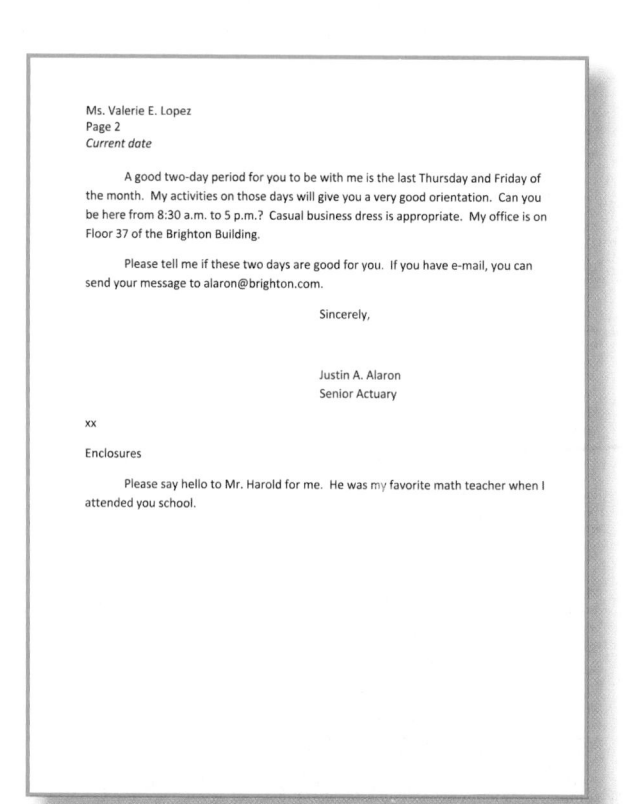

Ms. Valerie E. Lopez
Page 2
Current date

A good two-day period for you to be with me is the last Thursday and Friday of
the month. My activities on those days will give you a very good orientation. Can you
be here from 8:30 a.m. to 5 p.m.? Casual business dress is appropriate. My office is on
Floor 37 of the Brighton Building.

Please tell me if these two days are good for you. If you have e-mail, you can
send your message to alaron@brighton.com.

Sincerely,

Justin A. Alaron
Senior Actuary

xx

Enclosures

Please say hello to Mr. Harold for me. He was my favorite math teacher when I
attended you school.

Letter (p. 2) Showing Second-Page Heading

Envelope Guides

Return Address

Use block style, SS, and Initial Caps or ALL CAPS. If not using the Envelopes feature, begin as near to the top and left edge of the envelope as possible— TM and LM about 0.25".

Receiver's Delivery Address

Use block style, SS, and Initial Caps. If desired, use ALL CAPS instead of initial caps and omit the punctuation. Place city name, two-letter state abbreviation, and ZIP Code +4 on last address line. One space precedes the ZIP Code.

If not using the Envelopes feature, tab over 2.5" for the small envelope and 4" for the large envelope. Insert hard returns to place the first line about 2" from the top.

Mailing Notations

Key mailing and addressee notations in ALL CAPS.

Key mailing notations, such as SPECIAL DELIVERY and REGISTERED, below the stamp and at least three lines above the envelope address.

Key addressee notations, such as HOLD FOR ARRIVAL or PERSONAL, a DS below the return address and about three spaces from the left edge of the envelope.

If an attention line is used, key it as the first line of the envelope address.

Standard Abbreviations

Use USPS standard abbreviations for states (see list below) and street suffix names, such as AVE and BLVD. Never abbreviate the name of a city or country.

International Addresses

Omit postal (ZIP) codes from the last line of addresses outside the U.S. Show only the name of the country on the last line. Examples:

```
Mr. Hiram Sanders
2121 Clearwater St.
Ottawa, Onkia  OB1
CANADA

Ms. Inge D. Fischer
Hartmannstrasse 7
4209 Bonn 5
FEDERAL REPUBLIC OF GERMANY
```

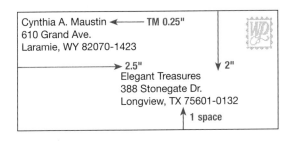

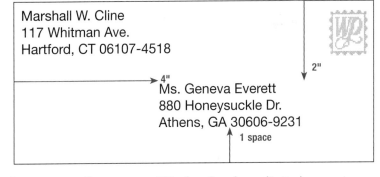

Folding Procedures

Small Envelopes (Nos. 6¾, 6¼)

1. With page face up, fold bottom up to 0.5" from top.
2. Fold right third to left.
3. Fold left third to 0.5" from last crease.
4. Insert last creased edge first.

Large Envelopes (Nos. 10, 9, 7¾)

1. With page face up, fold slightly less than one-third of sheet up toward top.
2. Fold down top of sheet to within 0.5" of bottom fold.
3. Insert last creased edge first.

Window Envelopes (Letter)

1. With page face down, top toward you, fold upper third down.
2. Fold lower third up so address is showing.
3. Insert sheet into envelope with last crease at bottom.
4. Check that address shows through window.

State and Territory Abbreviations

Alabama	AL	Illinois	IL	Nebraska	NE	South Carolina	SC
Alaska	AK	Indiana	IN	Nevada	NV	South Dakota	SD
Arizona	AZ	Iowa	IA	New Hampshire	NH	Tennessee	TN
Arkansas	AR	Kansas	KS	New Jersey	NJ	Texas	TX
California	CA	Kentucky	KY	New Mexico	NM	Utah	UT
Colorado	CO	Louisiana	LA	New York	NY	Vermont	VT
Connecticut	CT	Maine	ME	North Carolina	NC	Virgin Islands	VI
Delaware	DE	Maryland	MD	North Dakota	ND	Virginia	VA
District of Columbia	DC	Massachusetts	MA	Ohio	OH	Washington	WA
Florida	FL	Michigan	MI	Oklahoma	OK	West Virginia	WV
Georgia	GA	Minnesota	MN	Oregon	OR	Wisconsin	WI
Guam	GU	Mississippi	MS	Pennsylvania	PA	Wyoming	WY
Hawaii	HI	Missouri	MO	Puerto Rico	PR		
Idaho	ID	Montana	MT	Rhode Island	RI		

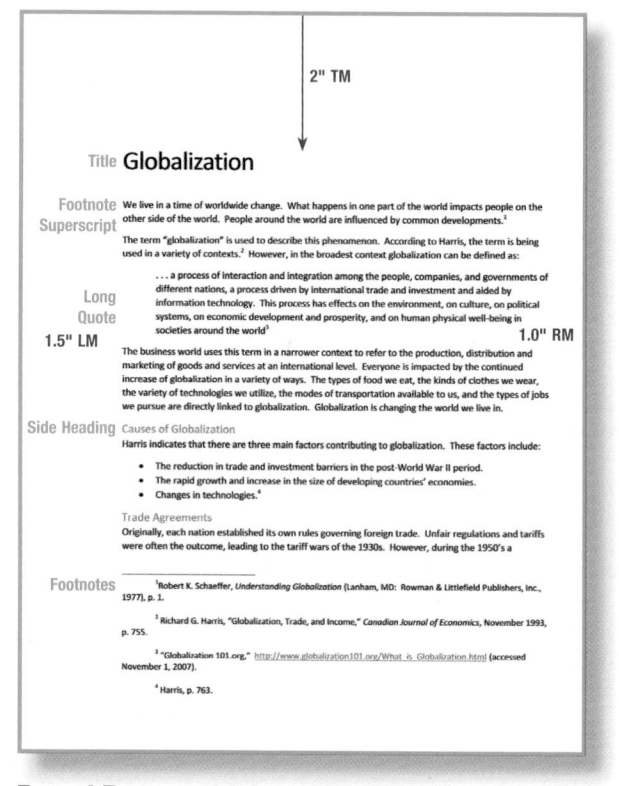

Unbound Report

Report is formatted in Word 2013 Normal Style (11-pt. Calibri with 1.08 Line Spacing and 8 pt. Space After Paragraph). The title is formatted in Title style, and side headings are formatted in Heading 1 style.

2" TM

Title

Unbound Report Guides

1" SM

Short reports are often prepared without binders. If they consist of more than one page, the pages are usually fastened together in the upper-left corner by a staple or paper clip. Such reports are called unbound reports.

Side heading

Margins and Spacing

The side and bottom margins on all pages are 1", the top margin on the first page is 2" and 1" on the second and subsequent pages. Use the default line spacing and spacing after paragraph for the paragraphs within the body of the report (1.08 line spacing and 8 pt. spacing after paragraph for Word 2013). Do not indent the first line of each paragraph.

Side heading

Titles and Headings

For the report title, use the default Title style (Calibri Light 28 pt. for Word 2013). For the side headings, use the default Heading 1 style (Calibri Light 16 pt. with Blue, Accent 1 for Word 2013). Capitalize the first letters of all words except prepositions in titles and side headings.

Side heading

Page Numbers

The first page of an unbound report may or may not include a page number. *The reports keyed for this unit will not include a page number on the first page.* On page 2 and subsequent pages, right-align the page number at the top of the page.

Side heading

Long Quotations, and Lists

Long quotations (four or more lines) are indented 0.5" (or at the first default tab setting) from the left margin. When bulleted or numbered lists are included in the body, use the default 0.25" indentation for the lists.

Side heading

Documentation

Textual citations, footnotes, or endnotes may be used to document the sources cited in the report. In this unit you will use the textual citations and footnotes methods. You will learn how to format the citations and the reference pages in an upcoming lesson.

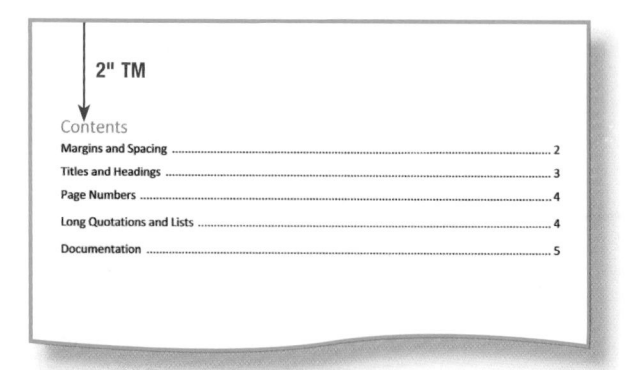

References Page

Number the References page if the report pages are numbered. Use the same page number alignment and position.

2" TM

1" SM

References   (Title Style)   1" SM

Magazine   Calloway, Sue. "Diary of an Electric Commuter." *Fortune*, January 17, 2011, 57-61.

Newspaper   Swartz, Jon. "Communications Overload." *USA Today*, February 2, 2011, 1b.

Website   "The Importance of Touch Keyboarding." *The Keyboard Teacher*. http://www.keyboardteacher.net/touchkeyguide_detailed.html (February 2, 2011).

Book   VanHuss, Susie H., Connie M. Forde, and Donna L. Woo. *Keyboarding & Word Processing Essentials*, Eighteenth Edition. Cincinnati: South-Western/Cengage Learning, 2011.

Hanging Indent

At least 1" BM

Bound Report with Long Quotation and Footnotes

2" TM

Title **Globalization**

Footnote Superscript

We live in a time of worldwide change. What happens in one part of the world impacts people on the other side of the world. People around the world are influenced by common developments.[1]

The term "globalization" is used to describe this phenomenon. According to Harris, the term is being used in a variety of contexts.[2] However, in the broadest context globalization can be defined as:

Long Quote

1.5" LM   1.0" RM

. . . a process of interaction and integration among the people, companies, and governments of different nations, a process driven by international trade and investment and aided by information technology. This process has effects on the environment, on culture, on political systems, on economic development and prosperity, and on human physical well-being in societies around the world[3]

The business world uses this term in a narrower context to refer to the production, distribution and marketing of goods and services at an international level. Everyone is impacted by the continued increase of globalization in a variety of ways. The types of food we eat, the kinds of clothes we wear, the variety of technologies we utilize, the modes of transportation available to us, and the types of jobs we pursue are directly linked to globalization. Globalization is changing the world we live in.

Side Heading   Causes of Globalization

Harris indicates that there are three main factors contributing to globalization. These factors include:

- The reduction in trade and investment barriers in the post-World War II period.
- The rapid growth and increase in the size of developing countries' economies.
- Changes in technologies.[4]

Trade Agreements

Originally, each nation established its own rules governing foreign trade. Unfair regulations and tariffs were often the outcome, leading to the tariff wars of the 1930s. However, during the 1950's a

Footnotes

[1] Robert K. Schaeffer, *Understanding Globalization* (Lanham, MD: Rowman & Littlefield Publishers, Inc., 1977), p. 1.

[2] Richard G. Harris, "Globalization, Trade, and Income," *Canadian Journal of Economics*, November 1993, p. 755.

[3] "Globalization 101.org." http://www.globalization101.org/What_is_Globalization.html (accessed November 1, 2007).

[4] Harris, p. 763.

Table of Contents

2" TM

Contents

Title Page

MLA Report, page 2

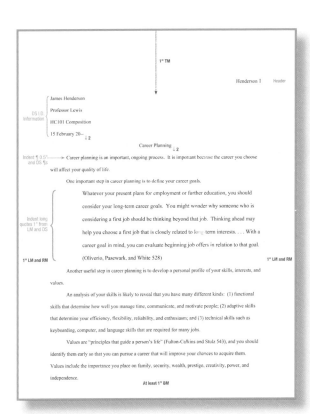

MLA Report, page 1

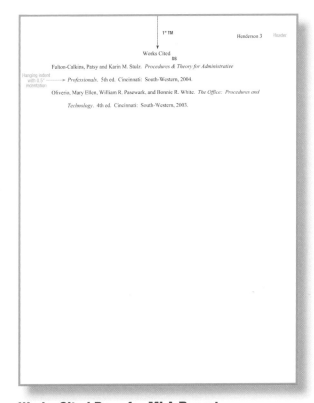

Works Cited Page for MLA Report

Report Documentation

Good report writing includes proof that the reported statements are sound. The process is called documenting. Most school reports are documented in the body and in a list. A reference in the body shows the source of a quotation or paraphrase. A list shows all references alphabetically.

In the report body, references may be noted (1) in parentheses in the copy (textual citations or parenthetical documentation); (2) by a superscript in the copy, listed on a separate page (endnotes); or (3) by a superscript in the copy, listed at the bottom of the text page (footnotes). A list may contain only the sources noted in the body (REFERENCES or Works Cited) or include related materials (BIBLIOGRAPHY). Two popular documenting styles are shown: Century 21 and MLA (Modern Language Association).

Century 21

Examples are listed in this order: (1) textual citation, (2) endnote/footnote, and (3) References/Bibliography page.

Book, One Author
(Schaeffer, 1997, 1)
[1]Robert K. Schaeffer. *Understanding Globalization*, (Lanham, MD: Rowman & Littlefield Publishers, Inc., 1997), p. 1.
Schaeffer, Robert K. *Understanding Globalization* (Lanham, MD: Rowman & Littlefield Publishers, Inc., 1997).

Book, Two or Three Authors
(Prince and Jackson, 1997, 35)
[2]Nancy Prince and Jeanie Jackson. *Exploring Theater* (Minneapolis/St. Paul: West Publishing Company, 1997), p. 35.
Prince, Nancy, and Jeanie Jackson. *Exploring Theater*. Minneapolis/St. Paul: West Publishing Company, 1997.

Book, Four or More Authors
(Gwartney, et al., 2014, 9)
[3]James D. Gwartney, et al., *Economics: Private and Public Choice* (Cincinnati: South-Western, Cengage Learning, 2014), p. 9.
Gwartney, James D., et al. *Economics: Private and Public Choice*. Cincinnati: South-Western, Cengage Learning, 2014.

Encyclopedia or Reference Book
(Encyclopedia Americana, 2008, Vol. 25, p. 637)
[4]*Encyclopedia Americana*, Vol. 25 (Danbury, CT: Grolier Incorporated, 2008), p. 637.
Encyclopedia Americana, Vol. 25. "Statue of Liberty." Danbury, CT: Grolier Incorporated, 2008.

Journal or Magazine Article
(Harris, 1993, 755)
[5]Richard G. Harris, "Globalization, Trade, and Income." *Canadian Journal of Economics*, November 1993, p. 755.
Harris, Richard G. "Globalization, Trade, and Income." *Canadian Journal of Economics*, November 1993, 755–776.

Website
(Railton, 2014)
[6]Stephen Railton, "Your Mark Twain." http://www.etext.lib.virginia.edu/railton/sc-as-mt/yourmt13.html (September 24, 2014).
Railton, Stephen. "Your Mark Twain." http://www.etext.lib.virginia.edu/railton/sc-as-mt/yourmt13.html (24 September 2014).

Modern Language Association

Examples include parenthetical reference (1) in documentation and (2) on Works Cited page.

Book, One Author
(Schaeffer 1)
Schaeffer, Robert K. *Understanding Globalization.* Lanham, MD: Rowman & Littlefield. 1997.

Book, Two or Three Authors
(Prince and Jackson 35)
Prince, Nancy, and Jeanie Jackson. *Exploring Theater.* Minneapolis/St. Paul: West Publishing. 1997.

Book, Four or More Authors or Editors
(Gwartney et al. 9)
Gwartney, James D., et al. *Economics: Private and Public Choice.* Cincinnati: South-Western. Cengage Learning, 2014.

Encyclopedia or Reference Book
(Encyclopedia Americana 637)
Encyclopedia Americana. "Statue of Liberty." Danbury, CT: Grolier, 2008.

Journal or Magazine Article
(Harris 755)
Harris, Richard G. "Globalization, Trade, and Income." *Canadian Journal of Economics.* Nov. 1993: 755–776.

Website
(Railton)
Railton, Stephen. *Your Mark Twain Page.* (24 Sept. 2014) http://www.etext.lib.virginia.edu/railton/sc-as-mt/yourmt13.html.

[Company/Department Name]

Agenda

[Date]

[Time]

Type of Meeting: **[Description of meeting]**

Meeting Facilitator: **[Name of meeting facilitator]**

Invitees: **[List of invitees]**

I. Call to order

II. Roll call

III. Approval of minutes from last meeting

IV. Open issues

    a) **[Description of open issue]**

    b) **[Description of open issue]**

    c) **[Description of open issue]**

V. New business

    a) **[Description of new business]**

    b) **[Description of new business]**

    c) **[Description of new business]**

VI. Adjournment

VII.

Agenda

TRAVEL ITINERARY FOR LISA PEROTTA			
222 Pine View Drive			
Coraopolis, PA 15108			
(412) 555-1320			
perotta@fastnet.com			
Pittsburgh, PA to Santa Ana, CA—April 18-22, 20--			
Date	**Time**	**Activity**	**Comments**
Tuesday April 18	3:30 p.m. (ET)	Depart **Pittsburgh International Airport** (PIT) for Santa Ana, CA Airport (SNA) on **USEast Flight 146.** *Arrival time is 5:01 p.m.(PT).*	The flight is non-stop on an Airbus A319, and you are assigned seat 22E.
	5:30 p.m. (PT)	Reservation with **Star Car Rental** (714-555-0190). Return by 12 noon (PT) on April 22.	Confirmation No.: 33-345. Telephone: 714-555-1030.
	6:00 p.m. (PT)	Reservations at the Hannah Hotel, 421 Race Avenue, Santa Ana for April 18 to April 22 for a single, non-smoking room at $145 plus tax. Telephone: 714-555-0200.	Confirmation No.: 632A-04/18. Check-in after 6 p.m. is guaranteed. Check out by 11 a.m.
Saturday April 22	1:25 p.m. (PT)	Depart **Santa Ana Airport** (SNA) for Pittsburgh International Airport (PIT) on **USEast Flight 148.** *Arrival time is 8:52 p.m. (ET).*	The flight is non-stop on an Airbus A319, and you are assigned seat 16A.
Travel Agency Contact Information—Agent is Mary Grecco; 444 Grant Street, Pittsburgh, PA 15219; Telephone: 412-555-0087; Fax: 412-555-0088; E-Mail: greccom@netway.com			

Itinerary

[Company/Department Name]

Meeting Minutes

[Date]

I. <u>Call to order</u>

    [Name of Meeting Facilitator] called to order the regular meeting of the **[Organization/Committee Name]** at **[time of meeting]** on **[date of meeting]** in **[Location of Meeting]**.

II. <u>Roll call</u>

    [Name of Organization Secretary] conducted a roll call. The following persons were present: **[List of Attendees]**

III. <u>Approval of minutes from last meeting</u>

    [Name of Organization Secretary] read the minutes from the last meeting. The minutes were approved as read.

IV. <u>Open issues</u>

    a) **[Open issue/summary of discussion]**

    b) **[Open issue/summary of discussion]**

    c) **[Open issue/summary of discussion]**

V. <u>New business</u>

    a) **[New business/summary of discussion]**

    b) **[New business/summary of discussion]**

    c) **[New business/summary of discussion]**

VI. <u>Adjournment</u>

    [Name of Meeting Facilitator] adjourned the meeting at **[time meeting ended]**.

Minutes submitted by: **[Name]**

Meeting Minutes

News Release

For Release: Immediate

Contact: Heidi Zemack

CLEVELAND, OH, May 25, 20--. Science teachers from school districts in six counties are eligible for this year's Teacher Excellence awards funded by The Society for Environmental Engineers.

Nominations can be submitted through Friday, July 31, by students, parents, residents, and other educators. Nomination forms are available from the participating school districts or on the Society's website at http://www.tsee.webhost.com.

An anonymous committee reviews the nominations and selects ten finalists. From that group, seven "teachers of distinction" and three award winners are selected. The top award winner receives $5,000, the second receives $2,500, and the third receives $1,500. Each teacher of distinction receives $500. The teachers of distinction and the award winners will be announced on September 5 at a dinner at the Cleveland Inn.

School districts participating in the program include those in these counties: Cuyahoga, Lorain, Medina, Summit, Lake, and Geauga.

###

News Release

Employment Application Form

Application for Employment
Regency Insurance Company
An Equal Opportunity Employer

PERSONAL INFORMATION

NAME LAST FIRST	SOCIAL SECURITY NO.	CURRENT DATE	PHONE NUMBER
Ruckert, Douglas H.	358-25-2850	5/22/2014	(713) 555-0121

ADDRESS NUMBER, STREET, CITY, STATE, ZIP CODE: 8503 Kirby Dr., Houston, TX 77054-8220

U.S. CITIZEN: ☑ YES   DATE YOU CAN START: 4/10/2014

ARE YOU EMPLOYED NOW? ☑ YES ☐ NO   IF YES, GIVE NAME AND NUMBER OF PERSON TO CALL:

EMPLOYED AT? Samuel Veloght, Manager (713) 555-0149   ☑ YES ☐ NO

POSITION DESIRED: Open   SALARY DESIRED: Customer Service

STATE HOW YOU LEARNED OF VACANCY: From Ms. Anne S. Salgado, Eisenhower Information Technology Instructor

HAVE YOU EVER BEEN CONVICTED OF A FELONY? ☐ YES ☑ NO   IF YES, EXPLAIN

EDUCATION

NAME AND LOCATION OF SCHOOL	YEARS ATTENDED	DID YOU GRADUATE?	SUBJECTS STUDIED
COLLEGE			
HIGH SCHOOL Eisenhower Technical High School, Houston, TX	2010 to 2014	Will graduate 06/2014	Information Technology
GRADE SCHOOL			
OTHER			

SUBJECTS OF SPECIAL STUDY/RESEARCH WORK OR SPECIAL TRAINING/SKILLS DIRECTLY RELATED TO POSITION DESIRED
Windows and Office Skills, including Word, Excel, Access, PowerPoint, and Publisher
Office Processing course with telephone training and interpersonal skills role playing

FORMER EMPLOYERS (LIST LAST POSITION FIRST)

FROM - TO (DATE & YEAR)	NAME AND ADDRESS	SALARY	POSITION	REASON FOR LEAVING
9/2012 to present	Hinton's Family Restaurant, 1106 S. Mayfield Avenue, Houston, TX 77205-8841	Minimum wage	Server	Want full-time position in my field
4/2010 to 6/2012	Tuma's Landscape and Garden Center, 10155 East Freeway, Houston, TX 77029-4419	Minimum wage	Sales	Employed at Hinton's

REFERENCES (LIST THREE PERSONS NOT RELATED TO YOU, WHOM YOU HAVE KNOWN AT LEAST ONE YEAR)

NAME	BUSINESS ADDRESS	PHONE NUMBER	TITLE	YEARS KNOWN
Ms. Anna S. Salgado	Eisenhower Technical High School, 100 N. Cavalcade, Houston, TX 77009-1451	(713) 555-0134	Information Technology Instructor	Four
Mr. Samuel R. Veloght	Hinton's Family Restaurant, 1106 S. Mayfield Avenue, Houston, TX 77205-8841	(713) 555-0149	Manager	Two
Mrs. Helen T. Lavall	Tuma's Landscape and Garden Center, 10155 East Freeway, Houston, TX 77024-4419	(713) 555-0182	Owner	Three

I UNDERSTAND THAT I SHALL NOT BECOME AN EMPLOYEE UNTIL I HAVE SIGNED AN EMPLOYMENT AGREEMENT WITH THE FINAL APPROVAL OF THE EMPLOYER AND THAT SUCH EMPLOYMENT WILL BE SUBJECT TO VERIFICATION OF PREVIOUS EMPLOYMENT DATA PROVIDED IN THIS APPLICATION, AND ANY RELATED DOCUMENTS. I KNOW THAT A REPORT MAY BE MADE THAT WILL INCLUDE INFORMATION CONCERNING ANY FACTOR THE EMPLOYER MIGHT FIND RELEVANT TO THE POSITION FOR WHICH I AM APPLYING, AND THAT I CAN MAKE A WRITTEN REQUEST FOR ADDITIONAL INFORMATION AS TO THE NATURE AND SCOPE OF THE REPORT IF ONE IS MADE.

SIGNATURE OF APPLICANT: *Douglas H. Ruckert*

Employment Application Letter

8503 Kirby Drive
Houston, TX 77054-8220
May 10, 2014

Ms. Jenna St. John
Personnel Director
Regency Insurance Company
219 West Greene Road
Houston, TX 77067-4219

Dear Ms. St. John:

Ms. Anne S. Salgado, my business technology instructor, informed me of the customer service position with your company that will be available June 15. She speaks very highly of your organization. After learning more about the position, I am confident that I am qualified and would like to be considered for the position.

As indicated on the enclosed resume, I am currently completing my senior year at Eisenhower Technical High School. All of my elective courses have been computer and business-related courses. I have completed the advanced computer application class where we integrated word processing, spreadsheet, database, presentation, and Web page documents by using the latest suite software. I have also taken an office technology course that included practice in using the telephone and applying interpersonal skills.

My work experience and school activities have given me the opportunity to work with people to achieve group goals. Participating in FBLA has given me an appreciation of the business world.

An opportunity to interview with you for this position will be greatly appreciated. You can call me at (713) 555-0121 or e-mail me at doug2@suresend.com to arrange an interview.

Sincerely,

Douglas H. Ruckert

Enclosure

Electronic Resume (Resume 1)

Douglas H. Ruckert
8503 Kirby Drive
Houston TX 77054-8220
(713) 555-0121
doug@suresend.com

SUMMARY
Strong communication and telephone skills; excellent keyboarding, computer, and Internet skills; and good organizational and interpersonal skills.

EDUCATION
Will graduate from Eisenhower Technical High School in June 2014 with a high school diploma and information technology emphasis. Grade point average is 3.75.

RELEVANT SKILLS AND COURSES
Proficient with most recent versions of Windows and Office, including Word, Excel, Access, PowerPoint, and Publisher.
Excelled in the following courses: Computer Applications, Business Communications, and Information Technology.

MAJOR ACCOMPLISHMENTS
Future Business Leaders of America: Member for four years, vice president for one year. Won second place in Public Speaking at District Competition; competed (same event) at state level.
Varsity soccer: Lettered three years and served as captain during senior year.
Recognition: Named one of Eisenhower's Top Ten Community Service Providers at end of junior year.

WORK EXPERIENCE
Hinton's Family Restaurant, Server (2012-present): Served customers in culturally diverse area, oriented new part-time employees, and resolved routine customer service issues.
Tuma's Landscape and Garden Center, Sales (2010-2012): Assisted customers with plant selection and responsible for stocking and arranging display areas.

COMMUNITY SERVICE
First Methodist Church Vacation Bible School teacher assistant (2012-2013).
Race for the Cure publicity committee (2013).
ETHS Senior Citizens Breakfast server (2011-2014).
United Youth Camp student helper (2013).

REFERENCES
Will be furnished upon request.

Formatted with default margins, line spacing, and font.

Print Resume (Resume 2)

Douglas H. Ruckert
8503 Kirby Drive
Houston TX 77054-8220
(713) 555-0121
doug@suresend.com

Objective: To use my computer, Internet, communication, and interpersonal skills in a challenging customer service position.

Education: Will graduate from Eisenhower Technical High School in June 2014 with a high school diploma and business technology emphasis. Grade point average is 3.75.

Relevant Skills and Courses:
☐ Proficient with most recent versions of Windows and Office.
☐ Excelled in the following courses: Keyboarding, Computer Applications, Business Communications, and Information Technology.

Major Accomplishments:
☐ Future Business Leaders of America: Member for four years, vice president for one year. Won second place in Public Speaking at the District Competition; competed (same event) at state level.
☐ Varsity soccer: Lettered three years and served as captain during senior year.
☐ Recognition: Named one of Eisenhower's Top Ten Community Service Providers at end of junior year.

Work Experience: Hinton's Family Restaurant, Server (2012-present): Served customers in culturally diverse area, oriented new part-time employees, and resolved routine customer service issues.
Tuma's Landscape and Garden Center, Sales (2010-2011): Assisted customers with plant selection and responsible for stocking and arranging display areas.

References: Will be furnished upon request.

Formatted as a 2" x 5" table. Default font and line spacing were used. All borders were removed.

The numbered parts are found on most computers. The location of some parts will vary.

1. **CPU (Central Processing Unit):** Internal operating unit or "brain" of computer.
2. **CD-ROM drive:** Reads data from and writes data to a CD.
3. **Monitor:** Displays text and graphics on a screen.
4. **Mouse:** Used to input commands.
5. **Keyboard:** An arrangement of letter, figure, symbol, control, function, and editing keys and a numeric keypad.

© Dmitry Melnikov/Shutterstock.com

KEYBOARD ARRANGEMENT

© PixAchi/Shutterstock.com

1. **Alphanumeric keys:** Letters, numbers, and symbols.
2. **Numeric keypad:** Keys at the right side of the keyboard used to enter numeric copy and perform calculations.
3. **Function (F) keys:** Used to execute commands, sometimes with other keys. Commands vary with software.
4. **Arrow keys:** Move insertion point up, down, left, or right.

5. **ESC (Escape):** Closes a software menu or dialog box.
6. **TAB:** Moves the insertion point to a preset position.
7. **CAPS LOCK:** Used to make all capital letters.
8. **SHIFT:** Makes capital letters and symbols shown at tops of number keys.
9. **CTRL (Control):** With other key(s), executes commands. Commands may vary with software.

10. **ALT (Alternate):** With other key(s), executes commands. Commands may vary with software.
11. **Space Bar:** Inserts a space in text.
12. **ENTER (RETURN):** Moves insertion point to margin and down to next line. Also used to execute commands.
13. **DELETE:** Removes text to the right of insertion point.

14. **NUM LOCK:** Activates/ deactivates numeric keypad.
15. **INSERT:** Activates insert or typeover.
16. **BACKSPACE:** Deletes text to the left of insertion point.

Repetitive stress injury (RSI) is a result of repeated movement of a particular part of the body. It is also known as repetitive motion injury, musculoskeletal disorder, cumulative trauma disorder, and by a host of other names. A familiar example of RSI is "tennis elbow." RSI is the number-one occupational illness, costing employers more than $80 billion a year in health-care fees and lost wages.

Of concern to keyboard and mouse users is the form of RSI called **carpal tunnel syndrome (CTS)**. CTS is an inflammatory disease that develops gradually and affects the wrists, hands, and forearms. Blood vessels, tendons, and nerves pass into the hand through the carpal tunnel (see illustration below). If any of these structures enlarge, or the walls of the tunnel narrow, the median nerve is pinched and CTS symptoms may result.

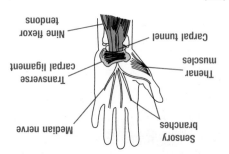

Palm view of left hand

Nine flexor tendons — Carpal tunnel — Transverse carpal ligament — Thenar muscles — Median nerve — Sensory branches

Symptoms of RSI/CTS

CTS symptoms include numbness in the hand; tingling or burning in the hand, wrist, or elbow; severe pain in the forearm, elbow, or shoulder; and difficulty in gripping objects. Symptoms usually appear during sleeping hours, probably because many people sleep with their wrists flexed.

If not properly treated, the pressure on the median nerve, which controls the thumb, forefinger, middle finger, and half the ring finger, causes severe pain. The pain can radiate into the forearm, elbow, or shoulder. There are many kinds of treatment, ranging from simply resting to surgery. Left untreated, CTS can result in permanent damage or paralysis.

The good news is that 99 percent of people with carpal tunnel syndrome recover completely. Computer users can avoid reinjuring themselves by taking the precautions discussed later in this article.

Causes of RSI/CTS

RSI/CTS often develops in workers whose physical routine is unvaried. Common occupational factors include (1) using awkward posture, (2) using poor techniques, (3) performing tasks with wrists bent (see below), (4) using improper equipment, (5) working at a rapid pace, (6) not taking rest breaks, and (7) not doing exercises that promote graceful motion and good techniques. Keying RSI/CTS is not limited to workers or adults. Keying school assignments, playing computer or video games, and surfing the Internet are increasing the incidence of RSI/CTS in younger people.

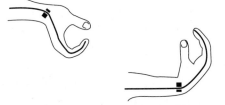

Improper wrist positions for keystroking

CTS is frequently a health concern for people who use a computer keyboard or mouse. The risk of developing CTS is less for those who use proper furniture or equipment, keyboarding techniques, posture, and/or muscle-stretching exercises than for those who do not.

Reducing the Risk of RSI/CTS

By taking the following precautions, keyboard and mouse users can reduce the risk of developing RSI/CTS and can keep it from recurring. Experts stress that good computer habits like these are very important in avoiding RSI/CTS. They can also help you avoid back, neck, and shoulder pain, and eyestrain.

Arrange the Work Area

Arrange your equipment in a way that is natural and comfortable for you. Position the keyboard at elbow height and directly in front of the chair. The front edge should be even with the edge of the table or desk.

Place the monitor for easy viewing. Some experts maintain that the top of the screen should be at or slightly below eye level. Others recommend placing the monitor even lower. Set it a comfortable distance from your eyes—at least an arm's length away.

Position the monitor to avoid glare (an antiglare filter can help). Close blinds or pull shades as needed. Adjust the brightness and contrast controls, if necessary, for readability. Keep the screen clean with a soft, lint-free cloth and (unless your instructor tells you otherwise) a nonalcohol, nonabrasive cleaning solution or glass cleaner.

If you cannot adjust your equipment and the desk or table is too high, try adjusting your chair. If that does not work, you can sit on a cushion, a coat, or even a stack of books.

Use a straight-backed chair that will not yield when you lean back. The chair should support your lower back (try putting a rolled-up towel or sweater behind you if it does not). The back of your knees should not be pressed against the chair. Use a seat that allows you to keep your feet flat on the floor, or use a footrest. Even a box or a backpack will do.

Position the mouse next to and at the same height as the keyboard and as close to the body as possible. Research has not shown conclusively that one type of pointing device (mouse, trackball, touch pad, stylus, joystick, etc.) is better than another. Whatever you use, make sure your arms, hands, and fingers are relaxed. If you change to a new device, evaluate it carefully first and work up gradually to using it all the time.

Arrange your work material so you can see it easily and maintain good posture. Some experts recommend positioning whatever you look at most often (the monitor or paper material) directly in front of you so you do not have to turn your head to the side while keying.

Exercise and Take Breaks

Exercise your neck, shoulders, arms, wrists, and fingers before beginning to key each day and often during the workday. Neck, shoulder, wrist, and other exercises appear at the Cornell University ergonomics website listed below.

Take a short break at least once an hour. Rest your eyes from time to time as you work by focusing on an object at least 20 feet away. Blink frequently.

Use Good Posture and Proper Techniques

Sit erect and as far back in the seat as possible. Your forearms should be parallel to the slant of the keyboard, your wrists and forearms low, but not touching or resting on any surface. Your arms should be near the side of your body in a relaxed position. Your shoulders should not be raised, but should be in a natural posture.

Keep your fingers curved and upright over the home keys. Strike each key lightly using the finger*tip*. Grasp the mouse loosely. Make a conscious effort to relax your hands and shoulders while keying.

For more information on mouse and keyboard use and CTS/RSI, visit the following Internet sites:

- http://kidshealth.org/kid/ (search for *ergonomics*)
- http://www.tifaq.org
- http://ergonomics.ucla.edu/
- http://www.office-ergo.com
- http://ergo.human.cornell.edu/

© InstinctDesign/Shutterstock.com

Ergonomic Keyboards

Ergonomic keyboards (see illustration at left) are designed to improve hand posture and make keying more comfortable. Generally they have a split design with left and right banks of keys and the ability to tilt or rotate the keyboard for comfort. More research is needed to determine just how effective ergonomic keyboards are in preventing RSI injuries and carpal tunnel syndrome.

Glossary

A

802.11 Another name for a wireless connection for accessing the Internet

active cell Current location of the insertion point that is highlighted with a thick border; stores information that is entered

agenda List of things to be done or actions to be taken, usually at a meeting

Align Left Software feature that starts all lines of the paragraph at the left margin; default paragraph alignment

Align Right Software feature that ends all lines at the right margin

application Software that allows a person to complete a specific task such as creating a report, browsing the Internet, editing a multimedia video, or calculating a math problem

ascending In order from A to Z for words and from lowest to highest for numbers

attachment notation Tells the reader that other material is attached to a letter or memo

audience People who will listen to a presentation

AutoFit Feature that adapts a table width to the current content

AutoFit Contents Option in the AutoFit feature that adjusts column widths to be just wide enough for all contents to fit within the cells

AutoFit Window Option in the AutoFit feature that adjusts column widths to fit within the left and right margins of a document

B

Back button Button located on the browser toolbar that returns the user to the previous page

BACKSPACE Key used to delete characters to the left of the insertion point

bank statement Report that lists all of the transactions in a bank account during the past month

bar chart Graph that compares values across categories of data

blind copy Feature used when the sender does not want the person receiving an email message to know that the sender also sent the message to another person

blog Internet site that allows a person to post messages for others to read; usually organized around a particular topic such as music or sports

Bluetooth Short-range wireless protocol for connecting different types of digital devices

body Contains the paragraphs that make up a report, memo, or letter; main or supporting points of a presentation

borders Printed line around cells in a table or around graphic objects such as text boxes or pictures

budget An itemized spending plan

bullets Character or graphic (square, circle, picture) that appears before each item in a list

business letter Letter sent from a person in a business to another person

C

CAPS LOCK Key used to create a series of capital letters

carpal tunnel syndrome (CTS) Form of RSI that affects keyboard users, causing numbness or pain in the hand, wrist, elbow, or shoulder

cell Place where a row and a column cross each other in a table; text, numbers, and formulas for calculating amounts can be entered in a cell

Center Software feature that places an equal (or nearly equal) space between the text and each side margin

central processing unit (CPU) Another name for a microprocessor

Charm bar The Windows 8/8.1 tool that can be displayed anytime to give access to searching, sharing, the Start screen, devices, and operating system settings

chart title Identifies chart contents

check register Form on which a person records information about his or her bank account

citation Note placed in a report body to mark material taken from other sources

clip art Ready-made drawings and photography that can be inserted or copied into a document

cloud Location on the Web where information or applications may be stored

column Information arranged vertically in a table

column chart Graph that compares values across categories of data

column heading Appears in a cell at the top of a range of data in a column and describes the data

compact disc (CD) Device used to store computer files; built into most personal computers

complimentary close Farewell for a letter

computer Machine that follows a set of instructions to change and store data

computer virus Destructive program that destroys or harms data on a computer; can be loaded onto a computer and run without the computer owner's knowledge

conclusion Summary of points presented and the action the presenter wants listeners to take

Convert Text to Table Feature that can be used to convert lists or other data that are separated by tabs into a table

Convert to Text Feature that can be used to convert a table into text that is separated by tabs, commas, or other separators

Copy Software command that copies selected text so it can be pasted to another location; original text is unchanged

copy notation Tells the reader that another person will receive a copy of the memo or letter

copyright Form of protection for certain works (books, articles, music, plays, movie scripts, artwork) granted by the U.S. government that states how the work may be legally used or copied

cover page Generally includes the report title, name and title of the writer, name of the writer's school or organization, and date of the report

Cut Software command that removes selected text from a document

cyber predator Someone who uses the Internet to hunt for victims whom they take advantage of in many ways

D

data Facts and figures such as words, pictures, and numbers

database Organized collection of facts and figures

data type Determines the kind of data in a database that a field can hold

Date & Time Feature that is used to insert the date and/or time into a document

demand Amount of a product or service consumers are willing and able to buy

descending In order from *Z* to *A* for words and from highest to lowest for numbers

desktop On-screen work area where windows, icons, tools, gadgets, and images appear

desktop publishing (DTP) Using a personal computer to produce high-quality printed documents; closely related to word processing

dialog box Area on a computer screen that lists the choices the user can make

digital Refers to performing calculations with two digits—0 and 1

digital certificate An attachment to a document that verifies the identity of a person sending a message or indicates the security of a website

DigiTools Another name for digital communication tools

discrimination Unfair treatment of people due to factors such as race, ethnic group, age, religion, disability, gender, or sexual orientation

distribution Involves sending and sharing information with the people who want or need it

domain name Internet address in alphabetic form, such as .gov or .edu, that can provide some insight into the purpose of the site

double-space (DS) To tap the ENTER key twice to move the insertion point down two lines

E

e-commerce Selling and buying of products on the Internet

economic indicator Measurement that describes how well the economy is doing

economy Refers to the business activities that take place in a region or country

edits Changes and corrections made to a database or another document

email Electronic transfer of messages

email address Contains a username and a domain name separated by the *at* sign (@)

employee benefits Payments other than wages that are made to workers in the form of cash, goods, or services

enclosure notation Tells the reader that other material is enclosed with a memo or letter

ENTER Key used to return the insertion point to the left margin and move it down one line

entrepreneur Person who organizes and manages a business, risking the money he or she invests in hopes of making a profit

Envelopes *Word* feature used to create envelopes

ethics Moral standards or values that describe how people should behave

F

facsimile (fax) Technology that sends a document by using standard telephone lines or an Internet connection capable of transmitting voice

fair use doctrine Rules pertaining to the use of a small portion of a copyrighted work for educational purposes

Favorites Browser feature that allows a person to create a list of links for sites

fax cover page Includes the name of the fax recipient, fax and regular phone numbers of the recipient, name of the sender, number of pages being sent, brief description of the document, and comments

field Contains one piece of information about a person or item in a database

file-sharing Searching for and copying files from someone else's computer

filter Database feature that hides records in a table that do not match the set criteria

Find and Replace Feature used to search for a word or phrase in a document and then replace the text with other words

firewall Hardware and software used to help prevent unauthorized users from accessing a person's data

flash memory Type of memory storage that is often used in portable devices such as USB flash drives, laptops, and PDAs; it is relatively inexpensive and characterized by quick read access time

flyer Announcement or advertisement usually intended for wide distribution

folder Used by *Windows* operating systems to organize computer files

footer Contains information that displays at the bottom of pages in a document

form Object used to enter or display data in a database

format To place text on a page so it looks good and is easy to read

formula Equation that performs calculations on values in a worksheet

Formula bar Displays contents of the active cell; used to enter or edit text or values

Forward button Button in an application window that allows a user to return to the page he or she just left

function Predefined formula that can be used to perform calculations

G

global marketplace Worldwide area where products are bought and sold

graphic Drawn picture, photo, or chart

graphical user interface (GUI) Computer interface that displays pictures, icons, and other images; allows the user to give commands and navigate by clicking the mouse or tapping a digital pen rather than keying commands

gridline Marks the outline of the area for each cell in a table; is not printed

gross words a minute (*gwam*) Number of standard words keyed in one minute

H

hacker Person who accesses computers or networks without proper permission

hacking Accessing computers or networks without proper permission

hanging indent Software feature that begins all lines except the first line away from the left margin

hard drive Most common storage device inside a computer

hardware Physical parts of a computer that a person can touch with his or her hands

header Contains information that appears at the top of pages in a document

History Browser feature that shows the user a list of links for sites he or she has visited recently

home-based business Company that is run primarily from a person's place of residence

Home button Button that allows the user to return to the home page or starting point

home keys Keys on which the keyboarder places his or her fingers to begin keying: **a s d f** for the left hand and **j k l ;** for the right hand

hyperlink Text, button, or graphic in an electronic document that, when clicked, takes the user to a new location

I

identity theft Finding out personal information about a person so as to impersonate that person by using his or her credit cards and damaging that person's good name

information processing Putting words, pictures, facts, or numbers into a meaningful form that can be used and understood

input Refers to the way a user puts data into a computer

instant messaging Allows users who are online to key text messages that are displayed almost instantly for others in a chat room

Internet Web of computer networks that spans the earth

Internet service provider (ISP) Company that provides customer connections to the Internet

introduction Opening remarks that tell listeners what a talk will be about

J

justify Software feature that starts all lines at the left margin and ends all full lines at the right margin

K

keyword Word that a person types into a search text box to search for information on the Web or on a single site

L

Landscape orientation Orientation in which the long side of the paper is positioned at the top

legend Key used to identify a chart's data categories; usually contains different colors or patterns

letter mailing address Name and address of the person to whom the sender of the letter is writing

letterhead Paper that has a business name and address printed on the paper

line spacing *Word* feature that is used to change the amount of blank space between lines of text

local area network (LAN) Network that connects computers that are close to each other, usually in the same building

login name Series of letters and/or numbers that identifies the user to the computer

M

main heading Describes the content of a table

margin Blank space between the edge of the paper and the print

market Company's customers or potential customers

market economy Economy in which consumer buying choices determine, to a great extent, the goods and services that will be produced or offered

marketplace Geographical area in which a company sells products

market price The price at which consumers are willing to buy and producers are willing to sell

Maximize Button that removes an application window from the taskbar so as to fill the entire screen

meeting minutes Serve as a historical record of what was discussed and decided at a meeting of an organization or a group of people

memo Written message in printed form used by people within an organization; sometimes called interoffice memo

memory Computer data storage for the operating system, applications, and data when a computer is on

merge To join cells

microprocessor Small circuit board that controls all of the work done by a computer; most important part of a computer

Minimize Button that sends an application window to the taskbar to hide it from the screen

minimum wage Minimum amount that a company must pay its workers by law

N

name box Identifies the active cell by the letter of the column and number of the row that it intersects

netiquette Rules for proper online behavior

network One computer linked to one or more other computers

Notes pane Window that allows the user to key notes about a slide

O

object Element of a database, such as a form or table

OneDrive *Microsoft's* cloud storage feature

online apps Applications that run over the Internet inside a web browser that permit completion of specific tasks such as sending email, creating reports, and viewing multimedia

operating system (OS) Software that controls the basic operations of a computer

organic results Main list of results returned after an online search that is not influenced by advertising dollars

outline Document that organizes facts and details by main topics and subtopics

output Way in which the user obtains data from a computer, such as reading a text message, printing a report, or viewing photos on a monitor

outsourcing Hiring another company or person to do work for a company

P

page break Used to signal the end of a page; both automatic and manual page breaks are used

page number Number assigned to each page of a document

paragraph Any amount of text that is keyed before the ENTER key is tapped; can be one word or several words or lines

paragraph spacing The amount of space before or after a paragraph

password Series of letters and/or numbers and symbols that a person keys to gain access to a computer

Paste Software command that places text that has been cut or copied into a document

path Drive and series of folders and subfolders that describe the location of a computer file, such as Documents\Computers\ Chapter 2\ < Name > Moon Project 2

peripheral Device that works with a computer, such as a printer, digital tablet, scanner, or headset

personal-business letter Type of letter used to deal with personal matters

personal computer (PC) Small computer designed for an individual user

phrase searching Turning individual words into exact phrases, such as "*big cottonwood canyon,*" by using quotation marks when conducting an online search

pie chart Graph that shows how much each value is of a total value

piracy Sharing or downloading copyrighted material without paying for it

placeholder Box with dotted borders that is part of most slide layouts; holds title and body text or objects such as charts, tables, and pictures

placeholder text Controls in a template that you replace with your own text

plagiarism Using material created by another person and claiming it as one's own

Portrait orientation Orientation in which the short side of the paper is positioned at the top

presentation Talk or speech given to inform, persuade, and/or entertain

primary key Field that uniquely identifies each record in a database table

Print screen Feature on the File tab that gives options for previewing and printing a document

privacy policy Document that tells how personal data collected by a company will be used

processing Refers to how data is changed or used

processor Another name for a microprocessor

productivity Measure of how much work can be done in a certain amount of time

profile Description of the audience

proofreaders' marks Letters and symbols used to show the errors or changes needed in a document

Q

query A search you make on the Internet; database object that displays certain data that meet the set criteria

R

Random Access Memory (RAM) Working memory of a computer that is erased or cleared when the computer is turned off

range Group of two or more cells on a worksheet

record Contains all of the information about one person or item in a database

reference Someone who knows you and can tell an employer what kind of person you are

reference initials Initials of someone other than the writer who keys a memo or letter

repetitive stress injury (RSI) Condition that is a result of repeated movement of a particular part of the body, such as tennis elbow

report Document that gives facts, ideas, or opinions about one or more topics; database object that is used to format and display data from tables or queries

resources Workers, goods (such as lumber and oil), money, and items used in making products

Restore Down Button used to restore an application window to its previous size

results Answer to a query

return address Writer's street address keyed at the beginning of a personal-business letter

ribbon Location in an application where all of the commands are displayed

row Information arranged horizontally in a table

row height Vertical amount of space in a row

S

salutation Greeting of a letter

scam Scheme used to take money under false pretenses or for a product that does not work as advertised

search Browser feature that allows a person to look for information related to a word or term

search box Location where a user can key keywords to conduct a search

select Highlight text using the mouse pointer so that you can manipulate it in some way

server Powerful computer that stores files for the Internet

shading Colored fill or background that can be applied to cells in a table or objects

shapes Ready-made shapes and a variety of lines that are available in *Word* in the Illustrations group on the Insert ribbon

single-space (SS) To tap the ENTER key once to move the insertion point down one line

sizing handle One of the small squares that appear on the border of a selected graphic

Slide pane Displays the current slide or the slide clicked on the Slides tab

Slide Sorter View that shows small images of slides and allows a person to rearrange slides easily

software Programs that give instructions to a computer

sort To arrange or group items in a particular order; *Access* feature that is used to arrange the information in a table or query in a certain order

Space Bar Key used to place a space between words

spam Unsolicited email messages sent to many addresses; "junk" email

split To divide cells

sponsored links Advertising links returned from an online search that are located at the right side (or sometimes at the top) of the results; sponsored by companies that want to sell products

spreadsheet software Computer program used to record, report, and analyze data in worksheets

standard format Criteria used when creating reports pertaining to such items as margins, spacing, styles, and references

standard word In keyboarding, five characters (letters, numbers, symbols, and/or spaces)

Start screen The tiled interface that displays when a user opens *Windows 8* or *8.1*

stem Main part of a search word (*ski*) that is referenced when related words with different endings or tenses are included in the search (*skis, skiing, skier, skied*)

storage Refers to saving data for later use

style Collection of format settings for font, font size, color, paragraph pacing, alignment, and so on that are named and stored together in a style set

Styles Group in which features can be used to enhance the text or appearance of a table

subfolder Folder stored inside another folder

supply Amount of a product or service producers (companies) are willing and able to offer for sale

system administrator Expert who manages a LAN

T

TAB Key used to move the insertion point to a specific location on the line

table Information arranged in rows and columns so readers can easily understand the information; database object used for organizing and storing data

Table Column Width Box into which a person can enter and set a column width to an exact size

Table Style Options Group in which features can be used to change table styles

Table Styles Group displaying formatting options for tables

tabs Set locations at which text can be placed

taskbar *Windows* feature that displays icons for open applications and files

template Master copy of a set of predefined styles for a particular type of document

text box Container or drawing object for text or graphics

theme Set of design elements that can be applied to slides

thumbnail pane Pane at the left side of the *PowerPoint* window in which you can click small thumbnails of slides to select them

U

unbound report Short report that is often prepared without covers or binders

uniform resource locator (URL) Address for a website

USB flash drive Device commonly used to store computer files

user interface (UI) Allows users to give commands to a computer

V

visual aid Something the presenter shows the audience to help them understand the message

W

web browser Program that lets the user find and view web pages

Wi-Fi (wireless fidelity) Another name for a wireless connection to the Internet

Wikipedia Online encyclopedia that can be edited by nearly anyone in the world, allowing people with different backgrounds and knowledge to collaborate and research together

window Framed screen in which an application opens

WordArt Decorative text gallery that has several predesigned font colors, shapes, and other effects that the user can select to change text into a graphic

wordwrap Causes text to move to a new line automatically when the current line is full

workbook Spreadsheet file that may contain one or more worksheets, usually with related data

worksheet Section in a workbook (spreadsheet file) where the user can enter data

worksheet title Describes the content of a worksheet table

World Wide Web System of computers on the Internet that can handle documents formatted in HTML; typically called "the Web"

Z

Zoom group Various features found on the View tab that allow the user to see close-up or reduced views of a document

S

Safety, Internet, 68–70

Saving
  files on the Internet, 28
  in *Microsoft Word,* 22, 23–24

Scams, computer, 67–68

Search box, 14

Search engines, 58

Search feature. *See also* Queries
  on websites, 56–60
  for Wikipedia, 64
  for World Wide Web, 58–60

Searching, phrase, 61

Search techniques, 61–64

Selecting cells, 243–246

Select pointer, 17

; (semicolon) key, learning, 79

Servers, Internet, 48

7 key, learning, 135–136

Shading, 268
  for tables, 251–252

Shapes feature, 271–274
  creating graphics with, 327

Shutting down, 12

Single spacing, 80

6 key, learning, 137–138

Sizing handles, 268

s key, learning, 79

/ (slash) key, learning, 139–141

Slide layouts, 321–323

Slides. *See also* Presentations
  adding graphics to, 318–319, 327–331
  adding sound to, 329–330
  copying and inserting, 324–325
  graphics for, 327–331
  with tables, 328

Slide Sorter view, 314–315, 329

SmartArt, 323–324

Software, 4–5

Sorting
  in databases, 410
  in tables, 253–254

Sound, adding to slides, 329–330

Space Bar, learning, 80, 81, 83

Space program, 47–48

Spacing, with punctuation, 103

Spam, 65

Spelling & Grammar feature, 184–185

Spinning circle pointer, 18

Splitting cells, 243–246

Sponsored links, 60

Spreadsheet software, 351. *See also* Worksheets
  functions in, 363–365

Spyware, 74

Standard, unbound reports, 187–189
  with proofreaders' marks, 191–192

Standard words, 105

Stems, word, 61

Storage spaces, 27–29

Styles feature, 186

Subfolders, 29
  creating, 40

Subtraction, 162–164

SUM function, in spreadsheets, 363, 364

Supply, 41

Symbol keys, learning, 127–170

System administrators, 27

T

TAB key, learning, 120–122

Tables, 236–262, 285–288
  adding records to, 391–394
  alignment of, 242–243
  borders and shading for, 251–252
  centering, 242
  changing row height for, 249–250
  changing vertical alignment for, 249–250
  column width, 240
  converting, 254–256
  creating, 237–239
  in databases, 389
  design, 389
  format of, 237–238
  heading styles, 241

letters with, 247–248

merging cells in, 243–246

print preview for, 394

research and design, 256

slides with, 328

sorting in, 253–254, 255–256

Styles, 241

Tablet PCs, 45

Tabs, 218–219, 220

Templates, 289–309, 342–350
  agenda, 300–301
  certificate, 293
  cover pages, 302–303
  fax cover pages, 301–302
  greeting card, 292
  invitation, 291–292
  meeting minutes, 296–299
  memo, 294–296

Text boxes, 267–269
  draw and size, 268
  formatting, 269
  preformatted, 267

Text, selecting, 172–173

Text select pointer, 17

Text wrapping, 278

Themes, 317–318

3 key, learning, 135–136

Three-column documents, 277

Time & Date feature, 219–220

Timed writings, 129, 134, 136, 138, 144, 147, 150, 153, 156

Title slides, 316

t key, learning, 92–93

Track pads, 10

Transitions, 335

2 key, learning, 137–138

Two-column documents, 275–277

U

UI (user interface), 8

u key, learning, 100–101

Unbound reports, standard, 187–189
  with proofreaders' marks, 191–192